Attribute-based Credentials for Trust

Kai Rannenberg · Jan Camenisch
Ahmad Sabouri
Editors

Attribute-based Credentials for Trust

Identity in the Information Society

Springer

Editors
Kai Rannenberg
Deutsche Telekom Chair of Mobile
Business and Multilateral Security
Goethe University Frankfurt
Frankfurt
Germany

Ahmad Sabouri
Deutsche Telekom Chair of Mobile
Business and Multilateral Security
Goethe University Frankfurt
Frankfurt
Germany

Jan Camenisch
IBM Zurich Research Laboratory
Rüschlikon
Switzerland

ISBN 978-3-319-14438-2 ISBN 978-3-319-14439-9 (eBook)
DOI 10.1007/978-3-319-14439-9

Library of Congress Control Number: 2014958890

Springer Cham Heidelberg New York Dordrecht London

Printed on acid-free paper

Springer International Publishing AG Switzerland is part of Springer Science+Business Media (www.springer.com)

Foreword

Data is the currency of the digital world. By 2020, European Data will be worth 1 trillion euro. Like any currency, it relies on trust. We need to engage to restore trust in the digital economy. That means, personal Data needs to be protected by a strong European regulation.

In 2011, European data was already worth 315 billion euro. Yet citizens' trust in the way in which data is used in the economy is low amongst Europeans. Even before the surveillance revelations, 92% of Europeans were concerned about the way their data is used without their consent.

The continuing data scandals both in the private and in the public sector had a deteriorating effect. We need to act to restore trust in the digital economy. In the sense, the PRISM scandal has been a wake-up call. European citizens want strong data protection rules and companies need a simple, clear and enforceable legal framework for doing business in the EU's internal market. Those are the two objectives of the European Data Protection Reform. It is conceived as a win-win deal for citizens and businesses alike.

For citizens, the goal is to secure that administrations and businesses do not collect and use more personal data than they need. Further, individuals should be back in control by updating their rights. The right to be forgotten, the right to data portability and the right to be informed of personal data breaches are key features. They will help close the growing rift between citizens and the companies with which they share their data.

For businesses, the reform will stimulate growth by establishing a true Digital Single Market. At the moment, a firm operating in all 28 Member States has to deal with a different legislation, as well as with different Data Protection authority in each country. The European Union wants to replace this complex and multilayer legal situation by one concise law that and valid in all of Europe: One continent, one law!

The proposal has been agreed by the European Parliament and is still under deliberation in the Council. I hope that strong and credible EU data protection rules can be approved as soon as possible, thereby setting a global standard for data protection.

The ABC4Trust project as a multidisciplinary and European project, gives a technological response to questions linked to data protection. Bringing together leading partner institutions from research and industry, ABC4Trust showed in two different pilots the feasibility of its advanced authentication solutions. Co-funding from the European Union's Seventh Framework Programme contributed to achieve these results. The presentation of a four-years work will take place one week ahead of the European Data Protection Day in Brussels on 20th January 2015. It will give a strong sign of European ambition in the filed of data protection. Work for improving data protection must continue politically and technologically for citizens and for businesses.

Strasbourg, 21st October 2014

Viviane Reding
Former Vice-president of the European Commission,
Member of European Parliament

Preface

When the preparations for the ABC4Trust proposal started in 2009, it could not be foreseen how much the world would change until today. However, the need for information privacy and security continued to grow and got increasingly recognized thereby making the results of ABC4Trust more relevant than ever.Also, we see confirmed one firm belief the project set out with: for privacy-friendly solutions to get accepted to a much larger degree, they need to be explained and trialled thoroughly and with a solid technical background. Editing and writing this book would not have been possible without the many helping hands that dedicated their knowledge, expertise, and time to make this endeavour a success. Among those who worked on this ABC4Trust volume and on the project as a whole, we would like to give a special thanks to:

- The partners, chapter editors, and researchers in ABC4Trust that contributed to this book and the deliverables (cf. Annex A) this book is based on;
- Viviane Reding MEP for kindly providing the foreword to this book;
- Christian Rauscher at Springer for accompanying us in the publishing endeavour towards a beautiful result;
- The Representation of the State of Hessen at the European Union for generously hosting the ABC4Trust summit event in its premises;
- The European Commission for funding ABC4Trust, as well as Rafael Tesoro Carretero, Gustav Kalbe, Jorge Gasos, Andrei Florea, and Dirk van Rooy, who as Project Officers took care of ABC4Trust;
- Kim Cameron for his invaluable efforts to facilitate international research;
- Last but not least, Christian Weber, without whom the successful ABC4Trust proposal would have never come into existence.

October 2014

Kai Rannenberg
Jan Camenisch
Ahmad Sabouri

Contents

Chapter 1
Introduction

Kai Rannenberg, Welderufael Tesfay, and Ahmad Sabouri

Abstract ABC4Trust advances trustworthy yet privacy-protecting ways of identity management. Therefore this chapter starts with an introduction to identity management and its privacy issues. Then it gives a first overview on Privacy-ABCs for privacy enhanced identity management and introduces the ABC4Trust Project goals and pilots.

Almost all applications and services based on computer systems require some authentication of participants to establish trust relations, either for only one endpoint of communication or for both. Username-password combination is the predominant form of authentication. Multiple other alternative techniques have been developed to provide a higher degree of access control to improve the drawbacks of simple password-based authentications. Cryptographic certificates are one known example of these. Although such certificates can offer sufficient security for many purposes, they do not typically cater to privacy requirements because they are bound to the identity of a real person. Any usage of such a certificate exposes the identity of the holder to the party requesting authentication.

1.1 Identity Management and its Privacy Issues

Most of the existing techniques for transferring trusted user attributes cause privacy issues. In systems where an online "Identity Provider" creates access tokens on demand, such as SAML, OpenID, or WS-Federation, this "Identity Provider" can impersonate its users or tracks their activities online. Systems with offline token creation, such as X.509 certificates, force the user to reveal more attributes than

Kai Rannenberg, Welderufael Tesfay, and Ahmad Sabouri
Chair of Mobile Business & Multilateral Security, Goethe University Frankfurt, Germany, e-mail: {kai.rannenberg, welderufael.tesfay, ahmad.sabouri}@m-chair.de

K. Rannenberg et al. (eds.), *Attribute-based Credentials for Trust*,
DOI 10.1007/978-3-319-14439-9_1

strictly needed (as otherwise the issuers signature cannot be verified) and make her online transactions linkable across different domains.

There are many scenarios where the use of classical certificates unnecessarily reveals the identity of their holders; for instance scenarios where a service provider only needs to verify the gender of a user but not the actual identity. These certificates often reveal the identity of the holder even though the respective application requires much less information. Revealing more information than necessary not only harms the privacy of the users but also increases the risk of abuse of information such as identity theft when the disclosed information falls in the wrong hands.

One example is the present setting of most ICT infrastructures and their security measures. These infrastructures and measures trigger more and more data collections that need to be analysed for their impacts on privacy and possible alternatives, that collect less data and have less negative impact. Moreover, advancements in digital data processing (ease of storage, transfer and reproduction) are disadvantageous for privacy unless followed by privacy friendly policies. For example, it is profitable to offer marginal discounts for disclosure of personal data and profiles, which are then subject to uncontrollable circulation afterwards.

Another area of privacy concern is the field of national electronic IDs, as a number of countries have already introduced or are about to introduce electronic identity cards (eID) and drivers' licenses. Electronic ticketing and toll systems are also widely used all over the world. As such systems become widespread for identification, authentication, and payment (which links them to people through credit card systems) in a broad range of scenarios, the users' privacy and untraceability will be increasingly threatened in the future internet society. If and when eIDs are rolled out, society and countries are well advised to build privacy protection techniques into them.

In summary, when designing identity management and access control systems inspired by the paradigm of Privacy by Design, the following concepts related to data thriftiness shall be of direct or indirect interest for bodies working on privacy-friendly ecosystems:

- Partial Identities and Partial Identifiers: More and more public and private parties are trying to overcome the natural borders between domains of activities, making users ever more transparent from ever more perspectives, e.g for many service providers offering services that relate to different parts of users' lives. Partial identities and Partial identifiers become more and more important for users to retain these borders by reducing the dangers of unwanted linkability across domains.
- Unlinkability: Unlinkability is related to Partial Identities and Identifiers, but in this context focusses on multiple uses of services within one domain. It ensures that a user may make multiple uses of resources or services without others being able to profile these activities.
- Minimal Disclosure: It is a common practice that service providers rely on the information about users provided by other entities that have an authentic profile of users' attributes. However, these entities typically possess a richer collection of information than is needed by the respective service provider. In this regard,

the users should have the possibility to calibrate the amount of disclosed information to the requested set only. Therefore on the side of the service providers risk management processes compatible with the minimal disclosure need to be established. One important building block for minimal disclosure is represented by Attribute Based Credentials, as they allow users to calibrate the amount of information they want to disclose.

1.2 Privacy-ABCs for Privacy Enhanced Identity Management

Privacy-preserving Attribute-based Credentials (Privacy-ABCs) are cryptographic schemes designed to enhance users' privacy. A credential is a means to establish a claimed identity, roles, or attributes about oneself with an entity, typically as part of an access control request. For instance, an ID card can serve as a credential to prove that one is between 13 and 16 years old, as might be required to access a teenage chat. Using a traditional ID card to establish such a proof would also reveal all the other information on the card, e.g. the residential address of the teenager, to the chat organizer. Privacy-ABCs overcome this: with such credentials, a user can selectively reveal any of the attributes contained in the credential without revealing any of their information whatsoever. Thus, Privacy-ABCs are a key ingredient to protecting one's privacy in an electronic world.

Over the past 20 to 30 years, a number of technologies have been developed to build Privacy-ABCs systems in a way that they can be trusted, like normal cryptographic certificates, while at the same time protecting the privacy of their holders (e.g., hiding the real holder's identity). Such credentials are issued just like ordinary cryptographic credentials (e.g., X.509 credentials) using a digital (secret) signing key. However, Privacy-ABCs allow their holders to transform them into new tokens that include only a subset of the attributes contained in the original credentials. Still, these transformed tokens can be verified just like ordinary cryptographic credentials (using the public verification key of the issuer) and offer the same strength of security.

Among the successful attempts of Privacy-ABC technologies, the most notable are IBM's Identity Mixer and Microsoft's U-Prove. Identity Mixer (idemix) is an anonymous credential system developed at IBM Research that enables strong authentication and privacy at the same time. U-Prove is also an innovative cryptographic technology that allows users to minimally disclose certified information about themselves when interacting with online resource providers. U- Prove provides a superset of the security features of Public Key Infrastructures (PKI), and also provides strong privacy protections by offering superior user control and preventing unwanted user tracking.

The future of Privacy-ABC technologies and partial identities becomes apparent as Internet applications become more and more personal, which raises major privacy problems. One example is the quest for strong identification for the use of Internet resources such as social networks or participation platforms. Anonymous access can address the privacy issues, but in many applications some reputation management is needed. The question is then, who can assure which claims, properties or attributes and which information is given to the relying party to enable the assurance.

The importance of anonymity on the Internet has been stressed by the Article 29 Working Party an association formed by a representative from the data protection authority of each EU Member State as early as 1997, when they stated that the possibility of remaining anonymous is essential if the fundamental rights to privacy and freedom of expression are to be maintained in cyberspace. Nonetheless, they also elaborated on the fact that public policies, e.g. prevention of crime, might require that the general anonymity can be lifted in specific circumstances and for specific individuals. The resulting conflict between on the hand the necessity to individualise someone and on the other hand the general requirement of anonymity can only be solved by striking a proportionate balance. Central to this balance will be an individual's ability to participate online in an anonymous fashion and the extent of this ability and the limits to it. ([Art], pp. 5, 6).

In contrast to the classical trustworthy credentials, Privacy-ABC technologies allow a holder to reveal just the minimal information required by the application, without giving away a full identity. Therefore, not only are Privacy-ABCs privacy-friendly, but they also prevent linking of different digital data and thus impede hidden and implicit profiling. These credentials thus facilitate the implementation of a trustworthy and at the same time privacy-preserving digital society.

1.3 The ABC4Trust Project Goals

The main existing implementations of Privacy-ABCs, U-Prove and Idemix, lack compatibility, which makes interoperability and interchangeability difficult. Consequentially, concerns about lock-in to one of the technologies and its provider can hinder the uptake of Privacy-ABC technologies. Therefore the major activities during the lifetime of the EU-funded Integrated Project ABC4Trust can be summarized as follows:

1. Develop a common, unified architecture for Privacy-ABC systems to allow comparing their respective features and combining them on common platforms.
2. Provide an open reference implementation of such architecture for selected Privacy-ABC systems.
3. Test the open reference implementation with actual production pilots, allowing provably accredited members of restricted communities to provide anonymous feedback on their community or its members.

The complexity of Privacy-ABC technologies and the client-server interactions they entail had so far overwhelmed potential users and consequently hindered the effective large-scale deployment of the technologies. Overcoming these hurdles required an in-depth comparative study of the functionalities of the different Privacy-ABC technologies and an analysis of their security and efficiency properties to provide a common understanding of their applicability to diverse application fields and scenarios.

A comparative understanding of these technologies makes it easier for different user communities to decide which technology best serves them in which application scenario. It also makes it easier to migrate to additional Privacy-ABC technologies, if and once they appear.

A further goal of the ABC4Trust project is to deepen the understanding of Privacy-ABC technologies, enable their efficient and effective deployment in practice, and their federation in different domains. Therefore project also involved the following activities:

- Raising the visibility of Privacy-ABCs and their visibility for relevant stakeholders.
- Serving as a "think tank" to the European Commission, regulators, and international standardization bodies.
- Working with standardisation bodies to standardise the matured elements of the concepts of Privacy-ABCs.

ABC4Trust built upon the work done in the EU-funded projects "Privacy and Identity Management for Europe" (PRIME[1]) [CLS11] and PrimeLife[2] [CFHR11], which had designed an architecture for privacy-enhancing identity management that combines anonymous credentials with attribute-based access control and anonymous communication. Those projects had also demonstrated the practical feasibility with a prototypical implementation of that architecture and demonstrators for application areas such as e-learning and location-based services. Moreover the Network of Excellence "Future of Identity in the Information Society" (FIDIS[3]) [RRD09] had provided the basic concepts for privacy-friendly identity management, considering identity as a collection of attributes and the concept of partial identities. The projects had, however, also uncovered that in order for these concepts to be applicable in practice, further research was needed in the areas of user interfaces, policy languages, infrastructures.

Also there was still effort needed to apply Privacy-ABC technology in concrete applications with cross-domain federation scenarios. Therefore, at the core of the ABC4Trust project were two small to medium-scale application scenario pilots. The project utilized these pilots to address possible tension between accountability and privacy in two different application fields. The Swedish school pilot deploys Privacy-ABCs for a communication network within a school in Söderhamn, Sweden. The Greek university pilot uses Privacy-ABCs to allow students anonymous evaluation of lectures. In these endeavours ABC4Trust profited from the experiences of the project "Privacy and Identity Management for Community Services" (PICOS[4]) [TKH+11], that had combined privacy-enhancing technologies and social networks.

[1] www.prime-project.eu

[2] www.primelife.eu

[3] www.fidis.net

[4] www.picos-project.eu

1.4 Overview of the Pilots

The ABC4Trust project realized the first ever implementation of Privacy-ABC systems in production environments. ABC4Trust gathered experiences on operation, interoperability, user acceptance, and so forth in two specific trials. Having these two pilots gave the opportunity to test Privacy-ABCs use and performance with two user groups of differing skills and needs. One user group was children at a school environment in Sweden, whereas the other was students at a Greek university. The use cases we designed were quite different in order to cover a broad variety of requirements and thus as well credentials.

1.4.1 Online Course Evaluation

A standard practice at the end of each term in most universities is to collect the opinions of the students who have taken a course and to evaluate different aspects of that course to further improve the quality of education. However, both the students and the professors have legitimate concerns about the process of course evaluation. The students might be worried about their identities being linked to their evaluation forms, resulting in negative impacts on their grades or education records. Meanwhile, professors consider a minimum level of participation in the lectures to be necessary for the students to get the real experience of the course and therefore to be eligible to evaluate it. The scenario becomes even more complex in terms of security, privacy, and trust, when electronic evaluation is desired.

Privacy-ABCs could help to address the aforementioned requirements in an online course evaluation system. In this regard, ABC4Trust launched two rounds of trials in Fall 2012 and Fall 2013 at the Patras University in Greece to realize such a system. Whilst the identity and privacy of the students were protected, the opinions of the students, who had attended more than a certain number of lectures, were collected via the evaluation portal.

At the beginning of the semester, the pilot participants were provided with their start-up kit including smart cards and necessary login information enabling the participants to bootstrap their access to the pilot system, register their smart cards and obtain their Privacy-ABCs from the identity management system. More specifically, the students were issued credentials certifying their enrolment in the university and the course, and both credentials were bound to the same secret key to prevent the students from credential pooling.

After the initialization actions were taken at the beginning of the semester, the students could record their participation in the lectures on their smart cards. Upon entering the lecture room, every student had to swipe her card in front of the device installed in the room in order to collect attendance units for that specific lecture. It is important to mention that these units were collected anonymously, meaning that no identifiable information was transferred to the system, which otherwise might have led to privacy breaches. Therefore, the attendance records were only stored on the smart cards of the students and not anywhere else.

During the evaluation period, the student could access the evaluation form online and submit their opinion if they could prove that:

1. they are a student of the university,
2. they are registered in the course,
3. they have attended at least a minimum number of the lectures from the course.

If all these conditions were met, the smart card could produce a Privacy-ABCs presentation proof that attested their eligibility to evaluate the course. While it was not possible to link the evaluations to the identity of the participants, the authentication step was designed based on "scope exclusive pseudonyms" (read more in Section 2.1) enabling the evaluation portal to force the user to generate the same pseudonym every time she visited the portal. This gave the possibility to recognize a returning user and therefore allow her to update her previous submission.

The second round of the trial aimed to further test the Privacy-ABCs' features developed in ABC4Trust in an actual deployment environment. New features such as revocation of credentials, advance issuance (i.e. carried-over attributes - read more in Section 2.1), and inspection of tokens (de-anonymization) were implemented and introduced into the pilot. The scenarios of the first round were extended in order to best integrate these new features. More specifically, after the students submitted their evaluations, they could receive a new credential that had their student ID blindly transferred to it from the university registration credential in their smart cards. In other words, they got a certificate of participation in the evaluation bound to their identity without the system being able to identify the students in the corresponding session. They could later use the new credential to anonymously take part in a tombola. When the winner was selected, her identity was revealed through the inspection of her presentation token. In this phase, there was no privacy risk for the winner with regard to the evaluation she provided, as the only information one could learn was that the winner had submitted an evaluation form.

1.4.2 School Community Interaction Platform

The Norrtullskolan school in Söderhamn, Sweden, hosted the second pilot of ABC4Trust, where a privacy-friendly platform, built upon Privacy-ABCs, was deployed to boost communication between pupils, their parents and school personnel. On the one hand, pupils were able to authenticate themselves in order to access restricted online activities and restricted information. On the other hand, they were able to remain anonymous when they asked private and sensitive questions to school personnel, while simultaneously assuring the school personnel that they were communicating with the authorised pupils of the respective school or class.

The platform was developed as a web-based application to be used for chat communication, counselling, political discussions, and exchange of sensitive and personal data between pupils, parents, and school personnel such as teachers, administrators, coaches, and nurses. This pilot specially helped to gather information on the usability of the Privacy-ABC systems under especially challenging usability conditions posed by children users. Due to the wide range of activities in this trial, the pilot was operated in two rounds where the first round was in a smaller scale to investigate the scalability of the platform and thus be able to address its shortcomings before a larger scale deployment.

All the pilot participants were equipped with the necessary hardware so that they could use the platform from their personal computers as well as the computers in the school. The smart cards were preloaded with a set of credentials that specified the participants' basic information such as first name, last name, and birthdate, their roles (i.e. pupil, parent, teacher, nurse, etc.), the classes and courses that the pupils were enrolled in, consequently giving the chance to define the access policies based on these attributes in the credentials. In order to mitigate the risk of credential sharing, all the credentials issued to a person were bound to the same secret key. Furthermore, the pilot benefited from the revocation feature of Privacy-ABCs to block the usage of credentials that had lost their validity.

The community interaction platform used an abstract model called "Restricted Area" (RA) that provided the virtual environment for the aforementioned communication activities. Every user could initiate such a private space and define access policies in order to restrict the participation to her desired target group. For example, a teacher could create an RA with "Chat" functionality to collect the opinions of the pupils about her teaching methods and limit the access to this chat room to participants of a specific class. In this case, the pupils of that class could join the discussion without being identified, while the other students from the school were prohibited to enter this chat room.

The users could choose to act anonymously or establish a partial identity. In the former case, users would have been assigned a temporary, one-time use, random alias that was usable only during that session, while in the latter case users could later claim the aliases again and resume their activities under that name. These aliases were mapped to cryptographic pseudonyms (read more in Section 2.1) underneath. The platform also supported the cases where identification of users was desired. For example, each participant owned a private RA that was used similar to an inbox for receiving messages or documents that were specifically addressed to that person. In order to access this RA, a user had to disclose her identity and prove her ownership of the RA. The third type of authentication that was offered in this platform provided conditional anonymity. An RA could be defined to be "Inspectable", meaning that the authentication token gave the possibility to the "School Inspection Board" to reveal the identity of a user under specific (extreme) circumstances that had been announced in advance. In that case, the participants were notified about the nature of this RA before entering it and could decide whether they want to join the activity or not. This mechanism was established to assist the school to fulfil some of its legal obligations such as controlling bullying threats.

References

[Art] Article 29 Working Party. Recommendation 3/97 - Anonymity on the Internet. WP 6, XV D /5022/97 final, adopted by the Working Party on 3 December 1997.

[CFHR11] Jan Camenisch, Simone Fischer-Hübner, and Kai Rannenberg, editors. *Privacy and Identity Management for Life*. Springer Berlin Heidelberg, 2011. ISBN: 978-3-642-20316-9.

[CLS11] Jan Camenisch, Ronald Leenes, and Dieter Sommer, editors. *Digital Privacy: PRIME - Privacy and Identity Management for Europe*, volume 6545 of *Lecture Notes in Computer Science*. Springer, 2011.

[RRD09] Kai Rannenberg, Denis Royer, and André Deuker, editors. *The Future of Identity in the Information Society Challenges and Opportunities*. Springer, 2009. ISBN: 978-3-540-88480-07.

[TKH+11] Markus Tschersich, Christian Kahl, Stephan Heim, Stephen Crane, Katja Böttcher, Ioannis Krontiris, and Kai Rannenberg. Towards privacy-enhanced mobile communitiesarchitecture, concepts and user trials. *Journal of Systems and Software*, 84(11):1947–1960, 2011.

Chapter 2
An Architecture for Privacy-ABCs

Patrik Bichsel, Jan Camenisch, Maria Dubovitskaya, Robert R. Enderlein, Stephan Krenn, Ioannis Krontiris, Anja Lehmann, Gregory Neven, Christian Paquin, Franz-Stefan Preiss, Kai Rannenberg, and Ahmad Sabouri

Abstract One of the main objectives of the ABC4Trust project was to define a common, unified architecture for Privacy-ABC systems to allow comparing their respective features and combining them into common platforms. The chapter presents an overview of features and concepts of Privacy-ABCs and introduces the architecture proposed by ABC4Trust, describing the layers and components as well as the high-level APIs. We also present the language framework of ABC4Trust through an example scenario. Furthermore, this chapter investigates integration of Privacy-ABCs with the existing Identity Management protocols and also analyses the required trust relationships in the ecosystem of Privacy-ABCs.

As we mentioned in the previous chapter, there are several implementations of Privacy-ABCs, based on different cryptographic primitives. Even though these schemes have similar features, they are realized with different cryptographic mechanisms and many times they are even called differently, making these technologies hard to understand and compare. Their differences and complexity also makes it difficult for application developers to use them in practice and it is almost impossible to switch between them once the application has been deployed.

The ABC4Trust architecture presented in this chapter aims to overcome these problems by defining an abstract interface to Privacy-ABCs, in such a way that they are independent from the concrete algorithms or cryptographic components used

Patrik Bichsel, Jan Camenisch, Maria Dubovitskaya, Robert R. Enderlein, Stephan Krenn, Anja Lehmann, Gregory Neven, and Franz-Stefan Preiss
IBM Research – Zurich, Switzerland, e-mail: {pbi, jca, mdu, enr, skr, anj, nev, frp}@zurich.ibm.com

Ioannis Krontiris, Kai Rannenberg, and Ahmad Sabouri
Chair of Mobile Business & Multilateral Security, Goethe University Frankfurt, Germany, e-mail: {kai.rannenberg, ahmad.sabouri}@m-chair.de

Christian Paquin
Microsoft Research, USA, e-mail: cpaquin@microsoft.com

K. Rannenberg et al. (eds.), *Attribute-based Credentials for Trust*,
DOI 10.1007/978-3-319-14439-9_2

underneath. The functional decomposition foresees possible architectural extensions to additional functional modules that may be desirable and feasible using future Privacy-ABC technologies or extensions of existing ones.

2.1 Concepts and Features of Privacy-ABCs

The predominant way to authenticate users on the Internet today is by usernames and passwords. When creating accounts, users often additionally have to provide a list of self-claimed attributes such as their name, address, or birth date. Only a few attributes, such as email addresses and credit card numbers, have some external mechanism to check their authenticity; all other attributes are essentially self-claimed.

Technical solutions such as the Security Assertion Markup Language (SAML), OpenID, or X.509 certificates let users authenticate and transfer trusted attributes, certified by issuers, to relying parties. Such technologies are slowly gaining momentum but present considerable security and privacy concerns. Briefly, either an online issuer unnecessarily exposes the issuance key to online attacks and learns the details of all transactions between users and relying parties, or the relying party learns more attributes than necessary, thereby becoming an attractive target for hackers.

Privacy-preserving attribute-based credentials (Privacy-ABCs) are a superior solution offering the best of both worlds: Issuers do not have to be involved during authentication, while users disclose only those attributes required by the relying parties and can do so without being easily traceable across their transactions.

2.1.1 User Attributes

We view a user's identity as a set of attributes. In most cases these attributes are information a party knows about a user. So, a user "identity" exists only in connection to a party. Because different parties know different things about the same user, every user has many different partial identities, possibly even multiple identities with each party he or she interacts with. To verify the authenticity of a user's attributes, a party (often called Relying Party (RP)) can either perform identity vetting on the attributes itself (for example, require the user to provide physical documents or take an exam) or rely on a specialized issuer whose identity-vetting procedures it trusts.

For example, in Figure 2.1, Alice has many different attributes, subsets of which make up Alice's different identities with the people and institutions she interacts with online. Alice should be able to manage these identities the same way she manages them in a paper-based world. Identities sharing a unique attribute can of course be linked; for example, her social security number can be linked across her healthcare-related identities, but her other identities should remain unlinkable.

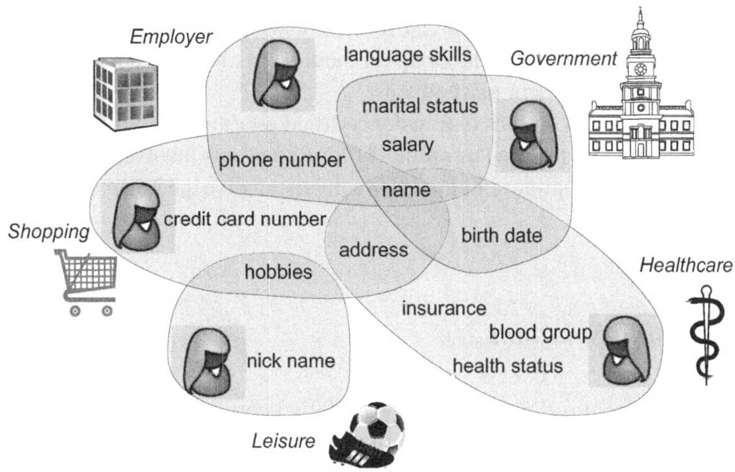

Fig. 2.1 Partial identities as subsets of attributes

Such user-centric identity management requires two basic mechanisms: one to transfer certified attributes from an issuer to a verifier, and one to authenticate (or re-authenticate) a user under a previously established identity. The former mechanism is essential to conduct trusted electronic transactions and requires cryptography. The latter mechanism can in principle be realized with a simple username and password, but this provides poor security guarantees. Indeed, passwords are well known to be vulnerable to password guessing, phishing, and social-engineering attacks. Their insecurity affects privacy, too. To alleviate these shortcomings, many service providers collect as much side information (for example, location or transaction history) about users as they can and analyze that data to detect suspicious behavior and potential breaches. So, a stronger cryptographic mechanism for authentication involving public-key cryptography seems advisable.

In our paper-based world, attribute transfer and authentication are often folded into one mechanism. For instance, a driver's license transfers the attribute "I'm allowed to drive a car" from the issuer to any relying party and, via the photo on it, provides an authentication mechanism. When realizing attribute transfer and authentication for the digital world, mimicking the paper-based solutions, as often happens, isn't enough. Instead, one must consider the very different environment: digital data is easily copied and virtually impossible to control once released. So, any digital realization must follow the principle of data minimization. When a user transfers an attribute from an issuer to a relying party, neither party should be able to learn any information that the transferred attribute hasn't already revealed, even if the parties collaborated.

Of course, an identity management system adhering to these principles doesn't eliminate all the digital world's dangers. Communication and stored information should always be encrypted. Sensitive data should be accompanied with usage policies defining how to treat it, who can use it, for what purpose it's to be used, and when to delete it. We do not elaborate on these issues here; rather, we concentrate on the identity management mechanisms.

Roughly, existing solutions to transfer certified user attributes from an issuer to a relying party are either offline or online. Offline solutions involve the issuer only at the time of issuance. Online solutions also actively involve the issuer during attribute transfer.

2.1.2 *Existing Solutions*

The most prominent offline solution are X.509 v3 certificates with attribute extensions. Here, the issuer or certificate authority (CA) signs the user's public key together with his or her attributes and includes the signature in the certificate. Since all attributes are needed to verify the CA's signature, the user is forced to reveal all of the attributes in the certificate when transferring an attribute. Moreover, the user's public key acts as a unique identifier that follows the user across all of his or her online transactions.

In online solutions, the user first authenticates directly to the issuer. The issuer then creates a verifiable token for the specific set of attributes required by the relying party. Popular examples following this approach include SAML and WS-Federation, as well as the more lightweight OpenID. The advantage of this approach is that only the required attributes are revealed. However, the issuer learns which user authenticates to which relying party at which time. Although some protocols may optionally hide the user's identity from the verifier or hide the verifier's identity from the issuer, this doesn't help when verifiers and issuers compare their transaction logs. Moreover, with online solutions, the issuance key must be on a system that's permanently connected to the Internet. This considerably increases the issuer's vulnerability to intruders, thus endangering the entire system's security.

2.1.3 *Basic Concepts of Privacy-ABCs*

Privacy-ABCs are similar to the offline approach in terms of the overall functionality and provided security guarantees, while letting users control and separate their different partial identities.

Similarly to X.509 certificates, users' credentials in Privacy-ABC systems are essentially signatures by the issuer on the attribute values assigned to the user. Unlike X.509 certificates, however, the user can hide some of the attribute values while keeping the issuer's signature verifiable to a verifier.

This section provides a detailed explanation on the features supported by Privacy-ABCs, on the different involved entities, and on the type of interactions that they engage in.

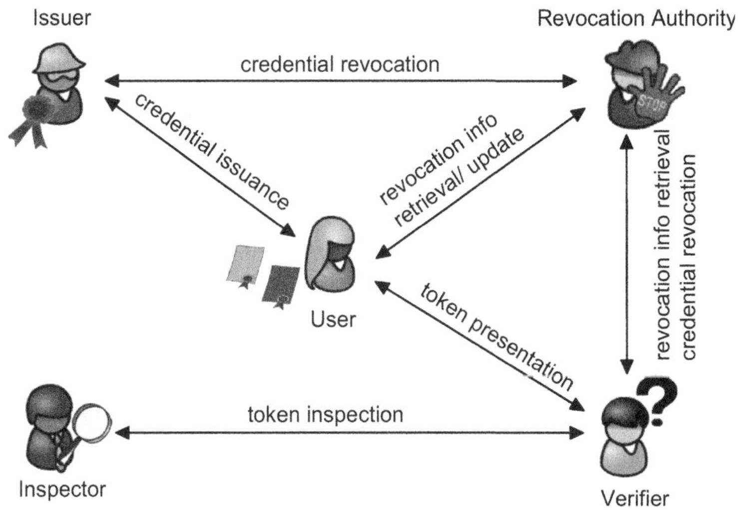

Fig. 2.2 Entities and interactions diagram

Figure 2.2 gives an overview of the different entities and the interactions between them.

- The *user* is at the center of the picture, collecting credentials from various issuers and controlling which information from which credentials she presents to which verifiers. The human user is represented by her user agent, a software component running either on a local device (e.g., on the user's computer or mobile phone) or remotely on a trusted cloud service. The user may own special hardware tokens to which credentials can be bound to improve security. In the identity management literature, the user is sometimes referred to as the requestor or subject.
- An *issuer* issues credentials to users, thereby vouching for the correctness of the information contained in the credential with respect to the user to whom the credential is issued. Before issuing a credential, the issuer may have to authenticate the user, which it may do using Privacy-ABCs, using a different online mechanism (e.g., username and password), or using out-of-band communication (e.g., by requiring the user to physically present herself at the issuer's office). In the identity management literature, the issuer is sometimes referred to as the identity (service) provider or attribute authority.
- A *verifier* protects access to a resource or service that it offers by imposing restrictions on the credentials that users must own and the information from these credentials that users must present in order to access the service. The verifier's restrictions are described in its *presentation policy*. The user generates from her credentials a *presentation token* that contains the information required by the presentation policy and the supporting cryptographic evidence. In the identity management literature, the verifier is sometimes also referred to as the relying party, server, or service provider.

- A *revocation authority* is responsible for revoking issued credentials, so that these credentials can no longer be used to generate a presentation token. The use of a particular revocation authority may be imposed by the issuer, in which case the revoked credentials cannot be used with any verifier for any purpose, or by the verifier, in which case the effect of the revocation is local to the verifier and does not affect presentations with other verifiers. Both the user and the verifier must obtain the most recent revocation information from the revocation authority to generate, respectively verify, presentation tokens.
- An *inspector* is a trusted authority who can de-anonymize presentation tokens under specific circumstances. To make use of this feature, the verifier must specify in the presentation policy which inspector should be able to recover which attribute(s) under which circumstances. The user is therefore aware of the de-anonymization options when the token is generated and actively participates to make this possible; therefore the user can make a conscious decision based on her trust in the inspector.

In an actual deployment, some of the above roles may actually be fulfilled by the same entity, or split among many. For example, an issuer can at the same time play the role of revocation authority and/or inspector, or an issuer could later also be the verifier of tokens derived from credentials that it issued.

Moreover, some of the flows presented in this document could be adapted for particular deployments and scenarios. It is assumed that verifiers have a reliable way of obtaining the public information of issuers and revocation authorities needed to validate presentation tokens, for example, by certifying the information through a classical public-key infrastructure (PKI).

2.1.3.1 Credentials

A *credential* is a certified container of attributes issued by an issuer to a user. An attribute is described by the attribute type, that describes the meaning of the attribute (e.g., first name), and the attribute value, that gives its contents (e.g., John). By issuing a credential, the issuer vouches for the correctness of the contained attributes with respect to the user. The user can then later use her credentials to derive presentation tokens that reveal partial information about the encoded attributes to a verifier.

The *credential specification* specifies the list of attribute types that are encoded in a credential. Since Privacy-ABCs natively only support integers of limited size (typically 256 bits) as attribute values, the credential specification also specify the *encoding mechanism* that maps attribute values to their integer representation. Depending on the data type and the size of the attribute value, this encoding may involve a cryptographic hash function.

At setup, the issuer generates public *issuer parameters* and a secret *issuance key*. The issuer parameters are used by verifiers to verify the authenticity of presentation tokens. Trust management and distribution are out of scope of this specification; a standard PKI, e.g., using hierarchical certification authorities, can be used to ensure that verifiers obtain authentic copies of the credential specifications and issuer parameters. Apart from cryptographic information, the issuer parameters also contain other meta-data such as the hash algorithm to use to create presentation tokens, as well as information for key binding, and revocation (see later). The issuer keeps the issuance key strictly secret and uses it only to issue credentials.

2.1.3.2 Presentation

To provide certified information to a verifier (for authentication or an access decision), the user uses one or more of her credentials to derive a *presentation token* and sends it to the verifier. A single presentation token can contain information from any number of credentials. The token can reveal a subset of the attribute values in the credentials (e.g., IDcard.firstname = "John"), prove that a value satisfies a certain predicate (e.g., IDcard.birthdate $< 1993/01/01$) or that two values satisfy a predicate (e.g., IDcard.lastname = creditcard.lastname). Apart from revealing information about credential attributes, the presentation token can optionally sign an application-specific message and/or a random nonce to guarantee freshness. Moreover, presentation tokens support a number of advanced features such as pseudonyms, key binding, inspection, and revocation that are described in more details below.

A verifier announces in its *presentation policy* which credentials from which issuers it accepts and which information from these credentials must be revealed in the presentation token. The verifier can cryptographically verify the authenticity of a received presentation token using the credential specifications and issuer parameters of all credentials involved in the token. The verifier must obtain the credential specifications and issuer parameters in a trusted manner, e.g., by using a traditional PKI to authenticate them or retrieving them from a trusted location.

The presentation token created in response to such a presentation policy consists of the presentation token description, containing a mechanism-agnostic description of the revealed information, and the presentation token evidence, containing opaque technology-specific cryptographic data in support of the token description. Presentation tokens based on Privacy-ABCs are cryptographically unlinkable and untraceable by default, meaning that verifiers cannot tell whether two presentation tokens were derived from the same or from different credentials, and that issuers cannot trace a presentation token back to the issuance of the underlying credentials. However, in what follows we will discuss additional mechanisms that, with the user's consent, introduce intentional linkability, or allow a dedicated third party to recover the user's identity.

Obviously, presentation tokens are only as unlinkable as the information that they intentionally reveal. For example, tokens that explicitly reveal a unique attribute (e.g., the user's social security number) are fully linkable. Moreover, pseudonyms and inspection can be used to purposely create linkability across presentation tokens (e.g., to maintain state across sessions by the same user) and create traceability of presentation tokens (e.g., for accountability reasons in case of abuse). Finally,

Privacy-ABCs have to be combined with anonymous communication channels (e.g., Tor onion routing) to avoid linkability in the "layers below", e.g., by the IP addresses in the underlying communication channels or by the physical characteristics of the hardware device on which the tokens were generated.

2.1.3.3 Key Binding

Credentials can optionally be *bound* to a user's secret key, i.e., a cryptographically strong random value that is generated by and known only to a particular user. The credential specification specifies whether the credentials issued according to this specification are to employ key binding or not. A presentation token derived from such a key-bound credential always contains an implicit proof of knowledge of the underlying secret key, so that the verifier can be sure that the secret key of the credential was involved in the creation of the presentation token.

Key-bound credentials can optionally be issued in such a way that the newly issued credential is bound to the same secret key as an existing credential already owned by the user — without the issuer learning the secret key in the process (see Section 2.1.3.6). A verifier can also optionally impose in its presentation policy that all key-bound credentials involved in the creation of the token must be bound to the same secret key.

Key binding can be used for several purposes. First, it can be used to prevent users from "pooling" their credentials, i.e., sharing their credentials with other users. In a presentation involving multiple credentials, the verifier can optionally insist that all credentials must be bound to the same user secret, so that credentials issued to different users cannot be used together. For this to work, users must be prevented from choosing the same secret key and from sharing their secret key with others. The former can be done by letting the secret be generated by a trusted hardware device such as a smartcard, through a joint generation between the issuer and user (see advanced issuance in Section 2.1.3.6), or by requiring the user to establish a scope-exclusive pseudonym at issuance and making sure that no two users have the same pseudonym (see Section 2.1.3.4). The latter can be enforced by making some highly valuable information or services accessible with the user secret alone, e.g., by protecting access to the user's main e-government account through a pseudonym derived from the same secret key.

Second, by storing the user secret on a trusted hardware device such as a smartcard, the credentials can be bound to the device. That is, if the key cannot be extracted from the device, but the device does participate in the generation of presentation tokens, then credentials cannot be used without the physical presence of the device.

Finally, key binding can be used to prevent users from being "framed" by a malicious issuer, i.e., from being impersonated by the issuer towards a verifier. A malicious issuer can of course always generate all the credentials that she wants, but she can only do so for a user secret that is different from the real user's secret. By letting users establish scope-exclusive pseudonyms at issuance and at presentation, the user can later prove that a presentation token was generated using a different user secret than the one used at issuance. Some external mechanism must be in place to prevent the issuer from tampering with the list of issued pseudonyms, for example, by letting the user sign (digitally or on paper) the pseudonym and then checking this signature.

2.1.3.4 Pseudonyms

There are many situations where a controlled linkability of presentation tokens is actually desirable. For example, web services may want to maintain state information per user or user account to present a personalized interface, or conversation partners may want to be sure to continue a conversation thread with the same person that they started it with.

Privacy-ABCs have the concept of *pseudonyms* to obtain exactly such controlled linkability. If the secret key from Section 2.1.3.3 is seen as the equivalent of a user's secret key in a classical public-key authentication system, then a pseudonym is the equivalent of the user's public key. Just like a public key, it is derived from the user's secret key and can be given to a verifier so that the user can later re-authenticate by proving knowledge of the secret key underlying the pseudonym. Unlike public keys of which there is only one for every secret key, however, users can generate an unlimited number of unlinkable pseudonyms for a single secret key. Users can thus be known under different pseudonyms with different verifiers, yet authenticate to all of them using the same secret key.

To be able to re-authenticate under a previously established pseudonym, the user may need to store some additional information used in the generation of the pseudonym. To assist the user in keeping track of which pseudonym she used at which verifier, the verifier's presentation policy specifies a pseudonym scope, which is just a string that the user can use as a key to look up the appropriate pseudonym. The scope string could for example be the identity of the verifier or the URL of the web service that the user wants to access.

We distinguish between the following three types of pseudonyms:

- *Verifiable pseudonyms* are pseudonyms derived from an underlying secret key as described above, allowing the user to re-authenticate under the pseudonym by proving knowledge of the secret key. Presenting a verifiable pseudonym does not involve presenting any related credentials and is useful in login scenarios, e.g., to replace usernames/passwords.
- *Certified pseudonyms* are verifiable pseudonyms derived from a secret key that also is bound to an issued credential. By imposing same-key binding in the presentation policy and token, a single presentation token can therefore prove ownership of a credential and at the same time establish a pseudonym based on the same secret key. As an example, a student could create several personas on a school discussion board using its core student credential, presenting the pseudonym associated with each persona, and without the possibility of anyone else (including

a malicious issuer) to present a matching pseudonym to hijack's the user's identity.
- *Scope-exclusive pseudonyms* are certified pseudonyms that are guaranteed to be unique for a specific scope string and secret key. For normal (i.e., non-scope-exclusive) pseudonyms, nothing prevents a user from generating multiple unlinkable pseudonyms for the same scope string. For scope-exclusive pseudonyms, it is cryptographically impossible to do so. By imposing a scope-exclusive pseudonym to be established, a verifier can be sure that only a single pseudonym can be created for each credential or combination of credentials that are required in the presentation. This feature can be useful to implement a form of "consumption control" in situations (e.g., online petitions or one-time coupons) where users must remain anonymous to the verifier but should not be allowed to create multiple identities based on a single credential. Note that scope-exclusive pseudonyms for different scope strings are still unlinkable, just like normal verifiable pseudonyms.

2.1.3.5 Inspection

Absolute user anonymity in online services can easily lead to abuses such as spam, harassment, or fraud. Privacy-ABCs give verifiers the option to strike a trade-off between anonymity for honest users and accountability for misbehaving users through a feature called inspection.

An inspector is a dedicated entity, separate from the verifier, who can be asked to uncover one or more attributes of the user who created a presentation token, e.g., in case of abuse. The inspector must on one hand be trusted by the user not to uncover identities unnecessarily, and must on the other hand be trusted by the verifier to assist in the recovery when an abuse does occur.

Presentation tokens are fully anonymous by default, without possibility of inspection. To enable an inspector to trace a presentation token when necessary, the presentation policy must explicitly specify the identity of the inspector, which information the inspector must be able to recover, and under which circumstances the inspector can be asked to do so. The user then creates the presentation token in a particular way so that the verifier can check by himself, i.e., without help from the inspector, that the token could be inspected under the specified restrictions if necessary.

In more technical detail, the inspector first sets up a public encryption key and a secret decryption key; he makes the former publicly available but keeps the latter secret. The presentation policy specifies

- (a reference to) the inspector's public key,
- which attribute(s) from which credential(s) which inspector must be able to recover, and
- the *inspection grounds*, i.e., an arbitrary human- and/or machine-readable string describing the circumstances under which the token can be inspected.

The user then prepares the presentation token so that it contains encrypted versions of the requested attribute values under the respective public key of the suggested inspector, together with a verifiable cryptographic proof that the encryption contains the same attribute values as encoded in the user's credentials and certified by the issuer.

When the situation described in the inspection grounds arises, the inspection requester can ask for an inspection. Besides the verifier, other entities such as criminal prosecutors, courts or the user herself are also potential requesters for inspection. Usually the verifier holds the stored copy of the presentation token and will send it to the inspector for inspection, possibly together with some kind of evidence (e.g., transaction logs, inquiry of competent authority, court order) that the inspection grounds have been fulfilled. The inspection grounds are cryptographically tied to the presentation token, so the verifier cannot change these after having received the token. The inspector uses its secret key to decrypt the encrypted attribute values and returns the cleartext values to the inspection requestor.

De-anonymization of presentation tokens is probably the main use case for inspection, but it can also be used to reveal useful attribute values to third parties instead of to the verifier himself. For example, suppose the verifier is an online merchant wishing to accept credit card payments without running the risk of having the stored credit card data stolen by hackers. In that case, he can make the user encrypt her credit card number under the public key of the bank by specifying the bank as an inspector for the credit card number with "payment" as inspection grounds.

2.1.3.6 Credential Issuance

In the simplest setting, an issuer issues credentials to users "from scratch", i.e., without relation to any existing credentials already owned by the users. In this situation, the user typically has to convince the issuer through some out-of-band mechanism that she qualifies for a credential with certain attribute values, e.g., by showing up in person at the issuer's office and showing a physical piece of ID, or by bootstrapping from a government-issued electronic identity. Credential issuance is a multi-round interactive protocol between the issuer and the user. The attribute values can be specified by either parties, or jointly generated at random (i.e., the issuer can be ensured that an attribute value is chosen randomly and not chosen solely by user, but without the issuer learning the attribute value).

Privacy-ABCs also support a more advanced form of credential issuance where the information embedded in the newly issued credential is *carried over* from existing credentials already owned by the user, without the issuer being able to learn the carried-over information in the process. In particular, the newly issued credential can

1. carry over attribute values from an existing credential,
2. contain "self-claimed" attribute values, i.e., values chosen by the user himself,
3. be bound to the same secret key as an existing credential or verifiable pseudonym,

all without the issuer being able to learn the carried-over attribute values or secret key in the process.

Moreover, the issuer can insist that certain attributes be generated jointly at random, meaning that the attribute will be assigned a fresh random value. The issuer does not learn the value of the attribute, but at the same time the user cannot choose, or even bias, the value assigned to the attribute. This feature is for instance helpful to impose usage limitation of a credential. To this end, the issuer first embeds a jointly random value as serial number in the credential. A verifier requesting a token based on such a credential can require that its serial number attribute must be disclosed by the user, such that it can detect if the same credential is used multiple times. The jointly random attribute hereby ensures that the verifier and issuer cannot link the generated token and issued credential together, and the user can not cheat by biasing the serial number in the credential.

The issuer publishes or sends to the user an *issuance policy* consisting of a presentation policy and a *credential template*. The presentation policy expresses which existing credentials the user must possess in order to be issued a new credential, using the same concepts and format as the presentation policy for normal token presentation. The user prepares a special presentation token that fulfills the stated presentation policy, but that contains additional cryptographic information to enable carrying over attributes and user secrets. The credential template describes the relation of the new credential to the existing credentials used in the presentation token by specifying

- which attributes of the new credential will be assigned the same value as which attributes from which credential in the presentation token,
- whether the new credential will be bound to the same secret key as one of the credentials or pseudonyms in the presentation token, and if so, to which credential or pseudonym.

The user and issuer subsequently engage in a multi-round issuance protocol, at the end of which the user obtains the requested credential.

2.1.3.7 Revocation

No identification system is complete without an appropriate revocation mechanism. There can be many reasons to revoke a credential. For example, the credential and the related user or device secrets may have been compromised, the user may have lost her right to carry a credential, or some of her attribute values may have changed. Moreover, credentials may be revoked for a restricted set of purposes. For example, a football hooligan's digital identity card could be blocked from accessing sport stadiums, but is still valid for voting or submitting tax declarations.

In classical public-key authentication systems, revocation usually works by letting either the issuer or a dedicated revocation authority publish the serial numbers of revoked certificates in a so-called certificate revocation list. The verifier then simply checks whether the serial number of a received certificate is on such a list or not.

The same approach does not work for Privacy-ABCs, however, as Privacy-ABCs should not have a unique fingerprint value that must be revealed at each presentation, as this would nullify the unlinkability of the presentation tokens. Nevertheless, there are cryptographically more advanced revocation mechanisms that provide the same functionality in a privacy-preserving way, i.e., without imposing a unique trace on the presentation tokens. We describe an abstract interface that covers all currently known revocation mechanisms.

Credentials are revoked by dedicated *revocation authorities*, which may be separate entities, or may also take the joint role of issuer or verifier. The revocation authority publishes its *revocation parameters* and regularly (e.g., at regular time intervals, or whenever a new credential is issued or revoked) publishes the most recent *revocation information* that verifiers use to make sure that the credentials used in a presentation token have not been revoked. The revocation parameters contain information where and how the verifiers can obtain the most recent revocation information. Depending on the revocation mechanism, the identifiers of revoked credentials may or may not be visible from the revocation information. It is important that verifiers obtain the most recent revocation information from the revocation authority directly, or that the revocation information is signed by the revocation authority if it is provided by the user together with the presentation token.

In order to prove that their credentials have not been revoked, users may have to maintain *non-revocation evidence* for each credential and for each revocation authority against which the credential must be checked. The first time that a user checks one of her credentials against a particular revocation authority, she obtains an initial non-revocation evidence. Later, depending on the revocation mechanism used, the user may have to obtain regular non-revocation evidence updates at each update of the revocation information. Also depending on the revocation mechanism, these evidence updates may be the same for all users/credentials or may be different for each user/credential. In the latter case, again depending on the mechanism, the users may fetch their updates from a public bulletin board or obtain their updates over a secure channel.

We distinguish between two types of revocation. Apart from a small list of exceptions, all revocation mechanisms can be used for either type of revocation.

- In *issuer-driven revocation*, the issuer specifies, as part of the issuer parameters, the revocation authority (and revocation parameters) to be used when verifying a presentation token involving a credential issued by his issuer parameters. Issuer-driven revocation is always global in scope, meaning that any presentation token must always be checked against the most recent revocation information from the specified revocation authority, and that the issuer denies any responsibility for revoked credentials. Issuer-driven revocation is typically used when credentials have been lost or compromised, or when the user is denied any further use of the credential. The revocation authority may be managed by or be the same entity as the issuer, or may be a separate entity. Issuer-driven revocation is performed through a *revocation handle*, a dedicated unique identifier that the issuer embeds as an attribute in each issued credential (but that should not be unnecessarily revealed in a presentation token). When the issuer, a verifier, or any third party wants to revoke a credential, it must provide the revocation handle to the revocation authority. How the party requesting the revocation learns the revocation handle is out of the scope of this document; this could for example be done digitally by insisting in the presentation policy that the revocation handle be revealed to a trusted inspector, or physically by arresting the person and obtaining his or her identity card.

- *Verifier-driven revocation* essentially allows the verifier to "black-list" certain credentials and prevent them from being used for authentication. The verifier specifies as part of the presentation policy against which revocation authority or authorities (and revocation parameters) the presentation must additionally be checked, i.e., on top of any revocation authorities specified by the issuer in the issuer parameters. The effect of the revocation is local to those verifiers who explicitly specify the revocation authority in their presentation policies, and does not affect presentations with other verifiers. Verifier-driven revocation is mainly useful for purpose-specific revocation (e.g., a no-fly list for terrorists) or verifier-local revocation (e.g., a website excluding misbehaving users from its site). Note that if unlinkability of presentation tokens is not a requirement, the latter effect can also be obtained by using scope-exclusive pseudonyms. The revocation authority may be managed by or be the same entity as the verifier, or may be a separate entity. Verifier-driven revocation can be performed based on any attribute, not just based on the revocation handle as for issuer-driven revocation. It is up to the verifier and/or the revocation authority to choose an attribute that on the one hand is sufficiently identifying to avoid false positives (e.g., the user's first name probably doesn't suffice) and on the other hand will be known to the party likely to request the revocation of a credential. Verifier-driven revocation is essentially a black list of attribute values, banning all credentials with a blacklisted attribute value.

2.1.4 Security and Privacy Features

Privacy-ABCs are a combination of several cryptographic building blocks, including signatures, pseudonyms, zero-knowledge proofs, encryption, and revocation mechanisms. Properly defining the security and privacy guarantees offered by such an encompassing framework is not an easy task. On a scientific level, the ABC4Trust project has made great advances in this respect by creating the most comprehensive formal security notions of Privacy-ABCs so far [CKL$^+$14]. In this section, we avoid technical details of cryptographic security notions, but rather give an intuitive description of the security and privacy features that application developers can expect when working with Privacy-ABCs.

Roughly, one could summarize the security and privacy features of Privacy-ABCs as security meaning that users cannot create valid presentation tokens without having the proper underlying credentials and keys, while privacy guarantees that presentation tokens do not reveal any more information than what was intentionally disclosed. The various features of Privacy-ABCs deserve a more detailed discussion, which we give in the following.

2.1.4.1 Basic Presentation

The most basic security guarantee is that credentials in a Privacy-ABC system are unforgeable. This means that users, without access to an issuer's secret key, cannot create new credentials or change attribute values in the credentials they obtained from that issuer. Presentation tokens are unforgeable as well, in the sense that in order to create a valid presentation token that discloses a number of attribute values or proves a number of (in)equality predicates, the user must possess credentials that satisfy the disclosed criteria. Note that this unforgeability only holds as long as the verifier can obtain authentic copies of the issuers' public keys, e.g., by certifying issuers' keys using an external PKI.

Presentation tokens can optionally "sign" a message that can contain a nonce, the intended verifier's identity, or any application-provided content. The information in that message is immutable: without the necessary credentials to regenerate a complete presentation token, one cannot change the message signed by the presentation token. The nonce in the signed message can be used to prevent replay attacks, where an eavesdropper or cheating verifier reuses a presentation token generated by an honest user to re-authenticate to the same or to a different verifier. Including the verifier identity (e.g., its URL or public key) in the signed message prevents man-in-the-middle attacks where a cheating verifier relays presentation tokens from honest users to authenticate itself to a second verifier. The application layer on the user's side must check that the verifier identity included in the signed message matches the application's intended verifier.

In terms of privacy, presentation tokens only reveal the information that is explicitly disclosed by the token. This means for example that presentation tokens reveal no information at all about the values of hidden credential attributes. If the presentation token includes attribute predicates, the token reveals nothing beyond the proof of the predicate, and in particular does not reveal the exact value of the involved attributes. It also means that presentation tokens are unlinkable, in the sense that even a collusion of issuers and verifiers cannot tell whether two presentation tokens were created by the same user or by different users, and cannot trace the presentation back to the issuance of the credentials.

Of course, unlinkability is only guaranteed to the extent that neither the disclosed attributes themselves nor the communication layer introduce trivial correlations between a user's presentations. In particular, it is important that presentation takes place over an anonymous communication channel, e.g., using Tor onion routing, to avoid that the verifier can link visits by the same user through his IP address. Achieving unlinkability at the physical layer can be particularly hard: intrinsic hardware characteristics of the user's device such as clock skews may be exploitable as unique device fingerprints [KBC05].

2.1.4.2 Key Binding

A key-bound credential cannot be used in a presentation without knowledge of the user secret. If the user secret is generated and stored on a trusted hardware device such as a smartcard, this means that the creator of the presentation token must have access to the device at the time of presentation. The presentation policy can optionally insist that different key-bound credentials or pseudonyms are bound to the *same* secret key. In this case, the policy cannot be satisfied using credentials or pseudonyms that are bound to or derived from different keys; the presentation token does not leak any information about the value of the key, however.

2.1.4.3 Advanced Issuance

In an advance issuance protocol, the user essentially performs a presentation before proceeding with the issuance. The same security and privacy properties hold for the issuance token as for normal presentation. Additionally, the issuance can carry over attribute values and user secrets from credentials involved in the presentation. In this case, the issuer is guaranteed that the attribute values or key in the newly issued credential are equal to those of the original credentials used in the presentation, but he doesn't see the actual value. For self-claimed attribute values, there is no such guarantee; the issuer blindly signs any attribute value that the user chooses. Jointly random attributes are guaranteed to be truly random, meaning that the user cannot steer or bias the distribution in any way, but the issuer again doesn't see the actual value. The user always sees all attribute values in his credentials.

2.1.4.4 Pseudonyms

Verifiable and certified pseudonyms can be seen as public keys corresponding to a user's secret key, with the main difference that the user can generate arbitrarily many pseudonyms from a single user secret. Pseudonyms are unlinkable, in the sense that verifiers cannot tell whether two pseudonyms originated from the same user secret or from different user secrets. Knowledge of the underlying secret key is required to create a valid presentation token involving a pseudonym. An attacker therefore cannot successfully authenticate under a pseudonym that was established by an honest user. This also implies that two honest users with independent user secrets will never accidentally generate the same pseudonym (because otherwise an adversary could generate pseudonyms for his own user secret until he hits an already established pseudonym).

Scope-exclusive pseudonyms are unique per scope and per user secret. Meaning, for a given scope string and a given user secret, there is only one scope-exclusive pseudonym for which a valid presentation token can be generated. Scope exclusive pseudonyms are unlinkable in the sense that, without knowing the user secret, one cannot tell whether two scope-exclusive pseudonyms for different scope strings were derived from the same or from different user secrets.

2.1.4.5 Inspection

Inspection allows the user to encrypt one or more attribute values under the public key of a trusted inspector. The encryption is secure against chosen-ciphertext attacks, meaning that the encrypted attribute values remain hidden even when the adversary can guess the encrypted value or can ask the inspector to inspect other presentation tokens. The user must encrypt his real attribute values for which he has valid credentials. Any attempt by the user to encrypt a different value, or to make the ciphertext undecryptable, will be detected by the verifier as an invalid presentation token. Finally, the inspection grounds are clear to the user at the time of presentation and are "signed" into the token, so that they cannot be modified afterwards. This prevents a malicious verifier from requesting a presentation token to be inspected based on different grounds than those that the user agreed with.

2.1.4.6 Revocation

When a credential is used in a presentation token with issuer-driven or verifier-driven revocation, the user merely proves that his revocation handle, respectively his combination of attribute values, was not revoked when the revocation authority published the stated revocation information. No other information about the value of the revocation handle or attributes is leaked. It is up to the verifier to check that the revocation information used in the presentation token is indeed the latest one as published by the revocation authority.

Revocation inherently opens up a subtle attack on user privacy by malicious revocation authorities. Namely, a cheating authority can always arbitrarily revoke valid credentials, just to test whether these credentials are involved in an ongoing presentation. The authority could even gradually "close in" on the user during subsequent presentations. External precautions must be taken to prevent such an attack, for example, by requiring that revocations must be logged on a public website or approved by an external auditor.

The communication pattern between users, issuers, and the revocation authority differs considerably for different revocation mechanisms. Some mechanisms follow a whitelist approach, where the revocation authority keeps track of valid revocation handles (attributes) and removes those of revoked credentials. These mechanisms usually require the revocation authority to be involved during credential issuance. Other revocation mechanisms use blacklists, where the revocation authority only keeps track of revoked values.

The revocation information may or may not hide the values of valid and revoked handles; this depends on the actual revocation mechanism that is used. Also depending on the mechanism, users may need to store non-revocation evidence with their credentials and update it before using it in a presentation. Some mechanisms require individualized updates, meaning that the user has to identify himself towards the revocation authority during the update. If the update occurs right before the presentation, this is a potential privacy leak. It is therefore better to let users perform the update of their non-revocation evidence at regular time intervals, rather than during presentation.

2.2 Architecture Highlights

The architecture of ABC4Trust is defined by following a layered approach, where all Privacy-ABC related functionalities are grouped together in a layer called ABCE (ABC Engine). It provides simple interfaces towards the application layer, thereby abstracting the internal design and structure. More specifically, this means that we define all the technology-agnostic components of the ABCE layer, as well as the APIs they provide. The APIs can be divided into two categories: first the interfaces that the ABCE components offer to the upper layers (e.g. Application), and second the interfaces that the different components within the ABCE layer expose to each other.

Equally important in the architecture is the specification of the data artefacts exchanged between the implicated actors, in such a way that the underlying differences of concrete Privacy-ABCs are abstracted away through the definition of formats that can convey information independently from the mechanism-specific cryptographic data. So the ABC4Trust architecture emphasizes on the XML based specification of the corresponding messages exchanged during the issuance, presentation, revocation, and inspection of privacy-enhancing attribute-based credentials.

The way that the ABC4Trust architecture is designed offers several benefits and facilitates their integration in today's applications. More specifically:

- The API defined by the architecture enables application developers to integrate Privacy-ABCs in their applications without having to think about their cryptographic realization.
- Application developers can implement their own UI for the interaction of the users with Privacy-ABCs, since it is considered to be an independent component and can be replaced and adapted according to the needs of different platforms.
- Users are able to benefit from different Privacy-ABC technologies at the same time on the same hardware and software platforms.
- Service providers and IdSPs are able to adopt whichever Privacy-ABC technology best suits their needs and switch among them with a minimal effort spent on adjusting their infrastructures. In this way, lock-in to specific technologies can be avoided.

The architecture described in this chapter has been implemented by the ABC4Trust project, it has been tested in the deployment of the two pilots and has been published as a reference implementation. Chapter 9 describes in more details the technical implementation of the architecture.

The architecture allows for deployments in actual production environments and in several application areas. Two specific cases are the ABC4Trust pilots, described in Chapters 6 and 7, where (1) minimal disclosure of identifying information when accessing resources, (2) and the anonymous feedback to a community by accredited members were in focus. Furthermore, some other application scenarios that could benefit from the ABC4Trust architecture are discussed in Chapter 10.

2.3 Architectural Design

Following standard design principles, our architecture uses a layered approach, where related functionalities are grouped into a common layer that provides simple interfaces towards other layers and components, thereby abstracting the internal design and structure. As mentioned in Chapter 1, the architecture focuses on the technology-independent components for Privacy-ABC systems, grouped in the ABCE layer, which can be integrated in various application and deployment scenarios. That is, we do not propose a concrete application-level deployment but provide generic interfaces to the ABCE layer that allow for a flexible integration. Note that we aim at an architecture that is capable of supporting all the privacy-enhancing features of Privacy-ABCs, but at the same time is not exclusive to those, i.e., it is also generic enough to support standard ABC technologies such as X.509 certificates.

The Privacy-ABC architecture defines for each entity the necessary components to operate with attribute-based credentials and to support the various features introduced in Section 2.1. A simplified overview of this architecture is depicted in Figure 2.3.

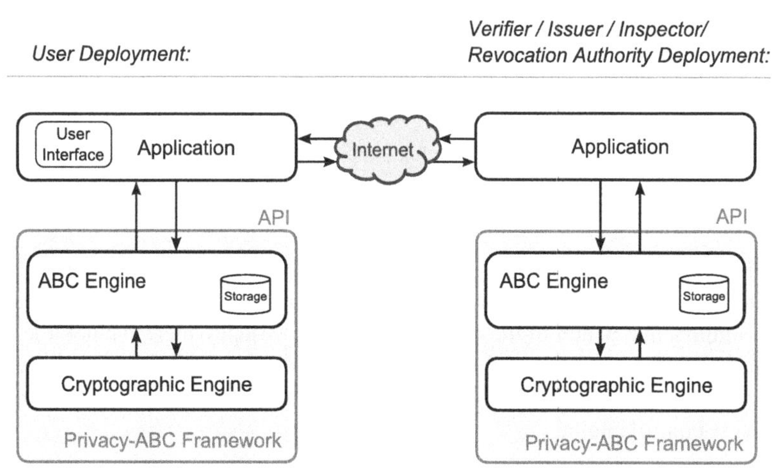

Fig. 2.3 Architecture of a Privacy-ABC System

2.3.1 *Overview of the Components*

We now briefly describe the different layers in our architecture and give an overview of the internal components of the ABCE layer. The latter is rather for informational purposes only, as the application developer does not have to deal with those internals of the ABCE but only invoked the external APIs. A more detailed view of the Privacy-ABC architecture and its components on the user side is shown in Figure 2.4.

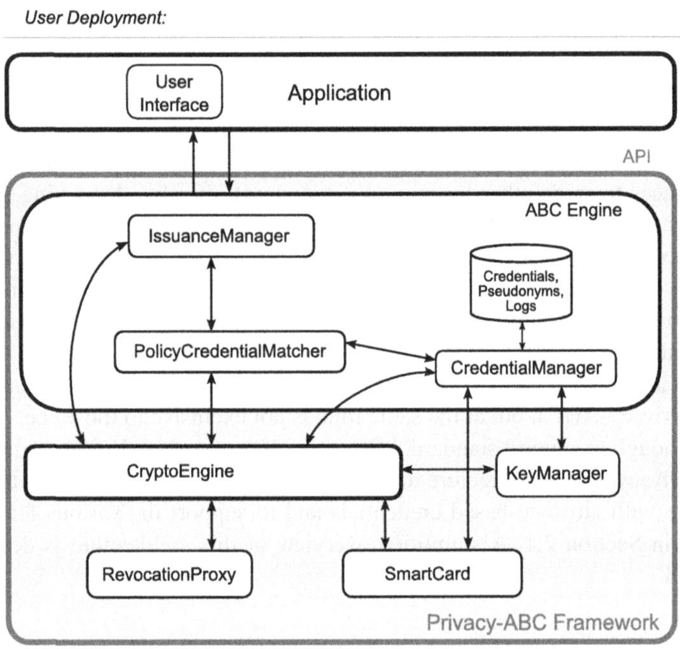

Fig. 2.4 Overview of the Privacy-ABC Architecture on the User Side

2.3.1.1 Application Layer

The application layer is actually not part of the Privacy-ABC architecture, but will operate on top of that. Roughly, the application layer comprises all application-level components, which in the case of the user-side deployment include the main application and the user interface for the identity selection (see description below). The application layer of verifiers and issuers will also contain the policy store and the access control engine.

UserInterface *(User)*: The UserInterface displays the possible choices of pseudonyms and credentials a user can apply in an issuance or presentation session. To this end, it shows a human-friendly description of the credentials and presentation/issuance token, namely, the information that will be revealed by presenting the token.

2.3.1.2 ABCE Layer

The ABCE layer is the core of our Privacy-ABC architecture and contains all technology-agnostic methods and components for a Privacy-ABC system. That is, it contains, e.g., the methods to parse an obtained issuance or presentation policy, perform the selection of applicable credentials for a given policy or to trigger the mechanism-specific generation or verification of the cryptographic evidence. The ABCE layer is invoked by the application-layer and calls out to the CryptoEngine to obtain the mechanism-specific cryptographic data. To perform their tasks, the internal components can also make use of other external components such as the KeyManager, Smartcard or the RevocationProxy.

IssuanceManager *(User, Issuer)*: The IssuanceManager receives the incoming issuance messages and routes them either to the CryptoEngine or to the PolicyCredentialMatcher, depending on the content of the message.

PolicyCredentialMatcher *(User)*: The PolicyCredentialMatcher prepares a list of choices of credentials, pseudonyms, and inspectors for the UserInterface, based on the policies it receives. When a choice was made by the user, the PolicyCredentialMatcher then provides the CryptoEngine with the description of the selected token and thereby starts the cryptographic proof generation.

PolicyTokenMatcher *(Verifier)*: The PolicyTokenMatcher is responsible for checking if a token received from the user matches a given policy. This verification is done in two main steps. First, it checks whether the statements made in the token description satisfy the required statements in the policy. If the policy requested the re-use of an established pseudonym, the PolicyTokenMatcher calls on the TokenManager (described below) to look up if a presented pseudonym already exists. When the first check succeeds, i.e., the token description matches the policy, it subsequently invokes the CryptoEngine which then verifies the validity of the crypto evidence. If the verification of the crypto evidence is successful as well, the PolicyTokenMatcher stores the token in a dedicated store (if requested by the application).

Token Manager *(Verifier, Issuer)*: The TokenManager stores the issuance and presentation tokens (including the used pseudonyms) that were accepted by the issuer and the verifier respectively. The issuer's token manager also stores a "history" of the issuances, which consists of the list of issuer-specified attributes (including the revocation handle) and the issuance token for all credentials that were issued.

CredentialManager *(User)*: The CredentialManager is responsible for storing all secret or privacy-sensitive info of the user, i.e., credentials, pseudonyms, secrets. It also seamlessly integrates the blobstore on the smartcards (via the smartcard manager) and is responsible for detecting smartcards and getting the PIN of the card from the user. In the course of an advanced issuance or presentation session the CredentialManager provides the PolicyCredentialMatcher with a list of all credentials and pseudonyms currently available in the storage and on all active smartcards. During issuance it further downloads and caches the default pictures associated with a credential, which are then passed to the PolicyCredentialMatcher and are possibly displayed in a UserInterface.

PrivateKeyStore *(Issuer, RevocationAuthority, Inspector)*: The PrivateKeyStore is available for the issuer, inspector and revocation authority and is responsible for storing private keys which are generated within the ABCE.

2.3.1.3 Crypto Layer

The crypto layer contains all the technology-specific methods needed in a credential life-cycle, e.g., to generate and verify presentation/issuance tokens, inspect attributes or maintain the revocation information. The ABC4Trust reference implementation of our Privacy-ABC framework also provides a rather generic CryptoEngine that currently incorporates U-Prove and Idemix as the main credential component, and also contains cryptographic realizations for all the additional features introduced in the previous Chapter. For a more detailed description of the CryptoEngine we refer to Section 3.1.

CryptoEngine *(User, Issuer, Verifier, Revocation Authority, Inspector)*: The CryptoEngine is responsible for all cryptographic computations in the Privacy-ABC framework. For instance, it creates pseudonyms, non-device-bound secrets, system parameters, key pairs and transforms the presentation/issuance token description into a cryptographic proof or verifies a given cryptographic proof. During issuance, the CryptoEngine of the issuer also interacts with the revocation authority (via the revocation proxy) to generate a new revocation handle and a non-revocation evidence for a new credential. Subsequently, the CryptoEngine also updates the non-revocation evidence of revocable credentials. Furthermore, the CryptoEngine provides mechanism-dependent and human-friendly proof descriptions which specify the information that is actually revealed in a presentation or issuance token and which can be used in the identity selection.

2.3.1.4 Storage & Communication Components

The Privacy-ABC architecture also contains several components that assist the work of the ABCE and Crypto layer, e.g., by providing a trusted public-key store or secure storage (and computation) on an external smartcard. As those components are rather use-case and technology-specific, they are described as individual modules and can be customized depending on the concrete scenario in which Privacy-ABCs are used.

KeyManager *(User, Issuer, Verifier, Revocation Authority)*: The KeyManager is responsible for storing trusted public keys, and if needed procuring these keys in an authenticated manner.

RevocationProxy *(User, Issuer, Verifier, Revocation Authority)*: The RevocationProxy is responsible for secure communication between the revocation authority and the user/issuer/verifier whenever dealing with revocable credentials. It creates, parses and dispatches revocation messages.

SmartcardManager *(User)*: The SmartcardManager is responsible for interacting with smartcards. It allows the seamless operation of several cards in parallel. The smartcard manager is NOT responsible for detecting new cards or asking for the user's PIN: that is the credential manager role.

Smartcard *(User, Inspector)*: The Smartcard stores the secret and sensitive data. It can be realized as software or as a physical device, and provides two different interfaces.The DataInterface allows one to store the credentials, inspector keys and other sensitive cryptographic objects in the card's blobstore. The CryptoInterface provides cryptographic functionality for issuance and presentation that is related to a secret stored on the card.

2.4 Deployment of the Architecture

In this section we describe the high-level APIs provided by our framework, and describe their usage along the main scenarios in a credential lifecycle. The API is based on the reference implementation of a Privacy-ABC framework that was created within the EU project ABC4Trust [abc, BCD+14, BBE+14]; the source code of that implementation is available at https://github.com/p2abcengine/p2abcengine. To focus on the main concepts of our architecture, the following description concentrates on the most significant methods and omits some convenience functions as well as simplifies the behaviour of some of the described methods.

The ABCE exposes technology-agnostic methods to the application developer that allow him to implement all the features introduced in the previous Chapter. In summary, those methods comprise the generation of cryptographic parameters and keys, import of these parameters, generation and verification of presentation tokens, issuance of credentials, inspection of tokens, and revocation of credentials or attributes.

2.4.1 Setup and Storage

To equip all parties in a Privacy-ABC system with the necessary key material, the API provides several methods for generating public and/or private cryptographic parameters.

However, before any entity can create its parameters, the global system parameters have to be generated. This is done by invoking the method `generateSystemParameters` with the desired security level as the input. The method then generates the global system parameters which define the security parameters (e.g., size of secrets, size of moduli, size of group orders, prime probability), the range of values the attributes can take, and the cryptographic parameters for the pseudonyms. To ensure interoperability, every user, issuer, inspector, and revocation authority in the system must use the same system parameters for generating their cryptographic keys and parameters. To achieve this, for example, a trusted authority such as a standardization body could generate and publish system parameters for various security levels, which are then used by all parties.

For each party, the ABCE then offers a dedicated method to create the corresponding key material. Thereby, the ABCE stores the private parameters in the trusted storage and outputs the public part of the parameters.

Issuer Parameters: When generating issuer parameters, one must (in addition to the system parameters) specify the concrete technology and the maximal number of attributes that can appear in credential specifications that are used in conjunction with these issuer parameters. That number is required as it can influence the issuer parameters, e.g., the issuer parameters of Idemix and U-Prove will contain a dedicated generator for each attribute. Further, if the issuer supports issuer-driven revocation, the method also needs the parameters of the corresponding revocation authority as additional input.

Revocation Authority Parameters: For the generation of the revocation authority parameters, one must specify the locations where users and verifiers can retrieve all the necessary information to obtain or update their state of revocation information and non-revocation evidence. Those comprise the location to obtain the latest revocation information, the location of the initial non-revocation evidence of newly issued credentials, and the location where users can obtain updates to their non-revocation evidence.

User Secret Keys: On the user side, the ABCE allows the creation of private keys to which subsequently credentials can be bound. We note that a user may generate multiple keys by calling this method multiple times. Our reference implementation also supports the storage of private keys on external devices such as smartcards.

The ABCE further provides APIs to store public parameters of other parties. As usual, it must be guaranteed that only authenticated parameters are imported and that the public key storage is kept up-to-date. To later retrieve public parameters from the ABCE again, they are stored together with a UID as unique identifier. Similarly, the ABCE includes methods to import credential specifications which define a particular type of credential.

The main methods to setup and maintain a credential system are listed in Table 2.1. Values in brackets denote that they are optional, i.e., can also be set to *null*.

Table 2.1 ABCE Interfaces for Setup and Storage

GLOBAL & STORAGE APIS

`generateSystemParameters`
input: int *securityLevel*
output: SystemParameters

`storeSystemParameters`
input: SystemParameters
output: boolean *success*

`storeIssuerParameters`
input: IssuerParameters
output: boolean *success*

`storeInspectorParameters`
input: InspectorParameters
output: boolean *success*

`storeRevocationAuthorityParameters`
input: RevocationAuthorityParameters
output: boolean *success*

`storeCredentialSpecification`
input: CredentialSpecification
output: boolean *success*

ISSUER

`generateIssuerParameters`
input: URI *id*, SystemParameters, URI *technology*, int *maximalNumberOfAttributes*, [URI *revocationAuthorityId*]
output: IssuerParameters

INSPECTOR

`generateInspectorParameters`
input: URI *id*, SystemParameters, URI *technology*
output: InspectorParameters

REVOCATION AUTHORITY

`generateRevocationAuthorityParameters`
input: URI *id*, SystemParameters, URI *technology*, URI *revocationInfoLocation*, URI *nonRevocationEvidenceLocation*, URI *nonRevocationUpdateLocation*
output: RevocationAuthorityParameters

USER

`generateUserSecretKey`
input: SystemParameters
output: URI *id*

2.4.2 Presentation of a Token

The process of presentation is triggered when the application on the user's side contacts a verifier to request access to a resource (Figure 2.5 – Step 1). Having received the request, the verifier responds with one or more presentation policies, which are aggregated in a *PresentationPolicyAlternatives* object. Recall that a presentation policy defines what information a user has to reveal to the verifier in order to gain access to the requested resource. For example, it describes which credentials from which trusted issuers are required, which attributes from those credentials have to be revealed, or which predicates the attributes have to fulfill. A detailed specification of a presentation policy is given in Section 2.5.

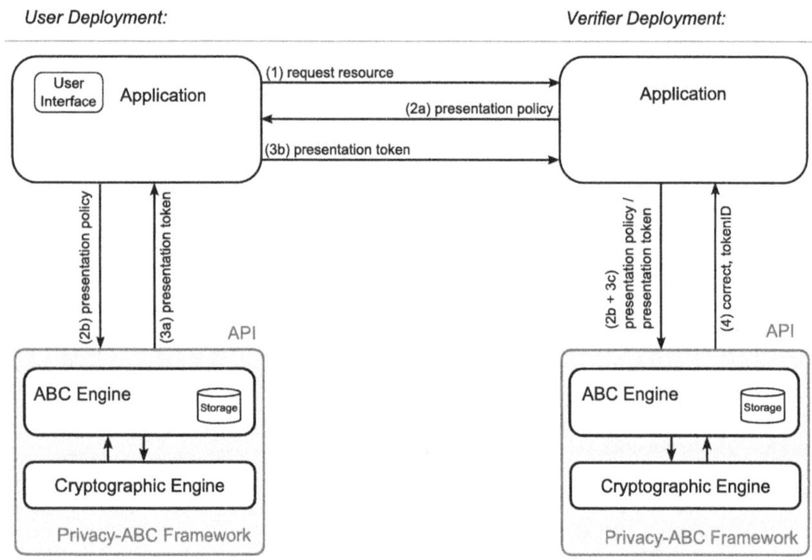

Fig. 2.5 Presentation of a Token (Application Level)

Upon receiving the policy (Figure 2.5 – Step 2.a), the application on the user's side invokes the Privacy-ABC system first with the `createIdentitySelectorArguments` method on input of the received presentation policy alternatives (Figure 2.5 – Step 2.b). The Privacy-ABC system then determines whether the user has the necessary credentials and pseudonyms to create a token that satisfies the policy. Based on that investigation, the method returns either an object of type *UiPresentationArguments* which describes all the possible combinations of the user's credentials and pseudonyms that satisfy the policy, or an error message indicating that the policy could not be satisfied. The user's application layer then performs an identity selection, that is, it invokes a component (such as a graphical user interface) that supports the user in choosing her preferred combination of credentials and pseudonyms and to obtain the user's consent in revealing her personal data.

The user's choice is recorded in an object of type *UiPresentationReturn* and passed to the `createPresentationToken` method. The Privacy-ABC system then invokes the Crypto Engine to obtain the corresponding cryptographic evidence for the selected token description. The method finally outputs a presentation token (Figure 2.5 – Step 3.a), consisting of the presentation token description and the crypto evidence, according to the user's choice. Afterwards, the presentation token is sent to the verifier (Figure 2.5 – Step 3.b).

When the verifier receives the presentation token from the user, it passes it to its ABCE layer with the method `verifyTokenAgainstPolicy` (Figure 2.5 – Step 2.b+3.c). This method verifies whether the statements made in the presentation token satisfy the corresponding presentation policy alternatives. The token verification is done in two steps. First, it is determined whether the statements made in the presentation token description logically satisfy the required statements in the corresponding presentation policy. Second, the validity of the cryptographic evidence for the given token description is verified. If both checks succeed, the ABCE outputs a boolean indicating the correct verification and, if requested, stores the presentation token in a dedicated token store, which allows the verifier to subsequently recognize established pseudonyms.

The ABCE interfaces available for the user and verifier in the context of generating and verifying a presentation token are summarized in Table 2.2 below.

Table 2.2 ABCE Interfaces for Token Presentation and Verification

USER

`createIdentitySelectorArguments`
input: PresentationPolicyAlternatives
output: UiPresentationArguments

`createPresentationToken`
input: UiPresentationReturn
output: PresentationToken

VERIFIER

`verifyTokenAgainstPolicy`
input: PresentationToken, PresentationPolicyAlternatives, boolean *storeToken*
output: boolean *isCorrect*, [URI *tokenId*]

`getPresentationToken`
input: URI *tokenId*
output: PresentationToken

2.4.3 Issuance of a Credential

Generally speaking, issuance is an interactive multi-round protocol between a user and an issuer, at the end of which the user obtains a credential. In fact, issuance can be seen as a special case of a standard resource request, where the resource is a new credential that the user wants to obtain. Thus, to handle such a credential request, the Privacy-ABC framework might invoke the same components and procedures as in the presentation scenario described above. However, depending on the scenario, the issuance transaction involves additional components to handle the case where the user wishes to (blindly) carry over her attributes or her secret key from one of her existing credentials to the new credential.

To start an issuance transaction, the user first authenticates towards the issuer (Figure 2.6 – Step 1) and indicates the credential type she wishes to obtain (Figure 2.6 – Step 2). Note that the exact details of the initial authentication are outside the scope of the Privacy-ABC framework and, for example, can be done using traditional means such as username and password. The issuer triggers the issuance of a credential through the API when receiving a correct credential request from a user. As described in Section 2.1 , there are two variants of issuance: *simple issuance* and *advanced issuance*, where the latter applies if attributes or a key need to be carried over from existing credentials.

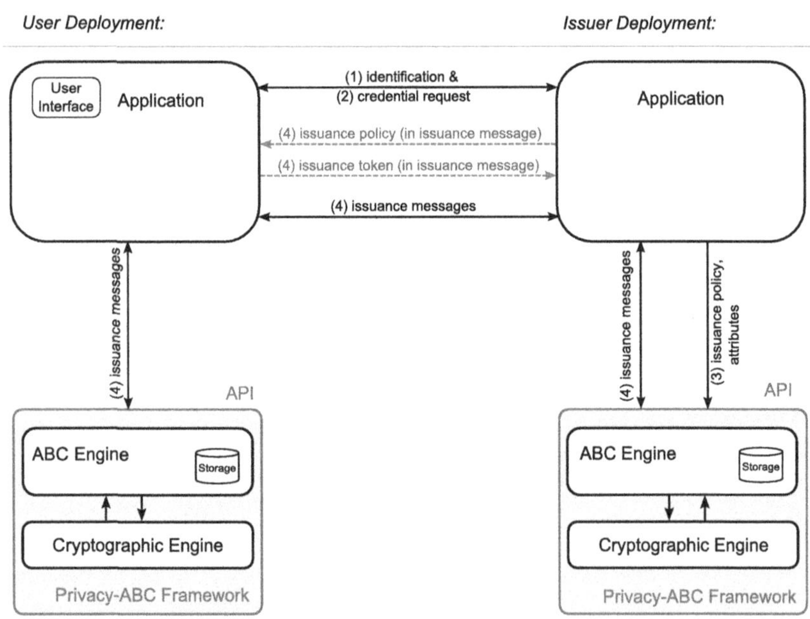

Fig. 2.6 Issuance of a Credential (Application Level)

2.4.3.1 Simple Issuance

In the simple issuance variant, an issuer issues the user a credential that is unrelated to any existing credentials or pseudonyms already owned by the user. In such a setting, the issuer first invokes the `initIssuanceProtocol` method of the ABCE with the set of attributes that shall be certified in the new credential, and with an *IssuancePolicy* that merely contains the identifiers of the credential specification and the issuer parameters of the credential that is to be issued (Figure 2.6 – Step 3). This call initiates the cryptographic issuance protocol by invoking the Crypto Engine. The method returns an *IssuanceMessage* containing cryptographic data (the format of the data is specific to the technology of the credential to be issued) and a reference that uniquely identifies the instance of the corresponding issuance protocol. The returned issuance message is then sent by the issuer to the user.

Upon receiving an issuance message, both the user and the issuer pass the message to their Privacy-ABC system using the `issuanceProtocolStep` method (Figure 2.6 – Step 4). If the output of that method in turn contains an issuance message, that message is sent to the other party until the method on the user's side completed the credential generation. At the end of a successful issuance protocol, the user's Privacy-ABC system stores the new credential in the local credential store and returns the description of the credential to the user.

2.4.3.2 Advanced Issuance

In the advanced issuance variant, the information embedded in the newly issued credential can be blindly carried over from existing credentials and pseudonyms that are already owned by the user. To this end, the issuance protocol is preceded by the generation and verification of an issuance token, which is generated on the basis of an issuance policy sent to the user. More precisely, the issuer triggers an advanced issuance transaction by invoking the `initIssuanceProtocol` method on input of an issuance policy and the set of known user attributes that shall be certified in the new credential (Figure 2.6 – Step 3). The issuance policy must require the user to present at least one credential or one pseudonym, otherwise simple issuance is performed. The method returns an issuance message (containing the issuance policy) which must then be sent to the user.

The user in turn invokes the method `issuanceProtocolStep` with the received message. The user's Privacy-ABC system recognizes that this is an advanced issuance scenario, and subsequently starts preparing an issuance token. This process is similar to the generation of a presentation token in that the method's output contains an object of type *UiIssuanceArguments* for the user to perform an identity selection. The method then expects the user's response in form of a *UiIssuanceReturn* object. Finally, based on the user's choice, her Privacy-ABC system (with the help of the Crypto Engine) generates an *IssuanceToken*, which includes additional cryptographic data needed for the subsequent issuance protocol. The issuance token is wrapped in an issuance message, which the user then forwards to the issuer (Figure 2.6 – Step 4).

As for simple issuance, the issuer's `issuanceProtocolStep` method is then called on input of the incoming issuance message from the user. The Privacy-ABC system then verifies the issuance token contained in the message with respect to the issuance policy (using similar methods as for the verification of a presentation token). If the verification succeeds, the cryptographic issuance protocol is started, again with the help of the Crypto Engine. The method outputs an issuance message containing cryptographic data depending on the technology of the credential. The issuer then sends the returned issuance message to the user (Figure 2.6 – Step 4).

Whenever the user or the issuer receive an issuance message, they invoke their local `issuanceProtocolStep` method. The output is then either another issuance message that must be sent to the other party, or an indication of the completion of the protocol. At the end of the protocol, the user's Privacy-ABC system stores the obtained credential and returns a description of that credential to the user.

Overall, the issuance-related APIs of the ABCE are summarized in Table 2.3.

Table 2.3 ABCE Interfaces for Credential Issuance

USER		
`issuanceProtocolStep`		
	input:	IssuanceMessage
	output:	IssuanceMessage, CredentialDescription, [UiIssuanceArguments]
`issuanceProtocolStep`		
	input:	UiIssuanceReturn
	output:	IssuanceMessage
ISSUER		
`initIssuanceProtocol`		
	input:	IssuancePolicy, List<Attribute> *issuerSpecifiedAttributes*
	output:	IssuanceMessage, boolean *isLastMessage*
`issuanceProtocolStep`		
	input:	IssuanceMessage
	output:	IssuanceMessage, boolean *isLastMessage*
`extractIssuanceToken`		
	input:	IssuanceMessage
	output:	IssuanceToken

Table 2.4 ABCE Interfaces for Inspection and Revocation

INSPECTOR

`inspect`
- input: PresentationToken, URI *credentialAlias*, URI *attributeType*
- output: Attribute

`inspect`
- input: IssuanceToken, URI *credentialAlias*, URI *attributeType*
- output: Attribute

REVOCATION AUTHORITY

`revoke`
- input: URI *revocationAuthorityId*, List<Attribute> *toRevoke*
- output: —

2.4.4 Inspection

As described in detail in Section 2.1.3.5 , the anonymity that is usually provided by Privacy-ABCs can be lifted through inspection if the policy allows it. In particular, if a policy mandates attributes to be inspectable, the user prepares her presentation tokens in a special way: the inspectable attributes are not revealed to the verifier, but are verifiably encrypted in the token under the public key of a trusted inspector and inseparably tied to some inspection grounds.

In case the event specified in the inspection grounds occurs, the inspection requestor (e.g., the verifier) contacts the inspector to request the de-anonymization of a presentation or issuance token. To do that, he sends the token (which he can retrieve, e.g., with the help of the `getPresentationToken` method described in Table 2.2) and the (non-cryptographic) evidence that the inspection grounds are fulfilled to the inspector. If the inspector determines by means of the evidence that these grounds are indeed fulfilled, he invokes the `inspect` method to decrypt the inspectable attributes in question (see Table 2.4).

2.4.5 Revocation

Our framework also supports revocation of credentials, thereby distinguishing whether a credentials may need to be revoked either globally (issuer-driven revocation) or for a specific context (verifier-driven revocation) (see Section 2.1 for details). To revoke a credential globally, the revocation authority calls the `revoke` method on input of the credential's revocation handle (see Table 2.4). For verifier-driven revocation, a conjunction of attributes can be revoked by calling the same method. In the latter case, all credentials that contain the combination of attribute values specified in the list will get revoked. The revocation authority typically knows the attribute values to revoke because they were either revealed in a former presentation token, or were decrypted by an inspector.

All entities that deal with revocable credentials must ensure that their respective revocation information is up-to-date. This is handled transparently by the ABCE which – if required – will internally contact the corresponding revocation authority through the Revocation Proxy and obtain the necessary updates or information. For instance, issuers have to contact their revocation authority during issuance in order to obtain a fresh revocation handle. On the verifier side, such a process is needed to guarantee that the verifier uses the latest revocation information from the revocation authority in order to correctly detect revoked credentials.

Similarly, users have to keep the non-revocation evidence of their credentials up-to-date. The Privacy-ABC system of a user should allow her to configure whether to contact the revocation authority only shortly prior to presenting a credential, or whether to perform proactive updates at regular intervals. The latter approach has the advantage that presentation is faster and that the revocation authority is not involved each single time a user wants to present her credential(s). Depending on the revocation technology, these updates may even fully preserve the anonymity of the user.

2.5 Language Framework

Given the multitude of distributed entities involved in a full-fledged Privacy-ABC system, the communication formats that are used between these entities must be specified and standardized.

None of the existing format standards for identity management protocols such as SAML, WS-Trust, or OpenID support all Privacy-ABCs' features. Although most of them can be extended to support a subset of these features, we define for the sake of simplicity and completeness a dedicated language framework which addresses all unique Privacy-ABC features. Our languages can be integrated into existing identity management systems.

In this section we introduce our framework covering the full life-cycle of Privacy-ABCs, including setup, issuance, presentation, revocation, and inspection. As the main purpose of our data artifacts is to be processed and generated by automated policy and credential handling mechanisms, we define all artifacts in XML schema notation, although one could also create a profile using a different encoding such as Abstract Syntax Notation One (ASN.1) [ASN08] or JavaScript Object Notation (JSON) [Cro06].

The XML artifacts formally describe and orchestrate the underlying cryptographic mechanisms and provide opaque containers for carrying the cryptographic data. Whenever appropriate, our formats also support user-friendly textual names or descriptions which allow to show a descriptive version of the XML artifacts to a user and to involve her in the issuance or presentation process if necessary.

For didactic purposes, we describe the different artifacts realizing the concepts and features of Privacy-ABCs (see Section 2.1) by means of an example scenario, which scenario is described in the following section. For the sake of space and readability, the artifact examples for the scenario do not illustrate all the features of Privacy-ABCs. We refer the reader to [BCD+14] for the full specification. In the following sections, we explicitly distinguish between user attributes (as contained in a credential) and XML attributes (as defined by XML schema) whenever they could be confused.

2.5.1 Example Scenario

In this section, we describe an example scenario for illustrating the language framework artifacts that are introduced in the following sections.

The Republic of Utopia issues electronic identity cards to all of its citizens, containing their name, date of birth, and the state in which they reside. These electronic identities are used for many applications, such as interactions with government and businesses. It is therefore crucial that any card that is reported lost or stolen will be quickly revoked.

All citizens of Utopia may sign up for one free digital membership card to the library of their state. To obtain a library card, the applicant must present her valid identity card and reveal her state of residence, but otherwise remains anonymous during the issuance of the library card.

The state library has a privacy-friendly online interface for borrowing both digital and paper books. Readers can log in to the library website to anonymously browse and borrow books using their library card based on Privacy-ABCs. Hardcopy books will be delivered in anonymous numbered mailboxes at the post office; digital books are simply delivered electronically. If paper books are returned late or damaged, however, the library must be able to identify the reader to impose an appropriate fine. Repeated negligence can even lead to exclusion from borrowing further paper books—but borrowing digital books always remains possible. Moreover, the library occasionally offers special conditions to readers of targeted age groups, e.g., longer rental periods for readers under the age of twenty-six.

2.5.2 Credential Specification

A credential specification describes the common structure and possible features of credentials. Remember that the Republic of Utopia issues electronic identity cards to its citizens containing their full name, state, and date of birth. Note that libraries and other verifiers may target different age groups in different policies, so hard-coding dedicated "over twenty-six" attributes would not be very sensible. Utopia may issue Privacy-ABCs according to the credential specification shown in Figure 2.7.

```
1  <CredentialSpecification KeyBinding="true" Revocable="true">
2    <SpecificationUID> urn:creds:id </SpecificationUID>
3    <AttributeDescriptions MaxLength="256">
4      <AttributeDescription Type="urn:creds:id:name" DataType="xs:string" Encoding="xenc:sha256">
5        <FriendlyAttributeName lang="EN"> Full Name </FriendlyAttributeName>
6      </AttributeDescription>
7      <AttributeDescription Type="urn:creds:id:state" DataType="xs:string" Encoding="xenc:sha256"/>
8      <AttributeDescription Type="urn:creds:id:bdate" DataType="xs:date" Encoding="date:unix:signed"/>
9      <AttributeDescription Type="urn:revocationhandle" DataType="xs:integer" Encoding="integer:unsigned" />
10   </AttributeDescriptions>
11 </CredentialSpecification>
```

Fig. 2.7 Credential specification of the identity card

The XML attribute **KeyBinding** indicates whether credentials adhering to this specification must be bound to a secret key. The XML attribute **Revocable** being set to *"true"* indicates that the credentials will be subject to issuer-driven revocation and hence must contain a special revocation handle attribute. The assigned revocation authority is specified in the issuer parameters.

To encode user attribute values in a Privacy-ABC, they must be mapped to integers of a limited length. The maximal length depends on the security parameter (basically, it is the bit length of exponents in the group) and is indicated by the **MaxLength** XML attribute (Line 3), here 256 bits. In our example, electronic identity cards contain a person's full name, state, and date of birth. The XML attributes **Type**, **DataType**, and **Encoding** respectively contain the unique identifier for the user attribute type, for the data type, and for the encoding algorithm that specifies how the value is to be mapped to an integer of the correct size (Lines 4,7,8,9). Attributes that may have values longer than **MaxLength** have to be hashed, as is done here for the name using SHA-256. The specification can also define human-readable names for the user attributes in different languages (Line 5).

2.5.3 Issuer, Revocation, and System Parameters

The government of Utopia acts as issuer and revocation authority for the identity cards. It generates an issuance key pair and publishes the issuer parameters, and generates and publishes the revocation authority parameters, which are illustrated in Figure 2.8.

The **ParametersUID** element assigns unique identifiers for the issuer and revocation authority parameters. The issuer parameters additionally specify the chosen cryptographic Privacy-ABC and hash algorithm, the maximal number of attributes that credentials issued under these issuer parameters may have, the parameter identifier of the system parameters that shall be used, and the parameters identifier of the revocation authority that will manage the issuer-driven revocation. The **CryptoParams** contain cryptographic algorithm-specific information about the public key.

```
<IssuerParameters>
  <ParametersUID> urn:utopia:id:issuer </ParametersUID>
  <AlgorithmID> urn:com:microsoft:uprove </AlgorithmID>
  <SystemParametersUID> urn:utopia:id:system </SystemParametersUID>
  <MaximalNumberOfAttributes> 4 </MaximalNumberOfAttributes>
  <HashAlgorithm> xenc:sha256 </HashAlgorithm>
  <CryptoParams> ... </CryptoParams>
  <RevocationParametersUID> urn:utopia:id:ra </RevocationParametersUID>
</IssuerParameters>
```

```
<RevocationAuthorityParameters>
  <ParametersUID> urn:utopia:id:ra </ParametersUID>
  <RevocationMechanism> urn:privacy−abc:accumulators:cl </RevocationMechanism>
  <RevocationInfoReference ReferenceType="url"> https:utopia.gov/id/revauth/revinfo
    </RevocationInfoReference>
  <NonRevocationEvidenceReference ReferenceType="url"> https:utopia.gov/id/revauth/nrevevidence
    </NonRevocationEvidenceReference>
  <CryptoParams> ... </CryptoParams>
</RevocationAuthorityParameters>
```

```
<SystemParameters>
  <ParametersUID> urn:utopia:id:system </ParametersUID>
  <CryptoParams> ... </CryptoParams>
</SystemParameters>
```

Fig. 2.8 Issuer, revocation authority, and system parameters

The revocation authority parameters can be used for both issuer- and verifier-driven revocation. They specify a unique identifier for the parameters, the cryptographic revocation mechanisms, and references to the network endpoints where the most recent revocation information and non-revocation evidence can be fetched.

The system parameters fix some cryptographic parameters that are needed by the Privacy-ABC system as a whole, such as the overall security level and the groups that are to be used with the pseudonyms. Every party in the Privacy-ABC system must use the same system parameters to ensure compatibility. Any trusted issuer can create fresh system parameters, but ideally system parameters should be standardized.

2.5.4 Presentation Policy with Basic Features

Assume that a user already possesses an identity card from the Republic of Utopia issued according to the credential specification depicted in Figure 2.7. To get her free library card the user must present her valid identity card and reveal (only) the state attribute certified by the card. This results in the presentation policy depicted in Figure 2.9.

We now go through the preceding presentation policy and describe how the different features of Privacy-ABCs can be realized with our language. We first focus on

```
1  <PresentationPolicy PolicyUID="libcard">
2    <Message>
3      <Nonce> bkQydHBQWDR4TUZzbXJKYUM= </Nonce>
4    </Message>
5    <Pseudonym Alias="nym" Scope="urn:library:issuance" Exclusive="true"/>
6    <Credential Alias="id" SameKeyBindingAs="nym">
7      <CredentialSpecAlternatives>
8        <CredentialSpecUID> urn:creds:id </CredentialSpecUID>
9      </CredentialSpecAlternatives>
10     <IssuerAlternatives>
11       <IssuerParametersUID> urn:utopia:id:issuer </IssuerParametersUID>
12     </IssuerAlternatives>
13     <DisclosedAttribute AttributeType= "urn:creds:id:state"/>
14   </Credential>
15 </PresentationPolicy>
```

Fig. 2.9 Presentation policy for an identity card

the basic features and describe extended concepts such as inspection and revocation in our second example.

Signing Messages

A presentation token can optionally sign a message. The message to be signed is specified in the policy (Figure 2.9, Lines 2–4). It can include a nonce, any application-specific message, and a human-readable name and/or description of the policy. The nonce will be used to prevent replay attacks, i.e. to ensure freshness of the presentation token, and for cryptographic evidence generation. Thus, when making use of the nonce, the presentation policy is not static anymore, but needs to be completed with a fresh nonce element for every request.

Pseudonyms

The optional **Pseudonym** element (Figure 2.9, Line 5) indicates that the presentation token must contain a pseudonym. A pseudonym can be presented by itself or in relation with a credential if key binding is used (which we discuss later).

The associated XML attribute **Exclusive** indicates that a scope-exclusive pseudonym must be created, with the scope string given by the XML attribute **Scope**. This ensures that each user can create only a single pseudonym satisfying this policy, so that the registration service can prevent the same user from obtaining multiple library cards. Setting **Exclusive** to *"false"* would allow an ordinary pseudonym to be presented. The **Pseudonym** element has an optional boolean XML attribute **Established**, not illustrated in the example, which, when set to *"true"*, requires the user to re-authenticate under a previously established pseudonym. The presentation policy can request multiple pseudonyms, e.g., to verify that different pseudonyms actually belong to the same user.

Credentials and Selective Disclosure

For each credential that the user is requested to present, the policy contains a **Credential** element (Figure 2.9, Lines 6–14), which describes the credential to present in detail. In particular, disjunctive lists of the accepted credential specifications and issuer parameters can be specified via **CredentialSpecAlternatives** and **IssuerAlternatives** elements, respectively (Figure 2.9, Lines 7-9 and 10–12). The credential element also indicates all attributes that must be disclosed by the user via **DisclosedAttribute** elements (Figure 2.9, Line 13). The XML attribute **Alias** assigns the credential an alias so that it can be referred to from other places in the policy, e.g., from the attribute predicates.

Key Binding

If present, the **SameKeyBindingAs** attribute of a **Credential** or **Pseudonym** element (Figure 2.9, Line 6), contains an alias referring either to another Pseudonym element within this policy, or to a Credential element for a credential with key binding. This indicates that the current pseudonym or credential and the referred pseudonym or credential have to be bound to the same key. In our preceding example, the policy requests that the identity card and the presented pseudonym must belong to the same secret key.

Issuance Policy

To support the advanced features described in Section 2.1 , we propose a dedicated *issuance policy*. A library card contains the applicant's name and is bound to the same secret key as the identity card. So the identity card must not only be presented, but also used as a source to carry over the name and the secret key to the library card. The library shouldn't learn either of these during the issuance process. Altogether, to issue library cards the state library creates the issuance policy depicted in Figure 2.10. It contains the presentation policy from Figure 2.9 and the credential template that is described in detail below.

```
1  <IssuancePolicy>
2    <PresentationPolicy PolicyUID="libcard"> ... </PresentationPolicy>
3    <CredentialTemplate SameKeyBindingAs="id">
4      <CredentialSpecUID> urn:utopia:lib </CredentialSpecUID>
5      <IssuerParametersUID> urn:utopia:lib:issuer </IssuerParametersUID>
6      <UnknownAttributes>
7        <CarriedOverAttribute TargetAttributeType= "urn:utopia:lib:name">
8          <SourceCredentialInfo Alias="id" AttributeType="urn:creds:id:name"/>
9        </CarriedOverAttribute>
10     </UnknownAttributes>
11   </CredentialTemplate>
12 </IssuancePolicy>
```

Fig. 2.10 Issuance policy for a library card. The presentation policy on Line 2 is depicted in Figure 2.9.

Credential Template

A credential template describes the relation of the new credential to the existing credentials that were requested in the presentation policy. The credential template (Figure 2.10, Lines 3–11) must first state the unique identifier of the credential specification and issuer parameters of the newly issued credential (notice that here those are different than the identifiers of the credential specification and issuer parameters of the credential that is presented). The optional XML attribute **SameKeyBindingAs** further specifies that the new credential will be bound to the same secret key as a credential or pseudonym in the presentation policy, in this case the identity card.

Within the **UnknownAttributes** element (Figure 2.10, Lines 6–10) it is specified which user attributes of the new credential will be carried over from existing credentials in the presentation token. The **SourceCredentialInfo** element (Figure 2.10, Line 8) indicates the credential and the user attribute of which the value will be carried over.

Although this is not illustrated in our example, an attribute value can also be specified to be chosen jointly at random by the issuer and the user. This is achieved by setting the optional XML attribute **JointlyRandom** to *"true"*.

2.5.5 *Presentation and Issuance Token*

A *presentation token* consists of the *presentation token description*, containing the mechanism-agnostic description of the revealed information, and the *cryptographic evidence*, containing opaque values from the specific cryptography that "implements" the token description. The presentation token description roughly uses the same syntax as a presentation policy. An *issuance token* is a special presentation token that satisfies the stated presentation policy, but that contains additional cryptographic information required by the credential template.

The main difference to the presentation and issuance policy is that in the returned token a **Pseudonym** (if requested in the policy) now also contains a **PseudonymValue** (Figure 2.11, Line 6). Similarly, the **DisclosedAttribute** elements (Figure 2.11, Lines 10–12) in a token now also contain the actual user attribute values. Finally, all data from the cryptographic implementation of the presentation token and the advanced issuance features are grouped together in the **CryptoEvidence** element (Figure 2.11, Line 17). This data includes, e.g., proof that the contained identity card is not revoked by the issuer and that it is bound bound to the same secret key as the pseudonym.

```
<IssuanceToken>
  <IssuanceTokenDescription>
    <PresentationTokenDescription PolicyUID ="libcard" >
      <Message> ... </Message>
      <Pseudonym Alias="nym" Scope="urn:library:issuance" Exclusive="true" />
        <PseudonymValue> MER2VXISHI=</PseudonymValue>
      </Pseudonym>
      <Credential Alias="id" SameKeyBindingAs="nym" >
        ...
        <DisclosedAttribute AttributeType="urn:creds:id:state" >
          <AttributeValue> Nirvana </AttributeValue>
        </DisclosedAttribute>
      </Credential>
    </PresentationTokenDescription>
    <CredentialTemplate SameKeyBindingAs="id" > ... </CredentialTemplate>
  </IssuanceTokenDescription>
  <CryptoEvidence> ... </CryptoEvidence>
</IssuanceToken>
```

Fig. 2.11 Issuance token for obtaining the library card

2.5.6 Presentation Policy with Extended Features

Recall that the state library has a privacy-friendly online interface for borrowing books, but that it wants to identify readers who don't properly return their books and potentially ban them for borrowing more paper books. Also recall that the library has a special program for young readers. Altogether, for borrowing books under the "young-reader"-conditions, users have to satisfy the presentation policy depicted in Figure 2.12.

A presentation policy that is used for plain presentation (i.e., not within an issuance policy) can consist of multiple policy alternatives, each wrapped in a separate **PresentationPolicy** element (Figure 2.12, Lines 2–34 and 35–63). The returned presentation token must satisfy (at least) one of the specified policies.

The example presentation policy requires two **Credential** elements, for the library and for the identity card, which must belong to the same secret key as indicated by the XML attribute **SameKeyBindingAs**.

Attribute Predicates

No user attributes of the identity card have to be revealed, but the **AttributePredicate** element (Figure 2.12, Lines 30–33) specifies that the date of birth must be after April 1st, 1988, i.e., that the reader is younger than twenty-six. Supported predicate functions include equality, inequality, greater-than and less-than tests for most basic data types, as well as membership of a list of values. The arguments of the predicate function may be credential attributes (referred to by the credential alias and the attribute type) or constant values. See [BCD$^+$14] for an exhaustive list of supported predicates and data types and note that an attribute's encoding as defined in the credential specification has implications on which predicates can be used for it and whether it is inspectable.

```
1  <PresentationPolicyAlternatives>
2    <PresentationPolicy PolicyUID= "young-reader" >
3      <Message> ... </Message>
4      <Credential Alias="libcard" SameKeyBindingAs="id" >
5        <CredentialSpecAlternatives>
6          <CredentialSpecUID> urn:utopia:lib </CredentialSpecUID>
7        </CredentialSpecAlternatives>
8        <IssuerAlternatives>
9          <IssuerParametersUID> urn:utopia:lib:issuer </IssuerParametersUID>
10       </IssuerAlternatives>
11       <DisclosedAttribute AttributeType= "urn:utopia:lib:name" >
12         <InspectorAlternatives>
13           <InspectorParametersUID> urn:lib:arbitrator </InspectorParametersUID>
14         </InspectorAlternatives>
15         <InspectionGrounds> Late return or damage. </InspectionGrounds>
16       </DisclosedAttribute>
17     </Credential>
18     <Credential Alias="id" >
19       <CredentialSpecAlternatives>
20         <CredentialSpecUID> urn:creds:id </CredentialSpecUID>
21       </CredentialSpecAlternatives>
22       <IssuerAlternatives>
23         <IssuerParametersUID> urn:utopia:id:issuer </IssuerParametersUID>
24       </IssuerAlternatives>
25     </Credential>
26     <VerifierDrivenRevocation>
27       <RevocationParametersUID> urn:lib:blacklist </RevocationParametersUID>
28       <Attribute CredentialAlias ="libcard" AttributeType="urn:utopia:lib:name" />
29     </VerifierDrivenRevocation>
30     <AttributePredicate Function= "...:date-greater-than" >
31       <Attribute CredentialAlias ="id" AttributeType= "urn:creds:id:bdate" />
32       <ConstantValue> 1988-04-01 </ConstantValue>
33     </AttributePredicate>
34   </PresentationPolicy>
35   <PresentationPolicy PolicyUID= "regular-reader" >
```

Lines 36–62 are identical to lines 3–29 (i.e., without the AttributePredicate element).

```
63   </PresentationPolicy>
64 </PresentationPolicyAlternatives>
```

Fig. 2.12 Presentation policy for borrowing books

Inspection

To be able to nevertheless reveal the name of an anonymous borrower and to impose a fine when a book is returned late or damaged, the library can make use of inspection. The **DisclosedAttribute** element for the user attribute *"...:name"* contains **InspectorParametersUID** and **InspectionGrounds** child elements, indicating that the attribute value must not be disclosed to the verifier, but to the specified inspector with the specified inspection grounds. The former child element specifies the inspector's public key under which the value must be encrypted, in this case belonging to a designated arbiter within the library. The latter element specifies the circumstances under which the attribute value may be revealed by the arbiter. Our language also provides a data artifact for inspector parameters, which we omit here for space reasons.

Issuer-Driven Revocation

When the presentation policy requests a credential that is subject to issuer-driven revocation (as defined in the credential specification), the credential must be proved to be valid with respect to the most recent revocation information. However, a policy can also require the use of a particular past version of the revocation information. In the latter case, the element **IssuerParametersUID** has an extra XML attribute **RevocationInformationUID** specifying the identifier of the specific revocation information. The specification of the referenced **RevocationInformation** is given in [BCD+14]. Presentation tokens can accordingly state the validity of credentials with respect to a particular version by using a **RevocationInformationUID** XML element in the corresponding Credential element.

Verifier-Driven Revocation

If customers return borrowed books late or damaged, they are excluded from borrowing further paper books, but they are still allowed to use the library's online services. In our example, this is handled by a **VerifierDrivenRevocation** element (Figure 2.12, Lines 26–29), which specifies that the user attribute *"...:name"* of the library card must be checked against the most recent revocation information from the revocation authority *"urn:lib:blacklist"*. Revocation can also be based on a combination of user attributes from different credentials, in which case there will be multiple **Attribute** child elements per **VerifierDrivenRevocation**. The presentation policy can also contain multiple **VerifierDrivenRevocation** elements for one or several credentials, the returned presentation token must then prove its non-revoked status for *all* of them.

2.5.7 Interaction with the User Interface

During a presentation, the user can potentially satisfy the presentation policy alternatives in many ways. In order to allow the user to choose which presentation policy he wishes to satisfy, to choose how to satisfy the chosen policy (e.g., if he has multiple credentials of one type), and to check what he reveals by doing so, the Privacy-ABC framework generates a **UiPresentationArguments** object and hands it over to the application, which in turn will probably want to forward it to some sort of user interface. The framework then expects an object of type **UiPresentationReturn** with the user's choice. There are similar objects **UiIssuanceArguments** and **UiIssuanceReturn** for issuance. Standardizing the format of these objects is less critical than the other described in the remained of this section as they remain confined to the user's machine; we show here one possible embodiment of these objects.

We designed the **UiPresentationArguments** object (Figure 2.13) such that the complexity of the user interface is minimized: (1) it contains enough information so that the application does not have to query additional data from the Privacy-ABC framework, and (2) it contains some redundant information so that it does not need to do complex parsing of the policy to figure out what exactly is being revealed. It

```
1  <UiPresentationArguments>
2    <data>
3      <credentialSpecification id="urn:utopia:lib">...</credentialSpecification>
4      <credentialSpecification id="urn:creds:id">...</credentialSpecification>
5      <issuer id="urn:utopia:lib:issuer">...</issuer>
6      <issuer id="urn:utopia:id:issuer">...</issuer>
7      <inspector id="urn:lib:arbitrator">...</inspector>
8      <revocationAuthority id="urn:utopia:id:ra">...</revocationAuthority>
9      <credentialDescription id="urn:utopia:lib:74bddfb3-6886-43ac-83f8-ca3b72ad050d">...</
           credentialDescription>
10     <credentialDescription id="urn:creds:id:14f22b9d-06e0-4110-a8d9-b1a922462cd1">...</
           credentialDescription>
11   </data>
12   <tokenCandidatePerPolicy policyId="0">
13     <policy>...</policy>
14     <tokenCandidate candidateId="0">
15       <tokenDescription>...</tokenDescription>
16       <credential ref="urn:utopia:lib:74bddfb3-6886-43ac-83f8-ca3b72ad050d" />
17       <credential ref="urn:creds:id:14f22b9d-06e0-4110-a8d9-b1a922462cd1" />
18       <revealedFact>
19         <description lang="EN">You prove that urn:creds:id:bdate from credential urn:creds:id
20             is greater than 1988-04-01 (26 years ago).</description>
21       </revealedFact>
22       <revealedFact>
23         <description lang="EN">You prove that 'Full Name' from credential 'Library Card'
24             is not revoked by the verifier urn:lib:blacklist.</description>
25       </revealedFact>
26       <revealedFact>
27         <description lang="EN">You prove that urn:creds:id is not revoked by urn:utopia:id:ra.</description>
28       </revealedFact>
29       <inspectableAttribute>
30         <credential ref="urn:utopia:lib:74bddfb3-6886-43ac-83f8-ca3b72ad050d" />
31         <attributeType>urn:utopia:lib:name</attributeType>
32         <inspectionGrounds>Late return or damage.</inspectionGrounds>
33         <inspectorAlternative ref="urn:lib:arbitrator" />
34       </inspectableAttribute>
35     </tokenCandidate>
36   </tokenCandidatePerPolicy>
37   <tokenCandidatePerPolicy policyId="1">...</tokenCandidatePerPolicy>
38 </UiPresentationArguments>
```


Fig. 2.13 Message sent to the User Interface for Presentation

consists of two parts: the first part is a **data** element, which lists all parameters and similar objects that are referred to in the second part: a list of all credential specifications (Lines 3–4), summaries of all issuer parameters (Lines 5–6), summaries of all inspector parameters (Line 7), summaries of all revocation authorities (Line 8), credential descriptions (Lines 9–10), and pseudonym descriptions (not shown for this example, but see Line 4 of Figure 2.14). The second part consists of a list of **tokenCandidatePerPolicy** elements, which in turn comprise a presentation policy (Line 13) and a list of **tokenCandidate** showing all possible alternatives to satisfy the policy. The latter consists of a partially filled out presentation token description (Line 15); the list of credentials that will be presented (Lines 16–17); all possible alternative lists of pseudonyms that are compatible with the presented credentials and that satisfy the policy (not shown in this example, but see Lines 9–11 in Figure 2.14), here the Privacy-ABC framework will tentatively create new pseudonyms each time and include those in the list, these pseudonyms are then only saved if the user actually

```
1  <UiIssuanceArguments>
2    <data>
3      ...
4      <pseudonym id="nym:urn:library:issuance:965999d1−25e9−49e5−8db6−ad8ae9705807">...</pseudonym>
5      ...
6    </data>
7    <tokenCandidate candidateId="0">
8      ...
9      <pseudonymCandidate candidateId="0">
10       <pseudonym ref="nym:urn:library:issuance:965999d1−25e9−49e5−8db6−ad8ae9705807" />
11     </pseudonymCandidate>
12     ...
13     </tokenCandidate>
14   <issuancePolicy>...</issuancePolicy>
15 </UiIssuanceArguments>
```

Fig. 2.14 Message sent to the User Interface for Issuance

selects them for inclusion in the presentation token; a list of facts that will be revealed as part of the presentation (Lines 18–28), such as equality between attributes, predicates over the attributes, revocation checks—the friendly names of credentials, attributes, and parameters are used whenever available; the list of attributes that are revealed (not shown in this example), including attributes that are proven to be equal to a revealed attribute; and the list of inspectable attributes (Lines 29–34) with a choice of possible inspectors (Line 33).

The **UiPresentationReturn** object (Figure 2.15) indicates which policy (Line 2), which presentation token within that policy (Line 3), and which inspector for each of the inspectable attributes (Line 4) the user chose. Not shown in this example, but also part of the **UiPresentationReturn** is the list of pseudonyms the user wishes to chose, and whether the user wishes to change the metadata of any of the stored pseudonyms (we show examples of those in Figure 2.16).

```
1  <UiPresentationReturn>
2    <chosenPolicy>0</chosenPolicy>
3    <chosenPresentationToken>0</chosenPresentationToken>
4    <chosenInspectors>urn:lib:arbitrator</chosenInspectors>
5  </UiPresentationReturn>
```

Fig. 2.15 Response from the User Interface for Presentation

The **UiIssuanceArguments** object (Figure 2.14) is similar to the **UiPresentationArguments** element. Since there is only one issuance policy per issuance transaction, we removed the **tokenCandidatePerPolicy** element; instead the **tokenCandidate** elements (Line 7) and **issuancePolicy** element (Line 14) are direct children of the root element.

The **UiIssuanceReturn** object (Figure 2.16) is similar to the **UiPresentationReturn** object. It indicates which presentation token within the policy (Line 2), which inspectors (not shown in this example), and which list of pseudonyms (Line 3) were

```
1  <UiIssuanceReturn>
2    <chosenIssuanceToken>0</chosenIssuanceToken>
3    <chosenPseudonymList>0</chosenPseudonymList>
4    <metadataToChange>
5      <entry>
6        <key>nym:urn:library:issuance:965999d1−25e9−49e5−8db6−ad8ae9705807</key>
7        <value>I used this to obtain my library card.</value>
8      </entry>
9    </metadataToChange>
10 </UiIssuanceReturn>
```

Fig. 2.16 Response from the User Interface for Issuance

chosen. In this example, the user has also chosen to associate new metadata to the pseudonym (Lines 4–9).

2.6 Applicability to Existing Identity Infrastructures

Many identity protocols and frameworks are in use today, and new ones are being developed by the industry, each addressing specific use cases and deployment environments. Privacy concerns exist in many scenarios targeted by these systems, and therefore it is useful to understand how they could benefit from Privacy-ABC technologies to improve their security, privacy, and scalability.

We consider the following popular systems: WS-*, SAML, OpenID, OAuth, and X.509.[1] A short description of each system is given to facilitate the discussion, but is by no means complete; the reader is referred to the appropriate documentation to learn more about a particular system. Moreover, we mostly describe how integration can be done, rather than discussing why as this is highly application-specific.

The last section describes the common challenges of these federated systems, and how Privacy-ABC technologies can help to alleviate them.

*2.6.1 WS-**

The set of WS-* specifications define various protocols for web services and applications. Many of these relate to security, and in particular, to authentication and attribute-based access (such as WS-Trust [WST09], WS-Federation [WSF09], and WS-SecurityPolicy [WSS07]). These specifications can be combined to implement various systems with different characteristics.

[1] Other popular frameworks, such as Facebook Login [Fac], OpenID Connect [Ope], and Fido Alliance [Fid] are similar or built on top of the schemes presented here, and will therefore be omitted in the discussion.

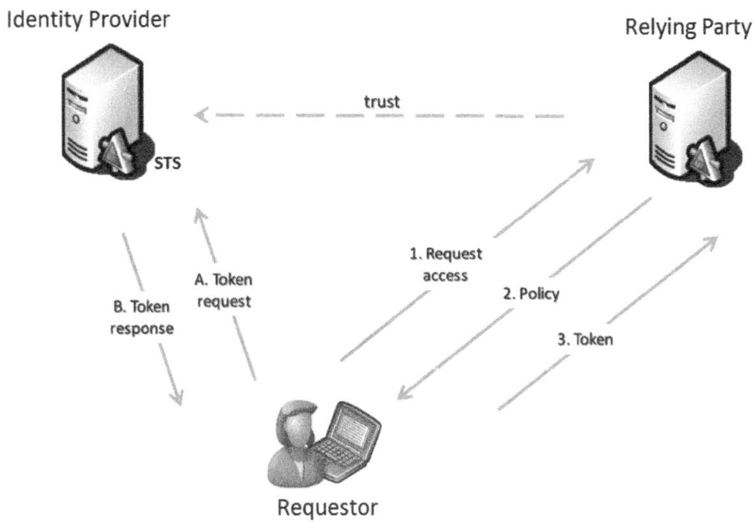

Fig. 2.17 WS-Trust protocol flow

The WS-Trust specification is the main building block that defines how *security tokens* can be obtained and presented by users. The specification does not make any assumption on the type of tokens exchanged, and provides several extensibility points and protocol flow patterns suitable for Privacy-ABC technologies.

In WS-Trust, a requestor (user) requests a security token from the Identity Providers Security Token Service (the issuer) encoding various certified claims (attributes), and presents it (either immediately or at a later time) to a Relying Party (the verifier); see Figure 2.17.

Integrating Privacy-ABC technologies in WS-Trust is straightforward due to the extensible nature of the WS-* framework. The issuance protocol is initiated by the requestor by sending, as usual, a `RequestForSecurityToken` message to the STS. The requestor and the STS then exchange as many `RequestForSecurityTokenResponse` messages as needed by the ABC issuance protocol (using the challenge-response pattern defined in Section 8 of [WS-12]). The STS concludes the protocol by sending a `RequestForSecurityTokenResponseCollection` message. Typically, this final message contains a collection of requested security tokens. Due to the nature of the Privacy-ABC technologies, the STS does not send the security tokens per se, but the requestor is able to compute its credential(s) using the exchanged cryptographic data. See Figure 2.18.

The issuance messages are tied together using a unique context, but otherwise do not specify the content and formatting of their contents. It is therefore possible to directly use the protocol artefacts defined in Section 2.5.

Presenting an ABC to a Relying Party is also straightforward. The exact mechanism to use depends on the application environment. For example, in a federated

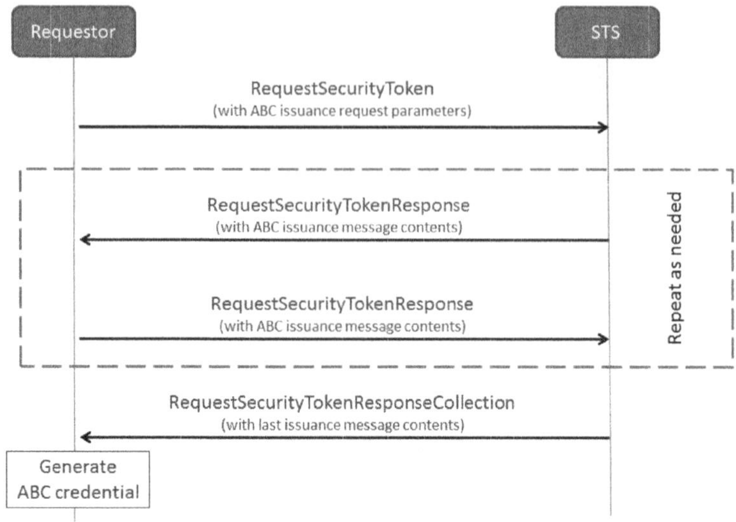

Fig. 2.18 WS-Trust issuance protocol

architecture using WS-Federation, the presentation token could be included in a `RequestForSecurity TokenResponse` message part of a `wresult` HTTP parameter. Given the support of extensible policy (using, e.g., WS-SecurityPolicy), the ABC verifier policy could be expressed by the Relying Party and obtained by the client; e.g., it could be embedded in a services federation metadata (see Section 3 of [WSF09]). Privacy-ABC technology integration into WS-Trust has been successfully demonstrated; see, e.g., [UPW11].

2.6.2 SAML

The Security Assertion Markup Language (SAML) is a popular set of specifications for exchanging certified assertions in federated environments. Different profiles exist addressing various use cases, but the core specification [SAM05] defines the main elements: the SAML assertion (a XML token type that can encode arbitrary attributes), and the SAML protocols for federated exchanges.

Typically, a User Agent (a.k.a. requester or client) requests access to a resource from a Relying Party (a.k.a. Service Provider) which in turn requests a SAML assertion from a trusted Identity Provider (a.k.a. SAML Authority). The User Agent is redirected to the Identity Provider to retrieve the SAML assertion (after authenticating to the Identity Provider in an unspecified manner) before passing it back to the Relying Party. Figure 2.19 illustrates the protocol flow.

Contrary to WS-*, the SAML protocols only permit the use of the SAML assertion token type. Therefore, one needs to profile the SAML assertion in order

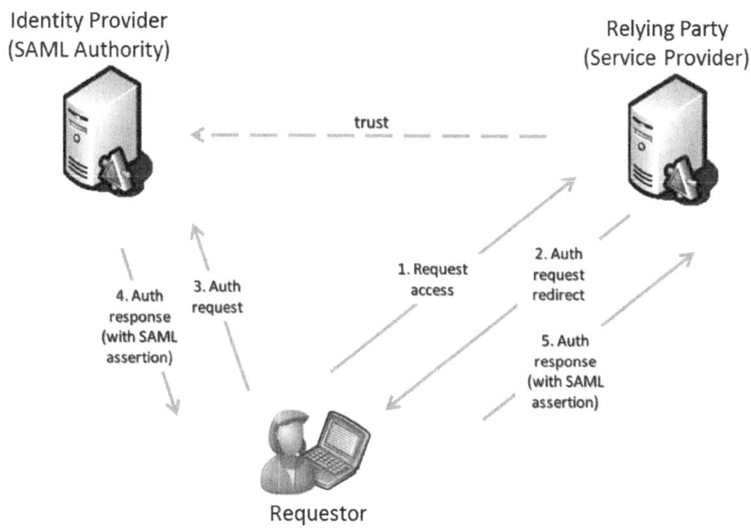

Fig. 2.19 SAML protocol flow

to use the Privacy-ABC technologies with the SAML protocols. The SAML assertion schema defines an optional `ds:Signature` element used by the Identity Provider to certify the contents of the assertion. If used, it must be a valid XML Signature [Bar02]. This means that XML Signature must also be profiled to support ABC issuer signatures.[2] The alternative would be to protect the SAML assertion using a custom external signature element. ABC-based SAML assertions could be used in the SAML protocols in various ways. One example would be for the client to create a modified SAML assertion using a Privacy-ABC in response to a Relying Partys authentication request rather than fetching it in real-time from the Identity Provider (replacing steps 3 and 4 in Figure 2.19). The assertion would contain the disclosed attributes, and encode the presentation tokens cryptographic data in the SAML signature. Essentially, the SAML assertion would be an alternative token type to the ABC presentation token. Additionally, the Identity Provider could issue an on-demand Privacy-ABC using the SAML protocol; this might require multiple roundtrips to accommodate the potentially interactive issuance protocol. Then the SAML assertion presented to the Relying Party would need to be created as explained above.

[2] This could be achieved by applying the appropriate XML transforms on the assertions contents before interpreting them as input to the ABC protocols.

2.6.3 OpenID

OpenID is a federated protocol allowing users to present an identifier[3] to Relying Parties by first authenticating to an OpenID Provider. The current specification, OpenID 2.0 [Ope07], specifies the protocol. Assuming that the user has an existing OpenID identifier registered with an OpenID Provider, we illustrate the steps in Figure 2.20.

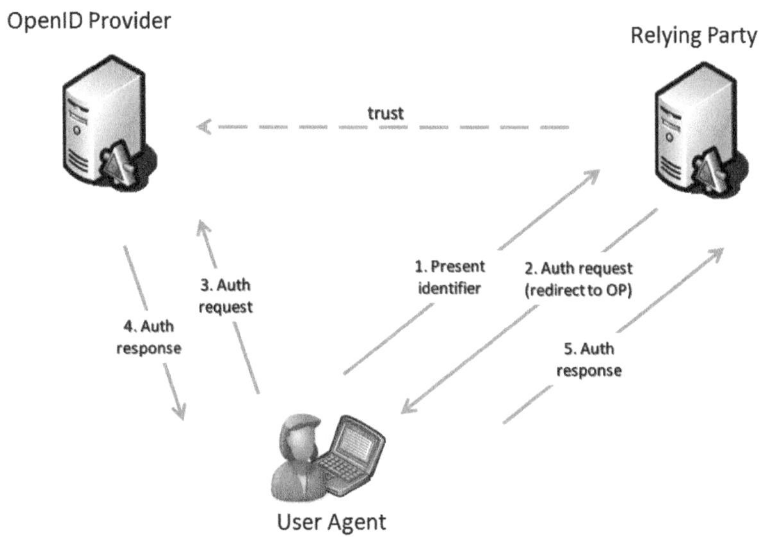

Fig. 2.20 OpenID protocol flow

1. To login to a Relying Party, the user presents her (unverified) OpenID identifier.
2. The Relying Party parses the identifier to discover the Users OpenID Provider and redirects the User Agent to it.
3. The user authenticates to the OpenID Provider; how this is achieved is out-of-scope of the OpenID specification (popular existing web deployments use usernames and passwords).
4. Upon successful authentication, the OpenID Provider redirects the User Agent to the Relying Party with a signed successful authentication message.
5. The Relying Party validates the authentication message using either a shared secret with the OpenID Provider or alternatively, by contacting the OpenID Provider directly.

OpenID follows a standard federated single sign-on model and therefore inherits the security and privacy problems of such systems. The OpenID specification de-

[3] The specification describe this as a URL or XRI (eXtensible Resource Identifier), but extensions used by popular deployments use email addresses.

scribes in Section 15 some countermeasures against common concerns, but nonetheless, the systems remains vulnerable to active attackers, especially to attacks originating from protocol participants (see, e.g., [Bra] for a summary of the issues).

Privacy-ABC technologies could be used to increase both the security and privacy of the protocol, and reduce the amount of trust needed on OpenID Providers. For example, certified or scope-exclusive pseudonyms derived from an ABC issued by an OpenID Provider could be used as local Relying Party identifiers, therefore providing unlinkability between the Users spheres of activities at different Relying Parties (using the Relying Parties URL as a scope string). The cryptographic data in the corresponding ABC presentation token would need to be encoded in extension parameters defined in an ABC profile. A similar integration has been demonstrated in the PseudoID prototype [DW10], using Chaums blind signatures [Cha83].

OpenID may also be used in attribute-based access scenarios. The OpenID Attribute Exchange [HBH07] extension describes how Relying Party can request attributes of any type from the OpenID Provider by adding fetch parameters in the OpenID authentication message, and how an OpenID Provider can return the requested attributes in the response. OpenID Connect [Ope] is a new scheme built on top of OAuth (see following section) that also addresses attribute exchange.

To generate an ABC-based response, the User Agent would create the OpenID response on behalf of the OpenID Provider using the contents of a presentation token, properly encoding the disclosed attributes using the OpenID Attribute Exchange formatting and by encoding the cryptographic evidence in custom attributes.

2.6.4 OAuth

OAuth is an authorization protocol that enables applications and devices to access HTTP[4] services on behalf of users using delegated tokens rather than the users main credentials. The current specification, OAuth 2.0 [Har12], is being developed by the IETF OAuth working group.[5] OAuth specifies four roles. Quoting from the spec:

resource owner: an entity capable of granting access to a protected resource (e.g. end-user).

resource server: the server hosting the protected resources, capable of accepting responding to resource requests using access tokens.

client: an application making protected resource requests on behalf of the owner and with its authorization.

authorization server: the server issuing access tokens to the client after successfully authenticating the resource owner and obtaining authorization.

An example scenario is as follows: an end-user (resource owner) can grant a printing service (client) access to her protected photos stored at a photo sharing service (resource server), without sharing her username and password with the printing

[4] Using a transport protocol other than HTTP is undefined by the specification.

[5] OAuth 2.0 evolved from the OAuth WRAP [HTEG10] profile which has been deprecated.

service. Instead, she authenticates directly with a server trusted by the photo sharing service (authorization server) which issues the service delegation-specific credentials (access token).

A typical OAuth interaction is illustrated in Figure 2.21:

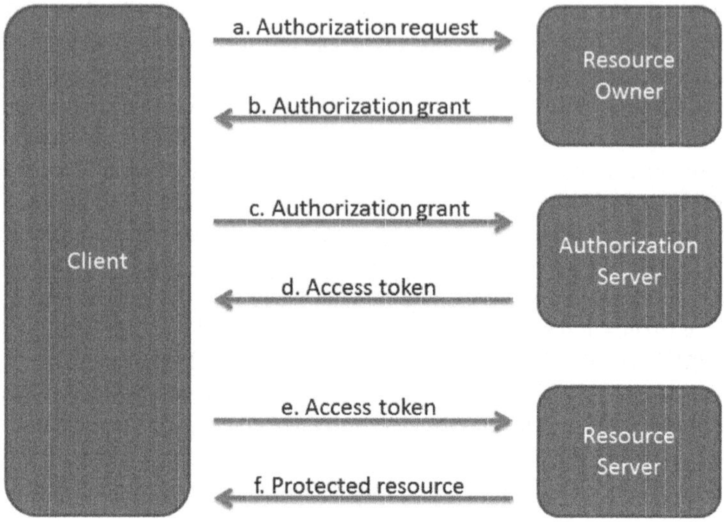

Fig. 2.21 OAuth 2.0 protocol flow

a. The client requests authorization from the resource owner. The authorization request can be made directly to the resource owner (as shown), or preferably indirectly via the authorization server as an intermediary.
b. The client receives an authorization grant which is a credential representing the resource owner's authorization, expressed using one of four grant types defined in this specification or using an extension grant type. The authorization grant type depends on the method used by the client to request authorization and the types supported by the authorization server.
c. The client requests an access token by authenticating with the authorization server and presenting the authorization grant.
d. The authorization server authenticates the client and validates the authorization grant, and if valid issues an access token.
e. The client requests the protected resource from the resource server and authenticates by presenting the access token.
f. The resource server validates the access token, and if valid, serves the request.

As we can see, two types of credentials are used in the protocol flow: the authorization grant and the access token. A Privacy-ABC could be used for either one, as we will describe in the following sections[6]. The OAuth protocol flow does not allow presenting a dynamic policy to the client; if this functionality is needed, the policy would need to be obtained and processed at the application layer; otherwise, the application may use an implicit policy that drives the clients behaviour.

2.6.4.1 Authorization grant

The first step in the OAuth flow is for the client to request authorization from the resource owner and getting back an authorization grant. The OAuth specification defines four grant types (authorization code, implicit, resource owner password credentials, and client credentials) and provides an extension mechanism for defining new ones.

Although one could use the authorization code or the client credential grant types, the extension mechanism is better-suited to integrate ABC-based grants. How the Privacy-ABC is obtained by the client is out-of-scope of the OAuth flow. To present the Privacy-ABC to the authorization server, one could define a profile similar to the SAML assertion one [MCM14]. For example, the client could send the following access token request to the authorization server:

```
POST /token HTTP/1.1
Host: server.example.com
Content-Type: application/x-www-form-urlencoded;charset=UTF-8
grant_type=http://abc4trust.eu/oauth&abctoken=PEFzc2VGlv...
```

where the `abctoken` parameter would contain an encoding of a presentation token (e.g., using a base64 encoding of the XML representation). As mentioned above, the policy driving the clients presentation behaviour would be dealt with at the application level (and might be fixed for an application).

2.6.4.2 Access token

An access token is issued by the authorization server to the client and later presented to the resource server. The format and contents of the access token is not defined in the OAuth specification, and therefore one could define a way to use a Privacy-ABC to create an access token. This can be done by defining a new access token type (as explained in Section 8.1 of [Har12]), or by encoding the presentation token content into an existing extensible token type, such as the JSON Web Token [JWT].[7]

Since access tokens are typically long-lived, the issuance of the Privacy-ABC can be done out-of-band of the OAuth protocol. It can also be done directly by

---

[6] The OAuth specification does not describe how the resource owner authenticates the client before issuing the authorization grant. Conceptually, this could also be done using an ABC.

[7] The JSON Web Token format contains a set of attribute name and value pairs and corresponding metadata (including a digital signature identified by an algorithm identifier). This is supported by ABC technologies, but does not allow the representation of the most advanced features. JWT extensions, such as the Proof-Of-Possession Semantics for JSON Web Tokens [JBT], might help to enable all the ABC features.

the authorization server by embedding the issuance protocol messages in multiple access token request-response runs (in which case the returned access tokens would be the opaque issuance messages). When this process concludes, the client would be able to create a valid ABC-based access token.

To present the ABC access token, client computes a valid presentation token using an application-specific resource policy (obtained out-of-band or implicitly defined), encodes it in the right access token format, and includes it in the OAuth protected resources access request.

2.6.5 X.509 PKI

Most of the schemes presented in this section require online interactions with an Issuer to present attributes to a Relying Party. This provides flexibility about what can be disclosed to the Relying Party, but impacts the privacy vis-à-vis the Issuer (which typically learns where the attributes are presented). A Public Key Infrastructure (PKI) uses a different approach: PKI certificates encoding arbitrary attributes and issued to users are typically long-lived. The decoupling of the issuance and presentation protocols provides some privacy benefits to the user, but removes the minimal disclosure aspect. Indeed, a Verifier will learn everything that is encoded in a certificate even if a subset of the information would have been sufficient to make its access decision. The integration of Privacy-ABC technology is therefore desirable to provide these privacy benefits while offering the same security level as in PKI.

X.509 [CSF$^+$08] is a popular PKI standard[8] that defines two types of credentials: public key and attribute certificates. A public key certificate contains a user public key associated to a secret private key, and other metadata (serial number, a validity period, a subject name, etc.) The certificate is signed by a Certificate Authority. An attribute certificate, also signed by the CA, is tied to a public-key certificate and can contain arbitrary attributes. Both types of certificates can also contain arbitrary extensions.

The X.509 protocol flow is as follows. The client starts by generating a key pair, and sends a certificate request that includes the generated public key to the Certificate Authority. The Certificate Authority creates, signs and returns the X.509 certificate to the client which stores it along with the associated private key. To authenticate to a Relying Party, the client later uses the certificates private key to sign a Relying Party-specified challenge (either a random number or an application-specific message). The Relying Party verifies the signature and validates the certificate. This involves verifying the certificates Certificate Authority signature, making sure that the Certificate Authority is a trusted issuer (is or is linked to a trusted root), and making sure that the certificate has not expired and is not revoked. Checking for non-revocation can be done by either checking that the certificates serial number

[8] Other PKI systems exist, such as PGP [CDF$^+$]. We will not consider them in this document, but ABC integration would look similar.

does not appear on a Certificate Revocation List (CRL), or by querying an Online Certificate Status Protocol (OCSP) responder.[9] See Figure 2.22.

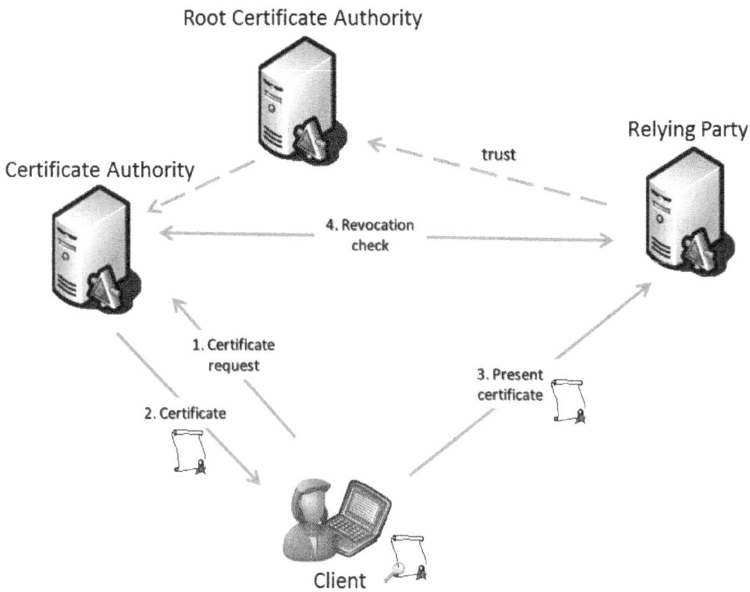

Fig. 2.22 X.509 protocol flow

Integrating Privacy-ABCs with X.509 certificates is possible and provides two immediate benefits:

- Long-lived certificates support minimal disclosure (only the relevant properties of encoded attributes are disclosed to the Relying Party rather than the full set of attributes), and
- The users public key and the Certificate Authority signatures on the certificates are unlinkable (the Certificate Authority and the Relying Parties cannot track and trace the usage of the certificate based solely on these cryptographic values).

Two integration approaches are considered next. The first one consists of encoding the ABC artefacts contents in X.509 artefacts using ABC-specific algorithm identifiers and extensions (i.e., the client would generate an X.509 certificate encoding the Privacy-ABCs contents at the end of the issuance protocol). Since the presentation protocol of an X.509 certificate is not specified, the presentation token artefact could be used almost as is, but including the modified X.509 certificate.

[9] The mechanism and endpoint to be used are specified by the CA and encoded into the certificate.

The second and preferred[10] approach would be to transform an existing X.509 certificate into a Privacy-ABC that can be presented to various Relying Parties. The following example illustrates the concept: The protocol flow would be as follows:

1. The client visits the ABC issuer and presents her X.509 certificate.
2. After validating the certificate and its ownership by the User, the ABC Issuer issues a Privacy-ABC encoding the certificates information into attributes:
    a. The certificates expiration date is encoded in an attribute.
    b. The certificates serial number is encoded as the revocation handle.
    c. The revocation information (e.g., the CRL endpoint)[11] is encoded in an attribute.
    d. The Certificate Authority identifier is encoded in an attribute.
    e. The other certificate fields might also be encoded in the Privacy-ABC if they need to be presented to Relying Parties.
3. The client later presents the ABC to the Verifier, disclosing the following information:
    a. Disclose the Certificate Authority identifier[12] and revocation information attributes.
    b. Prove that the underlying certificate is not expired by proving that the undisclosed expiration date is not before the current time.
    c. Prove that the serial number does not appear on the current CRL (this can be achieved using repetitive negation proofs on the CRL elements).[13]
4. The Verifier would perform these validation steps (on top of the normal ABC validation):
    a. Verify that the Certificate Authority is from a trusted set of issuers.
    b. Retrieve the current CRL (using the disclosed revocation information) and verify the non-revocation proof.
    c. Verify the non-expiration proof.

After these steps, the Verifier is convinced that the user possesses a valid (i.e., non-expired, non-revoked) X.509 certificate from a trusted Certificate Authority.

[10] We claim that this approach is preferred because of the broad existing code base implementing X.509. It would be easier to develop an conversion module on top of existing X.509 components.

[11] This example uses a CRL as the revocation mechanism. Using OCSP would also be possible by having the client prove to the OCSP responder directly that the ABC is not revoked, and presenting a freshly issued receipt to the Relying Party.

[12] Alternatively, the client could prove that the CA is from a trusted set specified by the Verifier.

[13] Alternatively, an ABC Revocation Authority could create an accumulator for the revoked values.

2.6.6 Integration Summary

The systems presented above follow a similar federated pattern of a Relying Party requesting, through the user, login or attribute information from a trusted Identity Provider. In PKI and OAuth the certified information (certificate and access token, respectively) are typically obtained in advance and reused over time, while in the other systems, the information is retrieved on-demand from the Identity Provider.

These architectures have some security, privacy, and scalability challenges that might be problematic in some scenarios:

- The Identity Provider can often access the Relying Party using a users identity without the users knowledge. This is trivial in systems where the Identity Provider creates the pseudonym (like in SAML, OpenID, OAuth, WS-Federation). In systems where a user secret is employed (like in PKI, or in some WS-Trust profiles), this is more complicated but still could be possible.[14] Moreover, Identity Providers can also selectively deny access to users by refusing to issue security tokens (discriminating on the requesting user or requested service).
- For authentication depending on knowledge of a user secret (e.g., username/password), phishing attacks on the credential provided to the Identity Provider result in malicious access to all Relying Parties that accept that identity.
- Strong authentication to the Identity Provider is often supported (including multi-factor asymmetric-based authentication), but the resulting security tokens (e.g., SAML assertion, OAuth access token, OpenID authentication response) are typically weaker software-only bearer token which can be intercepted and replayed by adversaries.
- The Identity Provider typically learns which Relying Party the user is trying to access. For on-demand security token issuance, this information is often provided to the Identity Provider in order to protect the security token (e.g., to encrypt it for the Relying Party) or to redirect the user to the right location. When security tokens are long-lived (like in PKI), this information is still available if the Identity Providers and Relying Parties compare notes (since signatures on security tokens generated using conventional cryptography are traceable).
- Central Identity Providers in on-demand federated systems limit the scalability of the systems because if they are offline, users will not be able to access any Relying Parties. This makes them interesting targets for denial of service attacks.

Privacy-ABC technologies help alleviate these issues by increasing the security, privacy, and scalability of these systems. Indeed:

- Since Privacy-ABCs are by default untraceable, even when obtained on-demand, Identity Providers are not able to track and trace the usage of the users information.

[14] As an example, in PKI, a Certificate Authority would not be able to re-issue a valid certificate containing the users public key, but could re-issue one with a matching serial number and subject and key identifiers often used for user authentication.

- Since Privacy-ABCs can be obtained in advance and stored by the user while still being able to disclose the minimal amount of information needed for a particular transaction, the real-time burden of the issuer is diminished, improving scalability.
- Since Privacy-ABCs are based on asymmetric cryptography, presenting login pseudonyms and certified attributes involve using a private key unknown to the Issuer, meaning that the Identity Provider (or another adversary) is unable to hijack the users identity at a particular Relying Party.

Privacy-ABC technologies offer a wide range of features; not all of them trivially compatible with the systems presented in this section. The important point is that Privacy-ABC technologies offer a superset of the functionality and of the security/privacy/scalability characteristics of these systems. Protocol designers and architects can therefore pick and choose which features and characteristics they would like to use to improve existing systems or their future revisions.

It is also important to note that Privacy-ABC technologies can be used in conjunction with these frameworks, since many real-life applications wont have the luxury to modify the existing standards and development libraries. Most of the privacy concerns occur in cross-domain data sharing, i.e., when information travels from one domain to another. Therefore, an ABC proxy can be used as a privacy filter between domains using well-known federated token transformer pattern (such as the WS-Trust STS). This is useful to avoid modifying legacy applications and infrastructure, and still benefit from the security and privacy properties of Privacy-ABC technologies.

2.7 Trust Relationships in the Ecosystem of Privacy-ABCs

Several incidents in the past have demonstrated the existence of possible harm that can arise from misuse of people's personal information such as blackmailing, impersonation, and so on. Giving credible and provable reassurances to people is required to build trust and make people feel secure to use the electronic services offered by companies or governments on-line. Indeed the use of Privacy-ABCs can help mitigate many serious threats to user's privacy. However, some risks still remain, which are not addressed by Privacy-ABCs, requiring some degree of trust between the involved entities. In this section, we focus on identifying the trust relationships between the involved entities in the ecosystem of Privacy-ABCs and provide a concrete answer to "*who needs to trust whom on what?*".

2.7.1 The Meaning of Trust

what do we mean by "trust"? A wide variety of definitions of trust exist in the bibliography [Har04][O'H04]. A comprehensive study of the concept has been presented in the work by McKnight and Chervany [MC96], where the authors provide a classification system for different aspects of trust. In their work, they define trust intention as *"the extent to which one party is willing to depend on the other party in a given situation with a feeling of relative security, even though negative consequences are possible."* [MC96]

Their definition embodies (a) the prospect of negative consequences in case the trusted party does not behave as expected, (b) the dependence on the trusted party, (c) the feeling of security, and the (d) situation-specific nature of trust. So, trust intention shows the willingness to trust a given party in a given context, and implies that the trusting entity has made a decision about the various risks of allowing this trust.

2.7.2 Related Work

Some work already exists in trust relationships in identity management systems. For example, Jøsang et al. [JP04] analyse some of the trust requirements in several existing identity management models. They consider the federated identity management model, as well as the isolated or the centralized identity management model and they focus on the trust requirements of the users into the service and identity providers, but also between the identity providers and service providers.

Delessy et al. [DFLP07] define the Circle of Trust pattern, which represents a federation of service providers that share trust relationships. The focus of their work however lies more on the architectural and behavioural aspects, rather than on the trust requirements which must be met to establish a relationship between two entities.

Later, Kylau et al. [KTMM09] concentrated explicitly on the federated identity management model and identify possible trust patterns and the associated trust requirements based on a risk analysis. The authors extend their scenarios by considering also scenarios with multiple federations. Nevertheless, their work does not match the ecosystem of Privacy-ABCs.

It seems that there is no work that discusses systematically the trust relationships in identity management systems that incorporate Privacy-ABCs. However, some steps have been done towards systematic threat analysis in such schemes, by the establishments of a quantitative threat modelling methodology that can be used to identify privacy-related risks on Privacy-ABC systems [LSK12].

2.7.3 Trust Relationships

To provide a comprehensible overview of the trust relationships, we describe the trust requirements from each entity's perspective. Therefore, whoever likes to realise one of the roles in the ecosystem of Privacy-ABCs could easily refer to that entity

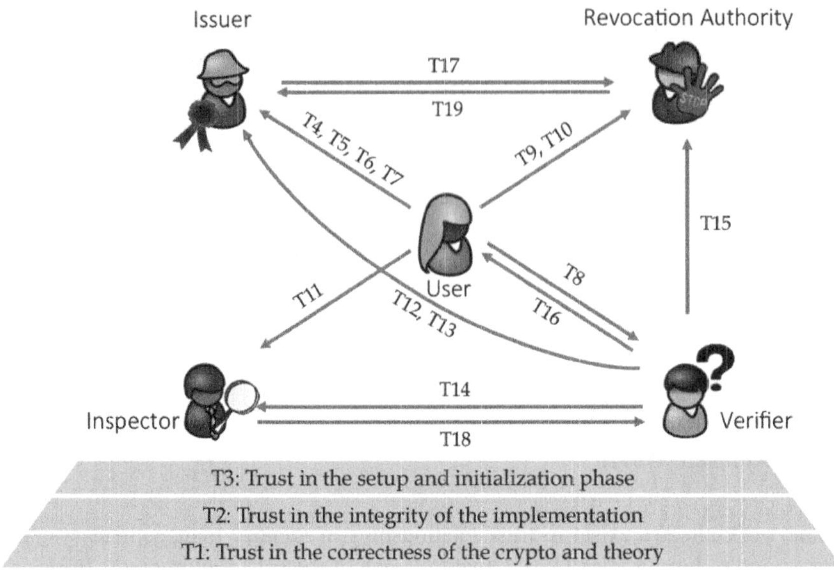

Fig. 2.23 Visualization of the trust relationships

and learn about the necessary trust relationships that need to be established. Figure 2.23 depicts an overview of the identified trust relationships between the involved parties, which we will describe in the next sections. On the bottom of Figure 2.23, the general trust requirements by all the parties are demonstrated.

2.7.3.1 Assumptions

Before delving into the trust relationships, it is important to elaborate on the assumptions that are required for Privacy-ABCs to work. Privacy-ABCs are not effective in case of tracking and profiling methods that work based on network level identifiers such as IP addresses or the ones in the lower levels. Therefore, in order to benefit from the full set of features offered by Privacy-ABCs, the underlying infrastructure must be privacy-friendly as well. If it is ensured that no additional information is being collected by the service providers, users can employ Privay-ABCs without any concern. Otherwise, the recommendation for the users would be to employ network anonymizer tools to cope with this issue.

Another important assumption concerns the verifiers' enthusiasm for collecting data. Theoretically, greedy verifiers have the chance to demand for any kind of information they are interested in and avoid offering the service if the user is not willing to disclose these information. Therefore, the assumption is that the verifiers reduce the amount of requested information to the minimum level possible either due to regulations or any other motivation such as not having to invest in technology to protect the data.

2.7.3.2 Trust by all the parties

Independent from their roles, all the involved parties need to consider a set of fundamental trust assumptions that relates to design, implementation and setup of the underlying technologies. It is worth noting that these kind of trust relationships exist for any kind of technologies. The most fundamental trust assumption by all the involved parties concerns the theory behind the actual technologies utilized underneath. Everybody needs to accept that in case of a proper implementation and deployment, the cryptographic protocols will offer the functionalities and the features that they claim. However, this trust relationship can be relaxed by making the security proofs publicly available so that different expert communities can verify them and vouch for their correctness.

T1 *All the involved parties need to put trust in the correctness of the underlying cryptographic protocols.*

Even a protocol that is formally proven to be privacy preserving does not operate appropriately when the implementation is flawed. Consequently, the realization of the corresponding cryptographic protocol and the related components must be trustworthy. For example, the Users need to trust the implementation of the so-called UserAgent and the smart card application meaning that they must rely on the assertion that the provided hardware and software components do not misbehave in any way and under any circumstances, which might jeopardise the User's privacy. It is worth noting that there are mechanisms such as *formal verification* and *code inspection* which can boost the users' trust in the implementations.

T2 *All the involved parties need to put trust in the trustworthiness of the implemented platform and the integrity of the defined operations on each party.*

A correct implementation of privacy preserving technologies cannot be trustworthy when the initialization phase has been compromised. For example, some cryptographic parameters need to be generated in a certain way in order to guaranty the privacy preserving features of a given technology. A diversion in the initialization process might introduce vulnerabilities to the future operation of the users. Nevertheless, it is possible to provide some information to the public so that the experts can check whether the initialization is done properly.

T3 *All the involved parties need to put trust in the trustworthiness of the system setup and the initialization process.*

2.7.3.3 Users' Perspective

In typical scenarios, verifiers grant access to some services based on the credentials that the users hold. A malicious issuer can trouble a user and cause denial of service by not providing credible credentials in time or deliberately embedding invalid information in the credentials. For example, in case of a discount voucher scenario, the issuer of the vouchers can block some specific group of users with fake technical failures of the issuance service until the offer is not valid anymore.

T4 *The users need to put trust in the issuers delivering accurate and correct credentials in a timely manner.*

When designing a credential, the issuer must take care that the structure of the attributes and the credential will not impair the principle of minimal disclosure. For example, embracing name and birth date in another attribute such as registration id is not an appropriate decision since presenting the latter to any verifier results in undesirable disclosure of data. In this regard, making the credential specifications public enables the independent auditors to review them and therefore reduce the concerns of the users who might not have the knowledge to evaluate the credentials on their own.

T5 *The users need to trust that the issuers design the credentials in an appropriate manner, so that the credential content does not introduce any privacy risk itself.*

Similar to any other electronic certification system, dishonest issuers have the possibility to block a user from accessing a service without any legitimate reason by revoking her credentials. Therefore the users have to trust that the issuer has no interest in disrupting users activities and will not take any action in this regard as long as the terms of agreement are respected.

T6 *The users need to trust that the issuers do not take any action to block the use of credentials as long as the user complies with the agreements.*

It is conceivable that a user loses control over her credentials and therefore contacts the issuer requesting for revocation of those credentials. If the issuer delays processing the user's request the lost or stolen credentials can be misused to harm the owner.

T7 *The users need to trust that the issuers will promptly react and inform the revocation authorities when the users claim losing control over their credentials.*

One of the possible authentication levels using Privacy-ABCs is based on a so-called *scope-exclusive pseudonym* where the verifier is able to impact the generation of pseudonyms by the users and limit the number of partial identities that a user can obtain in a specific context. For example, in case of an on-line course evaluation system, the students should not be able to appear under different identities and submit multiple feedbacks even though they are accessing the system pseudonymously. In this case, the verifier imposes a specific *scope* to the pseudonym generation process so that every time a user tries to access the system, it has no choice other than showing up with the same pseudonym as the previous time in this context. In this situation, a dishonest verifier can try to unveil the identity of a user in a pseudonymous context or correlate actives by imposing the "same" scope identifier in generation of pseudonyms in another context where the users are known to the system. However, similar to some other trust relationships, independent auditors could attest these policies when they are publicly available.

T8 *The users need to trust that the verifiers do not misbehave in defining policies in order to cross-link different domains of activities.*

If a revocation process exists in the deployment model, the user needs to trust the correct and reliable performance of the revocation authority. Delivering illegitimate information or hindrance to provide genuine data can disrupt granting user access to her desired services.

T9 *The users need to trust that the revocation authorities perform honestly and do not take any step towards blocking a user without legitimate grounds.*

Depending on the revocation mechanism setting, the user might need to show up with her identifier to the revocation authority in order to obtain the non-revocation evidence of her credentials for an upcoming transaction. If the revocation authority and the verifier collude, they might try to correlate the access timestamps and therefore discover the identity of the user who requested a service. A possible way to reduce this risk would be to regularly update the non-revocation evidence independent of their use of credentials.

T10 *The users need to trust that the revocation authorities do not take any step towards collusion with the verifiers in order to profile the users.*

Embedding encrypted identifying information within an authentication token for inspection purposes makes the users dependent of the trustworthiness of the inspector. As soon as the token is submitted to the verifier, the inspector is able to lift the anonymity of the user and disclose her identity. Therefore the role of inspector must be taken by an entity that a user has established trust relationship with. Nevertheless, there exist techniques that could help to avoid putting trust on a single entity but a group of inspectors. In this case, a minimum number of inspectors need to collaborate in order to retrieve the identity information from the presentation token.

T11 *The users need to trust that the inspectors do not disclose their identities without making sure that the inspection grounds hold.*

2.7.3.4 Verifiers' Perspective

Provisioning of the users in the ecosystem is one of the major points where the verifiers have to trust the issuers to precisely check upon the attributes that they are attesting. It holds for any certification scheme that the verifiers rely on the certified information by the issuers for the authentication phase, therefore the issuers assumed to be trustful.

T12 *The verifiers need to trust that the issuers are diligent and meticulous when evaluating and attesting the users' attributes.*

When a user loses her credibility, it is the issuer's responsibility to take the appropriate action in order to block the further use of the respective credentials. Therefore, the verifiers rely on the issuers to immediately request revocation of the user's credentials when a user is not entitled anymore.

T13 *The verifiers need to trust that the issuers will promptly react to inform the revocation authorities when a credential loses its validity.*

In an authentication scenario where inspection is enabled, the only party who is able to identify a misbehaving user is the inspector. The verifier is not able to deal with the case if the inspector does not to cooperate. Therefore, similar to trust relationship T11 by the users, the verifiers dependent of the fairness and honesty of the inspector. Moreover, in a similar fashion, the trust can be distributed to more than one inspector to reduce the risk of misbehaviour. In this case, a subset of all the inspectors would enough to proceed with the inspection.

T14 *The verifiers need to trust that the inspectors fulfil their commitments and will investigate the reported cases fairly and deliver the identifiable information in case of verified circumstances.*

The validity of credentials without expiration information is checked through the information that the verifier acquires from the revocation authority. A compromised revocation authority can deliver outdated or illegitimate information to enable a user to get access to resources even with revoked credentials. Therefore the revocation authority needs to be a trusted entity from the verifiers' perspective.

T15 *The verifiers need to trust that the revocation authorities perform honestly and deliver the latest genuine information to the verifiers.*

Often user credentials are designed for individual use, and sharing is not allowed. Even though security measures such as hardware tokens can be employed to support this policy and limit the usage of the credentials to their owners, the users can still share the tokens and let others benefit from services that they are not normally eligible for. The verifiers have no choice than trusting the users and the infrastructure on this matter.

T16 *The verifiers need to trust that the users do not share their credentials with the others, if this would be against the policy.*

2.7.3.5 Issuers' Perspective

As mentioned earlier T13, the issuer is responsible to take the appropriate steps to block further use of a credential when it loses its validity. The issuer has to initiate the revocation process with the revocation authority and trust that the revocation authority promptly reacts to it in order to disseminate the revocation status of the credential. For instance, when a user cancels her subscription for an online magazine, the publisher would like to stop her access to the service right after the termination of the contract. A compromised revocation authority can delay or ignore this process to let the user benefit from existing services.

T17 *The Issuers need to trust that the revocation authorities perform honestly and react to the revocation requests promptly and without any delay.*

2.7.3.6 Inspectors' Perspective

In order to have a fair inspection process, the inspection grounds must be precisely and clearly communicated to the users in advance. It can be said that presenting inspection grounds is as challenging as privacy policies where long, ambiguous and tedious texts would cause typical users to overlook or misunderstand the conditions. Therefore, in case of an inspection request, the inspector has to rely on the verifier that the users had been informed about these conditions properly.

T18 *The Inspector need to trust that the verifier has properly informed the users about the actual circumstances that entitle the verifier for de-anonymisation of the users.*

2.7.3.7 Revocation Authorities' Perspective

Revocation authorities are in charge of delivering up-to-date information about the credentials' revocation status to the users and the verifiers. However, they are not in a position to decide whether a credential must be revoked or not, without receiving revocation requests from the issuers. Therefore, their correct operations depends on the diligent performance of the issuers.

T19 *In order to provide reliable service, the revocation authorities need to trust that the issuers deliver legitimate and timely notice of the credentials to be revoked.*

2.8 Policy-based View of the Architecture

Policy can be represented at different levels, ranging from business goals to device-specific configuration parameters [WSS+01]. In this section, with the term "policy" we refer to a more abstract concept than the *issuance policy* and *presentation policy* artefacts of ABC4Trust. We consider policy to be "a definite goal, course or method of action to guide and determine present and future decisions", as defined in [WSS+01] . A view on the ABC4Trust architecture from this policy perspective delivers useful observations, even though policy handling is something that happens at a layer higher than the ABC4Trust architecture.

The ABC4Trust architecture does not define the roles and the corresponding operational processes for Policy Decisions Points (PDP) [WSS+01] and Policy Enforcement Points (PEP) [WSS+01], as this falls outside of its scope. However, we would like to emphasize that the ABC4Trust architecture offers valuable technical possibilities, awareness of which can be useful when designing and implementing PDPs. In the next step, it provides the technical means to support the Policy Actions [WSS+01] and enables the PEPs. To elaborate more, we consider an example for different stages in the life-cycle of Privacy-ABCs, namely, issuance, presentation, revocation and inspection. Specifically for the inspection and revocation phase, let us take the example of the Söderhamn pilot, which supports both.

One of the interesting features of Privacy-ABCs that concerns the credential issuance phase is the *carry-over attribute*. It allows blind transfer of an attribute value from another credential to the one being issued. A typical use of such mechanism is when the credential is issued to anonymous users but the issuer needs to make sure that the new credential cannot be transferred to anybody else. Therefore, the issuer binds the credential to the user's identity (e.g., Passport NR), retrieved as an attribute from another trusted credential that the users holds, but without actually being able to see the attribute value. Knowing about such a feature, which does not exist in the common identity management platforms, could prevent the decision makers from investing in much more expensive infrastructure and processes in order to achieve the same goal. When such a decision is made, it can be expressed in the XML artefact *issuance policy* and enforced when a credential issuance is taking place.

With regard to the presentation phase, the knowledge that attributes can be technically treated separately helps privacy advocates make the argument that credentials should only contain the minimum information, e.g. whether the user is of legal age and that there is no need to collect more information, while still all the required guarantees are offered to the relaying party.

Taking the Söderhamn pilot as an example: the school administration acted as a PDP by deciding (for compliance with Swedish regulations for schools) that the School Community Interaction Platform must make it possible for misbehaving students to be identified - in specific cases such as bullying or harassment. The decision was expressed in the *presentation policy* of the various sections of the system so that only Privacy-ABC *presentation tokens* with inspectable data would be considered to grant access to the activity area. As a result, there was a process to reveal the identity of misbehaving students in extraordinary circumstances. The PEP was where the system requested the users to include inspection data in their Privacy-ABC presentation tokens to access a resource. A possible further PEP would at the entity executing the inspection (possibly the school management together with another entity, so that the 4-eye principle would be followed). Note that Privacy-ABCs allow to change the policy requiring inspectable tokens at any point in time without the need to reissue credentials.

In the case of credential revocation, the school administration decided that whoever is not part of the school anymore should not be able to participate in the activities of the community platform. This decision was reflected by the application designers in the *credential specification* as well as the deployment architecture in order to enable the revocation process. We can consider two points where the policy enforcement was taking place: The first point was at the submission of the revocation request by the school administration to the revocation authority. In the next stage, the policy was enforced everytime the platform refused to give access to a user with a revoked credential.

References

[abc] ABC4Trust EU Project. https://www.abc4trust.eu.

[ASN08] Abstract syntax notation one (ASN.1), 2008. International Telecommunication Union - ITU-T recommendation X.680.

[Bar02] Bartel, Mark and Boyer, John and Fox, Barb and LaMacchia, Brian and Simon, Ed. XML-Signature Syntax and Processing. http://www.w3.org/TR/2002/REC-xmldsig-core-20020212/, February 2002.

[BBE+14] Thomas Baignères, Patrik Bichsel, Robert R Enderlein, Hans Knudsen, Kasper Damgård, Jonas Jensen, Gregory Neven, Janus Nielsen, Pascal Paillier, and Michael Stausholm. Final Reference Implementation. Deliverable D4.2, The ABC4Trust EU Project, 2014. Available at https://abc4trust.eu/download/D4.2%20Final%20Reference%20Implementation.pdf, Last accessed on 2014-11-08.

[BCD+14] Patrik Bichsel, Jan Camenisch, Maria Dubovitskaya, Robert R. Enderlein, Stephan Krenn, Ioannis Krontiris, Anja Lehmann, Gregory Neven, Janus Dam Nielsen, Christian Paquin, Franz-Stefan Preiss, Kai Rannenberg, Ahmad Sabouri, and Michael Stausholm. Architecture for Attribute-based Credential Technologies - Final Version. Deliverable D2.2, The ABC4Trust EU Project, 2014. Available at https://abc4trust.eu/download/Deliverable_D2.2.pdf, Last accessed on 2014-11-08.

[Bra] Stefan Brands. The ID Corner blog. The problem(s) with OpenID. http://www.untrusted.ca/cache/openid.html.

[CDF+] J. Callas, L. Donnerhacke, H. Finney, D. Shaw, and R. Thayer. OpenPGP Message Format. http://www.rfc-editor.org/rfc/rfc4880.txt.

[Cha83] David Chaum. Blind signatures for untraceable payments. In *Advances in cryptology*, pages 199–203. Springer, 1983.

[CKL+14] Jan Camenisch, Stephan Krenn, Anja Lehmann, Gert Læssø e Mikkelsen, Gregory Neven, and Michael østergaard Pedersen. Scientific Comparison of ABC Protocols: Part I Formal Treatment of Privacy-Enhancing Credential Systems. Deliverable D3.1, The ABC4Trust EU Project, 2014. Available at https://abc4trust.eu/download/Deliverable\%20D3.1\%20Part\%201.pdf, Last accessed on 2014-11-08.

[Cro06] Douglas Crockford. The application/json media type for JavaScript Object Notation (JSON). Technical Report RFC 4627, Internet Engineering Taskforce (IETF), 2006.

[CSF+08] D. Cooper, S. Santesson, S. Farrell, S. Boeyen, R. Housley, and W. Polk. RFC 5280 - Internet X.509 Public Key Infrastructure Certificate and Certificate Revocation List (CRL) Profile. Technical report, IETF, May 2008.

[DFLP07] Nelly Delessy, Eduardo B Fernandez, and Maria M Larrondo-Petrie. A pattern language for identity management. In *Computing in the Global Information Technology, 2007. ICCGI 2007. International Multi-Conference on*, pages 31–31. IEEE, 2007.

[DW10] Arkajit Dey and Stephen Weis. PseudoID: Enhancing Privacy in Federated Login. In *Hot Topics in Privacy Enhancing Technologies*, pages 95–107, 2010.

[Fac] Facebook Login. https://developers.facebook.com/products/login/.

[Fid] Fido Alliance. http://fidoalliance.org.

[Har04] Russell Hardin. *Trust and trustworthiness*, volume 4. Russell Sage Foundation, 2004.

[Har12] Dick Hardt. OAuth 2.0 Authorization Protocol. http://tools.ietf.org/html/rfc6749, October 2012.

[HBH07] Dick Hardt, Johnny Bufu, and Josh Hoyt. OpenID Attribute Exchange 1.0. http://openid.net/specs/openid-attribute-exchange-1_0.html, December 2007.

[HTEG10] D. Hardt, A. Tom, B. Eaton, and Y. Goland. OAuth Web Resource Authorization Profiles. http://tools.ietf.org/html/draft-hardt-oauth-01, January 2010. draft version 19 at time of writing.

[JBT] M. Jones, J. Bradley, and H. Tschofenig. Proof-Of-Possession Semantics for JSON Web Tokens (JWTs). http://tools.ietf.org/html/draft-jones-oauth-proof-of-possession-00.

[JP04] Audun Jøsang and Stéphane Lo Presti. Analysing the relationship between risk and trust. In *Trust Management*, pages 135–145. Springer, 2004.

[JWT] Json web token (jwt). http://datatracker.ietf.org/doc/draft-ietf-oauth-json-web-token. draft version 19 at time of writing.

[KBC05] Tadayoshi Kohno, Andre Broido, and Kimberly C Claffy. Remote physical device fingerprinting. *Dependable and Secure Computing, IEEE Transactions on*, 2(2):93–108, 2005.

[KTMM09] Uwe Kylau, Ivonne Thomas, Michael Menzel, and Christoph Meinel. Trust requirements in identity federation topologies. In *Advanced Information Networking and Applications, 2009. AINA'09. International Conference on*, pages 137–145. IEEE, 2009.

[LSK12] Jesus Luna, Neeraj Suri, and Ioannis Krontiris. Privacy-by-design based on quantitative threat modeling. In *Risk and Security of Internet and Systems (CRiSIS), 2012 7th International Conference on*, pages 1–8. IEEE, 2012.

[MC96] D. Harrison Mcknight and Norman L. Chervany. The Meanings of Trust. Technical report, University of Minnesota, 1996.

[MCM14] C. Mortimore, B. Campbell, and Jones M. SAML 2.0 Bearer Assertion Profiles for OAuth 2.0. http://tools.ietf.org/html/draft-ietf-oauth-saml2-bearer-19, March 2014. draft version 19 at time of writing.

[O'H04] Kieron O'Hara. *Trust: From Socrates to Spin*. Icon Books Ltd, 2004.

[Ope] OpenID Connect. http://openid.net/connect/.

[Ope07] OpenID Authentication 2.0. http://openid.net/specs/openid-authentication-2_0.html, December 2007.

[SAM05] Assertions and Protocols for the OASIS Security Assertion Markup Language (SAML) V2.0. http://docs.oasis-open.org/security/saml/v2.0/saml-core-2.0-os.pdf, March 2005.

[UPW11] U-Prove WS-Trust Profile V1.0. http://www.microsoft.com/u-prove, March 2011.

[WS-12] WS-Trust 1.4. http://docs.oasis-open.org/ws-sx/ws-trust/v1.4/ws-trust.html, April 2012.

[WSF09] Web Services Federation Language (WS-Federation) Version 1.2. http://docs.oasis-open.org/wsfed/federation/v1.2/os/ws-federation-1.2-spec-os.html, May 2009.

[WSS+01] Andrea Westerinen, John Schnizlein, John Strassner, Mark Scherling, Bob Quinn, Jay Perry, Shai Herzog, An-Ni Huynh, Mark Carlson, and Steve Waldbusser. Terminology for Policy-Based Management. Internet RFC 3198, November 2001.

[WSS07] WS-SecurityPolicy 1.2. http://docs.oasis-open.org/ws-sx/ws-securitypolicy/200702/ws-securitypolicy-1.2-spec-cs.html, April 2007.

[WST09] WS-Trust 1.4. http://docs.oasis-open.org/ws-sx/ws-trust/v1.4/os/ws-trust-1.4-spec-os.html, February 2009.

Chapter 3
Cryptographic Protocols Underlying Privacy-ABCs

Patrik Bichsel, Jan Camenisch, Maria Dubovitskaya, Robert R. Enderlein, Stephan Krenn, Anja Lehmann, Gregory Neven, and Franz-Stefan Preiss

Abstract In this chapter we present the Cryptographic Engine which provides the cryptographic functionality used in the ABC Engine, such as issuance or presentation of credentials. We first describe the architecture of the Cryptographic Engine, explain the building blocks it uses, and explain how they are bound together. We then describe the cryptographic primitives that the library uses to instantiate those building blocks.

As discussed in the previous chapter, the ABC Engine offers an abstract and cryptography-agnostic interface to Privacy-ABCs. In this chapter, we explain the Cryptographic Engine which is used as the underlying cryptographic library, cf. Figure 2.3.

The Cryptographic Engine provides all the functionality needed to realize Privacy-ABCs. In particular, it allows users to obtain credentials from issuers and to generate cryptographic evidence for the possession of such a credential. To achieve best possible modularity, our engine consists of two layers. The upper layer does not depend on concrete cryptographic primitives, but treats them as abstract building blocks, and only orchestrates how they play together. In the lower layer, the concrete primitives can run without having to worry about possible interactions with other primitives.

The design of the Cryptographic Engine is described in detail in Section 3.1. Then, in Section 3.2, we describe the concrete instantiations of the building blocks that we implemented in the lower layer of the engine.

Patrik Bichsel, Jan Camenisch, Maria Dubovitskaya, Robert R. Enderlein, Stephan Krenn, Anja Lehmann, Gregory Neven, and Franz-Stefan Preiss
IBM Research – Zurich, Switzerland, e-mail: {pbi, jca, mdu, enr, skr, anj, nev, frp}@zurich.ibm.com

K. Rannenberg et al. (eds.), *Attribute-based Credentials for Trust*,
DOI 10.1007/978-3-319-14439-9_3

3.1 Overview of Cryptographic Architecture

The main responsibilities of the Cryptographic Engine are to generate cryptographic key material, issue new credentials by means of a two-party protocol, generate the cryptographic evidence for a Presentation Token to prove that a user satisfies a Presentation Policy, and verify such a proof.

The Cryptographic Engine is shipped as a separate library and can operate without the ABC Engine. It replaces version 2 of IBM's Identity Mixer (Idemix) Library. Its main advantage compared to the old Idemix library is the increased modularity of its design. This modularity allowed us to implement additional features, such as supporting U-Prove credentials, and a predicate for checking linear combinations among attributes.

Structure

In the Crypto Engine, we have made a clear distinction between the *building blocks*, which implement the actual cryptographic algorithms, and the *framework* code, which is mostly cryptography-agnostic. The Building Blocks interact with the framework and with each other through implementation-agnostic interfaces. This clean separation allows one to easily substitute one implementation of a cryptographic primitive with another—or to provide a new implementation of a existing cryptographic primitive—and only minimally affect the framework code.

The framework comprises the following components:

- The Key Generation Orchestration, responsible for generating cryptographic key material.
- The Proof Generation Orchestration, which, with the help of the Proof Engine, is responsible for generating the cryptographic evidence of a Presentation Token.
- The Proof Verification Orchestration, which, with the help of the Proof Engine, is responsible for verifying the cryptographic evidence contained in a Presentation Token.
- The Issuance Orchestration, which is responsible for the whole process of issuing a credential. It also uses the Proof Engine. This component operates in two modes: Issuer and Recipient.
- A Proof Engine, which is tasked with generating, and later verifying, a non-interactive zero-knowledge proof. This component also operates in two modes: Prover and Verifier.
- A Building Block Factory, which keeps track of all known building blocks and is responsible for returning the appropriate block or list of blocks for a given task.
- State Storage, for keeping the intermediate state during the issuance protocol.

The framework of the Crypto Engine also accesses several other components of the ABC Engine, such as the Credential Manager, the Key Manager, the Smartcard Manager, and the Revocation Proxy. In case the Crypto Engine runs without a ABC Engine, an alternative implementation of these components must be provided.

In what follows, we describe how the various Orchestration components work. We then describe the Proof Engine and the proof interface of the Building Blocks.

3.1.1 Key Generation Orchestration

Let us describe the generation of parameters/keys such as the System Parameters, the Issuer Key Pair, Inspector Key Pair, and Revocation Authority Key Pair. For the Crypto Engine, this is stateless two-step process: first, upon receiving a request from a user, the Key Generation (KG-) Orchestration generates a *Configuration Template* and returns it to the user; second, the user submits the completed configuration to the KG Orchestration, which then initiates the generation of the parameters/keys proper.

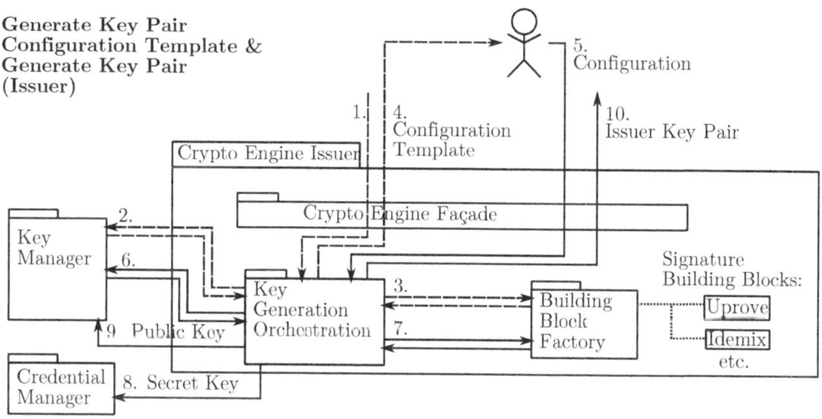

Fig. 3.1 Example of generating an Issuer Key Pair including the creation of the intermediate Key Pair Configuration Template.

In Figure 3.1 we depict the setup of an Issuer Key Pair as an example of the parameter/keys generation process. The generation of System Parameters, or of a key pair of another entity is similar.

Template Generation

The user starts by requesting a Key Pair Configuration Template (1) from the Crypto Engine. This request is forwarded to the Key Generation (KG-) Orchestration. The latter requests the System Parameters from the Key Manager (2) as well as all signature Building Blocks from the Building Block Factory (3). Further, it adds a few default entries to the Configuration Template, and asks each signature Building Block in turn to add its own implementation-specific entries to the Configuration Template. The Configuration Template is then returned to the user (4).

A template is configured with default values that serve as suggestion for a general purpose use; the actual settings (including which implementation of a specific cryptographic primitive) must be set manually and in accordance with the planned use. While all implementations of a given cryptographic primitive can add parameters to the template; the user only needs to fill out the general entries and the entries corresponding to the chosen implementation—the entries corresponding to non-chosen implementations will be ignored.

Parameter Generation

After completing the configuration by overriding the appropriate default settings of the Template Configuration, the user calls the Crypto Engine again to request the generation of an Issuer Key Pair (5). The KG-Orchestration queries the Key Manager for the System Parameters again (6), and the Building Block Factory for the chosen implementation of the signature Building Block (7). It then asks that Building Block to generate an Issuer Key Pair based on the configuration. It then stores the secret key of the pair in the Credential Manager (8), and the public key in the Key Manager (9), before returning the whole key pair to the user (10).

3.1.2 Presentation Orchestration

Let us now illustrate the generation of a Presentation Token as depicted in Figure 3.2.

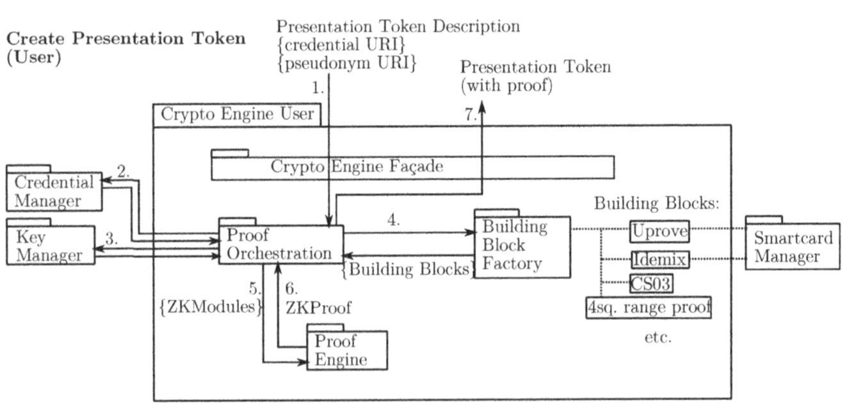

Fig. 3.2 Creation of a Presentation Token.

When a user wants to create a Presentation Token she needs to pass the Presentation Token Description, a list of credential URIs, and a list of pseudonym URIs to the Crypto Engine (recall that the credential and pseudonym URIs have meaning only on the user's machine, and might de-anonymize the user if exposed; these URIs must therefore not be included in the Presentation Token Description). These elements get forwarded to the Proof Orchestration (1). The Proof Orchestration first fetches the credentials and pseudonyms based on their URI from the Credential Manager (2). Second, it loads the System Parameters, Issuer Public Keys, Credential Templates, Inspector Public Keys, and Revocation Authority Public Keys from the Key Manager (3). Third, it queries the Building Block Factory for the Building Blocks required for the Presentation Token at hand (4). For Building Blocks that have several implementations, the Proof Orchestration may mandate a specific implementation, or it may ask the Building Block Factory for any implementation that is supported by the verifier. In any case, the prover must record his choice of implementation so that the verifier can retrieve the exact same Building Block.

The Proof Orchestration asks these Building Blocks each generate one or more Zero-knowledge–proof Modules (*ZkModules*) (5), and configures each ZkModule with the appropriate parameters such as the keys, credentials, or pseudonyms. These ZkModules will be used later inside the Proof Engine. Each ZkModule will independently perform one part of the overall zero-knowledge proof and encapsulates needed algorithms and state while exposing a uniform interface to the Proof Engine. We point out that ZkModules responsible for proving ownership of a credential or a pseudonym receive a reference to the Smartcard Manager, as they may delegate part of the proof process to the Smartcard Manager, which in turn interacts with a smartcard to generate the proof elements needed during proof creation.

The Proof Orchestration then asks the Proof Engine to generate a Zero-knowledge Proof (6) supporting the validity of the Presentation Token based on this list of ZkModules. The Proof Orchestration finally updates the Presentation Token Description and then combines the former with the Zero-knowledge Proof to form the final Presentation Token (7).

3.1.3 Verification Orchestration

In Figure 3.3 we show the verification of a Presentation Token. After the verifier has matched the Presentation Token to the Presentation Policy, he sends the Presentation Token to the Crypto Engine for cryptographic verification (1). The Crypto Engine forwards the Presentation Token to the Proof Verification (PV-) Orchestration. The PV-Orchestration fetches the relevant System Parameters, Issuer Public Keys, Credential Templates, Inspector Public Keys, and Revocation Authority Public Keys from the Key Manager (2). It then needs to fetch the same set of Building Blocks from the Building Block Factory (3) as the prover did. Thereafter, it can generate a list of ZkModules using these Building Blocks, where the ZkModules correspond to the ones generated by the prover (4). The ZkModules for creden-

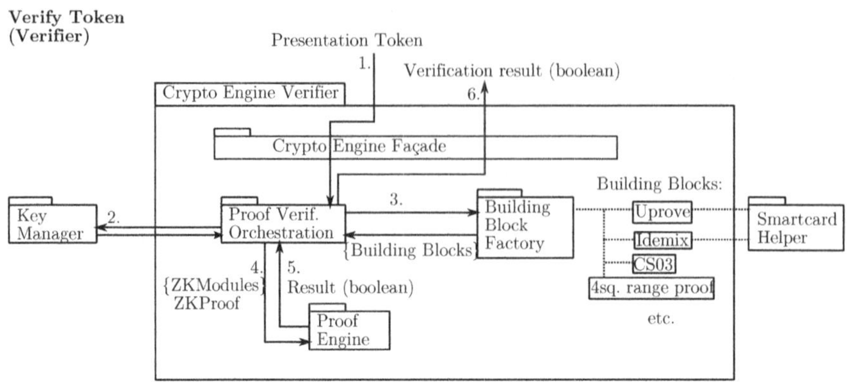

Fig. 3.3 Verification of a Presentation Token.

tials and pseudonyms receive a reference to a Smartcard Helper, which provides the functionality required to verify the part of the proof generated by a smartcard. All ZkModules together with the Zero-knowledge Proof in the token are sent to the Proof Engine for verification. The result of the verification (5) is then forwarded to the verifier (6).

3.1.4 Issuance Orchestration

We now describe the issuance protocol in the case of advanced issuance of a revocable credential where the signing of the credential needs only one round (as is the case for CL signatures) and where no jointly-random attributes are present. We point out that the issuance protocol continues for as many rounds as the used signature building block specifies. Figures 3.4 and 3.6 show the issuance process on the issuer's side and Figures 3.5 and 3.7 show the process on the recipient of the credential's side.

Issuer: Create Issuance Policy

The first step of the issuance protocol is shown in Figure 3.4. The issuer invokes the Crypto Engine with an Issuance Policy and a list of issuer-set attributes (1). The Crypto Engine forwards those to the Issuance Orchestration. The Issuance Orchestration saves the Issuance Policy and list of attributes in the State Storage (2), wraps the Issuance Policy in an Issuance Message, and returns that message to the issuer (3). The issuer should then transmit the message to the recipient.

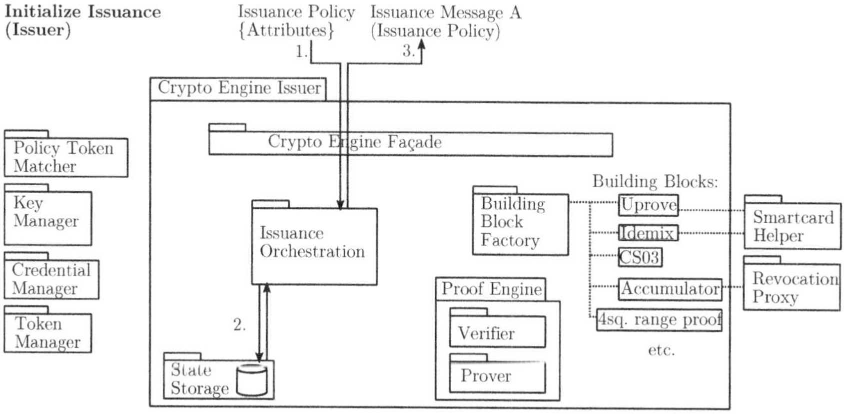

Fig. 3.4 Initiation of the issuance protocol on the issuer's side.

Recipient: Generate Issuance Token

The second step of the issuance protocol is shown in Figure 3.5. The recipient must choose how to satisfy the Issuance Policy contained in the issuer's Issuance Message similar to a presentation. The recipient then calls the Crypto Engine with the Issuance Token Description, a list of credential URIs, a list of Pseudonym URIs, and the original Issuance Message (4). These elements are forwarded to the Issuance Orchestration. The latter first checks with the State Storage that the Issuance Context (contained in the Issuance Message) has never been seen before (5). Steps (6) to (10) are similar to a presentation proof (see Section 3.1.2), with the exception that

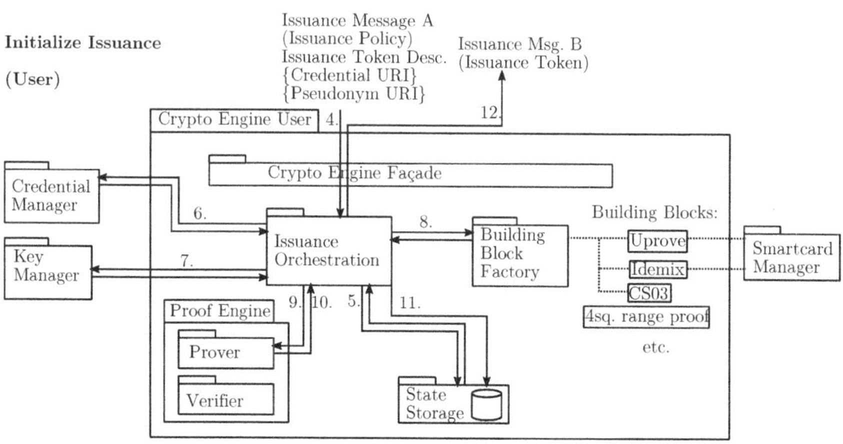

Fig. 3.5 Recipient computes an Issuance Token proving properties used for the credential to be issued.

the Issuance Orchestration additionally generates a ZkModule from the signature building block that enables the carry-over of attributes.

The Issuance Orchestration also retrieves state pertaining to the carry-over of attributes from the aforementioned ZkModule after the Proof Engine finished the proof generation. It then completes the Issuance Token Description with data generated during the proof, generates an Issuance Token from the proof and the Issuance Token Description, wraps the Issuance Token in an Issuance Message, saves its current state in the State Storage (11), and returns the Issuance Message to the recipient (12).

Issuer: Create Signature

The third step of the issuance protocol is shown in Figure 3.6. The issuer should forward the recipient's Issuance Message (containing the Issuance Token) to his Crypto Engine directly. The latter forwards it to the Issuance Orchestration (13). The Issuance Orchestration first recovers the state associated with the Issuance Context from the State Storage (14). Then, it checks the proof contained in the recipient's Issuance Token similar to the PV-Orchestration (see Section 3.1.3) (15)–(18).

If the verification succeeded, the Issuance Orchestration then recovers the Revocation Authority's Public Key from the Key Manager (19), the issuer's Secret Key from the Credential Manager (20), and a Building Block for revocation of the correct implementation from the Building Block Factory (21). It then recovers state from the ZkModule for carry-over and uses that state to initialize a ZkModule for issuance from the signature Building Block; that ZkModule is also initialized with the issuer-set attributes, and the Issuer Secret Key. It also generates a ZkModule for issuance from the Building Block for revocation. During creation time, the ZkModule contracts the Revocation Authority (through the Revocation Proxy) to retrieve a

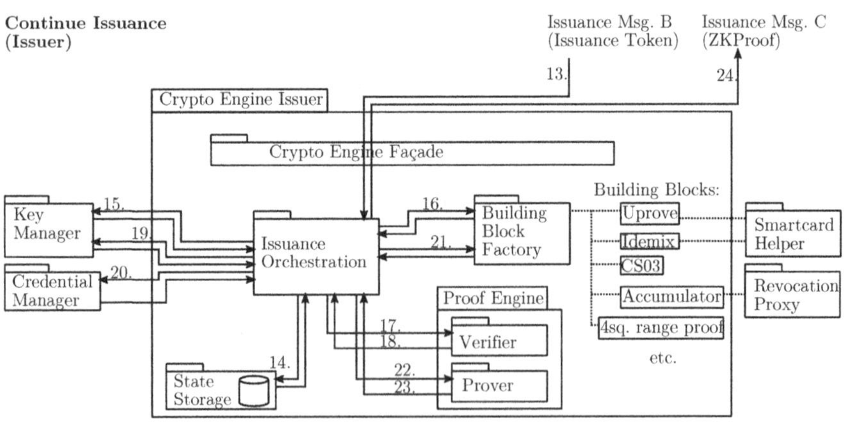

Fig. 3.6 Issuer creates signature.

new Revocation Handle and the associated Non-revocation Evidence. The Issuance Orchestration then passes these two ZkModules to the Proof Engine (22).

During the proof generation, the ZkModule for signature issuance will blindly sign the new credential. The Proof Engine returns the created zero-knowledge proof to the Issuance Orchestration (23). This zero-knowledge proof also contains the issuer's blind signature on the credential, the issuer-set attributes, the value of the Revocation Handle, and the Non-revocation Evidence. The Issuance Orchestration then queries the ZkModule for signature issuance for the list of attribute values it knows about (including the revocation handle), and generates an issuance log entry containing that list. Finally, it wraps the zero-knowledge proof into an Issuance Message, and returns it to the issuer (24).

Recipient: Complete Credential

The last step of the issuance protocol is shown in Figure 3.7. The recipient should forward the issuer's Issuance Message (containing the zero-knowledge proof) to her Crypto Engine directly. The latter forwards it to the Issuance Orchestration (25). The Issuance Orchestration first recovers the state associated with the Issuance Context from the State Storage (26), retrieves the necessary parameters, specifications, and keys from the Key Manager (27). It then queries for a Building Block for signatures and a Building Block for revocation of the appropriate implementation from the Building Block Factory (28).

The Issuance Orchestration creates a ZkModule for signature issuance from the first Building Block, initializing it with the issuer's Public Key and state from the ZkModule for carry-over from last round. It also creates a ZkModule for revocation issuance from the second Building Block. It then sends these two ZkModules and the zero-knowledge proof to the Proof Engine for verification (29). After the Issuance Orchestration gets back the results of the proof verification (30), it extracts

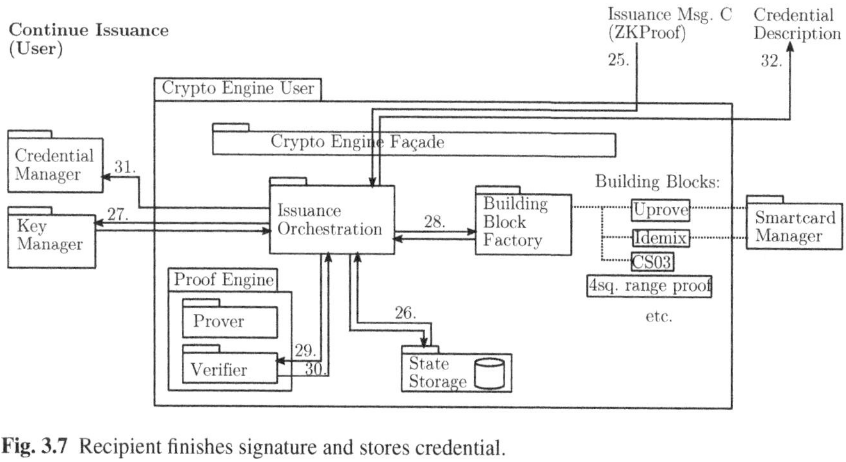

Fig. 3.7 Recipient finishes signature and stores credential.

the issuance state from the ZkModule for signature issuance. It asks the signature Building Block to combine the states of the ZkModule for issuance and the ZkModule for carry over from last round to generate the complete credential, including signature and Non-revocation Evidence. It then saves the credential in the Credential Manager (31) and returns the Credential Description to the recipient (32).

3.1.5 Building Blocks

The Building Blocks are singleton classes that implement the actual cryptographic algorithms. We have defined an interface for Building Blocks for each of the cryptographic primitives (signatures, pseudonyms, inspection, revocation, range proofs, not-equal proofs, set-membership proofs) plus a few interfaces for helper Building Blocks (e.g., reveal attribute, attribute equality, add message to proof). There may be several implementations of a given cryptographic primitive (e.g., CL-signatures and U-Prove signatures), but the Building Blocks corresponding to the various implementations expose the same interface to the rest of the library. This strong encapsulation ensures the modularity of the library.

The Building Block for signatures for example has the following interfaces:

- Functions to populate a template for an Issuer Key Pair and to generate an Issuer Key Pair.
- One *proof interface* for presenting the signature (i.e., proving possession of the signature).
- One proof interface for carry-over, in which it is proven that a freshly generated commitment contains all the user-specified or carried over attributes, and which allows the prover and verifier to extract that commitment and later use the commitment for issuance.
- One proof interface for issuance, in which it is proven that a blind signature was performed correctly, and which allows the verifier to extract the blind signature.
- Functions to continue with the issuance process after the issuance proof (used only for implementations that have a multi-step issuance process, like U-Prove).
- A function that extracts a complete signature from the issuance proof.
- Bookkeeping functions, for example one that returns the identifier of the cryptographic primitive, and one that returns the name of the implementation.

Other Building Blocks have interfaces that are adapted to the needs of the specific cryptographic primitive they implement. The interface of helper Building Blocks typically comprises only a single proof interface and the bookkeeping functions.

3.1.5.1 Proof Interfaces and ZkModules

The proof interface of a Building Block consists of two functions: one factory for so called prover *ZkModule* (zero-knowledge–proof modules) objects and one factory for verifier ZkModule objects. These ZkModules are the actual objects that are sent to the Proof Engine. Each ZkModule is responsible for performing one part of a zero-knowledge proof (for example the proof of a single cryptographic commitment) without needing to explicitly care about interaction with other ZkModules—it the Proof Engine's responsibility to coordinate the ZkModules behind the scenes.

All prover ZkModules in the library expose the same interface towards the Proof Engine, allowing the latter to handle them uniformly. (Some specialized ZkModules also have additional functions, for example to retrieve values after the proof is completed, but those functions are not visible to the Proof Engine.) This interface consists of four callback functions that are called sequentially by the Proof Engine during the course of the proof:

- `initializeModule`, in which the ZkModule must tell the ZkBuilder (a component of the Proof Engine) the name of all attributes it intends to use, the acceptable range of values each attribute can take, whether each attribute should be revealed or not, whether it knows the value of that attribute or not, whether this attribute is an external attribute (i.e., one which resides on a smartcard), and whether it needs to know the value of some other attribute (provided by another ZkModule) before it can set the value of that attribute. In this phase, the ZkModule may also declare that an attribute is equal to another attribute (possibly an attribute that appears in another ZkModule).
- `collectAttributes`, in which the ZkModule must provide the value of all attributes for which it knows that value (and where the ZkModule is allowed to query for the value of the attributes it requested in the initialize phase).
- `firstRound`, in which the ZkModule must help the ZkBuilder perform the first phase of the zero-knowledge proof, that is determine all the values that will be used to compute the challenge: the ZkModule can ask if any of its attributes is revealed, query for the value of all revealed attributes, and query for the R-Value (randomizers—see Table 3.1) of all unrevealed non-external attributes; and must generate T Values (commitment values). At this point the ZkModule may also add data to its hash contribution by adding D-Values (which are delivered to the verifier) or N-Values (which are not delivered to the verifier as he is supposed to know the value already).
- `secondRound`, in which the ZkModule receives the value of the challenge from the ZkBuilder and must provide the S-Value (response values) for all external attributes.

Similarily, all verifier ZkModules expose the same interface towards the Proof Engine. This interface consists of two callback functions that are called sequentially by the Proof Engine during the course of a proof verification:

- `initializeModule`, in which the ZkModule must tell the ZkVerifier (a component of the Proof Engine) the name of all attributes it intends to use, the acceptable range of values each attribute can take, whether each attribute should be revealed or not, and whether it knows the value of that attribute or not. In this phase, the ZkModule may also declare that an attribute is equal to another attribute (possibly an attribute that appears in another ZkModule). The verifier

Table 3.1 Glossary for values inside a zero-knowledge proof. More details are given in Section 3.2.2.

Name	Explanation
R-value	**R**andomizers. The random values that replace the attribute values when computing the T-values.
T-value	Commi**t**ment values. Values that are derived from the R-Values and the statement to be proven, and which will be used to compute the challenge (together with the D-values, N-values, and revealed attributes).
D-value	**D**elivered values. Values that are sent to the verifier together with the proof, and which are also used to compute the challenge.
N-value	Co**n**text values. Values that the prover and the verifier agree on during the proof and that don't need to be transmitted to the verifier. These values are also used to compute the challenge.
S-value	Re**s**ponse values. Values that are computed based on the challenge.

ZkModule must make the equivalent calls as the corresponding prover ZkModule in this function.

- `verify`, in which the ZkModule receives the value of the challenge, the S-Values of all of its attributes, and the value of all revealed attributes; and must re-compute the T-Values. The ZkModule must also provide the N-Values and may perform additional checks in this function (for example by doing implementation-specific checks on the S-Values and D-Values).

3.1.6 Proof Engine

The Proof Engine is responsible for orchestrating the construction of a zero-knowledge proof following the Fiat-Shamir heuristic on input a list of ZkModules. We designed the Proof Engine according to the Builder pattern: the zero-knowledge proof is build step-by-step by the ZkBuilder (the builder in the Builder pattern) following the directions of a ZkDirector class and of the individual ZkModules (both collectively fulfilling the role of the director in the Builder pattern).

In Figure 3.8 we show the sequence diagram of the construction of a proof in the Proof Engine. The ZkDirector's role is simply to call the methods of the ZkModules and the ZkBuilder in the right order:

- First, it calls `initializeModule` on all ZkModules (with a reference to the ZkBuilder), so that the latter can register their attributes with the ZkBuilder. The ZkBuilder needs to keep track of which attributes are equal (and handle all equivalences implied by transitivity); and for each disjoint set of attributes, it needs to keep track of the properties, such as acceptable range, whether the attributes are external. The ZkBuilder will later also need to keep track of the attribute values, R-Values and S-Values.
- Second, if some ZkModules need to know the value of attributes of other ZkModules, the ZkDirector asks the ZkBuilder to topologically sort the ZkModules.

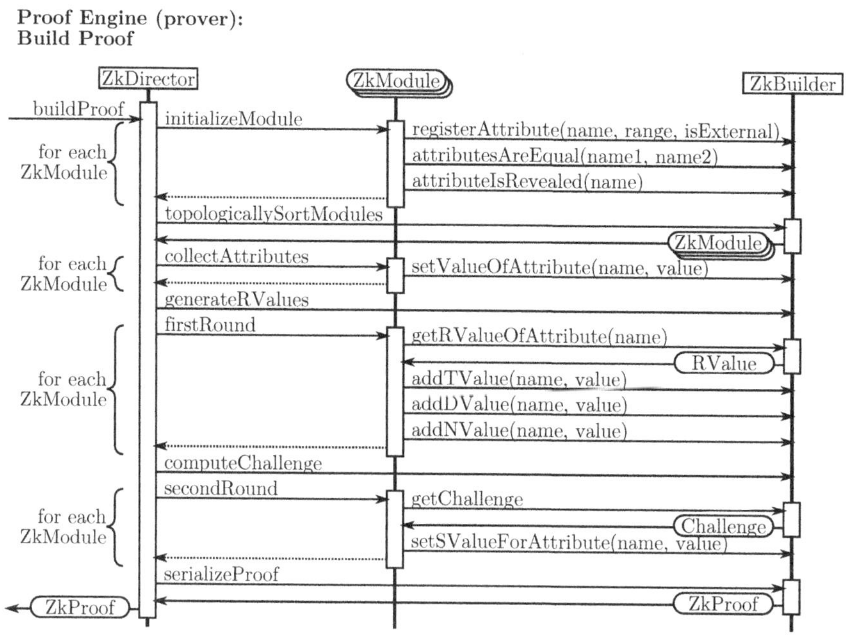

Fig. 3.8 Sequence diagram for the construction of a proof in the Proof Engine

- Third, the ZkDirector calls `collectAttributes` on all ZkModules. In this phase, the ZkBuilder will learn the value of all non-external attributes.
- Fourth, it asks the ZkBuilder to compute R-Values for all unrevealed non-external attributes.
- Fifth, it calls `firstRound` on all ZkModules. In this phase, the ZkBuilder learns the T-Values of all equations in the proof and collects the D-Values and N-Values from the ZkModules.
- Sixth, it asks the ZkBuilder to compute the value of the challenge of the proof. This computation requires two steps: the ZkBuilder computes a *hash contribution* for each ZkModule that includes all the T-, N-, and D-Values (including revealed attributes) used by that ZkModule; and finally the overall challenge is computed by hashing all hash contributions. After the ZkBuilder computed the challenge, it also computes the S-Value of all unrevealed non-external attributes.
- Seventh, it calls `secondRound` on all ZkModules. In this phase, the ZkModules tell the ZkBuilder the S-Values of all external attributes.
- Finally, it asks the ZkBuilder to build the zero-knowledge proof object from: the list of ZkModule names, the list of ZkModule hash contributions, the list of D-Values (including revealed attributes), and the list of S-Values.

The Proof Engine uses a similar construction for verifying a proof. In Figure 3.9 we show the sequence diagram for the verification of a proof in the Proof Engine. The ZkDirector does the following:

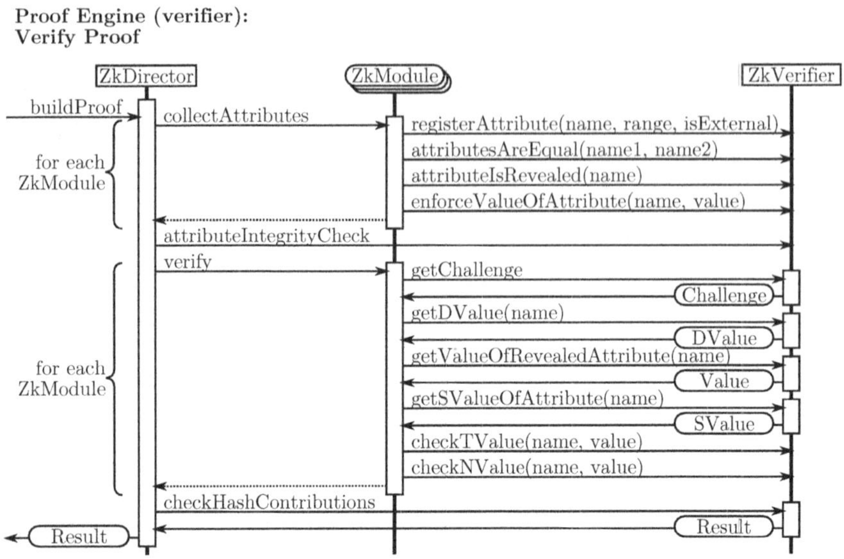

Fig. 3.9 Sequence diagram for the verification of a proof in the Proof Engine

- First, it calls `collectAttributes` on all ZkModules, so that the latter can register their attributes with the ZkVerifier. The ZkVerifier needs to re-construct a similar attribute database as the ZkBuilder during the construction of the proof. We note that for revealed attributes, the ZkModules may choose to request a specific value of an attribute—if no ZkModule provides such a value, the corresponding D-Value from the proof object is taken.
- Second, it asks the ZkVerifier to check that all S-Values are within their acceptable range. At this point, the ZkVerifier also re-computes the value of the challenge from the list of hash contributions.
- Third, it calls `verify` on all ZkModules. The ZkModules now have access to the value of the challenge, the D-Values, and the S-Values; and must re-compute the T-Values and provide the N-Values to the ZkVerifier. ZkModules may also perform additional checks with the D-Values and S-Values (e.g., for the U-Prove signatures, the verifier must check that the U-Prove token —a D-Value—sent by the prover is valid).
- Finally, it asks the ZkVerifier to check the hash contributions of all ZkModules. If the list of re-computed hash contributions matches the list in the proof, the ZkVerifier reports that the proof verification was successful.

3.2 Cryptographic Primitives

After describing the cryptographic architecture implemented within this project, we next give a detailed summary of the diverse building blocks that are used. In particular, all the building blocks mentioned in Figures 3.2, 3.3, 3.4 and 3.5 will be discussed in the following.

For each building block, we give a high-level description of the primitive and the security properties that need to be satisfied, as well as a cryptographic description of the instantiations we use. However, we refrain from giving implementation specific details for any of the building blocks, but refer the interested reader to the documentation of the implementation [VLG$^+$14].

3.2.1 Algebraic Background

We now briefly explain the mathematical background that is required for the rest of this chapter, as well as the cryptographic hardness assumptions that underly the security proofs of the given instantiations.

3.2.1.1 Groups

The concept of groups is central for all the primitives and protocols presented in the following. Informally, a group is a set of elements, on which one can operate as one is used to from addition on the integers: combining two elements yields another element of the group (the sum of two integers is an integer), the order in which elements are combined does not matter (parentheses are not important for addition), there is an element which does not change the value of any other element when combined with that element (adding zero to any integer yields the very same integer), and for every element there is an inverse element (there exists the negative inverse for every integer).

The following now formally defines this idea:

Definition 1. A pair $(\mathscr{G},\otimes)$, where $\mathscr{G}$ is a set and $\otimes$ is a binary operation, is called a *group* if the following properties are satisfied:

Closure. For all $a,b \in \mathscr{G}$ the result $a \otimes b \in \mathscr{G}$.
Associativity. For all $a,b,c \in \mathscr{G}$ it holds that $(a \otimes b) \otimes c = a \otimes (b \otimes c)$.
Identity element. There exists $e \in \mathscr{G}$ such that for all $a \in \mathscr{G}$ it holds that $a \otimes e = e \otimes a = a$.
Inverse element. For all $a \in \mathscr{G}$ there exists an element $b \in \mathscr{G}$ such that $a \otimes b = b \otimes a = e$, where e is the identity element.

Now and in the following, we will typically omit the binary operation when denoting the group, i.e., we will just write $\mathscr{G}$ instead of $(\mathscr{G},\otimes)$.

In cryptography, we are mainly concerned with finite groups, i.e., groups where $\mathcal{G}$ only contains a finite number of elements, which we will assume for the rest of this chapter.

A group is called *cyclic* if there exists an element $a \in \mathcal{G}$ such that any element $b \in \mathcal{G}$ can be written as $b = a \otimes \cdots \otimes a = a^n$ for some positive integer n. In this case, a is called a *generator* of $\mathcal{G}$. The smallest positive integer such that $e = a^n$, where e is the identity element, is called the *order of* a, and the number of elements in $\mathcal{G}$ is called the *order of* $\mathcal{G}$.

Finally, for two elements $a, b \in \mathcal{G}$ we say that an integer n is the *discrete logarithm of* b *in base* a, if it holds that $b = a^n$.

3.2.1.2 Hardness Assumptions

The security of most cryptographic primitives cannot be proved directly using information-theoretic arguments, but can only be proved assuming that solving some mathematical task is computationally infeasible. Here, computationally infeasible means that no algorithm whose running time is bounded by a polynomial in the length of its input, can solve the given task with more than negligible probability, where a function is negligible if it vanishes faster than any inverse polynomial.

The following hardness assumptions have been analyzed for decades, and are widely believed to be satisfied for the groups that we are going to use in the following descriptions.

Definition 2. Let $\mathcal{G}$ be a cyclic group, and let a be a generator of $\mathcal{G}$. Given a random $b \in_R \mathcal{G}$, the *discrete logarithm problem* is to compute the discrete logarithm of b in base a, i.e., to find an integer n such that $b = a^n$. The *discrete logarithm assumption* holds for $\mathcal{G}$ if no efficient (i.e., polynomial time) algorithm can solve the discrete logarithm problem with more than negligible probability.

Definition 3. Let $\mathcal{G}$ be a cyclic group of order q, and let a be a generator of $\mathcal{G}$. Let further be $x, y, z \in_R \mathbb{Z}_q$. The *decisional Diffie-Hellman problem* is to distinguish (a, a^x, a^y, a^z) from (a, a^x, a^y, a^{xy}). The *decisional Diffie-Hellman assumption* (DDH) holds for $\mathcal{G}$ if no efficient (i.e., polynomial time) algorithm can solve the decisional Diffie-Hellman problem with more than negligible probability.

The next assumption is related to factoring large integers, and is also commonly believed to be computationally hard. It is a generalization of the RSA assumption [RSA78] and was introduced by Fujisaki and Okamoto [FO97] and Barić and Pfitzmann [BP97].

Definition 4. Let n be a random safe RSA modulus, i.e., $n = pq$ where $p := 2p' + 1, q := 2q' + 1$ and p, q, p', q' are all primes, and p and q are about the same size. Then the *strong RSA problem* is to find, given n and a random $b \in_R \mathbb{Z}_n^*$, an element $a \in_R \mathbb{Z}_n^*$ and a positive integer $e > 1$ such that $b = a^e \bmod n$. The *strong RSA assumption* says that no efficient (i.e., polynomial time) algorithm can solve the strong RSA problem with more than negligible probability.

The following assumption was first introduced by Paillier [Pai99].

Definition 5. Let n, p, q, p', q' be as in Definition 4. Let further $\mathcal{G}$ be the subgroup of $\mathbb{Z}^*_{n^2}$ consisting of all n^{th} powers of elements in $\mathbb{Z}^*_{n^2}$, i.e., $\mathcal{G} := \{a^n : a \in \mathbb{Z}^*_{n^2}\}$. The *decisional composite residuosity problem* is to, given n, distinguish random elements of $\mathbb{Z}^*_{n^2}$ from random elements of $\mathcal{G}$. The *decisional composite residuosity assumption* says that no efficient (i.e., polynomial time) algorithm can solve the decisional composite residuosity problem with more than negligible probability.

3.2.2 Zero-Knowledge Proofs of Knowledge

Zero-knowledge proofs of knowledge are a fundamental primitive for privacy-enhancing cryptography. They are two-party protocols between a prover and a verifier, where the prover claims to know some secret piece of information and needs to convince the verifier about this fact in a private manner.

Zero-knowledge proofs of knowledge have to satisfy the following security properties. First, *correctness* says that honest provers can always convince honest verifiers. Furthermore, they have to satisfy the following seemingly contradictory goals: On the one hand, *soundness* guarantees that a prover that can convince the verifier really knows the claimed secret, except for a negligibly small probability. On the other hand, the *zero-knowledge* property says that the proof does not reveal any information about the secret to the verifier, except for what is already revealed by the claim itself.

What is typically being proved in our applications is knowledge of discrete logarithms or similar statements. Now and in the following we use the notation introduced by Camenisch and Stadler [CS97] to denote such proof in an abstract way. For instance, an expression like:

$$ZKP\left[(\alpha,\beta,\gamma) \,:\, y_1 = g_1^{\alpha} g_2^{\beta} \,\wedge\, y_2 = y_1^{\alpha} g_3^{\gamma} \,\wedge\, \alpha > 0\right]$$

denotes a zero-knowledge proof of knowledge of integers α, β, γ such that the relations on the right hand side are satisfied. We stick to the convention that knowledge of values denoted by Greek letters has to be proved, while all other values are assumed to be publicly known.

We next show how such proof goals are compiled to real-world protocols on hand of the following simple example proof goal:

$$ZKP\left[(\alpha,\beta) \,:\, y = g^{\alpha} h^{\beta}\right], \tag{3.1}$$

where g and h are generators of a group $\mathcal{G}$ of prime order q, and y is the public image. Let further be H a collision resistant hash function such as, e.g., SHA-2, and $\mathsf{desc}_{\mathcal{G}}$ be a description of the group $\mathcal{G}$. Then Figure 3.10 illustrates the protocol run.

Prover		Verifier
$r_a, r_b \in_R \mathbb{Z}_q$ $t := g^{r_a} h^{r_b}$	`firstRound`	
$c := \mathsf{H}((t), (y, g, h, \mathsf{desc}_{\mathcal{G}}), ())$	`computeChallenge`	
$s_a := r_a + c\alpha$ $s_b := r_b + c\beta$	`secondRound`	
	$\xrightarrow{(c, (s_a, s_b))}$	
	`verify`	$t' := g^{s_a} h^{s_b} y^{-c}$ Output accept if and only if: $c \stackrel{?}{=} \mathsf{H}((t'), (y, g, h, \mathsf{desc}_{\mathcal{G}}), ())$

Fig. 3.10 Protocol flow of the zero-knowledge proof of knowledge specified in (3.1). The given method names correspond to those discussed in Section 3.1.6.

On hand of this example, we next explain the concepts of T-values, etc. that were introduced in Table 3.1:

R-values. These are the internal random coins the prover draws. In Figure 3.10, the R-values are given by r_a and r_b. R-values are never revealed to the verifier in the clear.

T-values. Using the R-values the T-values are computed, essentially by evaluating the proof goal on the randomnesses instead of the secrets. T-values do not need to be sent to the verifier, but the verifier can re-compute them himself. They are hashed in order to compute the challenge c for the proof. In our example, the only T-value is t.

S-values. S-values are derived from the R-values, the challenge and the secrets. They are always computed as a sum of an R-value and the product of the challenge and the respective secret value, cf. Figure 3.10. S-values are sent to the verifier together with the challenge c. In our example, the S-values are given by s_a and s_b.

N-values. N-values contain all public values that are required to perform the proof, and that are already known to both parties before the proof starts. They typically specify the entire algebraic setting such as the groups and group elements being used, as well as the public images for which the prover claims to know the corresponding secrets. In Figure 3.10, the algebraic setting is given by $g, h, \mathsf{desc}_{\mathcal{G}}$ and the public image is given by y.

D-values. Finally, D-values are public values that are required to perform the proof, but that are not already known to both parties before the proof starts. Such values often arise when algebraic claims about secrets are to be proved, such as, e.g., $\alpha > 0$ or $\alpha = \beta\gamma$ or the like. Technically, such proof goals are realized by first reformulating such claims as claims related to discrete logarithms, i.e., to claims of the form $z = v^{\mu} w^{\nu}$, etc.. In this case often temporary public values need to be computed, which are then added as D-values and which are also used when computing the challenge c. In our example no D-values are required, and therefore the empty list is hashed in Figure 3.10.

For a deeper discussion of the design of efficient zero-knowledge proofs of knowledge for practically relevant proof goals we refer the interested reader to the original literature, in particular Schnorr [Sch91] and generalizations [FO97, DF02, CKY09], and Fiat and Shamir [FS87].

3.2.2.1 Four Square Range Proof

Many practically relevant proof goals require a user to prove that same secret value is larger (or smaller) than some threshold value. For instance, when claiming some senior citizen discount, a user has to prove that his secret birth date was before some public reference date. In this case, the proof goal contains an algebraic claim of the form $\alpha < \mathsf{date}$, where α is the secret attribute specifying the birth date of the user. As stated before, such claims need to be rewritten to discrete logarithm based claims before they can be proved efficiently.

By Lagrange's Four Square Theorem, every non-negative integer can be written as the sum of four squares, and this is obviously not the case for negative integers. Furthermore, efficient algorithms for computing this decomposition are known in the literature [RS86]. Therefore, a proof goal of the form:

$$ZKP\left[(\alpha,\rho)\ :\ y = g^{\alpha}h^{\rho}\ \wedge\ \alpha > \mathsf{date}\right]$$

can be rewritten to:

$$ZKP\left[(\chi_1,\chi_2,\chi_3,\chi_4,\rho)\ :\ y = g^{\chi_1^2+\chi_2^2+\chi_3^2+\chi_4^2+\mathsf{date}}h^{\rho}\right],$$

where $\chi_1^2+\chi_2^2+\chi_3^2+\chi_4^2-\alpha\quad\mathsf{date}$.

Now, standard techniques found in the literature allow this to be rewritten to a conjunction of the form $z = v^{\mu}w^{\nu}$, which can then be proved as discussed before. The complexity of such a proof is roughly nine times the complexity of a proof for a statement of the form $z = v^{\mu}w^{\nu}$.

We refer the interested reader to the original literature [Lip03] for details.

3.2.3 Commitment Schemes

Informally, a commitment scheme can be seen as the digital equivalent of a sealed envelope: A party can commit to a chosen value, while keeping it secret from others. The committing party can later reveal (or *open*) the commitment to another party, which can verify the correctness of this opening.

There are three security requirement a commitment scheme has to satisfy. First, if an honest party commits to a message and later opens the commitment to another party, the latter will always be convinced that the opening is correct. This property is referred to as *correctness*. Second, the *hiding* property guarantees that only given the commitment, one cannot learn any information about the contained message. Third, it is infeasible to open a commitment to two different messages, i.e., to convince the receiver that two different openings are correct for the same commitment. This property is known as *binding*.

In our implementation, commitments are used in multiple places. They are used for advanced issuance to make an issuance protocol depend on a preceding credential presentation proof. At presentation, a user shows that he knows a credential, and additionally proves that the same attributes are contained in a freshly computed commitment. Then, for issuance, the value contained in this commitment is injected into the new credential. The hiding property guarantees that the issuer does not learn the attribute value, while the binding property guarantees the issuer that he issues a credential on an attribute that was already contained in a previous credential. Furthermore, we use commitments to realize protocol extensions such as inequality proofs, i.e., to prove that an attribute is larger than some (potentially public) other value. For this to be possible, we need commitment schemes that allow one to commit to arbitrarily large integer values, which is the case for the scheme presented in the following.

3.2.3.1 Pedersen/Damgård-Fujisaki Commitments

Our implementation uses the so-called Damgård-Fujisaki-Okamoto scheme [DF02], which is a generalization of the Pedersen commitment scheme [Ped91] to messages of arbitrary length.

Key generation. A commitment key is computed by drawing a random safe RSA modulus n, S randomly in $\mathbb{Z}_n^*$ and $R_1, \ldots, R_L$ randomly in $\langle S \rangle$.

Message space. The commitment scheme supports arbitrary messages in $\mathbb{Z}^L$.

Committing to a message. Given a message $m = (m_1, \ldots, m_L)$, the commitment is computed as follows:

1. Choose a random $r \in_R [0, \lfloor n/4 \rfloor]$ and
2. compute the commitment as $com := \prod_{i=1}^{L} R_i^{m_i} S^r \bmod n$.

Verifying a commitment. Given a commitment com, a message m and an opening r, the validity can be checked by checking whether the following equation is satisfied:

$$com \stackrel{?}{=} \prod_{i=1}^{L} R_i^{m_i} S^r \bmod n\,.$$

We note that it is important that the committing entity is not privy of the factorization of n. For our instantiation, we can use $R_1, \ldots, R_L$, S and n from the public key of an issuer.

Theorem 1 ([DF02]). *Under the strong RSA assumption, the above commitment scheme is correct, statistically hiding and computationally binding.*

3.2.4 Blind Signature Schemes

A blind signature scheme allows a user to obtain signatures on messages (or attributes) from a signer, without the signer learning the attributes he signed. As a non-digital example, one could think of the following scenario. A voter privately makes his choice in a voting booth, and then puts his ballot into a carbon paper envelope. He then authenticates himself towards the voting authorities, proving that he is indeed eligible to vote, e.g., by showing his passport. The authorities approve this by signing the envelope, and therefore also the ballot. The signed envelope is then put into the ballot box. Now, when counting the votes, it can be verified whether or not a ballot was voted by an eligible voter, but the authorities never learned the choice of any specific citizen.

Informally, a blind signature scheme should satisfy the following security properties. First, an honest user should always be able to obtain a signature on messages of his choice. This property is referred to as *correctness*. Second, *blind issuance* ensures that the signer does not learn any information about the messages he signed. Third, *untraceability* guarantees that when proving possession of a blindly obtained signature, this cannot be linked to a specific issuance session. Finally, the *unforgeability under chosen message attacks* property says that only the signer is able to produce valid signatures, i.e., no other party is able to produce a signature on a message that has not been signed by the signer before, even if it can request signatures on arbitrary message of its choice.

Blind signatures are at the heart of all known anonymous credential systems. The scheme underlying IBM's idemix are so-called CL-signatures [CL02a], whereas the scheme underlying Microsoft's U-Prove is Brand's blind signature scheme [Bra93].

3.2.4.1 CL-Signatures

CL-signatures were first proposed by Camenisch and Lysyanskaya [CL02a]. They are at the heart of IBM's identity mixer (aka *idemix*), and many other real world applications such as Direct Anonymous Attestation that allows one to remotely authenticate a machine while preserving privacy.

Key generation. On input ℓ_n, choose an ℓ_n-bit RSA modulus n such that $n := pq$, $p := 2p' + 1$, $q := 2q' + 1$, where p, q, p', and q' are primes. Choose, uniformly at random, $R_1, \ldots, R_L, S, Z \in \mathbb{QR}_n$.

Output the public key $(n, R_1, \ldots, R_L, S, Z)$ and the secret key p.

Message space. Let ℓ_m be a parameter. The message space is the set

$$\{(m_1, \ldots, m_L) : m_i \in \pm\{0,1\}^{\ell_m}\} \ .$$

Signing. Let ℓ_r, $\ell_e > \ell_m + 2$ and $\ell_v := \ell_n + \ell_m + \ell_r$ be security parameters. A signature on messages $m_1, \ldots, m_L$ is then generated by the protocol depicted in Figure 3.11. There, $R \subseteq \{0, \ldots, n-1\}$ denotes the set of indices of the messages

User		Issuer
$r \in [0,n]$ $t = \prod_{j \notin R} R_j^{m_j} S^r$		
	$\xrightarrow{t}$	
	$ZKP\left[((\mu_j)_{j \notin R}, o, \rho) : t = \prod_{j \notin R} R_j^{\mu_j} S^{\rho} \wedge com = \prod_{j \in C} R_j^{\mu_j} S^{o} \wedge \mu_j \in \pm\{0,1\}^{\ell_m}\right]$	
		$v' \in_R 1\|\{0,1\}^{\ell_v - 1}$ $e \in_R \mathbb{P} \cap 1\|\{0,1\}^{\ell_e - 1}$ $A = \left(\frac{Z}{t \prod_{i \in R} R_i^{m_i} S^{v'}}\right)^{1/e}$
	$\xleftarrow{(A, e, v')}$	
	$ZKP\left[(\varepsilon, v') : A = \left(\frac{Z}{t \prod_{i \in R} R_i^{m_i} S^{v'}}\right)^{1/\varepsilon}\right]$	
Check that $Z = A^e S^{v'}$ Check that $e \in \mathbb{P} \cap 1\|\{0,1\}^{\ell_e - 1}$ Output $sig = (e, A, v = v' + r)$		

Fig. 3.11 Issuance of a signature for attributes $(m_1, \ldots, m_L)$. In the first zero-knowledge proof, the user acts as the prover, while in the second proof the issuer acts as the verifier. If any of the checks fails or proofs fails, the protocol aborts.

which are revealed to the signer, and $C \subseteq \{0, \ldots, n-1\} \setminus R$ denotes the set of indices of the messages which are to be carried over from a previous signature. That is, as discussed earlier, the commitment *com* is the output of a preceding presentation proof, and the values of the contained messages are carried over into the new signature, ensuring security to both parties.

Signature presentation. When proving possession of a signature, the user can again decide to reveal a subset R of the messages, and additionally generate a commitment *com* for a subset C of different messages. The latter can then be used in a follow-up issuance session to show that the attributes where actually blindly carried-over correctly as describe above.

Presentation is now done as follows:

1. The user first re-randomizes the signature (e, A, v) by choosing a random $r \in_R [0,n]$ and computing $(e, A' = AS^{-r}, v' = v + er)$. Note that A' is statistically close to the uniform over $\mathbb{Z}_n^*$ and therefore does not leak any information to the verifier.
2. The user computes a commitment *com* to the attributes with indices in C as described in Section 3.2.3.1.
3. The user then sends A' and *com* to the adversary.
4. The user and the verifier run the following zero-knowledge proof of knowledge:

$$ZKP\Big[((\mu_j)_{j\notin R},\rho,v',\varepsilon) : Z\prod_{i\in R} R_i^{-m_i} = A'^{\varepsilon}\prod_{j\notin R} R_j^{\mu_j} S^{v'} \wedge com = \prod_{j\in C} R_j^{\mu_j} S^{\rho} \wedge$$
$$\bigwedge_{j\notin R} \mu_j \in \pm\{0,1\}^{\ell_m} \wedge 2^{\ell_e-1} < \varepsilon < 2^{\ell_e}\Big].$$

5. The verifier accepts if and only if this proof output accept.

Theorem 2 ([CL02a]). *Under the strong RSA assumption, the above scheme is secure against adaptive chosen message attacks. Furthermore, for any polynomially bounded number of presentations, it is computationally infeasible to link presentation sessions among each other, or presentation sessions to an issuance session, even if verifiers and issuers collude.*

The original scheme considered messages in the interval $[0, 2^{\ell_m} - 1]$. Here, however, we allow messages to be from $[-2^{\ell_m} + 1, 2^{\ell_m} - 1]$. The only consequence of this is that we need to require that $\ell_e > \ell_m + 2$ holds instead of $\ell_e > \ell_m + 1$.

3.2.4.2 Brands Signatures

The signature scheme presented in the following was introduced by Brands [Bra93]. It is the core building block of Microsoft's U-Prove anonymous credential system.

In the following, let H be a collision resistant hash function, i.e., it is hard to find to different values which map to the same output.

Key generation. Choose random primes p and q such that $q|(p-1)$ and computing discrete logarithms in the unique subgroup of order q of $\mathbb{Z}_p^*$ is hard for the given security parameter. Choose further a random generator g of this subgroup, and random values $y_i \in_R \mathbb{Z}_q$ for $i = 0,\ldots,L$, and define $g_i := g^{y_i}$ for all i. Output the public key $(g,p,q,g_0,\ldots,g_L)$ and the secret key y_0.

Message space. Let ℓ_m be such that $2^{\ell_m} < q$. The message space is the set

$$\{(m_1,\ldots,m_L) : m_i \in \{0,1\}^{\ell_m}\} .$$

Signing. Using the same notation as for the signing algorithm in Section 3.2.4.1, Figure 3.12 shows how messages can blindly be signed.

Signature presentation. Again using the notation from Section 3.2.4.1, knowledge of a signature is done as follows:

1. The user computes a commitment com to the attributes with indices in C as described in Section 3.2.3.1.
2. The user sends (h,z',c',r') and com to the verifier.
3. The user and the verifier run the following zero-knowledge proof of knowledge:

$$ZKP\Big[((\mu_j)_{j\notin R},\sigma,\rho) : h = \Big(g_0\prod_{j\in R} g_i^{m_i}\prod_{j\notin R} g_i^{\mu_j}\Big)^{\sigma} \wedge com = \prod_{j\in C} R_j^{\mu_j} S^{\rho}\Big].$$

User		Issuer
$s \in_R \mathbb{Z}_q^*$ $v \in_R \mathbb{Z}_q$ $b_1, b_2 \in_R \mathbb{Z}_q$ $h = (g_0 \prod_{j=1}^{L} g_j^{m_j})^s$ $t_1 = g_0^{b_1} g^{b_2}$ $t_2 = h^{b_2}$ $t' = \prod_{j \notin R} g_j^{m_j} g^v$		
	$\xrightarrow{t'}$	
	$ZKP\left[\left((\mu_j)_{j\notin R}, o, v\right) : t' = \prod_{j\notin R} g_j^{\mu_j} g^v \wedge com = \prod_{j\in C} R_j^{\mu_j} S^o\right]$	
		$w \in_R \mathbb{Z}_q$ $a = g^w$ $t = g_0 t' \prod_{j\in R} g_j^{m_j}$ $b = t^w$ $z = t^{y_0}$
	$\xleftarrow{(a,b,z)}$	
$z' = (z/g_0^v)^s$ $a' = t_1 a$ $b' = (z')^{b_1} t_2 (b/a^v)^s$ $c' = H(h, z', a', b') \in \mathbb{Z}_q$ $c = c' + b_1 \bmod q$		
	$\xrightarrow{c}$	
		$r = c y_0 + w \bmod q$
	$\xleftarrow{r}$	
$r' = r + b_2 \bmod q$ Output $sig = (s, h, z', c', r')$		

Fig. 3.12 Issuance of a signature for attributes $(m_1, \ldots, m_L)$. In the zero-knowledge proof the user acts as the prover. If any of the checks or proofs fails, the protocol aborts.

4. The verifier accepts if and only if $c' \stackrel{?}{=} \mathsf{H}(h, z', g^{r'} g_0^{-c'}, h^{r'} (z')^{-c'})$ and the above proof output accept.

Theorem 3. *For any polynomially bounded number of presentations, it is infeasible to link presentation sessions to an issuance session, even if verifiers and issuers collude.*

Note here that in contrast to CL-signatures it is possible to link multiple presentations of the same signature among each other. This can easily be seen by the way presentations are done: there, the user reveals parts of the signature to the verifier. Therefore, if presentations should be unlinkable, every signature must only be used in a single presentation session.

Furthermore, note that there does not exist a formal proof that Brands signatures are unforgeable under chosen message attacks. However, they have been well studied for almost two decades and are widely believed to be secure.

3.2.5 Verifiable Encryption

In public key encryption schemes, each user has two keys: a public key, which others can use to encrypt message for this user, and a secret key, which the user can use to decrypt these ciphertexts. Such schemes can be thought of as digital equivalents of standard letter boxes: Each other user can post a letter in this box, but only the legitimate owner of the letter box is able to open it and extract the letter from the box.

Informally, the public key encryption schemes used for anonymous credentials have to satisfy the following security properties. First, they have to be *correct*, i.e., decrypting a ciphertext always yields the message that was originally encrypted. Second, they should be *indistinguishable under chosen-ciphertext attacks*. This means, that given a ciphertext, no adversary knowing the public key but not the secret key can tell which message got encrypted. This has to hold even if the adversary knows that the ciphertext is an encrypted of one out of two adversarially chosen plaintexts, and if the adversary is allowed to obtain decryptions of arbitrary different ciphertexts.

Verifiable encryption schemes are an extension of public key encryption schemes, where the sender is additionally able to prove certain statements about the message he encrypted, without having to reveal the message. In particular, a sender is able to prove that he knows the message contained in a ciphertext, or, e.g., that the ciphertext contains the same message as a given commitment.

3.2.5.1 The Camenisch-Shoup Encryption Scheme

The scheme described here was proposed by Camenisch and Shoup [CS03] and is a variation of an encryption scheme put forth by Cramer and Shoup [CS02]. The scheme makes use of a keyed hash scheme $\mathscr{H}$ that uses a key hk, chosen at random from an appropriate key space associated with the security parameter. Every hash function $\mathsf{H} \in \mathscr{H}$ maps triples of the form (u,e,L) to integers in the set $[0, 2^{\ell}-1]$. The hash functions have to be collision resistant, i.e., given a random hash key hk it is infeasible to find two different triples mapping to the same value.

We further define $\mathsf{abs} : \mathbb{Z}^*_{n^2} \to \mathbb{Z}^*_{n^2}$ as the function mapping $(a \bmod n^2)$ to $(n^2 - a \bmod n^2)$ if $a > n^2/2$, and to $(a \bmod n^2)$, otherwise. Note that $v^2 \equiv (\mathsf{abs}(v))^2$ holds for all $v \in \mathbb{Z}^*_{n^2}$.

Key generation. On input ℓ_n, choose an ℓ_n-bit RSA modulus n such that $n := pq$, $p := 2p'+1$, $q := 2q'+1$, where p, q, p', and q' are primes. Let further $n' := p'q'$. Choose random $x_1, x_2, x_3 \in_R [0, \lfloor n^2/4 \rfloor]$, and a random $g' \in_R \mathbb{Z}^*_{n^2}$, and compute $g := (g')^{2n}$, and $y_i := g^{x_i}$, for $i = 1,2,3$.

Also, generate a hash key hk from the key space of the hash scheme $\mathscr{H}$ associated with the given security parameter.

The public key is $(\mathsf{hk}, n, g, y_1, y_2, y_3)$. The secret key is $(\mathsf{hk}, n, x_1, x_2, x_3)$.

Message space. The message space is given by $[0, n]$.

Encryption. To encrypt a message m with label $L \in \{0,1\}^*$ under a public key as above, choose a random $r \in_R [0, \lfloor n/4 \rfloor]$ and compute

$$u := g^r \ , \qquad e := y_1^r (n+1)^m \ , \quad \text{and} \qquad v := \mathsf{abs}\left((y_2 y_3^{\mathsf{H}(u,e,L)})^r \right) \ .$$

The ciphertext is (u, e, v).

Decryption. To decrypt a ciphertext $(u, e, v) \in \mathbb{Z}^*_{n^2} \times \mathbb{Z}^*_{n^2} \times \mathbb{Z}^*_{n^2}$ with label L under a secret key as above, first check that $\mathsf{abs}(v) \equiv v$ and $u^{2(x_2+\mathsf{H}(u,e,L)x_3)} \equiv v^2$. If this does not hold, then output reject and halt. Next, let $t := 2^{-1} \bmod n$, and compute $\hat{m} := (e/u^{x_1})^{2t}$. If $\hat{m}$ is of the form h^m for some $m \in [0, n]$, then output m; otherwise, output reject. This can efficiently be tested using the fact that $h^m \equiv 1 + mn \bmod n^2$ for $0 \leq m < n$, and therefore in this case $m = \frac{\hat{m}-1}{n}$.

Theorem 4. *Under the decisional composite residuosity assumption and if the deployed hash function is collision resistant, the scheme described above is indistinguishable under chosen-ciphertext attacks.*

In a credential scheme, typically some attribute uniquely identifying the credential and/or the owner of the credential is encrypted for a presentation proof, under the public key of some public authority such as, e.g., a judge, commonly referred to as *inspector*. When presenting the credential, the user additionally shows that the computed ciphertext is indeed the same as the corresponding attribute value in the credential. While the user's privacy is maintained, the verifier is thereby ensured that he has a valid encryption of the user's identity. Upon misbehavior of the user, the verifier can now request the public authority to reveal the identity of the user by decrypting the ciphertext, and thus the user can, e.g., be held accountable for any damage he caused.

3.2.6 Scope-Exclusive Pseudonyms

Pseudonyms are aliases that users assume for particular applications or settings. That is, a user may be known under different pseudonyms to different entities, such that those entities cannot decide whether two pseudonyms belonged to the same user or not. A pseudonyms is scope-exclusive, if for a given string specifying the scope of the session, e.g., the URL of a webpage or the name of a service, the user can only take a unique pseudonym. This means that within a given scope users can be recognized, but that they are still unlinkable across scopes. If for a certain service it is not required to be recognizable, the scope can just be set to a fresh random string every time, thereby becoming fully unlinkable.

Technically, a user is identified with a secret key that is only known to that specific user. A scope-exclusive pseudonym is then derived deterministically from the scope string and the user's secret key. Whenever a user gives a pseudonym to a verifier, he further proves that he knows the secret key that was used to derive the pseudonym without revealing it.

Such a scheme has to satisfy the following security properties. The scheme must be *complete*, meaning that an honest user deriving a pseudonym from his secret key can convince the verifier that he is indeed privy of this secret key, i.e., that he owns the identity hidden behind the given pseudonym. On the other hand *soundness* guarantees that only an honest user can convince a verifier about this fact. The *scope-exclusiveness* property says that for each scope string, every user secret key maps to a unique pseudonym. *Collision resistance* ensures that for every fixed scope, no two different identities map to the same pseudonym. Finally, *unlinkability* says that given pseudonyms to two different scopes, it is infeasible to decide whether or not they were derived from the same user secret key.

3.2.6.1 Efficient Scope Exclusive Pseudonyms

In the following we present the algorithms for an efficient pseudonym system.

Key generation. The public key of the scheme consists of a group $\mathcal{G}$ of prime order q, and a hash key hk specifying a collision resistant hash function H as in Section 3.2.5.1.

User key generation. A user's secret key is computed by randomly choosing an $x \in_R \mathbb{Z}_q$.

Pseudonym generation. Given a scope string scope and a user secret key x, the pseudonym is given by $\mathsf{nym} := \mathsf{H}(\mathsf{scope})^x$.

Pseudonym presentation. To convince a verifier that the user knows the identity behind a given pseudonym, they perform the following zero-knowledge proof of knowledge:

$$ZKP\left[(\chi) : \mathsf{nym} = \mathsf{H}(\mathsf{scope})^{\chi}\right].$$

Theorem 5. *Under the DDH-assumption for $\mathcal{G}$ and if the deployed hash function is collision resistant, the given scope-exclusive pseudonym system is secure.*

In practice, the user's secret key is embedded as an attribute into a credential. Then, when presenting a credential under a pseudonym, the user shows that the same user secret key was used in the presentation of the credential and to derive the pseudonym.

3.2.7 Revocation

In real-world applications of anonymous credentials it is vital to have efficient means to revoke credentials. On the one hand, users might want to revoke their credentials, e.g., if they loose the device they used to store the credential, or if it gets stolen. On the other hand, service providers might want to revoke credentials upon misbehavior such as credential sharing.

In a revocation scheme, a revocation authority gives secret pieces of information to every user, and publishes some publicly available revocation information. Now, whenever presenting a credential, the user simultaneously proves that his credential has not yet been revoked by showing that he possesses such an unrevoked secret piece of information, and that this data is somehow linked to the presented credential.

Informally, revocation schemes have to satisfy the following security properties. First, *correctness* ensures that honest holders of unrevoked credentials can always convince the verifier that this is indeed the case. Second, by the *soundness* property, verifiers are ensured that only honest users can make them accept. Finally, to protect the user's privacy, the *zero-knowledge* property guarantees the user that no personal information is leaked to the verifier when proving that the credential has not yet been revoked.

3.2.7.1 Camenisch-Lysyanskaya Accumulators

The scheme described in the following was presented by Camenisch and Lysysanskaya [CL02b]. On a very high level, the scheme works as follows: The revocation authority publishes some revocation information v in $\mathbb{Z}_n^*$, and hands a secret pair (e,u) to the user, where $e > 1$ is an integer, and u is an eth root of v, such that no two users receive the same e. If a user wants to prove that his secret has not yet been revoked, he proves that he knows such a pair (e,u) in a zero-knowledge manner. If a user's secret key is to be revoked, the revocation authority just computes a root of v, obtaining $v^{e^{-1}}$ as the new revocation information. Unrevoked users can update their pairs efficiently, while the revoked user would now have to compute a fresh root of the new revocation information, as his secret exponent was "divided out". However, the latter is impossible under the strong RSA assumption, cf. Definition 4.

Key generation. The revocation authority, on input ℓ_n, chooses an ℓ_n-bit RSA modulus n such that $n := pq$, $p := 2p' + 1$, $q := 2q' + 1$, where p, q, p', and q' are primes. It further chooses $v, g, h \in_R \mathbb{QR}_n$.
The public key is given by (u,g,h,n) and the secret key is given by (p,q).

Join. Whenever a user joins joins the group, the revocation authority hands over a random prime e and $u \in \mathbb{QR}_n$ such that $u^e \equiv v \bmod n$. Using the secret key, such a u can always be computed efficiently as $u = v^{e^{-1} \bmod (p-1)(q-1)}$ using the extended Euclidean algorithm.

Revoking a user. If a user's certificate is to be revoked, the revocation authority updates the public revocation information v as $v := v^{e'^{-1} \bmod (p-1)(q-1)} \bmod n$, where e' denotes the exponent the user received when he joined the group. The revocation authority then further published the value e'.

Updating the revocation information. Every time a user's certificate gets revoked, all the remaining users have to update their secret values u and e. Let therefore e' denote the revoked value, $v_{\texttt{new}}$ be the new revocation information published by the revocation authority, and $v_{\texttt{old}}$ be the public revocation information from before e' was revoked.

In a first step, a user uses the extended Euclidean algorithm to compute integers a and b such that $ae + be' = 1$. In a second step, the user then updates his private group element u to $u := u^b v_{\texttt{new}}^a$.

Proving unrevokedness. A user can prove to a verifier that his certificate has not been revoked by performing the following steps:

1. The user first draws $r_1, r_2, r_3 \in_R [0, \lfloor n/4 \rfloor]$.
2. The user then computes $C_e = g^e h^{r_1}$, $C_u = uh^{r_2}$ and $C_r = g^{r_2} h^{r_3}$, which he sends to the verifier.
3. The user and the verifier together run the following zero-knowledge proof of knowledge:

$$ZKP\Big[(\varepsilon, \rho_1, \rho_2, \rho_3, \phi, \psi) \ : C_e = g^{\varepsilon} h^{\rho_1} \ \wedge \ C_r = g^{\rho_2} h^{\rho_3} \ \wedge \\ v = C_u^{\varepsilon} h^{-\phi} \ \wedge \ 1 = C_r^{\varepsilon} g^{-\phi} h^{-\psi}\Big] .$$

   Here, the user uses $r_2 e$ for ϕ and $r_3 e$ for ψ.
4. The verifier accepts if and only if this proof output accept.

Theorem 6 ([CL02b]). *Under the strong RSA assumption, the scheme described above is a secure revocation scheme.*

The above revocation scheme is linked to the credential scheme by embedding the user's revocation key e as an attribute into a credential. The user then shows that he knows an unrevoked revocation key, and that the very same key is contained in the credential, thereby proving that the credential has not been revoked.

References

[BP97] Niko Barić and Birgit Pfitzmann. Collision-Free Accumulators and Fail-Stop Signature Schemes Without Trees. In W. Fumy, editor, *EUROCRYPT*, volume 1233 of *LNCS*, pages 480–494. Springer, 1997.

[Bra93] Stefan A Brands. An Efficient Off-line Electronic Cash System Based On The Representation Problem. Technical report, 1993.

[CKY09] Jan Camenisch, Aggelos Kiayias, and Moti Yung. On the Portability of Generalized Schnorr Proofs. In A. Joux, editor, *EUROCRYPT 09*, volume 5479 of *LNCS*, pages 425–442. Springer, 2009.

[CL02a] Jan Camenisch and Anna Lysyanskaya. A Signature Scheme with Efficient Protocols. In S. Cimato, C. Galdi, and G. Persiano, editors, *SCN 02*, volume 2576 of *LNCS*, pages 268–289. Springer, 2002.

[CL02b] Jan Camenisch and Anna Lysyanskaya. Dynamic Accumulators and Application to Efficient Revocation of Anonymous Credentials. In M. Yung, editor, *CRYPTO*, volume 2442 of *LNCS*, pages 61–76. Springer, 2002.

[CS97] Jan Camenisch and Markus Stadler. Efficient Group Signature Schemes for Large Groups (Extended Abstract). In B. S. Kaliski Jr., editor, *CRYPTO*, volume 1294 of *LNCS*, pages 410–424. Springer, 1997.

[CS02] Ronald Cramer and Victor Shoup. Universal Hash Proofs and a Paradigm for Adaptive Chosen Ciphertext Secure Public-Key Encryption. In L. R. Knudsen, editor, *EUROCRYPT*, volume 2332 of *LNCS*, pages 45–64. Springer, 2002.

[CS03] Jan Camenisch and Victor Shoup. Practical Verifiable Encryption and Decryption of Discrete Logarithms. In D. Boneh, editor, *CRYPTO*, volume 2729 of *LNCS*, pages 126–144. Springer, 2003.

[DF02] Ivan Damgård and Eiichiro Fujisaki. A Statistically-Hiding Integer Commitment Scheme Based on Groups with Hidden Order. In Y. Zheng, editor, *ASIACRYPT 02*, volume 2501 of *LNCS*, pages 125–142. Springer, 2002.

[FO97] Eiichiro Fujisaki and Tatsuaki Okamoto. Statistical Zero Knowledge Protocols to Prove Modular Polynomial Relations. In B. S. Kaliski Jr., editor, *CRYPTO 97*, volume 1294 of *LNCS*, pages 16–30. Springer, 1997.

[FS87] Amos Fiat and Adi Shamir. How to Prove Yourself: Practical Solutions to Identification and Signature Problems. In A. M. Odlyzko, editor, *CRYPTO 86*, volume 263 of *LNCS*, pages 186–194. Springer, 1987.

[Lip03] Helger Lipmaa. On Diophantine Complexity and Statistical Zero Knowledge Arguments. In C.-S. Laih, editor, *ASIACRYPT 03*, volume 2894 of *LNCS*, pages 398–415. Springer, 2003.

[Pai99] Pascal Paillier. Public-Key Cryptosystems Based on Composite Degree Residuosity Classes. In J. Stern, editor, *EUROCRYPT*, volume 1592 of *LNCS*, pages 223–238. Springer, 1999.

[Ped91] Torben Pryds Pedersen. Non-Interactive and Information-Theoretic Secure Verifiable Secret Sharing. In J. Feigenbaum, editor, *CRYPTO 91*, volume 576 of *LNCS*, pages 129–140. Springer, 1991.

[RS86] Michael O Rabin and Jeffery O Shallit. Randomized Algorithms in Number Theory. *Communications in Pure and Applied Math*, 39:239–256, 1986.

[RSA78] Ronald L Rivest, Adi Shamir, and Len Adleman. A Method for Obtaining Digital Signatures and Public-Key Cryptosystems. *Communications of the ACM*, 21(2):120–126, 1978.

[Sch91] Claus-Peter Schnorr. Efficient Signature Generation by Smart Cards. *Journal of Cryptology*, 4(3):161–174, 1991.

[VLG+14] Fatbardh Veseli, Jesus Luna, Hamza Ghani, Tsvetoslava Vateva-Gurova, Harald Zwingelberg, Katalin Storf, Felix Bieker, Daniel Deibler, and Marit Hansen. Benchmarking Criteria. Deliverable D2.3, The ABC4Trust EU Project, 2014. Available at `https://abc4trust.eu/download/D2.3%20-%20Benchmarking%20Criteria.pdf`, Last accessed on 2014-11-08.

Chapter 4
Comparison of Mechanisms

Michael Østergaard Pedersen, Gert Læssøe Mikkelsen, Fatbardh Veseli, Ahmad Sabouri, and Tsvetoslava Vateva-Gurova

Abstract In this chapter we compare Privacy-ABC schemes based on the security, functionality and efficiency they offer. The aim of this is to help researchers and application developers choose an schemes and parameters most suitable for their application.

Different Privacy-ABC schemes have different properties when it comes to security, functionality, and efficiency. For researchers and application developers who want to utilize Privacy-ABC technology, it is very important to understand these differences.

The first part of this chapter supplies the reader with background information needed to be able to reason about security aspects of Privacy-ABC schemes, and the second part compares functionality and efficiency of Privacy-ABC schemes. These comparisons are based on a set of comparison metrics developed in the ABC4Trust project.

Functionality and efficiency are parameters which can be compared using practical tests and measurements, whereas security needs a more theoretical approach. Therefore the first part is more theoretical, and the last part is more practical based on concrete implementations.

Michael Østergaard Pedersen
Miracle A/S, Denmark, e-mail: mop@miracle.dk

Gert Læssøe Mikkelsen
Alexandra Institute, Denmark, e-mail: gert.l.mikkelsen@alexandra.dk

Fatbardh Veseli and Ahmad Sabouri
Chair for Mobile Business & Multilateral Security, Goethe University Frankfurt, Germany, e-mail: {fatbardh.veseli, ahmad.sabouri}@m-chair.de

Tsvetoslava Vateva-Gurova
Department of Computer Science, Technische Universität Darmstadt, Germany, e-mail: vateva@deeds.informatik.tu-darmstadt.de

K. Rannenberg et al. (eds.), *Attribute-based Credentials for Trust*,
DOI 10.1007/978-3-319-14439-9_4

4.1 Theoretical Comparison – Security Properties and Claims

Before we can compare the security of any mechanism, including Privacy-ABCs, we need to know what security actually means. First of all, it is important to realize that the different entities of a system might have different views on what security properties are relevant. In the Privacy-ABC settings for example, a scheme might be secure for the Issuer and the Verifier in the sense that a malicious User cannot forge a credential. The same scheme, however, might leak information about hidden attributes to the Verifier during presentation. We consider the following security properties of a Privacy-ABC scheme:

Pseudonym Collisions Resistance No cheating User, Issuer or Verifier is able to present a pseudonym of an honest User.

Unforgeability Security for the Issuer and Verifier against cheating users, trying to impersonate other users, forge credentials, forge presentation proofs, or present revoked credentials.

Privacy This covers the following properties:

- *Untraceability* means that the Issuer is not capable of tracing the use of an issued credential, even when the Issuer and the Verifier colludes, except in trivial cases such as when a unique attribute known by the Verifier is revealed during presentation or when an attribute is revealed in case of inspection.
- *Attribute Hiding* means that the Verifier does not get any information about undisclosed attributes, even if the Issuer and the Verifier colludes. This includes inspectable attributes, unless they are revealed by the Inspector.
- *Unlinkability* means that a Verifier cannot tell if two presentations are done using the same credential or two different credentials even from different users. This must hold even in the case where the Issuer and the Verifier colludes.

Weak Privacy As the above except only *untraceability* and *attribute hiding* are provided.

When considering the above security properties it is also important to take the attacker trying to break the security properties into account. What methods can he use for his attack and how much computational power does he have. Some security properties are said to hold unconditionally which means that no adversary, no matter how powerful, will ever be able to break that security property of the scheme. Unfortunately only a few schemes are unconditionally secure for all their security properties especially for the settings where we want to use Privacy-ABCs. In fact for many types of cryptographic primitives it can be proven that an unconditionally secure scheme cannot exist. A classical example of such schemes are commitment schemes, where it is relatively easy to prove that no scheme can exist where both the hiding and binding properties hold unconditionally. We can, however, base the security on computational assumptions instead. Computational assumptions are assumptions about some computational problems being infeasible to compute for sufficiently large inputs. In Section 4.1.1 we have a closer look at the different assumptions used by the building blocks in Chapter 3. For the security properties of

Privacy-ABC schemes it is more important that the privacy features holds unconditionally, than the unforgeability feature. This is because over time it is possible to update a system with new schemes or new parameters to preserve unforgeability, whereas for the privacy properties an attacker might try to attack presentation tokens presented years ago. Moreover, if the privacy is broken and values are revealed, these values cannot be unrevealed again.

A security proof (sometimes also called a security reduction) of a cryptographic scheme is a reduction showing that if there exists an adversary that can break the security of the scheme, then there exists an algorithm turning this attack on the scheme into an efficient algorithm solving the computational problem. This means that if in fact the assumption (that the underlying computational problem is hard) is true then the scheme is secure. One could argue that this does not actually prove the security of the scheme as it only moves the trust from the scheme to the assumption. This is of course true, however, many assumptions have been very well studied for many years, and are still expected to hold. Moreover, it is a lot easier to analyse a simple assumption than it is to analyse the security of a complex scheme without a proof. There also exist schemes used in practice where it is unknown whether there exist proofs of their security except assuming that the scheme is secure. Despite the weaker security guarantees, some of these schemes are used in practice either because they are more efficient or due to other properties.

For computationally secure schemes, we can affect the security level by changing the key size. The security level can vary from being able to solve the computational problem underlying the scheme in hours with a standard computer to taking millions of years with current technology. In Section 4.1.3 practical values for key sizes are discussed. One additional note regarding the key size is the tightness of a security proof. For some proofs we can only conclude that if an adversary can break the scheme then we can turn this into a solution of the underlying computational problem for much smaller numbers than the actual key size of the scheme. In that case one needs to choose a larger key size so that the reduction results in a key size of the underlying computational problem that is still secure. When a reduction shows that the key size for a scheme and the corresponding computational problem are of about the same size, we say that the reduction is tight. Reductions that are not tight are called loose. In practice tightness of the reduction is rarely taken into account when determining the key size for a given scheme.

4.1.1 Computational Assumptions

The building blocks implemented in the Cryptographic Engine relate to the following computational assumptions that were introduced in Chapter 3:

- Discrete Logarithm (DL) assumption
- Decisional Diffie-Hellman (DDH) assumption
- Strong RSA (SRSA) assumption
- Decisional Composite Residuosity (DCR) assumption

These computational assumptions are directly linked to the security of one or more building blocks. However, there are also other assumptions that are essential for the security of the composition of the building blocks in the Cryptographic Engine:

Collision Resistance Collision resistance is a security property of a hash function and not a general computational assumptions. It says that for a hash function H, it is difficult to find two different inputs x and y such that $\mathsf{H}(x) = \mathsf{H}(y)$.

Fiat-Shamir Heuristic The Fiat-Shamir Construction is a way to turn an interactive zero-knowledge proofs into a non-interactive version. The Fiat Shamir Heuristic is the assumption that the Fiat-Shamir Construction is secure. This assumption can actually be proven secure in some theoretical models, but its security in real world applications remain an assumption.

When looking at computational assumptions one always has to keep in mind in which group the assumption is believed to hold. For example there are groups in which the DDH problem is easy to solve, yet computing discrete logarithms is still believed to be hard. The ability to compute discrete logarithms in a group would imply that it would be easy to solve the DDH problem in that group as well, but this is not the case in the opposite direction. Therefore DDH is a stronger assumption than DL since requiring that the DDH assumption holds in a group is a more restrictive requirement.

There are many different assumptions in use in the cryptographic literature. Some of them are fairly new and only used to reason about security of a very small number of protocols, while others are widely used and have been studied for many years. All the computational assumptions in this section are well studied.

4.1.2 Security Aspects of Privacy-ABC Schemes

Since Privacy-ABC schemes are composed of building blocks, we need to know which building blocks a scheme is based on in order to evaluate its security, and we also need to know which assumption each of the building blocks are based on. In Table 4.1 each building block from Chapter 3 is listed together with the assumptions they are based on. We note that the listed assumptions might only be a requirement for some security properties of the building block, meaning that other security properties can have a stronger security guarantee than the listed assumptions, e.g. be unconditionally secure.

A combination of two building blocks requires at least the assumptions of both building blocks to hold. However, the other way, that the combination is secure given that the assumptions of both building blocks hold is not necessarily true. In fact, the building blocks are only proven secure as standalone protocols and combining them might in general not preserve their security properties. Nevertheless, using underlying building blocks with security proofs is still a big step in the direction of a secure system.

Table 4.1 Building Blocks and their Computational Assumption

Type	Instantiation	Computational Assumption
Commitment	Pedersen/Damgård-Fujisaki Commitments	Strong RSA assumption
Blind Signature	Camenisch-Lysyanskaya Signatures	Strong RSA assumption
Blind Signature	Brands Signatures (Subgroup or Elliptic Curve)[a]	Unknown - No security proof exists. However, at least the Discrete Logarithm assumption must hold in the group[b]
Verifiable Encryption	Camenisch-Shoup Encryption Scheme	Decisional Composite Residuosity assumption
Pseudonym	Scope-Exclusive Pseudonym	Decisional Diffie-Hellman assumption
Revocation	Camenisch-Lysyanskaya Accumulators	Strong RSA assumption

[a]Brands Signatures can be instantiated over a subgroup of a group defined by multiplication modulo a prime or over elliptic curves. U-Prove, as it is available directly from Microsoft [PZ13], can do both whereas the ABC4Trust Cryptographic Engine only implements the former.
[b]According to Baldimtsi and Lysyanskaya [BL13], it is not possible to prove that any of the assumptions listed in this section are sufficient to prove security of the Brands signature scheme.

Since the different security properties of Privacy-ABC schemes rely on different security properties of the underlying building blocks, not all security properties require all assumptions of the underlying building blocks to hold. As an example of this, consider the two Privacy-ABC schemes defined in Table 4.2.

Looking more closely at how these Privacy-ABC schemes are implemented using the building blocks, we can map the computational assumptions of the building blocks to the security properties of Privacy-ABC schemes. This mapping is shown in Table 4.3. Note especially that *Privacy* and *Weak-Privacy* are unconditionally se-

Table 4.2 Two Examples of Privacy-ABC Schemes

Scheme	Building Blocks
PABC-CL	Pedersen/Damgård-Fujisaki Commitments Camenisch-Lysyanskaya Signatures Camenisch-Shoup Encryption Scheme Scope-Exclusive Pseudonym Scheme Camenisch-Lysyanskaya Accumulators
PABC-Brands	Pedersen/Damgård-Fujisaki Commitments Brands Signatures Camenisch-Shoup Encryption Scheme Scope-Exclusive Pseudonym Scheme Camenisch-Lysyanskaya Accumulators

Table 4.3 Underlying Computational Assumptions for Security Properties of Privacy-ABC Schemes

Scheme	Pseudonym Collision-Resistance	Unforgeability	Privacy	Weak-Privacy
PABC-CL	Security of hash function[a]	SRSA	Unconditional, DCR[d]	Unconditional, DCR[d]
PABC-Brands	Security of hash function[a]	Unknown[b], SRSA[c]	No	Unconditional, DCR[d]

[a] Only applicable for scope exclusive pseudonyms. Non-scope exclusive pseudonyms are unconditionally secure.
[b] There does not exist a security proof for Brands signatures, but the best currently known attack is to solve the DL problem.
[c] This assumption is only relevant if the revocation feature is used.
[d] This assumption is only relevant if the inspection feature is used.

cure. This is because the computational assumptions listed for the signature building blocks in Table 4.1 are only needed for the *unforgeability* property.

4.1.3 Key Sizes in Practice

Increasing the key size of a secure cryptographic scheme leads to an increased security level at the cost of lower performance of the cryptographic operations. Since different cryptographic schemes often require different key sizes to provide the same level of security it is important that when comparing the performance of different cryptographic schemes, they are compared at the same security level instead of comparing the actual key size.

The ECRYPT II project [Sma12] has defined actual key sizes for various groups corresponding to different security levels. Their definition of security level ℓ corresponds to the security of an ideal symmetric cipher with key size ℓ bits, meaning a cipher where the only possible attack is a brute force attack. Furthermore they have picked a few common security levels which are summarized in Table 4.4.

Table 4.5 shows the relation between security level and actual key size for computational problems in various groups. The table uses groups instead of assumptions since for most well-known assumptions they are equally hard for a given key size in a given group. In the ECRYPT II report they provide more details about how the size of parameters in a given group can be affected by different computational assumptions.

The columns in Table 4.5 are taken from the ECRYPT II report and refer to the following: *Symmetric* refers to the desired security level from Table 4.4; *RSA Based* is in our case the size of the RSA modulus in the schemes relying on the Strong RSA assumption, and the size of n before being squared (not the size of n^2) in the schemes

Table 4.4 Security Levels from ECRYPT II

Security Level	Protection	Comment
32	Attacks in real-time by individuals.	Only acceptable for auth. tag.
64	Very short-term protection against small organizations.	Should not be used for confidentiality in new systems.
72	Short-term protection against medium organizations, medium-term protection against small organizations.	
80	Very short-term protection against agencies, long term protection against small organizations.	Smallest general-purpose level, ≤ 4 years protection.
96	Legacy standard level.	Approx. 10 years protection
112	Medium term protection.	Approx. 20 years protection.
128	Long-term protection.	Good, generic application independent recommendation (approx. 30 years protection).
256	Foreseeable future	Good protection against quantum computers unless Shor's algorithm applies.

Table 4.5 Key Sizes for Given Security Levels from ECRYPT II

Symmetric	RSA Based	Subgroup	Logarithm Group	Elliptic Curve	Hash
64	816	128	816	128	128
72	1008	144	1008	144	144
80	1248	160	1248	160	160
96	1776	192	1776	192	192
112	2432	224	2432	224	224
128	3248	256	3248	256	256
256	15424	512	15424	512	512

relying on the DCR assumption; *Subgroup* and *Logarithm Group* refer to the size of the subgroup and the size of the group for schemes based on DL and DDH, when these are instantiated as a subgroup of a group defined by multiplication modulo a prime; *Elliptic Curve* refers to the size of the group for schemes based on DL and DDH, when these are instantiated as groups over elliptic curves. Note that this does not necessarily cover schemes relying on bilinear maps as some accumulator schemes do; *Hash* refers to the output size of a hash function.

The design of the Cryptographic Architecture allows for different implementations of the cryptographic building blocks, so in general it is not possible to talk about a single key size for the entire Privacy-ABC scheme. However, the building blocks that are currently implemented in the Cryptographic Engine all use key sizes from the *RSA Based* and *Logarithm Group* columns of Table 4.5. Since they are

Table 4.6 Actual Key Sizes of Building Blocks for Various Security Levels

Security Level	Pedersen/ Damgård-Fujisaki Commitments	CL Signatures	Brands Signatures (Sub-group)	Brands Signatures (Elliptic Curve)	Camenisch-Shoup Encryption Scheme	Scope-Exclusive Pseudonym	CL Accumulators
64	816	816	816	128	816	816	816
72	1008	1008	1008	144	1008	1008	1008
80	1248	1248	1248	160	1248	1248	1248
96	1776	1776	1776	192	1776	1776	1776
112	2432	2432	2432	224	2432	2432	2432
128	3248	3248	3248	256	3248	3248	3248
256	15424	15424	15424	512	15424	15424	15424

identical, the current version of the Cryptographic Engine only takes a single key size as input. If one were to implement additional building blocks with key sizes from e.g. the *Elliptic Curve* column, one would need to do this differently, e.g. by supplying a key size for each building block, or by specifying a security level as input and letting each building block generate keys of the correct length for that level of security.

In Table 4.6 the numbers from Table 4.5 are combined with our building blocks from Table 4.1 to give an actual key size for the different building blocks. For simplicity, we ignore the tightness of the security reduction. Brands signature scheme does not have a security reduction to any assumption, and it is therefore unknown whether more efficient attacks exist than solving the discrete logarithm problem. The numbers for Brands signatures in Table 4.6 are, however, based on the assumption that solving the discrete logarithm problem is the most efficient attack. If other attacks exist, this might influence the actual key size, or render the scheme insecure for any key size.

Most of the building blocks also rely on a hash function. For simplicity the Cryptographic Engine always uses SHA256, with provides a security level of 128, even for lower security levels, as hashing is a very efficient operation compared to the other cryptographic operations. Microsoft U-Prove [PZ13] internally chooses between SHA256 and SHA1 for hashing based on the security level and the ABC4Trust Cryptographic Engine mimics this behaviour when instantiated with the Brands signature scheme in order to allow for compatibility with U-Prove.

4.2 Practical Comparison

This section presents the practical part of the comparison. It is organised into two subsections, namely one that defines the criteria for comparing the technologies, and the other section that present the results of the practical comparison of two Privacy-ABC technologies using those criteria.

4.2.1 Comparison Criteria for Privacy-ABC Technologies

Despite the availability of implementations of Privacy-ABC technologies, there remain additional challenges towards their wider adoption in practice, one of which is the lack of understanding of their differences in terms of applicability to different scenarios. A first step towards improving this is the identification of the criteria, which could be used to compare these Privacy-ABC technologies. Such criteria would in the best case apply to existing, but also to potential future Privacy-ABC technologies.

In this regard, as a result of our extensive study of these technologies in the ABC4Trust project, we have come up with a set of comparison criteria covering the main aspects of Privacy-ABC technologies. The work on the identification of the benchmarking criteria is based on the unified architecture, concepts and features of Privacy-ABCs [CDL+13, BCD+14]. Furthermore, we try to identify additional challenges, which are inherent to certain Privacy-ABC technologies, providing an indication to the specific challenges and important considerations in their deployment in real life applications.

Privacy-ABC technologies are mainly investigated as part of anonymous credential systems. As the underlying technology relies heavily on cryptographic primitives [CL03, Bra00], much of the work has been focused on individual aspects, such as efficiency [CL03, VA13, MV11, Sch91, LKDDN10, CL02], or support for additional features [BCKL08, LLX07]. In addition, there are a number of proposed mechanisms for revocation of anonymous credentials, which also need to be benchmarked. An analysis of revocation schemes for PKI is presented in [ÅJK+00], but it does not take into account the specific aspects of Privacy-ABCs (e.g. privacy features). In this regard, tradeoffs between revocation schemes for anonymous credentials have been analysed in [LKDDN11, LKDDN10, CL02].

From a methodological perspective, elicitation of benchmarking criteria in general is studied also in other areas, e.g. on benchmarking security [LGLS12, LGVS12, PF09], although not particularly focusing on Privacy-ABC technologies. However, there is currently no comprehensive work on benchmarking Privacy-ABC technologies with a broader perspective covering a wider range of aspects as in our approach.

4.2.1.1 Comparison Dimensions, Criteria, and Impacting Factors

With the set of identified criteria being quite extensive, we have organised them into three main subsets, namely into *Functionality, Efficiency,* and *Security Assurance*. Each of these subsets represents a separate benchmarking dimension and con-

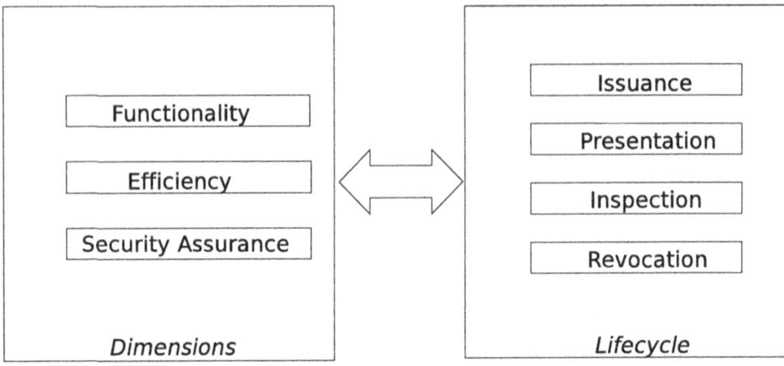

Fig. 4.1 The organisational structure of the benchmarking criteria

tains a list of criteria, which are chronologically organised following the lifecycle of Privacy-ABCs, including *Issuance, Presentation, Inspection,* and *Revocation*, as presented in Figure 4.1. Furthermore, we also identify typical impacting factors for the benchmarks related to the given criteria, following a user-centered approach.

4.2.1.2 Functionality

The functionality criteria are mostly qualitative and they aim at benchmarking different Privacy-ABC technologies based on their native support for different features, as introduced in Section 3. Here we also identify additional factors for distinguishing different Privacy-ABC technologies. We list these functional criteria in Table 4.7, organised following the lifecycle of Privacy-ABCs.

Issuance

The lifecycle of the Privacy-ABCs starts with the issuance of the credential and ends with its revocation. As mentioned in the ABC4Trust architecture deliverable

Table 4.7 Functionality Benchmarking Criteria

Stage	Functionality Criteria
Issuance	Supported issuance privacy features
Presentation	Combination of different credentials in presentation
	Supported predicates over attributes
	Support for multiple-presentation unlinkability
	Support for key binding
	Supported pseudonymity types
Inspection	Support for multi-party inspection
Revocation	Support for immediate revocation
	Key- vs. attribute revocation
	Offline non-revocation proof

D2.2 [BCD+14], and in the language framework by Camenisch *et al.* [CDL+13], besides the "simple issuance" of a credential, Privacy-ABC technologies can also support "advanced" forms of issuance, such as issuance binding two credentials to the same key, or carrying over attributes from another credential, which provide additional privacy features for the User. The fact whether or not a certain Privacy-ABC technology supports these advanced forms of issuance can be an important criterion for comparing fsuch technologies.

Presentation

Presentation can be considered the most important stage in the Privacy-ABC life-cycle as it is supposed to be the one that the User most often will be experiencing. The first criteria for benchmarking would be the support for the basic Privacy-ABC features, namely the types of unlinkability (issuance-presentation and multiple presentation unlinkability), as well as selective disclosure of attributes. Moreover, the support for more advanced Privacy-ABC features, such as support for predicates over attributes (e.g. comparison of dates or other mathematical operations over different credential attributes), support for non-revocation proof, or having all credentials used in a proof bound to a single key (key binding - to avoid credential pooling, for instance) represent further criteria for benchmarking.

While it is usually not the case, it may be that the Privacy-ABC technology only supports presentations using a single credential, whereas in many scenarios may require a combination of different Privacy-ABCs might be desired. In some scenarios, a certain level of linkability may be desired, where users may want to create different types of pseudonyms. Users can create unlimited number of *verifiable pseudonyms*, enabling them to create unlinkable profiles. Furthermore, by imposing *scope-exclusive pseudonyms*, a User can create no more than one pseudonym for a given *scope* (e.g. application), whenever that is needed (such as in cases of voting scenarios, where Users can cast only one vote, but are able to change it).

Certain Privacy-ABC technologies may support unlinkability of issuance and presentation, but not the multiple-presentations unlinkability. In case this feature is required for an application and such a technology is desired, a workaround could be to use Privacy-ABCs only one time, requiring re-issuance of such credentials (before every presentation). In order to overcome potential privacy implications, it is possible to automate the process of issuance by issuing a batch of such credentials at once. However, this approach has not only storage implications for the User, but also influence the usability of the technology due the fact that the User needs to engage in additional issuance instances with the Issuer (which also may require the User needs to be online). Therefore, the fact whether a certain Privacy-ABC technology poses this additional requirement on the User or not is an important benchmarking criterion related to the practical viability of such a technology.

Inspection

Inspection is the process of uncovering the identity of the person behind a conditionally inspectable presentation token. This is considered to be an important feature of

Privacy-ABCs, as it can enable accountability in an otherwise-anonymous scenario. However, it may be important to distinguish technologies that enable a stronger limitation of authority abuse of the Inspection Authority by a single person, by e.g. enabling "four-eyes" principle or requiring k out of n inspectors to be present for inspection. This and other abuse-limitation techniques could help establish more trust in the sensitive role of the Inspector. The comparison criterion here would investigate the mechanism that a chosen implementation of a Privacy-ABC technology supports to limit the potential of authority abuse by the Inspector.

Revocation

As there are a number of proposed schemes for revocation, the first benchmark would be the support for immediate revocation. Furthermore, some revocation schemes may revoke credentials based on a secret key (thus being able to revoke all credentials bound to that key, e.g. in case of theft or loss), whereas other schemes may only enable attribute-revocation (revoking a special attribute in the credential, requiring revocation of each credential separately).

Proving non-revocation of the credentials is especially challenging for Privacy-ABC technologies if the privacy property of unlinkability has to be preserved. Unlike in X.509 and related technologies, the User must not reveal any unique value (serial number), which the Verifier could check against a public CRL (Credential Revocation List). For this purpose, alternative solutions have been proposed in the literature, each of which comes with certain limitations. Most of the proposals that support immediate revocation, such as those based on cryptographic accumulators [LLX07, CL02], impose additional efforts on either the User or the Verifier. Typically, the User needs to prove during the presentation not only that she fulfils the presentation policy of the Verifier, but also prove in zero-knowledge that her Privacy-ABCs are not included in an accumulated value (accumulator).

This accounts for not only performance overhead for the User (i.e. delay), but also requires periodical connectivity of the User with the Revocation Authority during the presentation, as presented in step (3b) of Figure 4.2, to update the "evidence" that her credentials are not revoked. Such revocation mechanisms limit the deployability of these technologies on devices with network capability (making it infeasible to use in "offline devices", such as smart cards). A number of studies in this area show the different overhead distribution of revocation (non-revocation proof) on the presentation [LKDDN11, LKDDN10], whereas [CL02] claims a non-interactive proof-of-knowledge scheme, confirming the importance non-interactive scheme in practice.

4.2.1.3 Efficiency

Privacy-ABC technologies can be built using different cryptographic building blocks, such as signature schemes, encryption, zero-knowledge proofs, commitments, and revocation schemes. Efficiency has been identified as an important fac-

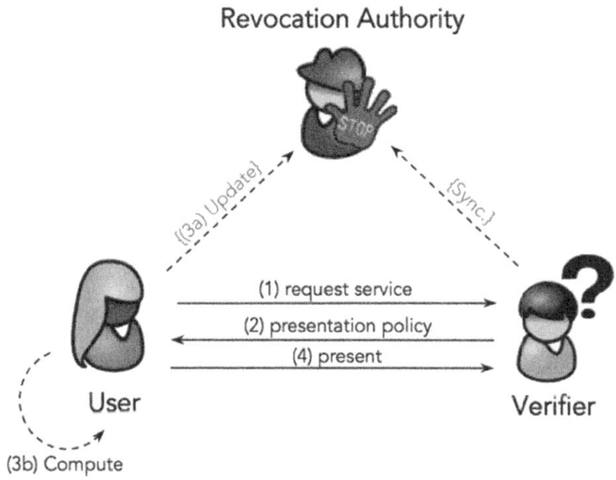

Fig. 4.2 "Online" connectivity of the User with the Revocation Authority - revocation information update during presentation

tor for Privacy-ABCs already in previous research [CL03, VA13, MV11, Sch91, LKDDN10, CL02, LLX07], as it directly affects the performance of the applications using these technologies, and is thus considered to have an important influence on a wider acceptance of Privacy-ABC technologies. As it is seen an important challenge, efficiency continues to be an important research area. In our work, we identify a set of criteria for benchmarking the efficiency, which are mostly quantitative, and organise them in three main aspects, namely into *computational*, *communication* and *storage* efficiency criteria.

Computational and Communication Efficiency (CCE)

Although computational and communication efficiency represent two different benchmarking aspects, they can be benchmarked together as they usually refer to the same cryptographic operations and are impacted by common factors. *Computational efficiency* is in direct relation with the complexity of the underlying cryptographic scheme. In theoretical terms, the computational complexity of the underlying cryptographic scheme can be assessed in mathematical terms. Some of the factors, such as the cryptographic group size, as well as the key size used for cryptographic operations may impact all three efficiency parameters, namely both CCE and storage efficiency. In practice, the computational efficiency reflects the time (in milliseconds) required to perform a given proof on a certain platform, e.g. computer, mobile phone, smart card, etc.

Communication efficiency deals with the data sizes exchanged during the interaction of the User with the other entities, i.e. during issuance, presentation, and so on.

Table 4.8 Efficiency Benchmarking Criteria

Stage	Criteria	Impacting Factors
Issuance	CCE for simple issuance CCE for advanced issuance	Number of attributes Use of "carry-over" feature Use of "same-key binding" feature Use of "jointly random" issuance feature
Presentation	CCE for "simple" proof CCE using advanced proofs	Number of credentials proven Number of hidden attributes Number of revocable credentials Use of "same-key binding" feature Use of predicates over attributes Use of inspection
Revocation	Distributivity	
All stages		Chosen security level (key size)

Table 4.8 presents the main criteria for benchmarking different Privacy-ABCs on the CCE, and the most important factors, which influence such benchmarks. As we can see from the table, the security level is a common factor influencing all the efficiency benchmarks, including issuance and presentation.

Issuance efficiency benchmarking criteria distinguish between the "simple" and the "advanced" forms of issuance, as mentioned in Section 2.1 . Advanced forms of issuance (if supported) include additional proofs for each advanced feature used (key binding, carry over, etc.), making them less efficient than the simple ones. However, the actual CCE for the same operations may differ for different Privacy-ABC technologies, and this is exactly what is important to compare.

Presentation is certainly the most important stage for efficiency benchmarking, as it is the one in which the User is mostly involved. The CCE for presentation can vary for different Privacy-ABC technologies, depending on the building blocks used. However, there are common factors impacting the CCE of presentations on different Privacy-ABC technologies, which typically depend on the complexity of the proof being made, which is defined in the presentation policy. In "simpler" types of proofs, presentation only requires a proof of possession of a credential, whereas more "advanced" proofs use additional features, as presented in Table 4.8.

Similar to the issuance, each of advanced features used, such as predicates over attributes (e.g. age proof), use of same-key binding, or attribute hiding (disclosure), has a direct impact on the CCE of presentation. On top of that, a significant overhead on the presentation efficiency can be the use of inspection, where the User needs to verifiably encrypt the inspectable attributes. Depending on the revocation scheme, proving non-revocation of credentials used in the presentation may be additional overhead for the User, reducing the overall efficiency. Finally, the security level, which corresponds to the cryptographic key length used, has a direct impact on the efficiency of presentation.

Revocation benchmarking includes the distributivity of the service of dissemination of revocation information (the Revocation Authority) to enable better performance and avoid delays in peak usage times.

Table 4.9 User-related Data to be Stored and their Impacting Factors

Data type	Impacting factors
Credential(s)	Number of credentials and attributes Size of Issuer's public key
Revocation information	Number of revocable credentials Type of revocation scheme Size of the Revocation Authority's public key
Keys of other entities	Other keys stored (Public key(s) of the Issuer(s), Verifier(s), Rev. Authorities)
Pseudonyms	Number and type of pseudonyms
All data	Cryptographic key and group sizes

Storage Efficiency

The amount of user-related data is an important element for comparison between different Privacy-ABC technologies. In principle, the User may need to store the Privacy-ABCs themselves, but potentially also additional data, which are necessary for the credentials to be useful. Among such additional information is shown in Table 4.9 and includes pseudonyms of the User, but also other cryptographic data, such as public key(s) of the Issuer, Revocation Authority, etc.

Key and group size are certainly a factor that has an influence on the size data that the User needs to store, including the public key of the Issuer, which in turn has an impact on the size of the credential(s) and other credential-related information for most of the Privacy-ABC technologies. On top of that, the number of attributes may impact the size of the credentials for the User, whereas also different pseudonyms may also be stored locally on the chosen storage medium. However, the impacts of the identified factors on the storage efficiency may vary, which can be a good benchmarking criterion for the different Privacy-ABC technologies.

4.2.1.4 Security Assurance

To be able to assess the security assurance provided by a specific Privacy-ABC technology, we propose the usage of security assurance criteria with respect to different stages of the lifecycle of Privacy-ABCs, and with respect to the security of the basic schemes. The aim of these criteria is to assess the effectiveness of the technology-specific security assurance mechanisms in order to evaluate how the security requirements are met by the respective Privacy-ABC technology.

Table 4.10 presents the security assurance benchmarking criteria we are proposing. We distinguish between the Inspection and Revocation stages of the Privacy-ABC's lifecycle. Apart from that, as can be seen from the table, security assumptions and security proofs related to the basic schemes are taken into account. It has to be considered whether the security proofs and assumptions of the basic schemes are information theoretic, computational or without security reduction. In the case they are computational, the hardness assumptions have to be described.

Table 4.10 Benchmarking security criteria along the credential lifecycles

Stage	Security Assurance Benchmarking Criteria
Inspection	Preventive measures against authority misuse
Revocation	Mechanisms to guarantee the authenticity and integrity of Revocation Information Access to the Revocation Handles
Basic schemes	Security proofs Security assumptions

In addition, means to assess the security of the conventional mechanisms, which are specifically applied and customized to enhance the security assurance of Privacy-ABCs (e.g. access control mechanisms for the Revocation Information), are necessary; therefore security assurance benchmarks for these mechanisms are to be considered. With regard to Inspection, the security assurance for preventing authority misuse by the person in charge of inspection has to be investigated. It has to be assessed whether the technology supports measures for preventing this, e.g. by applying key sharing mechanisms, where k out of n keys must be combined in order to be able to conduct inspection.

Additional security assurance criteria are needed also for the Revocation. On the one hand, the guarantees the technology provides for the integrity and authenticity of the Revocation Information have to be studied. The mechanisms applied by the Privacy-ABC technology to protect both the integrity and authenticity of Revocation Information need to be specified. Moreover, the access restrictions to the Revocation Handles that are posed through the technology have to be analyzed. The different possibilities, e.g. public vs. private access and whether the Revocation Handles are learnt only by the Verfier or also by the Revocation Authority have to be studied.

4.2.2 Functionality Comparison

This section provides a brief comparison of the Privacy-ABC technologies employed within the ABC4Trust project, namely U-Prove and Idemix, in terms of their functionalities. It is important to mention that the cryptographic libraries of U-Prove and Idemix presented here differ from the currently official version of Idemix and U-Prove, as they have further been improved and developed as part of ABC4Trust and the work on the new crypto architecture of ABC4Trust. The new crypto architecture provides a better modularity so that U-Prove and Idemix can be supported on the same Crypto Engine sharing various building blocks such as for pseudonyms, revocation, inspection, predicates proofs, and so on.

Table 4.11 Functionality Comparison - Issuance

Stage	Functionality Criteria	Result
Issuance	Supported issuance privacy features	ABC4Trust version of both U-Prove and Idemix support – issuance from scratch – carry-over-attribute – key-bound credentials

4.2.2.1 Issuance

Privacy-ABC technologies may differ in terms of the functional features that they support during the issuance phase and that might affect the choice of technology by an adopter. More specifically, apart from the simplest case where the credentials are issued based on the attributes known to the issuers from certified sources, some more advanced scenarios for issuance could be a matter of interest.

In this regard, we consider the advanced issuance with *carry-over attributes* in our comparison, which essentially enables the issuance of a credential with some attribute value being "carried-over" from another credential of the User. Another flavour of that mechanism called issuance with *self-claimed carry-over attributes* relies on the user as the source of information and the issuer vouches for a claimed attribute value by the user without knowing the value. This is shown in Table 4.11, which also compares the two technologies in terms of their support for different features.

Furthermore, additional feature we consider important in this comparison is the possibility of binding the credentials to a secret (e.g. users' secret key) or even binding two different credentials to the same secret (i.e. same-key binding), which can be useful in order to avoid, e.g., credential pooling.

The last comparison criterion here concerns the issuance of *jointly-random* attributes where the issuer can be ensured an attribute value is chosen randomly and not chosen solely by the user, but without the issuer learning the attribute value.

With regard to the issuance of *self-claimed carry-over attributes*, it is technically possible to support it in the ABC4Trust version of U-Prove and Idemix. However, the upper layer interfaces are not provided yet. Concerning *jointly-random attributes*, none of the technologies support this type of issuance.

4.2.2.2 Presentation

Looking into the functionalities that Privacy-ABCs offer during the presentation phase provides a proper view on the types of proofs that one could expect from the given technologies. In this section, we compare the ABC4Trust version of U-Prove and Idemix with respect to their support for combination of credentials to produce a proof, predicates that one could use over attributes, unlinkability across different presentations, key binding, and different types of pseudonyms.

As a result of the new crypto architecture proposed by ABC4Trust, U-Prove and Idemix could benefit from some shared libraries which allows them to provide the exact same set of functionalities such as for the predicates over attributes or the supported types of pseudonyms. However, these two technologies behave differently when it comes to aspects such as offering unlinkability between different presentation sessions. Table 4.12 provides in details the comparison of the presentation phase for the ABC4Trust version of U-Prove and Idemix.

4.2.2.3 Inspection

The inspection mechanism was implemented as a shared functionality to be used by both U-Prove and idemix in the ABC4Trust project, so a comparison is not applicable in this case. However, responding to the criterion "Support for multi-party inspection" in Table 4.7, it would be theoretically possible to have multi-party inspection mechanism working with both U-Prove and Idemix, but the implemented inspection mechanism in ABC4Trust considered only one inspector. Table 4.13 summarizes our benchmark of the inspection mechanism used in ABC4Trust.

4.2.2.4 Revocation

The answers to the questions like how fast the revocation of a credential will be effective, or whether revocation would work for the credentials in the offline world or not, can highly influence the decision on the adoption of a Privacy-ABC technology. For instance, the importance of revocation status is much less critical in the case of transportation tickets compared to access control in a corporate premises. One day delay in the propagation of the revocation status will not introduce so much risk to the former case while it can result in severe damages for the latter one. In this regard, we provide a benchmark of the revocation strategy implemented in the ABC4Trust project. Since both Privacy-ABCs (U-Prove and Idemix) use the same revocation scheme, we cannot provide a comparison, but rather a benchmark of the implemented revocation scheme.

The revocation scheme used in ABC4Trust is based on *accumulators*. In this scheme, a verifier is not informed about the revocation of a credential as long as she does not refresh her *Revocation Information*. As soon as she synchronizes with the revocation authority, the revoked credential will not be usable in the realm of that verifier. This revocation mechanism also requires a valid user to have connectivity with the revocation authority and update the so-called *Non-Revocation Evidence*, in case it is out-dated, before taking part in a presentation proof. Therefore, it is not suitable for offline scenarios. Furthermore, the revocation scheme works based on a specific attribute in the credentials called *revocation handle* and it can block further use of the credentials that contain a revoked revocation handle. Thus, if revocation

Table 4.12 Functionality Comparison - Presentation

Stage	Functionality Criteria	Result
Presentation	Combination of different credentials in presentation	ABC4Trust version of both U-Prove and Idemix can use multiple credentials from the same or different issuers in the same presentation proof.
	Supported predicates over attributes	ABC4Trust version of both U-Prove and Idemix support the following predicates over attributes: – equality of strings – equality of integers – equality of booleans – equality of times – equality of dates – inequality of strings – inequality of integers – inequality of booleans – inequality of times – inequality of dates
	Support for multiple-presentation unlinkability	In the case of Idemix, the same credential can be shown multiple times without the concern of being linkable across different sessions. However, in the case of U-Prove the process is different and a credential contains a bunch of single-use U-Prove tokens. If the user consumes the same token in two different sessions, they will be linkable.
	Support for key binding	ABC4Trust version of both U-Prove and Idemix support key binding for credentials and pseudonyms.
	Supported pseudonymity types	ABC4Trust version of both U-Prove and Idemix support the following types of pseudonyms. – verifiable pseudonyms – certified pseudonyms – scope exclusive pseudonyms

Table 4.13 Functionality Comparison - Inspection

Stage	Functionality Criteria	Result
Inspection	Support for multi-party inspection	The implemented inspection mechanism in ABC4Trust considered only one inspector.

Table 4.14 Functionality comparison - Revocation

Stage	Functionality Criteria	Result
Revocation	Support for immediate revocation	Immediate revocation is only achieved when the verifiers fetch the latest Revocation Information upon any changes by the revocation authority, and enforce them immediately.
	Key- vs. attribute revocation	The revocation scheme implemented in ABC4Trust does not offer key revocation.
	Offline non-revocation proof	The revocation scheme implemented in ABC4Trust does not offer Offline Usage.

of all the credentials bound to a secret key is desired, this scheme is a not proper choice. Table 4.14 summarizes our benchmark of the revocation scheme used in ABC4Trust.

4.2.3 *Efficiency Comparison*

In the efficiency comparison of Privacy-ABC technologies, we distinguish between three different types of efficiency, namely the *computational efficiency*, which measures to time to perform certain operations (features) of Privacy-ABCs; the *communication efficiency*, which focuses on measuring the data sizes produced by certain operations and exchanged between parties during those operations; and *storage efficiency*, which focuses on comparing how the Privacy-ABC technologies differ in terms of the size of the data the User needs to store.

4.2.3.1 Computational efficiency

Computational efficiency is an important factor for the acceptance of a Privacy-ABC technologies. A computationally efficient Privacy-ABC technology enables better performing applications that use the Privacy-ABC technology, e.g. a seamlessly quick presentation. However, as the Privacy-ABC features are built on cryptographic tools, this may be a challenge. For this purpose, the first dimension we would like to compare between the two instantiations of Privacy-ABC technologies is the computational efficiency. For our purposes, the computational efficiency is expressed in time units (seconds), and the following section presents a summary of the most important comparison results for issuance and presentation.

Issuance efficiency

As there are different types of issuance possible, the computational efficiency for each of them may differ. In the case of a “simple issuance”, the issuance policy requires no prior proof from the User in order to get the credential issued. An excerpt from an issuance policy for the simple issuance is shown in Figure 4.3 , where we can see that the issuance policy contains an empty presentation policy (see the empty definition of the <abc:PresentationPolicy> element).

```
<abc:IssuancePolicy ...>
    <abc:PresentationPolicy PolicyUID="urn:SimpleIssuance">
    </abc:PresentationPolicy>
    <abc:CredentialTemplate >
        <abc:CredentialSpecUID>urn:soderhamn:credspec:credSchool_simple</abc:CredentialSpecUID>
        <abc:IssuerParametersUID>urn:soderhamn:issuer:credSchool_simple</abc:IssuerParametersUID>
    </abc:CredentialTemplate>
</abc:IssuancePolicy>
```

Fig. 4.3 Excerpt from the issuance policy for "Simple Issuance"

In contrast to this type of issuance, it is interesting to compare the efficiency of performing simple issuance to the advanced forms of issuance, including the case of an issuance with "nym proof", "same key binding", and the issuance with "carry-over attributes", as shown in the excerpt from the issuance policy in Figure 4.4, Figure 4.5, and Figure 4.6 respectively. As we can see, the "advanced" factor is defined within the <abc:PresentationPolicy> element.

A comparison of the computational efficiency of these types of issuance is shown in Figure 4.7 for two different technologies, namely for U-Prove and Idemix. As we can also assume, the simple issuance is the most efficient one, because of its empty presentation policy, as compared to the advanved forms of issuance. On the other hand, the advanced forms of issuance are approximately similarly efficient, where there is a small overhead for performing "same-key binding" and "carrying over" attribute to the new credential.

```
    <abc:PresentationPolicy PolicyUID="urn:NymProof">
        <abc:Pseudonym Exclusive="true" Scope="urn:someScope" Established="true" Alias="#nym"/>
    </abc:PresentationPolicy>
```

Fig. 4.4 Exceprt from issuance policy for "Nym Proof"

```
<abc:IssuancePolicy ...>
    <abc:PresentationPolicy PolicyUID="urn:NymProof">
      <abc:Pseudonym Exclusive="true" Scope="urn:someScope" Established="true" Alias="#nym"/>
    </abc:PresentationPolicy>
    <abc:CredentialTemplate SameKeyBindingAs="#nym">
      ...
    </abc:CredentialTemplate>
</abc:IssuancePolicy>
```

Fig. 4.5 Excerpt from issuance policy for "Same Key as Nym"

```
<abc:IssuancePolicy ...>
    <abc:PresentationPolicy PolicyUID="urn:soderhamn:policies:issuance:credCarryOver">
        <abc:Credential Alias="#credSchool"> ... </abc:Credential>
  </abc:PresentationPolicy>
   <abc:CredentialTemplate>
    ...
       <abc:UnknownAttributes>
          <abc:CarriedOverAttribute TargetAttributeType="credCarryOver:firstname">
               <abc:SourceCredentialInfo Alias="#credSchool" AttributeType="school:firstname"/>
          </abc:CarriedOverAttribute>
       </abc:UnknownAttributes>
...
</abc:IssuancePolicy>
```

Fig. 4.6 Excerpt from issuance policy "Carry-over"

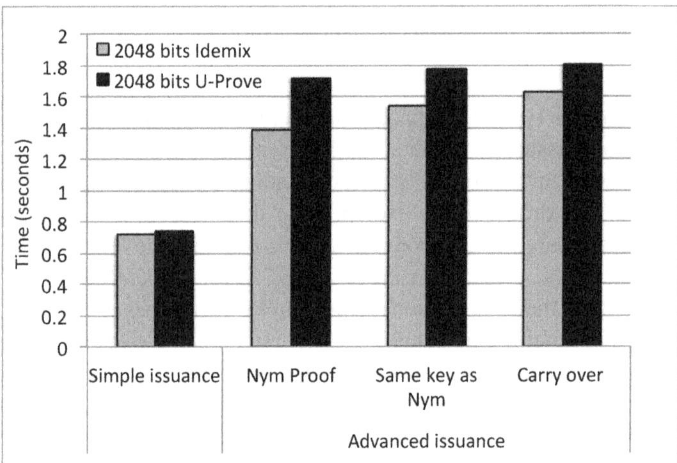

Fig. 4.7 Comparison of the computational efficiency for different types of issuance for with two different Privacy-ABC technologies, namely two different signature schemes

Presentation efficiency

For the User, presentation will be the most frequently used operation normally, and this makes it central to our comparison focus. In this regard, it is important not only to compare the computational efficiency for performing a proof of a credential between the two Privacy-ABC technologies, but also to understand the impact of additional features used in the presentation policy on the efficiency of presentation. For this purpose, we have provided in Figure 4.8 an overview of the time to complete the presentation for different presentaiton policies. In addition, we identify the amount of time that it spent on the User side to generate a presentation token for a given policy (proving), as well as the time spent at the Verifier side to verify the respective presentation token of the User (verification).

Excerpts from the presentation policies labelled "Cred", "Cred + Nym", "2 Creds", "Equality with attribute", and "Cred + Inspection" are presented in Figures

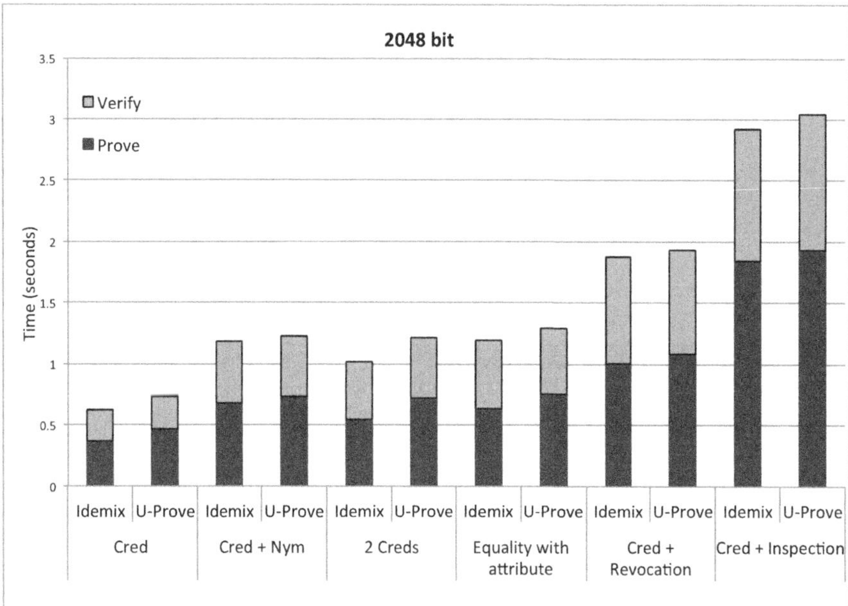

Fig. 4.8 Comparison of the computational efficiency for presentation between two instantiantions of Privacy-ABC technologies

4.9 - 4.12, respectively, whereas the "Cred + Revocation" policy can be a simple policy proving one credential, but with the difference that the credential is revocable (which is defined in the issuance policy).

Figure 4.8 shows an overview of the efficiency for different types of presentation for the above-mentioned presentation policies for the two instantiations of Privacy ABC technologies (Idemix and U-Prove) using cryptographic key size of 2048 bits. For all of the tested cases, there is a slight advantage of Idemix compare to U-Prove, whereas the additional features used in presentation affect to a similar extent both Idemix and U-Prove respectively.

The basic policy is considered "Cred", which, as shown in Figure 4.9, only requires a proof possesion of a credential, and is the simplest form of a presentation policy, and is therefore more efficient to do (taking least time), whereby both technologies have a similar computational efficiency close to 0.6 seconds for Idemix and close to 0.7 for U-Prove. Furthermore, we can notice that more efforts are spent in proving than in verification.

In addition to that, we can compare the overhead of proving a different (possesion of a) number of credentials by comparing the time required to perform presentation for "Cred" and "2 Creds", parts of the presentation policies of which are shown in Figure 4.9 and Figure 4.10, respectively. Clearly, the time to do the presentation grows linearly by the number of credentials being proven for both Idemix and U-Prove. As shown in the the figure, a similar impact as of an additional credential can be noticed by proving a pseudonym besides the credential, which is represented in

```
<abc:PresentationPolicy PolicyUID="uri:showCredentialCredSchool">
    <abc:Credential Alias="#credSchool" >
        <abc:CredentialSpecAlternatives>
          <abc:CredentialSpecUID>urn:soderhamn:credspec:credSchool</abc:CredentialSpecUID>
      </abc:CredentialSpecAlternatives>
      <abc:IssuerAlternatives>
        <abc:IssuerParametersUID>urn:soderhamn:issuer:credSchool</abc:IssuerParametersUID>
        </abc:IssuerAlternatives>
    </abc:Credential>
</abc:PresentationPolicy>
```

Fig. 4.9 Exceprt from presentation policy for "Cred"

```
<abc:PresentationPolicy PolicyUID="uri:prove2Creds">
     <abc:Credential Alias="#credSchool" >
       ...
     </abc:Credential>
  <abc:Credential Alias="#credSchool2" >
  ...
     </abc:Credential>
  </abc:PresentationPolicy>
```

Fig. 4.10 Excerpt from the presentation policy for "2 Creds"

the figure by "Cred + Nym", and whose excerpt of the presentation policy is shown in Figure 4.11. Again, there is a slight advantage of Idemix in the efficiency over U-Prove.

```
<abc:PresentationPolicy PolicyUID="uri:Cred+Nym">
  <abc:Pseudonym Exclusive="true" Scope="urn:soderhamn:registration" Established="true" Alias="#nym"/>
  <abc:Credential Alias="#credSchool" >
  ...
  </abc:Credential>
</abc:PresentationPolicy>
```

Fig. 4.11 Excerpt from the presentation policy for "Cred + Nym"

Further from the figure, "Equality with attribute" is a policy that requires the User to prove possession of a credential and that one of the attributes equals a the value of another credential attribute (proving two credentials, doing the equality proof without revealing its value).

An important factor that influences the time to do presentation in both technologies is the use of features revocation and inspection. On one hand, the chart element labelled "Cred+revocation" shows the efficiency of proving a credential and proving that it is not revoked, which clearly shows that the overhead of proving non-revocation is bigger than proving two credentials (compare to "Cred"). On the other hand, an even stronger impact on the computational efficiency of presentation, for both U-Prove and Idemix, is caused by the use of inspection. The time to prove a credential, which has inspection enabled is shown in the graph element "Cred +

Inspection", where one of the attributes is verifiably encrypted with the public key of the Inspector (to be inspectable). While the fact whether or not a non-revocation proof is required depends on whether or not a credential is revoked (which is defined in the issuance policy), the fact on the use of inspection is defined in the presentation policy. An excerpt from the presentation policy for "Cred + Inspection" is shown in Figure 4.12.

```
<abc:DisclosedAttribute AttributeType="urn:soderhamn:credspec:credSchool:firstname">
        <abc:InspectorAlternatives>
          <abc:InspectorPublicKeyUID>http://thebestbank.com/inspector/pub_key_v1</abc:
                InspectorPublicKeyUID>
        </abc:InspectorAlternatives>
        <abc:InspectionGrounds>
          Description of circumstances and process under which token may be inspected.
        </abc:InspectionGrounds>
      </abc:DisclosedAttribute>
```

Fig. 4.12 Excerpt from the presentation policy for "Cred + Inspection"

4.2.3.2 Communication efficiency

The messages exchanged between the Issuer and the User during the issuance protocol are XML-formatted messages, as defined in the ABC4Trust architecture deliverable [BCD+14]. For this reason, the size of the messages contains not only the cryptographic part of the message, but also the additional structure of an XML document, resulting in some overhead in the overall message size. Depending on the type of issuance ("simple" vs. "advanced") and on the technology used (Idemix vs. U-Prove), the number of issuance rounds, as well as the size of the messages exchanged during each round may be different. For Idemix, simple issuance has only one round of communication between the Issuer and the User, whereas for U-Prove there are two rounds, according to the protocol specification of U-Prove. For the advanced issuance, both technologies require an additional round of communication, which consists of a presentation session, where the User needs to prove the fulfillment of the required presentation policy.

Issuance efficiency

A summarized presentation of the total size of the incoming and outgoing (for the User) traffic (message sizes) for both signature schemes and different issuance scenarios is presented in Figure 4.13, where one can see also the overhead of the other forms of issuance on the communication efficiency, namely that advanced forms of issuance are less efficient in terms of communication size. In general, the issuer messages are longer in Idemix than in U-Prov. However, as U-Prove requires an additional round of communication between the User and the Issuer, this has to be

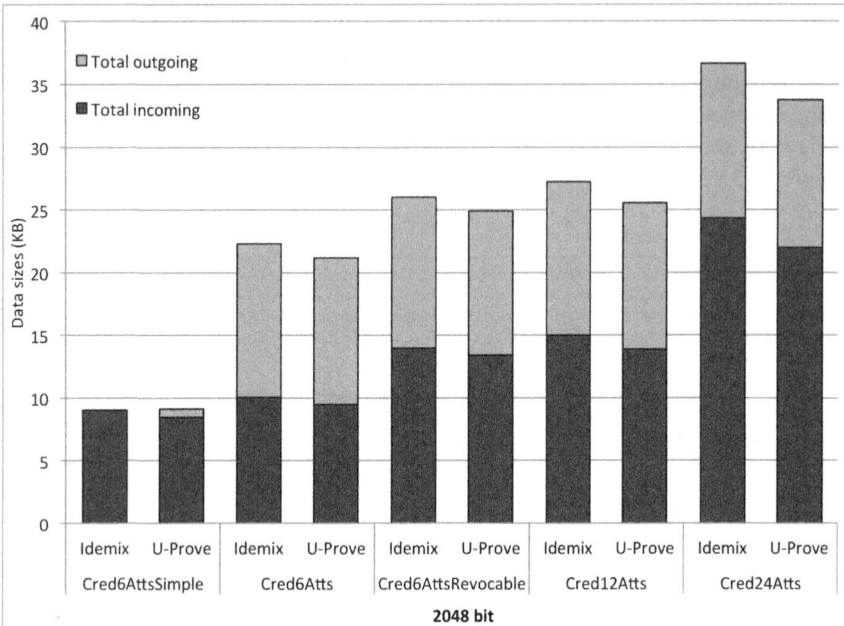

Fig. 4.13 Comparison of total incoming and outgoing messages during issuance for the two signature schemes

taken into account if issuance communication efficiency is important, as it can result in time delays, depending on the network connectivity.

Furthermore, we can also clearly notice that the number of attributes has a direct impact on the communication size (compare Cred6Atts, Cred12Atts, and Cred24Atts) for both technologies.

Presentation efficiency

For presentation, we investigated the impact of different features used in the presentation phase on the size of the presentation tokens. A brief summary of the size of the presentation tokens for different types of presentation policies for the two implementations is presented in Figure 4.14. The results show varying sizes of presentation tokens for different presentation policies, starting from basic proof of a credential (Cred), combination of a credential and a pseudonym (Cred + Nym) as well as binding them to the same secret key (Cred+Nym+Key Binding), use of predicates (equality proof) of an attribute with a constant (Equality with constant) and with a different credential attribute (Equality with attribute), presentation of two credentials (2Creds), and presentation with three credentials (3Creds).

On top of that, we investigated how the number of attributes impacts the size of the presentation token by testing presentation for credentials using respectively 6, 12 and 24 attributes (Cred, Cred 12 Atts, and Cred 24 Atts).

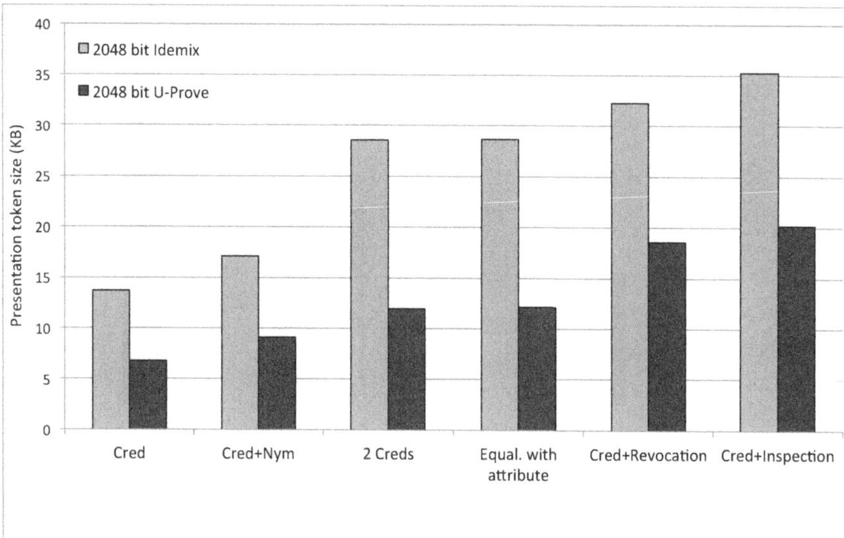

Fig. 4.14 Comparison of sizes of the presentation tokens for different presentation policies for the two instantiations of Privacy-ABC technologies

4.2.3.3 Storage efficiency

The size of the credentials may differ under different technologies and using different key sizes. Following are the comparison results for the issuance scenarios described in the previous sections of this chapter, namely simple issuance, issuance with key binding, issuance with carry over attributes, and the issuance with different number of credentials. Figure 4.15 shows a comparison of credential sizes (in kilobytes) for the two signature schemes both schemes depending on the number of attributes, respectively credential with six (Cred6Atts), twelve (Cred12Atts), and 24 attributes (Cred24Atts). As shown in the figure, both technologies perform similarly-efficient for storage, namely the size of the same type of credentials in both technologies is similar, with a slight advantage of Idemix (CL-based signatures) being slightly more efficient.

For revocable credentials, the User has to store an additional piece of information that can be used during presentation to prove non-revocation. As both technologies tested used the same revocation technology in our comparison, the impact of the revocation information on the overall storage efficiency was constant and independent on the signature scheme. The storage overhead of revocation can be assesed by comparing the size of the revocable credential together with the revocation information in "6Atts+Revoc." with the one without revocation, namely "6Atts." in the figure.

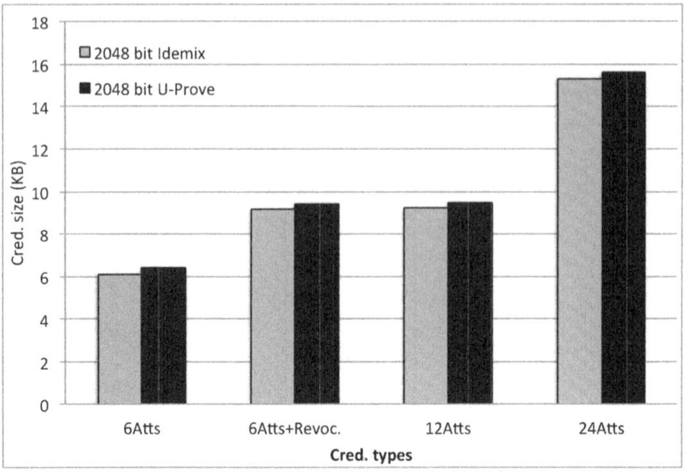

Fig. 4.15 Comparison of the credential sizes for the two signature schemes and the impact of revocation and number of attributes

4.2.4 Security Assurance Comparison

As a basis for the security assurance comparison of Privacy-ABC technologies, we are using the security assurance benchmarking criteria proposed in 4.2.1.4 where applicable. These benchmarking criteria were mainly developed by taking into account the specific properties of the technologies. As we are taking into consideration the benchmarking criteria shown in the previous section, the comparison is also done with regard to the different stages of the lifecycle of the Attribute-based credentials and the security of the basic schemes. The security assurance benchmarking criteria that are applied for the practical comparison are:

- Technical Preventive Measures Against Authority Misuse;
- Mechanisms used along with the Privacy-ABC Technology to guarantee the Integrity and Authenticity of the Revocation Information [1];
- Support in case of compromised end-user's Private Key;
- Access to Revocation Handles;
- Security proofs and assumptions;

This group of metrics was mainly developed taking into consideration the specific properties of the technologies, and are explained in more detail in the following paragraphs.

[1] Defined by the reference implementation, but might be out of the scope of Privacy ABCs

Table 4.15 Security Assurance Practical Comparison - Inspection

Stage	Security Assurance Criteria	Result
Inspection	Technical Preventive Measures Against Authority Misuse	The measures applied to eliminate the ways of misusing User's data are related to the design of the respective technology. Important is that the User is provided the information relevant for the inspection e.g., the inspection grounds or who is in charge of the actual revealing of attributes.

4.2.4.1 Inspection

With regard to the inspection stage of the Privacy-ABC lifecycle, we apply the metric:

- Technical Preventive Measures Against Authority Misuse for the practical comparison.

The intuition behind it is to provide information regarding how authority misuse is prevented from the person in charge of inspection. It considers the measures applied to eliminate the ways of misusing User's data, and is related to the design of the respective technology.

The Inspector is trusted not only by the Verifier to assist by providing the required information in case of abuse, but also by the User not to uncover identities unnecessarily. At the time of creating the presentation token the User is aware of the inspection grounds related to specific attributes, of the identity of the Inspector who will be contacted to reveal information, as well as of the information that will be revealed in case of evidence for inspection grounds. This can be considered as a measure against authority misuse. A summary of this result is given in Table 4.15. The interested reader is referred to [BCD$^+$14] for further information.

4.2.4.2 Revocation

Regarding the practical comparison at the Revocation-stage of the Privacy-ABC lifecycle, we apply the metrics:

- Mechanisms used along with the Privacy-ABC technology to guarantee the integrity and authenticity of the Revocation Information
- Support in case of compromised end-user's Private Key
- Access to Revocation Handles

The mechanisms that have been implemented along with the Privacy-ABC technology to protect the Revocation Information's integrity and authenticity are studied. The results show that in ABC4Trust only the issuer-driven revocation is implemented currently. The Verifier can use an authenticated channel to the Revocation Authority responsible for publishing the Revocation Information. This was demonstrated in Patras Pilot (see Chapter 7) in which the Verifier connects to the Revocation Authority via an SSL/TLS channel. More detailed information on the implementation evidence can be found in [BCD$^+$14].

The support in case of compromised end-user's Private Key is concerned with the existence of a process (i) to request the automatic revocation of all the credentials bound to a specific end-user's Private Key or (ii) to block all the pseudonyms generated from that Private Key for future authentication. The current implementation of ABC4Trust supports only the revocation of credentials or specific attributes. Implementation evidence on that and further information is given in [BCD$^+$14].

The access to Revocation Handles implemented by the technology is also to be studied for the practical comparison. It considers what access restrictions apply to Revocation Handles, or what is the access level to Revocation Handles. It can be either public or private. Keeping the Revocation Handles confidential might have an impact on the security and enhance the security assurance. The Revocation Handles can be learnt by RA or by the Verifier only. For the current implementation of ABC4Trust, the list of revoked Revocation Handles is contained within the Revocation Information. Consequently, the Verifier can learn or disclose the Revocation Handles. The interested reader is referred to [BCD$^+$14] for information on the implementation evidence. A summary of the results of the revocation-related comparison is given in Table 4.16.

4.2.4.3 Security of the basic schemes

The security comparison of the two instantiations of Privacy-ABC technologies in terms of security proofs for the used basic scheme is given in this part of the chapter. Our aim is to compare the two instantiations with respect to the schemes they are based on, and depending on whether the implementation is made with security reductions or not. The proposed security metrics related to the security proofs and assumptions aim at providing information regarding whether security proofs are given and under which assumptions. They should state whether the security proofs and assumptions are (i) information theoretic, (ii) computational or (iii) without security reduction/proof. Table 4.17 provides the information regarding the security proofs and assumptions. As can be seen from the table, the basic schemes usually rely on schemes that have security reduction. We do not provide a security reduction for the full scheme, as the composition of secure scheme does not imply that the composed scheme is secure.

Table 4.16 Security Assurance - Revocation

Stage	Security Assurance Criteria	Result
Revocation	Mechanisms used along with the Privacy-ABC Technology to guarantee the Integrity and Authenticity of the Revocation Information	One possibility for guaranteeing the Integrity and Authenticity of Revocation Information in the currently implemented issuer-driven revocation, is that the Verifier uses an authenticated channel to the Revocation Authority responsible for publishing the revocation information e.g., transmitting the data via an SSL/TLS channel in order to enhance the security of the Revocation Information. There are some other mechanisms that can be used as well.
	Support in case of compromised end-user's Private Key	In the currently implemented version the revocation of credentials or specific attributes is supported as a measure to address compromised end-user's Private Key.
	Access to the Revocation Handles	The Verifier can have access to the Revocation Handles, because the list of revoked Revocation Handles is contained within the Revocation Information.

Table 4.17 Security assurance - Security Proofs and Assumptions

Stage	Security Assurance Criteria	Result
Basic schemes	Security proofs and assumptions	Regarding assumptions we do not have any security reductions. However, the schemes are still based on other schemes that in most cases do have a security reduction. We do not have a security reduction for the full scheme since the composition of various secure schemes does not imply security of the composed scheme, etc.

References

[ÅJK+00] André Årnes, Mike Just, Svein J Knapskog, Steve Lloyd, and Henk Meijer. Selecting Revocation Solutions for PKI, 2000.

[BCD+14] Patrik Bichsel, Jan Camenisch, Maria Dubovitskaya, Robert R. Enderlein, Stephan Krenn, Ioannis Krontiris, Anja Lehmann, Gregory Neven, Janus Dam Nielsen, Christian Paquin, Franz-Stefan Preiss, Kai Rannenberg, Ahmad Sabouri, and Michael Stausholm. Architecture for Attribute-based Credential Technologies - Final Version. Deliverable D2.2, The ABC4Trust EU Project, 2014. Available at `https://abc4trust.eu/download/Deliverable_D2.2.pdf`, Last accessed on 2014-11-08.

[BCKL08] Mira Belenkiy, Melissa Chase, Markulf Kohlweiss, and Anna Lysyanskaya. P-signatures and Noninteractive Anonymous Credentials. In *Theory of Cryptography*, volume 4948, pages 356–374. Springer, 2008.

[BL13] Foteini Baldimtsi and Anna Lysyanskaya. Anonymous credentials light. In *Proceedings of the 2013 ACM SIGSAC conference on Computer & communications security*, pages 1087–1098. ACM, 2013.

[Bra00] Stefan A Brands. *Rethinking Public Key Infrastructures and Digital Certificates: Building in Privacy.* MIT Press, 2000.

[CDL+13] Jan Camenisch, Maria Dubovitskaya, Anja Lehmann, Gregory Neven, Christian Paquin, and Franz-Stefan Preiss. Concepts and Languages for Privacy-Preserving Attribute-Based Authentication. In *IDMAN*, volume 396, pages 34–52. Springer, 2013.

[CL02] Jan Camenisch and Anna Lysyanskaya. Dynamic Accumulators and Application to Efficient Revocation of Anonymous Credentials. In *Advances in Cryptology*, pages 61–76. Springer, 2002.

[CL03] Jan Camenisch and Anna Lysyanskaya. A Signature Scheme with Efficient Protocols. In *Proceedings of the 3rd International Conference on Security in Communication Networks*, pages 268–289. Springer, 2003.

[LGLS12] Jesus Luna Garcia, Robert Langenberg, and Neeraj Suri. Benchmarking Cloud Security Level Agreements Using Quantitative Policy Trees. In *CCSW*, pages 103–112. ACM, 2012.

[LGVS12] Jesus Luna, Hamza Ghani, Tsvetoslava Vateva, and Neeraj Suri. Quantitative Assessment of Cloud Security Level Agreements: A Case Study. In *SECRYPT*, pages 64–73. SciTePress, 2012.

[LKDDN10] Jorn Lapon, Markulf Kohlweiss, Bart De Decker, and Vincent Naessens. Performance Analysis of Accumulator-Based Revocation Mechanisms. In *SEC*, volume 330, pages 289–301. Springer, 2010.

[LKDDN11] Jorn Lapon, Markulf Kohlweiss, Bart De Decker, and Vincent Naessens. Analysis of Revocation Strategies for Anonymous Idemix Credentials. In *Communications and Multimedia Security*, volume 7025, pages 3–17. Springer, 2011.

[LLX07] Jiangtao Li, Ninghui Li, and Rui Xue. Universal accumulators with efficient nonmembership proofs. 2007.

[MV11] Wojciech Mostowski and Pim Vullers. Efficient U-Prove Implementation for Anonymous Credentials on Smart Cards. In *SecureComm*, volume 96, pages 243–260. Springer, 2011.

[PF09] Pierre Parrend and Stéphane Frénot. Security benchmarks of OSGi platforms: toward Hardened OSGi. *Softw., Pract. Exper.*, 39(5):471–499, 2009.

[PZ13] Christian Paquin and Greg Zaverucha. U-prove Cryptographic Specification v1.1 (Revision 2). Technical report, Microsoft Corporation, 2013.

[Sch91] Claus-Peter Schnorr. Efficient signature generation by smart cards. *Journal of Cryptology*, 4:161–174, 1991.

[Sma12] Nigel Smart. ECRYPT II yearly report on algorithms and keysizes (2011-2012). `www.ecrypt.eu.org/documents/D.SPA.20.pdf`, 2012.

[VA13] Pim Vullers and Gergely Alpár. Efficient Selective Disclosure on Smart Cards Using Idemix. In *IDMAN*, volume 396, pages 53–67. Springer, 2013.

Chapter 5
Legal Data Protection Considerations

Marit Hansen, Felix Bieker, Daniel Deibler, Hannah Obersteller, Eva Schlehahn, and Harald Zwingelberg

Abstract This chapter gives an overview of relevant legal issues for the use of Privacy-ABCs. However, only legal issues stemming from privacy or data protection laws are examined. Further considerations regarding general civil or contractual problems are left aside, since they would require specific knowledge of the intended use-case and the involved entities.
The chapter is in particular aimed at researchers and application developers, who are not only provided with a general outline of the requirements that have to be observed when processing personal data (Section 5.1) but also with considerations regarding specific issues arising when deploying Privacy ABCs (Section 5.2).

When applying Privacy-ABCs to real use-cases, the requirements of data protection norms and standards have to be taken into account. Although the cryptographic foundations of Privacy-ABCs have been known for decades, this is not widely reflected in legislation. During the lifetime of the ABC4Trust project, several partners worked on interpreting the landscape of today's legal frameworks and also gave feedback to lawmakers on the European level. Therefore, when writing these sections, the authors were able to not only rely on theoretical research regarding the issues at stake but also on the experience from the legal supervision of the pilots over the last three years.

5.1 Legal Requirements

The subsequent sections will elaborate on the general legal requirements for a compliant data processing.

Marit Hansen, Felix Bieker, Daniel Deibler, Hannah Obersteller, Eva Schlehahn, and Harald Zwingelberg
Unabhängiges Landeszentrum für Datenschutz Schleswig-Holstein, Germany, e-mail: {ULD6, ULD63,ULD68,ULD66,ULD67,ULD2}@datenschutzzentrum.de

K. Rannenberg et al. (eds.), *Attribute-based Credentials for Trust*,
DOI 10.1007/978-3-319-14439-9_5

As a foundation the concept of *"personal data"* and the relating issue of pseudonymity and anonymity will be discussed shortly. In a next step the question of the applicable law will be examined. Subsequently, the general principles of privacy protection as well as the different actors and their legal roles will be outlined. After these general considerations, the following sections will elaborate on the relevant provisions of European law providing the legal grounds for a processing of personal data including the requirements for a valid consent of minors as well as outline the obligations concerning data security.

5.1.1 Concepts of Anonymity and Pseudonymity

Every processing of data raises questions regarding the privacy of data subjects (the concerned person whose personal data is processed) since the fundamental right to respect for private life (e. g. Art. 8 European Convention on Human Rights [Con]) includes amongst other things the right to privacy and protection of personal data. As data protection and privacy laws aim at safeguarding these rights (cf. Art. 1 Directive 95/46/EC [Dir]), their limitations towards data processing operations have to be respected. However, the connection to those fundamental rights also means that these limitations are only applicable for the processing of personal data. Personal data, in its legal sense, is understood as *"any information relating to an identified or identifiable natural person"* (Art. 2 a) Directive 95/46/EC). Consequently, the concept of personal data does not presuppose that a person is al-ready identified but that he or she is identifiable. Nevertheless, identification has to be possible by *"means likely reasonably to be used"* (Recital 26 Directive 95/46/EC) and not just exist as a hypothetical possibility. Therefore, the categorisation of data can only be done on a case-by-case basis since ascertaining what is reasonable depends on the circumstances and the purpose of the data processing operation.

In this context, and in particular in the context of Privacy-ABCs, the concepts of anonymity and pseudonymity also have to be considered. Anonymisation is commonly understood in international standards, such as ISO 29100, as well as in European law as the process of altering personal data irreversibly in such a way that the data subject cannot be re-identified directly or indirectly by anyone ([Art14], pp. 5, 6). Therefore, anonymity means that identification is impossible; pseudonymisation on the other hand can be defined as *"disguising identities in a re-traceable way"* [Art13] and therefore allowing a re-identification of the data subject. Consequently, data protection rules apply if pseudonymous data is processed, since only the linkability of a dataset with the original identity has been reduced but not removed ([Art14], p. 3). Moreover, it has to be stressed that even further encryption of the pseudonymised data does not change this conclusion since encryption does not change the nature of the data even though it might technically protect it.

5.1.2 Applicable Law

After establishing that data protection laws apply, since personal data will be processed, the question arises whose law is applicable.

The Directive 95/46/EC set out to establish a common European data protection framework and to adjust the national laws of the Member States to a minimum level of data protection. Nevertheless, the directive is not self-executing and therefore had to be transferred into each national law by the respective states. Since the Directive permitted a higher standard of protection and furthermore explicitly encouraged the adoption of more protecting provisions in the national legislation (Recital 10 Directive 95/46/EC) the different national laws still differ to a certain degree from each other. Nevertheless, the issue of the applicable law is solved consistently in the national laws and based on the so-called principle of domicile. According to this principle European laws allow data controllers to "export" their national data protection laws, when they are processing data in other EEC Member States (Recital 18, Art. 4 (1a) Directive 95/46/EC). Consequently, the national law of that EEC Member State is applicable in which the controller, who is responsible for the data processing, has established his place of business. Therefore, the applicability is only dependent on where the controller has its headquarter but independent on where in the EEC states the data is processed. Furthermore, at the moment there are new efforts to further harmonise national laws in the field of privacy laws. The new General Data Protection Regulation (GDPR) [EUP] is expected to be adopted in 2014 or 2015 and as a Regulation it would be self-executing across the EU. The Regulation will update the Directive, which was adopted in 1995, when hardly anybody could imagine to which dimension the information technology, and especially the internet, would grow. It aims at bringing the data protection law into the digital age, but holds on to the well-known principles of data protection, which will be outlined in the following section.

5.1.3 General Principles and Protection Goals

The above mentioned principles of data protection are not only based on the fundamental rights to privacy and data protection but can also be found to a certain extent in the respective national and European law. Therefore, to achieve a legally compliant processing of personal data the following seven principles should be observed. This section will provide a clear and concise checklist to evaluate a data processing operation.

According to the first principle each processing of personal data needs a specific legal ground. Legal grounds can be provided either by law, contract, factual necessity (as conclusively stipulated in Art. 7), or by a valid consent given from the data subject. While each one of these offer a legal basis for personal data processing, in the private sector the consent of the concerned person whose personal data is processed the data subject will be relevant most of the times. A closer scrutiny of the relevant legal grounds can be found in Section 5.1.5.

The second principle stipulates that only a valid consent of the data subject can provide an effective legal ground. This validity can only be achieved if the data subject was sufficiently informed about the data processing prior to the collection of the data. Moreover, the consent must be given freely, i.e. without negative consequences for the data subject in case of refusal. According to Art. 10 Directive 95/46/EC, data subject should be given information about the identity of the controller and of his representative, if any, as well as the purpose of the processing. Furthermore, the information must entail every recipient of the data, or whether any kind of response is required of the data subject and which consequences a missing reaction has. Moreover, the data subject must be informed about his or her rights, such as the right to access and the right to rectify the data concerning her or him. However, the amount of information strongly depends on the specific circumstances of the collection and processing of personal data. Therefore, the data subject should be provided with any information that seems necessary to guarantee a fair processing. More detailed information regarding the necessary information will be given below, in the context of the principle of transparency and in Section 5.1.5 addressing the mandatory elements for obtaining a valid consent from the data subject. In cases where the concerned person needs to accept pre-formulated clauses, like the Terms of Service (ToS) of a digitally proved service, these clauses must emphasis the parts concerning the consent to enable a clear understanding of what the data subject is agreeing to. Moreover, consent should in principle be given in written form.

The third principle can be described as purpose limitation, according to which the service or offered task determine and in particular limit the scope of the personal data that will be collected and processed. The purpose(s) of the processing must be stipulated as precise as possible already prior to the collection of the personal data. One very broad purpose, commonly used in the private sector, is the fulfilment of rights and obligations deriving from a contract. This purpose is also stipulated in Art. 7 (b) Directive 95/46/EC as a legal ground. Furthermore, in case of subsequent alterations or added purposes, these require a specific legitimation on their own, either by another explicit consent of the data subject, or by another legal ground as stipulated in Art. 7.

The fourth principle, which is closely linked to the principle of purpose limitation, is necessity. Meaning that the collection, processing and usage of personal data is only legitimate as far as it is necessary to fulfil contractual obligations, or other purposes stated in Art. 7. The principle of necessity consequently requires data minimisation. Data should not only be limited to the least amount possible at the time of collection but also should be erased as soon as possible, i.e. when it is no longer needed for the intended purpose.

The fifth principle can be summarised as transparency. Transparency entails that the data subject knows all relevant circumstances and factors regarding the processing of the personal data related to her or him. This way, the individual is enabled to decide freely about the handling of her or his data and equipped with knowledge about the consequences resulting from this decision. In accordance with Art. 10 Directive 95/46 EC and correlating to the above mentioned necessary information, the data subject must be able to understand for which purposes which personal data of her or him is collected, processed or used. Moreover, information about the recipients of the data, and the data subject's rights are a crucial element of transparency. These rights entail amongst others the right of access, right to rectification, erasure and blocking of data, as well as the right to notification in cases of deletion, rectification, blocking of data, and first disclosure of information to third parties (Art. 12 Directive 95/46 EC). Moreover, the data subject has a right to object to the processing of her personal data. This objection may not result in any negative consequences (Art. 14 Directive 95/46 EC). Beyond this core information, there might be cases where personal data is not collected directly from the data subject but from a third party. In these cases Art. 11 Directive 95/46 EC demands a notification of the data subject as well as additional information about the data collection, the identity of the respective person or entity and the purpose(s). Furthermore, all the other information as outlined above is still necessary to comply with the principle of transparency. In summary, providing comprehensive in-formation about all the aforementioned aspects is not only a central part of the transparency principle but also a prerequisite for receiving a valid informed con-sent from the data subject.

According to sixth principle, ensuring a legitimate personal data processing, appropriate measures for achieving data security have to be deployed. This derives from the fact that a sufficient data protection is only possible if the data are also secure. Data security is primarily realised by implementing technical and organisational measures meeting the classical IT security goals of confidentiality, integrity, and availability. Specific measures supporting these goals will be explained below (Section 5.1.6).

Last but not least, the seventh principle requires an efficient internal and external supervision. This principle demands continuous and comprehensive evaluation of any processing operation in its whole lifecycle by routinely implemented measures and procedures. To provide for internal supervision an entity should em-ploy a designated data protection officer. Concerning external oversight, each entity processing personal data should be prepared to meet requests of supervisory data protection authorities, e. g. granting access to procedural documentations and supporting evaluation actions of the authority. While the provision of such measures might at a first glance deem arduous, it can also be useful to obtain beneficial audits and certifications for specific processing operations, and thus creating a competitive advantage to other service providers.

All these seven principles help to guarantee the lawfulness of the personal data processing. Thereby, they serve the privacy protection goals of unlinkability, transparency, and intervenability [ZH12]. The goal transparency was already elaborated on above. Unlinkability ensures that data cannot be linked across different do-mains and/or used for a different purpose than originally intended. Therefore, unlinkability can be supported by the principles of purpose limitation and data minimisation, aiming at a separation of personal data. Intervenability means that the data subjects, as well as the controller or supervisory authorities, have control over the personal data processing. Especially concerning the data subject, this goal is closely linked to an effective realisation of his or her legally guaranteed rights.

These three goals, combined with the classical IT security goals confidentiality, integrity, and availability are helpful in assessing and evaluating data protection and data security risks. Thereby, they serve as corrective cornerstones to deter-mine the necessary and appropriate requirements regarding technical and organisational measures.

5.1.4 Legal Roles

As shown above, the general principles establish different rights and obligations for different entities. Therefore, this section will elaborate on the different legal roles and entities normally involved in a data processing. These different roles are also foreseen in the legal framework on a European level.

Art. 1 Directive 95/46/EC stipulates that the Directive is applicable once personal data is concerned. As explained in Section 5.1.1 and according to Art. 2 (a), *personal data* means any information relating to an identified or identifiable natural person. This person is then called *data subject*. Therefore, the data must always relate to a specific individual, which consequently means that data relating to a legal entity are not protected by the Directive 95/46. Personal information can relate to factual circumstances (e. g. the individual being a PC user or a licensed doctor) as well to personal traits (like the data subject's gender or characteristics of his or her physical appearance). However, the legal data protection framework is not only applicable once a person is identified by name or otherwise, but also when only the possibility exists that an individual can be identified with the information available. The Directive is not applicable anymore once the data are anonymised and the individual can no longer be identified. However, the Directive is still applicable if the data are only pseudonymous, meaning that there is still some kind of identifier available linking the data to the individual.

Another role in the context of personal data processing is the *responsible party*, the so-called *controller* according to Art. 2 (d) Directive 95/46/EC. Usually each person or entity which alone or jointly with others determines the purpose(s) and means of the personal data processing is categorised as a controller. This party is, in general, legally responsible for the legality of the processing, thus bound by the preconditions manifested in the legal European data protection framework. There-fore, this entity will be addressed by the supervisory authorities. However, the controller is by no means obliged to perform all processing operations by himself; rather the Directive foresees the possibility of assigning a processor entity.

According to Art. 2 (e) of the Directive, a *processor* is a person or entity processing personal data on behalf of the controller. This is legally permitted as long as the correlating mandatory requirements of the Directive are met. The same holds true for further processor-relationships (sub-processing), as long as the processing entities are bound to the instructions of and supervised by the controller.

Further entities mentioned in the Directive 95/46 EC are the "third party" (Art. 2 (f)) and the "recipient of the data" (Art. 2 (g)). A third party is a person or entity not fulfilling any of the roles mentioned above, while a recipient is a party to whom data are transferred or disclosed, no matter if it is a third party or has one of the roles mentioned above.

5.1.5 Legal Grounds

The general principles of data protection require further that every processing of personal data is based on a specific legal ground. The Directive 95/46/EC adopted this principle by containing an exhaustive list of legal grounds for data processing (Art. 7 Directive 95/46/EC) and by stating that every data processing must be fair and lawful (Art. 6 (1)(a) Directive 95/46/EC).

In the context of private and business-oriented deployments of Privacy-ABCs on a big scale, several of the listed legal grounds can be neglected, since they rarely provide a viable legal ground:

- Art. 7 (c) Directive 95/46/EC allows data processing only for compliance with a legal obligation; therefore every exceeding data cannot be processed based on this paragraph.
- Art. 7 (d) Directive 95/46/EC requires that the data processing is necessary to protect the vital interests of the data subject; as business and economic interests do not constitute vital interests it seems difficult to envisage that this paragraph will provide a viable legal ground.
- Art. 7 (e) Directive 95/46/EC permits data processing only in the public interest or in the exercise of official authority and can thus not justify any private processing of data.
- Art. 7 (f) Directive 95/46/EC requires a legitimate interest of the controller that is not overridden by fundamental interests of the data subject; while this paragraph theoretically can provide a legal ground for data processing in a business environment, the practical implementation would require a weighing of the opposing interests on a case by case basis.

In summary, the deployment of Privacy-ABCs in the private sector will most likely be based on the consent of data subjects which will be elaborated in detail below or on Art. 7 (b) Directive 95/46/EC which permits the necessary data processing *"for the performance of a contract to which the data subject is party or in order to take steps at the request of the data subject prior to entering into a contract"*.

However, in this context the principles of necessity, purpose limitation and data minimisation have to be reiterated. Consequently, only the absolutely necessary data can be processed lawfully. Therefore, when deploying Privacy-ABCs, only those attributes have to be disclosed and processed which are absolutely needed for the performance of the contract. Nevertheless, the exact amount of necessary data can only be determined with in-depth knowledge of the use-case, the purpose of the processing and the used credential.

The last but definitively not the least legal ground is the consent of the data subject, as already introduced under Section 5.1.3. According to Art. 2 (h) Directive 95/46/EC the data subject's consent *"shall mean any freely given specific and informed indication of his wishes by which the data subject signifies his agreement to personal data relating to him being processed"*. This definition provides the two core prerequisites for a valid and legally binding even though the consent can be withdrawn at any time consent, namely voluntariness and awareness.

Firstly, the consent has to be given freely. Nevertheless, voluntariness requires more than the sheer lack of coercion and compulsion. In general it demands that no disadvantages are linked to not consenting or that at least all disadvantages are openly communicated to the data subjects, so that they are able to freely evaluate the benefits and disadvantages of consenting.

Secondly, the data subjects have to be informed prior to consenting to the data processing. Even though the Directive 95/46/EC does not stipulate the exact scope of the information that has to be provided, some national laws do, so for example Art. 2 (k) Greek Data Protection Law [Law]. Furthermore, since this obligation is closely linked to the duty to inform and notify the data subject during or after the data processing, the scope of information can be derived from the relevant provisions ([Art11], p. 19). While the exact scope will always depend on the exact use-case of Privacy-ABCs, the general goal has to be to enable the data subject to make an informed decision. Consequently, the *"consent by the data subject must be based upon an appreciation and understanding of the facts and implications of an action. The individual concerned must be given, in a clear and understandable manner, accurate and full information of all relevant issues, [...]"* ([Art07], p. 9).

The least information provided should entail the identity of the controller, the purpose of the data processing as well as which data will be stored and for how long. Furthermore, if further data processors or third parties are involved in the data processing their identities should be communicated as well.

Furthermore, in cases where sensitive data such as racial or ethnic origin, political opinions, religious or philosophical beliefs is processed, the processing of this sensitive personal data has to be explicitly mentioned in the consent form.

Last but not least, the issue of consenting minors requires special attention. In principle, a minor is a data subject just like an adult and as such holder of the same rights. This can be concluded directly from the Directive, which states that it applies to any "natural person" ([Art09], p. 7). Therefore, the consent generally has to be sought from the minor him- or herself. Nonetheless, it has to be taken into account, that minors are not yet (fully) legally capable. Due to the fact that children and adolescents have not yet achieved physical and psychological maturity, they need more protection than grown-up data subjects ([Art09], p. 4). This applies not only to the field of data protection, but in general to all legal transactions. Thus, minors are legally incapable of most transactions and their rights are usually exercised by their legal guardians in the best interest of the child. However, taking into account the individual level of development of a minor and the fact, that there is also a right to partake, he or she should be involved in the execution of his or her rights. Depending on the degree of maturity, this can be done by consulting the minor, making a joint decision with him or her or even by allowing him or her to make an autonomous decision ([Art09], p. 6).

In addition, the not yet fully existing capabilities of minors also have to be taken into account when providing them with information. Since, according to the Directive, a valid consent requires the provision of understandable information beforehand this information and the way of providing it needs to be adjusted to the minors' physical and psychological capabilities. Therefore, an information sheet has to be written in a clear, educational and understandable manner ([Art09], p.10). While the information still has to include all relevant facts as explained above -, at the same time it may not be too long or overwhelming. The information, as far as it concerns the data subjects' rights, must also elaborate on the special requirements that arise from the fact, that the data subject is a minor. For example, the general right of access to data might when concerning under aged data subjects additionally include the right to exercise this right alone and exclude the guardians from it. This might be the case if the minor has reached a sufficient degree of maturity and the personal data concern e.g. his or her sexual life ([Art09], pp. 10, 11).

5.1.6 Data Security Measures

As mentioned before, the protection of personal data can only be guaranteed if the data is processed and stored securely. Art. 16 and 17 of Directive 95/46 EC explicitly require the confidentiality and security of the processing. Art. 17 (1) stipulates that appropriate technical and organisational measures must be implemented to protect the data subject's personal information against unlawful destruction, accidental loss, alteration, unauthorised disclosure or unauthorised access. This applies even more for processing operations in a network. Technical measures are those that are achieved through technical settings and precautions, like technically implemented access restrictions via password protection, or smart cards. The organisational measures complement the technical ones and consist mostly of regulations which determine the scope and the responsibility regarding the data processing in question. This is often realised in company-internal guidelines and agreements. In this context, exemplary standard security measures could be standardised processes and procedures for access limitation, access authorisation, data separation, encryption, logging and documentation for audits, predefined deletion periods, and sticky policies. This list, however, is by no means conclusive and in general, it is not necessary to implement all technical and organisational measures. Nonetheless, it must be evaluated which measures are necessary by striking a balance between the effort of implementation and the risks inherent to the intended data processing. Thereby, the three classical IT security goals confidentiality, integrity, and availability must be considered and balanced as well. Furthermore, when a controller mandates a data processor acting on his behalf, Art. 17 (2) Directive 95/46 EC demands that the processor must also provide guarantees regarding the data security and compliance with the necessary measures implementation.

5.2 Applying Legal Requirements to Privacy-ABCs

This section will address the question how to actually realise the aforementioned data protection requirements in the context of a real world deployment of Privacy-ABCs. Firstly, ways are shown how to implement the privacy protection goals of transparency and intervenability. These two goals are centrepieces of not only a pleasant and convenient User experience, but also mandatory for a valid informed consent given by the User and other aspects of informational self-determination. Secondly, it is explained which content processing contracts in the controller-processing relationships have to include. Thirdly, it will be explained how to properly set up an inspection process, compliant to the European data protection requirements.

5.2.1 Transparency and Intervenability for Privacy-ABCs

Especially for digital means of processing personal data, there is a great need of direct support for the aforementioned privacy protection goals. Moreover, the IT system providing the service or good demanded by the customer shall be able to enhance the overall User experience by providing an interface with sufficient transparency and intervenability features also meeting usability necessities. Generally, a transparent system, which offers convenient functions for the data subject to exercise his or her rights, significantly increases the trust into the system as well as in the entity providing it. The same applies for intervenability, which empowers all entities involved. Even though usability is not a specific privacy protection goal, it is, in this context, a correlating factor. An improved usability also enables the data subject to navigate and use the service more efficiently. Therefore, it is also in the service provider's interest to offer such features for an enhanced competitive edge in its field of business.

The obvious basic criteria supporting the User experience is that a system works without any errors or disruptions. This is not only important for availability and integrity reasons but also for preventing data corruption or loss. Therefore, the system should be tested thoroughly prior to a real life deployment. Moreover, in the context of a Privacy-ABC system, ensuring a seamless User experience when obtaining credentials, using presentation tokens, and accessing the service is a crucial factor for acceptance of this fairly new technology.

Furthermore, since this technology is still quite unfamiliar to lay persons, some efforts should be invested in displaying correct and sufficient information assisting the user. The provision of such information is not only a prerequisite to realise sufficient transparency in favour of the User, but also a legal precondition for a valid informed consent. Consequently, several measures were undertaken to enhance transparency for the Users during the ABC4Trust pilots. In both pilots, the Users were informed prior to their consent about what Privacy-ABCs are, how to use the system, the terms of use, as well as the means and purposes of the necessary data processing. Adapted to the specifics of the individual pilots, the Users were also informed about the inspection process, the correlating purpose, and the specific preconditions under which an identity may be revealed. When using the system after the start of the pilot, this information was still accessible for them via a website link, under which this information was always accessible. Moreover, in the Söderhamn pilot, the User interface supported transparency in such a fashion that the Users were enabled to access their data on their own. If the User chooses to, she was able to see the list of her credentials, to access a dashboard, and to view the Restricted Area's access policies. Moreover, when a User wanted to access a Restricted Area, the system explicitly showed which attributes were necessary to gain the desired access. While it was possible to use the default alias (the real name), Users were also able to choose an anonymous or pseudonymous alias. Moreover, the interface always displayed in a dedicated field in the top right corner of the screen under which alias the User was currently acting.

All these measures could even be improved in future Privacy-ABC settings. For example a more fine-grained display of the respective anonymity status, a more prominent display of the active aliases, and even a User tutorial on how to use Privacy-ABCs and aliases are possible. However, it should be avoided to give information about anonymity status in form of a bar or percent rating/scaling. Such a determination could prove legally challenging due to varying and partially unforeseeable minimum anonymity sets.

Still, other measures are more appropriate to enhance transparency sufficiently, like affirmation messages from the system after submitting personal information to demonstrate the proper functioning of the User-system interaction. Thereby, the User can actively check if something worked to her satisfaction. Correlating to such affirmation messages, in case of system failures error messages should be easily comprehensible. This principle especially applies to warning messages concerning information relevant to the data subject's personal data. For example, the system could provide automated notifications to the User once any deletion, rectification, blocking, or first disclosure to third parties occurs. A well thought-through logging concept can support both the transparency in favour of the User, and also provide a useful evaluation tool, for example for data protection supervisory authorities. All of these exemplary mentioned verification functionalities are a good way to empower the User and to increase her trust into the system. In addition, further measures such as backup or recover functionalities, as well as a help desk interface, or any other working contact point are even easier to implement. This can also include offline organisational precautions to help Users in case they have any problems.

To achieve the goal of intervenability, the system should provide sufficient and comprehensible means for the data subjects to exercise her right to rectify, delete, or block her data, especially if it is incorrect. Thereby the User interface should provide meaningful, understandable and reachable functions. Of course, such intervening activities of the User concerning her personal data must also affect eventually existing backup data sets. Furthermore, other involved parties should have means to exercise their influence on the system as well within their own rights and obligations.

It goes without saying that transparency and intervenability are important throughout the entire lifecycle of a data processing and in particular for all processes such as issuance of credentials, using credentials and presentation tokens, revoking credentials, and for the workflows concerning inspection (in more detail elaborated in Section 5.2.3). Privacy-ABCs have the potential of realising the privacy protection goal of unlinkability in an exemplary manner. However, since Privacy-ABCs add a certain degree of complexity to the data processing by involving more parties (e. g. for potential inspection), it is a challenge to achieve exemplary transparency and intervenability as well.

5.2.2 *Contractual Fixation of Processing on Behalf of the Controller*

As explained in the description of the different legal roles, it is possible that the data is processed on behalf of the controller. Nonetheless, since the controller stays responsible for the data processing and the data processor is only functioning as an aide to the controller, their dependent relationship has to be ensured. Ac-cording to Art. 16 Directive 95/46/EC the personal data shall not be processed by anyone except on instructions from the controller or if it is required by law. Furthermore, for safeguarding this limitation as well as the dependency between controller and processor Art. 17 (3) Directive 95/46/EC requires that the *"processing on behalf"* has to be governed by a contract or other binding legal act. This con-tract shall further stipulate, that

- the processor is bound to the instructions of the controller;
- the processor must implement appropriate technical and organisational measures to protect personal data against accidental loss, alteration, unauthorised disclosure or access;
- the national data protection laws of the state, where the processor is established, are applicable regarding the appropriate technical and organisational measures.

Moreover, the data controller shall only choose *"a processor providing sufficient guarantees in respect of the technical security measures and organisational measures governing the processing to be carried out, and must ensure compliance with those measures"* (Art. 17 (2) Directive 95/46/EC).

However, as explained in regards to the applicable law (Section 5.1.2), these requirements are only the minimum ones provided by the Directive 95/46/EC and the different national laws might ask for a written contact or for additional provisions in the contract. One example would be 11 (2) German Federal Data Protection Act

(Bundesdatenschutzgesetz, BDSG [BGB]) which contains a list of ten minimum requirements in regard to the content of each outsourcing contract. To ensure a higher level of privacy protection 11 BDSG [BGB] was used as the foundation of the processing contracts in the project pilots. Further elaborations on the specific contracts of the pilots as well as the contracts themselves can be found in [BDD$^+$14].

A similar list of requirements for the relation between controller and processor and the respective contract can be found in the draft for a new General Data Protection Regulation adopted by the European Parliament. According to Art. 26 (2) Draft-GDPR:

> *"The controller and processor (...) shall provide that the processor shall:*
> *(a) process personal data only on instructions from the controller, unless otherwise required by Union law or Member State law;*
> *(b) employ only staff who have committed themselves to confidentiality or are under a statutory obligation of confidentiality;*
> *(c) take all required measures pursuant to Article 30 (Security of Processing);*
> *(d) determine the conditions for enlisting another processor only with the prior permission of the controller, unless otherwise determined ;*
> *(e) insofar as this is possible given the nature of the processing, create in agreement with the controller the appropriate and relevant technical and organisational requirements for the fulfilment of the controller's obligation to respond to requests for exercising the data subject's rights laid down in Chapter III;*
> *(f) assist the controller in ensuring compliance with the obligations pursuant to Articles 30 to 34, taking into account the nature of processing and the information available to the processor;*
> *(g) return all results to the controller after the end of the processing, not process the personal data otherwise and delete existing copies unless Union or Member State law requires storage of the data;*
> *(h) make available to the controller all information necessary to demonstrate compliance with the obligations laid down in this Article and allow on-site inspections."*

Moreover, the new Regulation will introduce further obligations for the processor regarding documentation of the data processing (Art. 28 Draft-GDPR), cooperation with the supervisory authority (Art. 29), notification, communication and prior-authorisation (Art. 31, 32, 34). Furthermore, processors will be required to carry out a data protection impact assessment (Art. 33) and designate data protection officers (Art. 35).

5.2.3 Modelling the Inspection Process

Privacy-ABCs add the benefit of conditional identification where needed through the inspection feature. Under pre-defined and specific circumstances it allows the

Inspector, who is the sole holder of the secret key, to reveal attributes of the inspectable tokens. In order to comply with legal requirements, this process needs to be well-defined and foreseeable for the User concerned. Figure 5.1 provides an overview of a generic inspection process [BZH14].

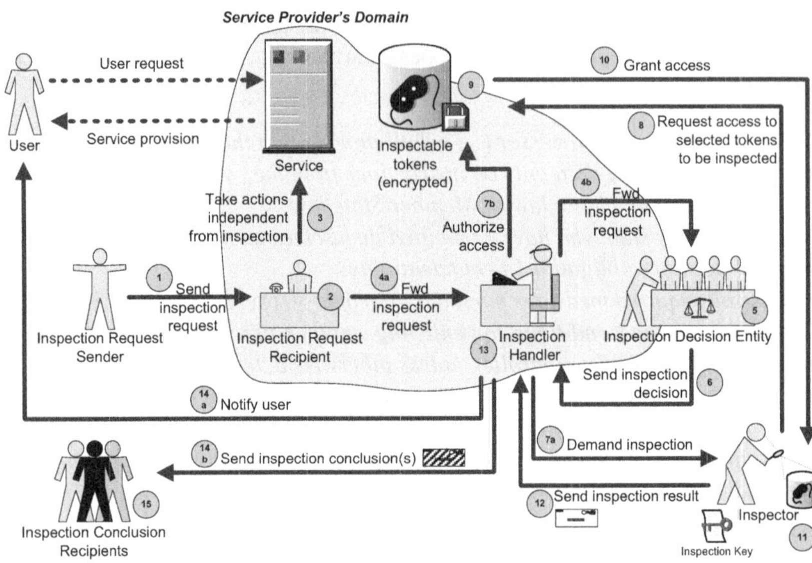

Fig. 5.1 Generic model of the inspection process

The entire process can be divided into four phases: Phase 1 takes place before the Inspection Handler becomes involved, Phase 2 occurs until the Inspector takes ac-tion. Phase 3 encompasses the activities of the Inspector and in the final phase, the inspection result is post-processing.

At the start of the inspection process an Inspection Request Sender submits a request for an inspection to the Inspection Request Recipient. The request can inter alia be submitted by a report function. As the request is received an automated ticket system creates an automatic reply (1). The Inspection Request Recipient, acting as first-level support, filters the requests received. In limited instances, the process may be aborted directly, in cases of evident abuse (2). Optionally, the Inspection Request Recipient may act below the threshold of an inspection and delete or block the reported content. Thus, there is a low-level possibility to abort the process before an inspection is carried out (3).

As the request is escalated to the Inspection Handler (4a), Phase 2 begins and the Inspection Handler forwards the request to the Inspection Decision Entity (4b). This entity can be a board and should be independent from the Service Provider to assure a neutral decision-making process. In emergency situations only may the Inspection Handler forego the involvement of the Inspection Decision Entity and directly demand an inspection. As to allow review this step has to be logged. In step (5), the Inspection Decision Entity generates a reasoned decision whether the inspection grounds are fulfilled and thereby decides whether or not an inspection may occur. In its decision, the entity can also define the scope and further requirements of the inspection. The entire deliberation of the Inspection Decision Entity is logged to allow review. Upon arriving on a decision, it is sent to the Inspection Handler (6). If the decision is that an inspection may not occur, the process is aborted. At this point, the process can also be de-escalated by referring it back to the Inspection Request Recipient to take action according to step (3).

If the decision is that an inspection may be carried out, the Inspection Handler instructs the Inspector to perform an inspection as defined by the inspection decision (7a) and thereby initiates Phase 3. At the same time, the Inspection Handler authorises access to the selected encrypted tokens in the database (7b). The Inspector then requests access to the predefined encrypted tokens (8). It is then technically checked whether the request of the Inspector is authorised (9) and, where this is not the case, the process is aborted. If access is authorised, it is granted (10) and logged to enable oversight by the Inspection Handler. By decrypting the to-kens, the Inspector generates the inspection result (11) and sends it to the Inspection Handler (12).

In the final phase, the Inspection Handler matches the information received with own information to create target-specific responses, i.e. inspection conclusions for those who should be informed or take action (13). This may be done ac-cording to the inspection request (in case of inter alia judicial decisions) or the inspection decision. The Inspection Handler then, in order to promote transparency, notifies the affected User(s) (14a) where not legally banned (as may be the case with judicial decisions) and ideally at the same time sends the inspection conclusions to the Inspection Conclusion Recipients (14b), one of whom could be the Inspection Request Sender. Accordingly, the Inspection Conclusion Recipients may take action (15).

In order to fully comply with the legal and transparency requirements set out inspection should be a rare exception. Thus, a narrowly and pre-defined list of inspection grounds is warranted, which must be presented to the User before any personal data is submitted. The inspection grounds have to balance the interests of Users and the Service provider. Where necessary and justified, the Service Provider has to have the option to identify Users. Under the current legal framework, the Service Providers may collect vast amounts of data, even if they are only necessary in specific cases. When refraining from such collection, this must not lead to a surrender of legitimate interests.

Two types of inspection grounds can be distinguished: formal and substantive reasons. The former category encompasses state-issued orders, which have binding effect on the Service Provider. This includes court orders and those of other competent authorities. In these instances a weighing of interests will usually al-ready have been accomplished by the competent authority. Yet, in most instances these may be challenged according to national law.

Any other kind of reason is a substantive reason and requires a weighing of interests. Usually, the interest of the party interested in an inspection (which may be the Service Provider, the Inspection Request Sender or the Inspection Conclusion Receiver), will have to be weighed against the rights and interests of the User. This exercise can best be achieved through an independent Inspection Decision Entity. In the decision-making process, the rights and interests of both parties, which may stem from the EU Data Protection framework, but also fundamental rights of individuals as laid down in the EU Charter of Fundamental Rights [CFR], need to be correctly identified and properly balanced. The rights laid out in the Charter are binding on all EU Member States according to Art. 51 (1) of the Charter. In all instances should it be borne in mind, that, at the very least, the User affected by the inspection is protected by the rights to privacy and data protection according to Art. 7 and 8 of the Charter. Where a User expresses an opinion, she is also protected by the right to free speech under Art. 11 of the Charter.

In order to weigh these rights against the rights and interests of the potentially aggrieved party (which might inter alia be intellectual property rights or the instigation of judicial proceedings against the User), it should be ascertained whether an inspection is suitable to accomplish the defence of the latter party's rights and interests. In a second step it has to be ensured that the data processing does not go beyond what is necessary to achieve the aim. At this stage it should be determined whether there are less invasive measures to protect the rights and interests of the potentially aggrieved party. In this context, it has to be borne in mind, that identifying the User has *ultima ratio* character and the removal of the offending content should always be considered as a remedy. Additionally, informing the User of a pending inspection can also be an incentive for her to become proactive and serve to de-escalate the conflict. At the last stage, it should be considered whether an inspection is appropriate with regard to the User's rights and interests. This step is reserved for manifestly disproportionate interferences with the User's rights.

Once an inspection has occurred, a reasoned decision must be submitted to at least allow for a defence before further definite measures are taken. Also, it should be pointed out, that in cases when there are high-level rights at issue, such as cases of threats of suicide or violence, the inspection process as modelled here requires no additional time. Such threats evidently take precedence over a User's right to privacy. Furthermore, a well-defined and documented inspection procedure facilitates the production of a reasoned decision for the User.

5.2.4 Considerations Concerning the Revocation Process

The revocation authority is empowered to revoke credentials if necessary, for instance in cases of loss or misuse. If a credential is revoked, it can no longer be used for authentication. Just like the inspection grounds mentioned above, the revocation grounds have to be made known to the user in advance.

The revocation of credentials and their grounds raise similar issues as discussed with regards to the inspection process and grounds. But the consequences from revocation are even more severe: Once a credential is revoked, it becomes invalid and the user can no longer use it. This means, she cannot access the desired service anymore. Therefore, the revocation grounds have to be pre-defined and made accessible for users as well.

In certain cases, such as loss or when she withdrew the consent to the data processing, it is in the user's own interest that the credential is revoked. But there are cases conceivable, where the user does not want her credential to be revoked. For instance, if the user misused the credential or corrupted it (accidentally). However, in the school context, revocation due to misuse should rather be addressed through educational measures. Nevertheless, the revocation grounds need to be defined precisely, since otherwise the revocation authority may be subject to claims for damages due to the unavailability of the service. For reasons of transparency, the user should be able to understand that her credential has been revoked prior to relying on it to provide proof towards the service provider. Therefore, information of potential revocation should be accessible from the user interface. The user should be notified of the reason for the revocation. Additionally, the revocation authority should log all revocation requests it receives.

Especially with respect to time-sensitive request, e.g. credentials which concern monetary affairs and consequently make interesting targets for third party attacks, it must be guaranteed that the inspection authority is sufficiently available.

Another issue to be solved is the replacement of credentials. Due to the fact that the user is not supposed to be identified, the recovery of data submitted by use of the now revoked credential is impossible. But recovery of this data may be achieved through the introduction of "replacement credentials". The user may get this additional credential and can then present it in conjunction with a token generated from the revoked credential towards the service provider. By doing so, she could still provide proof that she is the same person. While this approach obviously is susceptible to third party attacks, it cannot be discussed in detail at this point.

As with inspection, cases of revocation should be strictly limited. As described above, when revoking a credential, the revocation authority invalidates it and puts it on a list which is disseminated to users and service providers, possibly even issuers. This is achieved through a unique identifying number contained in every credential, which is however never disclosed to service providers. Generally, the consequences can be serious if a user can no longer access a certain service. Therefore, revocation has similar requirements as inspection: it should be the exception, this means only applied as ultima ratio. In any case, the option of suspending a credential, as a less invasive measure, should be considered first. A suspension can be useful, whenever it is desirable to only temporarily limit access. In case of scheduled of unscheduled absence, when the user cannot access the service, suspension can ensure that there is no fraudulent use. Accordingly, in case of the potential loss of the storage device containing a credential, if a user cannot yet ascertain whether it has been misplaced, actually lost or stolen.

However, not only must the conditions under which a credential will be revoked be made known to the user in advance, but she must also be enabled to intervene in the process or at the very least be informed during all stages. This means, for instance, to allow the user to check prior to the start of a transaction whether the credentials she intends to use are still valid or perhaps revoked. This requirement of transparency can be met, by having the user actively transmit non-revocation evidence to the service provider along with the presentation token. Another possible way of implementation would be to oblige the service provider to constantly updating revocation list.

References

[Art07] Article 29 Data Protection Working Party. Working Document on the processing of personal data relating to health in electronic health records (EHR). WP 131, 00323/07/EN, adopted on 15 February 2007, 2007.

[Art09] Article 29 Data Protection Working Party. Opinion 2/2009 on the protection of childrenś personal data (General Guidelines and the special case of schools), WP 160, 398/09/EN, adopted on 11 February 2009, 2009.

[Art11] Article 29 Data Protection Working Party. Opinion 15/2011 on the definition of consent. WP 187, 01197/11/EN, adopted on 13 july 2011, 2011.

[Art13] Article 29 Data Protection Working Party. Statement of the Working Party on current discussions regarding the data protection reform package. Brussels, 27 February 2013, 2013.

[Art14] Article 29 Data Protection Working Party. Opinion 05/2014 on Anonymisation Techniques. WP 216, 0829/14/EN, adopted on 10 April 2014, 2014.

[BDD+14] Souheil Bcheri, Kasper L. Damgård, Daniel Deibler, Norbert Götze, Hans G. Knudsen, Maxim Moneta, Apostolos Pyrgelis, Eva Schlehahn, Michael B. Stausholm, and Harald Zwingelberg. Experiences and Feedback of the Pilots. Deliverable D5.3, The ABC4Trust EU Project, 2014. Available at `https://abc4trust.eu/download/D5.3_ExperiencesAndFeedback_Final.pdf`, Last accessed on 2014-11-08.

[BGB] Bundesdatenschutzgesetz in der Fassung der Bekanntmachung vom 14. Januar 2003 (BGBl. i s. 66), das zuletzt durch Artikel 1 des Gesetzes vom 14. August 2009 (bgbl. i s. 2814) geändert worden ist (German Federal Data Protection Act) (2009).

[BZH14] Felix Bieker, Harald Zwingelberg, and Marit Hansen. Towards a privacy-preserving inspection process for authentication solutions with conditional identification. In *Open Identity Summit 2014 – Proceedings*, GI-Edition - Lecture Notes in Informatics (LNI), 2014.

[CFR] Charter of Fundamental Rights of the European Union (2000/C 364/01). Official Journal of the European Union C 83, 30.03.2010, pp. 389-403 (2010).

[Con] Convention for the Protection of Human Rights and Fundamental Freedoms (European Convention of Human Rights) as amended by Protocols No. 11 and No. 14 (2010).

[Dir] Directive 95/46/EC of the European Parliament and of the Council of 24 October 1995 on the protection of individuals with regard to the processing of personal data and on the free movement of such data (1995).

[EUP] European Parliament legislative resolution of 12 March 2014 on the proposal for a regulation of the European Parliament and of the Council on the protection of individuals with regard to the processing of personal data and on the free movement of such data (General Data Protection Regulation) (COM(2012)0011 – C7-0025/2012 – 2012/0011(COD)).

[Law] Law 2472/1997 on the Protection of Individuals with regard to the Processing of Personal Data as amended by Laws 2819/2000 and 2915/2000. English translation of the Greek Data Protection Act (1997).

[ZH12] Harald Zwingelberg and Marit Hansen. Privacy Protection Goals and their implications for eID systems. In *Privacy and Identity Management for Life*, pages 245–260. Springer, 2012.

Chapter 6
School Community Interaction Platform: the Söderhamn Pilot of ABC4Trust

Ahmad Sabouri, Souheil Bcheri, Jimm Lerch, Eva Schlehahn, and Welderufael Tesfay

Abstract The Norrtullskolan school in Söderhamn, Sweden, hosted one of the ABC4Trust trials, where a privacy-respecting School Community Interaction Platform, built upon Privacy-ABCs, was deployed to boost communication between pupils, their parents and school personnel. In this chapter, we present an overview of the scope and the scenarios, and elaborate on the results we achieved through the design, deployment, operation and evaluation phases of this pilot.

According to 2013 statistics [Fin13], 86 to 97 percent of Swedish children between the ages of 12-15 were accessing the Internet on a daily basis. Concurrently, Internet usage has become much more common in Swedish schools in recent years. More specifically, the daily Internet use in schoolwork has increased from 11% in 2009 to 53% in 2013 among the students in the aforementioned age group. A similar trend has been observed in the use of social networks. For example, statistics indicate that some children start using social networking sites at the age of eight, even though there is often a higher minimum age requirement (i.e. 13 years of age for Facebook). Focusing on children between the ages of 12 to 15, Facebook was visited daily by 59% of the boys and 68% of the girls in 2013. The observed growth in Internet and social networks usage among Swedish teenagers affirmed the choice of the pilot environment by ABC4Trust.

The Norrtullskolan school in Söderhamn, Sweden, hosted the school trial of ABC4Trust. A privacy-friendly platform, built upon Privacy-ABCs, was deployed

Ahmad Sabouri and Welderufael Tesfay
Chair of Mobile Business & Multilateral Security, Goethe University Frankfurt, Germany, e-mail: {ahmad.sabouri,welderufael.tesfay}@m-chair.de

Souheil Bcheri and Jimm Lerch
Eurodocs AB, Sweden, e-mail: sosso@eurodocs.net, jimmlerch@gmail.com

Eva Schlehahn
Unabhängiges Landeszentrum für Datenschutz Schleswig - Holstein, Germany, e-mail: ULD67@datenschutzzentrum.de

K. Rannenberg et al. (eds.), *Attribute-based Credentials for Trust*,
DOI 10.1007/978-3-319-14439-9_6

to boost communication between pupils, their parents and school personnel. On the one hand, pupils were able to authenticate themselves in order to access restricted online activities and restricted information. On the other hand, they were able to remain anonymous when they asked private and sensitive questions to school personnel, while simultaneously assuring the school personnel that they were communicating with the authorised pupils of the respective school or class.

The trial covered a wide range of activities; therefore, the pilot was operated in two rounds.The first round was smaller in scale, ten teachers and twenty-two students, in order to better investigate the scalability of the platform as well as be able to address any system shortcomings before the larger-scale second round deployment. The first round participants tested the overall functionality of the system with regard to them downloading their respective credentials onto their PIN-protected smart cards and testing the features. The feedback that was provided with regard to response times, optimization and usability proved to be vital in preparing for a successful second round.

6.1 Application Description

The School Community Interaction Platfrom for the Söderhamn pilot was developed as a web-based application to be used for chat communication, counselling, political discussions and exchange of sensitive and personal data between pupils, parents, and such school personnel as teachers, nurses, and counsellors. This pilot particularly helped to gather information on the usability of the Privacy-ABC systems under the especially challenging, usability conditions posed by having child participants.

The preparation for the pilot began with a deep analysis of the pilot environment. In this regard, the specialists focused primarily on the elicitation and elaboration process to identify the application scenarios, fix the boundaries and create a list of requirements. The rest of this section contains a brief description of the main use case scenarios, an overview of the identified requirements, a summary of the key design elements and further information regarding security and privacy highlights of the design.

6.1.1 Pilot Key Scenarios

The Söderhamn pilot of ABC4Trust aimed at providing a School Community Interaction Platform. The precise definition of the use-case scenarios in this pilot experienced several changes prior to the deployment phase, as the scholars obtained further knowledge about the environment and the requirements. In this section, we provide the final scenario definitions in relation to their actual implementation. Figure 6.1 demonstrates an abstract overview of the scenarios and types of activities in the School Community Interaction Platform.

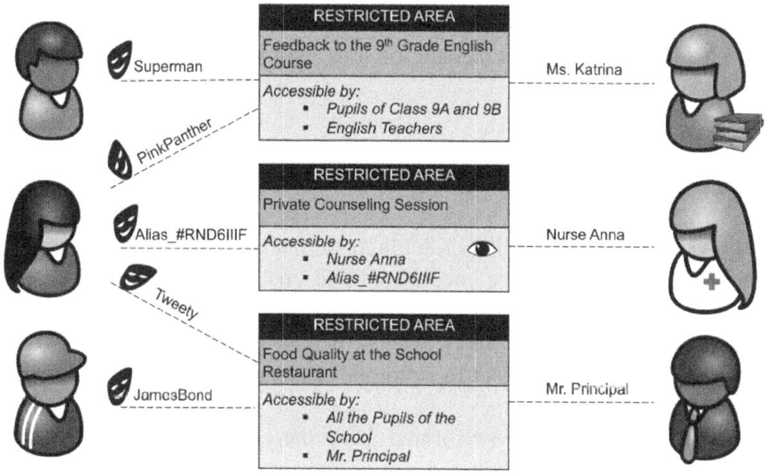

Fig. 6.1 School Community Interaction Platform

6.1.1.1 Counselling

In this scenario, a pupil who needed counselling would have been able to contact the authorised professionals regarding various social or health related problems, above and beyond the general school-related issues. In this case, the pupil was the one who initiated such a counselling communication. The counselling session began immediately if the school personnel were available online. Otherwise, the communication could be performed asynchronously (send a message and receive the answer later).

Due to the fact that the school should be able to rescue the pupil in extreme circumstances, such as a case of depression where the pupil threatens to commit suicide, the so-called Inspection functionality was enabled for the counselling sessions by default (read more about Inspection in 6.1.1.5). As it is shown in Figure 6.1, upon entering a counselling session, the pupil would have received a new alias generated randomly by the system to avoid linkability to any other activity of the pupil in the case of an Inspection.

6.1.1.2 Restricted chat rooms

The live chat feature was expected to be one of the more widely used services in the platform. The users had the possibility to create chat rooms and limit the access to their desired target group. For example, a pupil could initiate a chat room to discuss the quality of the English language course for the 9th grade and make it accessible to the English teachers and pupils in classes 9A and 9B (see Figure 6.1).

In addition to group chat, it was possible to create private chat rooms and limit the participation to specific persons by using their Aliases in the policy. For example, the pupil *Superman* enjoyed the discussion with *PinkPanther* in a public chat room and subsequently invited her to a private chat room only accessible to these two users to better express and exchange opinions, without actually knowing who the other person was.

6.1.1.3 Political discussions

Political discussions are very important in modern and democratic societies. Therefore, young citizens should be encouraged and enabled to participate in political discourse as an integral part of their education. Anonymous political discussions can encourage some pupils to freely express their opinions. This can be useful to allow for the expression of dissenting opinions on sensitive subjects against a settled majority of the participants.

Political discussions were performed using the chat and wall functionality. In order to overcome the fear of being identified and accused for an opinion, the system configuration settings did not allow for Inspection (read more about Inspection in 6.1.1.5) of political discussions.

6.1.1.4 Document sharing

Schools typically produce many documents, e.g. exam results, grades and individual development plans, that need to be shared with or distributed to the pupils and their parents/guardians. Furthermore, the users communicating in a chat room might need to share some documents such as photos to boost their discussions. To accommodate these needs, a "Document Sharing" functionality feature was introduced within the system. Every user, entitled to participate in an activity (e.g., chat), was able to upload documents there. The uploaded documents were then available and accessible by all users who had access to that activity.

By default a *Personal Restricted Area* existed for every user in the system and important documents were uploaded to this area to be picked up by the user. These areas were set to be accessible by the *Default Alias* (real identity) of the users only.

6.1.1.5 De-anonymization under special circumstances

In exceptional situations, such as the protection from immediate threat to life or health, the *inspection board* of the school could decide to request the inspector to reveal the identity of a user. The conditions to initiate an inspection process clearly defined in the contractual relationship beforehand and announced in advance. The inspection board consisted of the schoolmaster and a combination of teachers, nurses, pupils and parents, while the inspector was a trusted third party who held the smart card containing the inspection cryptographic key.

In the context of the Community Interaction Platform, the special circumstances of inspection were defined at the beginning of the trial and known to the users as the *inspection grounds*. All the activities within the system that had the inspection feature enabled were visibly marked and the users were informed about the inspection grounds before they joined the activity. Therefore, the users were completely aware of the condition and could decide to join or abandon the activity. Nevertheless, to relieve concern during the political discussions, the system did not allow any political discussion to be inspectable. To further assist the users, upon entering an inspectable domain the system automatically checked whether the current alias had been used in an inspectable activity before and, if not, warned the user about the possibility of being linked to their previous activities under this alias in the event of an inspection.

6.1.2 Requirements

During the design phase, the requirement engineering process resulted in the following list of conditions to be fulfilled. These requirements were considered generic and not specific to this pilot since they had been identified in a collaborative effort with the other ABC4Trust pilot in Patras. The requirements were:

1. The pilot participants needed to be equipped with:
   - Smart cards as the hardware token and the storage for the secret keys; and
   - Smart card readers.
2. Use of smart cards to obtain or present credentials must be PIN protected.
3. Except for the secret keys, which remain covert, the users must be provided with tools to browse the information stored on the smart card.
4. The users must be able to change the PIN of their smart cards.
5. Upon continuous use of the smart card the PIN must be cached to improve the usability.
6. Personal Unlock Key (PUK) is needed to avoid losing control over smart cards in case the PIN is forgotten.
7. The performance must be acceptable by the users.
8. User-friendly administrative interfaces must be integrated within the system.
9. Log files must be generated by the reference implementation libraries in order to provide input for debugging issues.
10. A mechanism to revoke the credentials must be in place.
11. The users must not be able to share or exchange their credentials.
12. Credentials, Privacy-ABC presentation and issuance tokens must be resilient against unauthorised manipulation.
13. Combining attributes from different credentials in the same presentation token must be possible.
14. The issuance and presentation processes must be resilient against replay attacks.
15. In an anonymous session, the Privacy-ABC presentation token must be unlinkable to the credentials' issuance.

16. It must be possible to request users to include specific pseudonyms in their presentation and issuance tokens.
17. Users should be able to authenticate themselves under previously established pseudonyms.
18. A mechanism to identify a returning user in a specific context (scope) must be in place.
19. All processing of personal data requires a legal ground. Such a legal ground may be stipulated by the applicable national law. Further grounds for lawful data processing can be consensual or contractual.
20. Personal data stored in the system must be deleted once it is not needed anymore (e.g. when the pilot is over). For this purpose, the retention periods and a deletion process must be defined prior to the processing so that if smart cards were returned the data stored on them must be erased as well.

In addition to the generic requirements listed above and in order to be considered successful in terms of legal compliance, the following criteria were defined to estimate the Söderhamn pilot's success as it should:

1. Meet the legal requirements of the Swedish Data Inspection Board.
2. Meet the legal requirements of The Swedish National Agency for Education.
3. Meet other legal requirements to which a Swedish School must comply.

6.1.3 The Key Design Elements

In this section, we introduce the design of the pilot application at a glance. In particular, the four key elements in the design of the application that will be further elaborated upon include: the involved actors, the structure of the credentials, the abstract model for the Community Interaction Platform, and management of identities.

6.1.3.1 Involved Actors

The analysis conducted in the early phases led in the identification of several types of actors in the context of the pilot. Here we briefly describe which actors were involved in the operation of the School Community Platform:

Administrator: A major effort had to be taken during the setup and initialisation phase, as well as the running period of the pilot, to administer the processes and manage the operation of the pilot. The administrators were responsible for setting up the system, provisioning of the users, rolling-out the smart cards and coordinating all the technical support in the operation phase.

User: A user was considered to be one of the active participants of the School Community Interaction Platform. The users received smart cards, readers and the necessary credentials that enabled them to access the system. The following list contains the final set of users' roles:

- Pupil
- Counsellor
- Teacher
- Guardian

Inspector: The Inspector was a trusted entity in the pilot who was able to assist the school in the event of extraordinary circumstances to de-anonymize a Privacy-ABC presentation token, thereby revealing the identity of the corresponding user. The inspection process had well-defined conditions, procedures and was known to the users in advance. Please see Section 6.1.1.5 for further information

6.1.3.2 Credentials

Designing Privacy-ABCs required a deep understanding of the scenarios, infrastructure and environment. In the case of the ABC4Trust Söderhamn pilot, the credentials' structure had to change with the lessons learnt from the tests conducted in the earlier round until they reached a stable state. There were several factors that impacted the final design of the credentials. Apart from the scenarios and the requirement analysis, limitations on computation capabilities and storage capacity on smart cards affected the design of the credentials. In this section, we report on the final design of the credential formats employed in the trial.

The primary credential used in the pilot was named *CredSchool* and contained the personal information of the users. Table 6.1 demonstrates the structure of this credential. A major decision made about the attribute values was to avoid using the Swedish national unique identifier (known as Civic Registration Number) within the pilot, even though it is widely used in Sweden. Therefore, the Pilot User Number (PUN) was introduced with the same format, but replaced part of the Civic Registration Number with a random value. This credential was the key to access the

Table 6.1 School Registration Credential Structure

CredSchool	
Attribute	*Comment*
First name	
Last name	
Pilot User Number (YYMMDD-RRRR)	*Used instead of Civic Registration Number (YYMMDD-XXXX). PUN uses random numbers RRRR instead of the Swedish unique identifier XXXX in the pattern.*
Gender	
School	*In this case it is the Söderhamn school: Norrtullskolan*
Revocation handle	*This attribute is embedded by the issuer to enable revocation of this credential.*

Community Interaction Platform in the first step. Due to the storage and computation overhead within the revocation process, in addition to providing better usability in terms of the delay experienced by the user, it was decided to have only this credential revocable and use it as a master credential whenever a revocation check was desired.

One of the other points where the storage limitation of the smart card impacted the credential design was in the case of *CredSubject* (Table 6.2), which was designed to attest pupils' enrolment in different courses. The credentials could have been implemented as separate instances for each course. However, considering the storage overhead of each new credential on the smart card, the decision was made to have only one credential containing all the subjects as Boolean values. Therefore, whoever was enrolled in a subject would have had the corresponding attribute set to "True" rather than "False".

Investigation of the pilot scenarios required the addition of another credential to authenticate enrolment of the pupils in a certain class or grade. As show in Table 6.3, the so-called *CredClass* was utilized to address this requirement.

In addition to the aforementioned credentials, *CredRole* was designed to distinguish between the different types of users in the pilot, introduced in Section 6.1.3.1.

Table 6.2 Subject Credential Structure

CredSubject	
Attribute	*Comment*
MA	*Maths (Boolean)*
SVA	*Swedish as a Second Language (Boolean)*
TK	*Technology (Boolean)*
BL	*Art (Boolean)*
SLT	*Needlework (Boolean)*
SLTM	*Wood and Metal Craft (Boolean)*
MU	*Music (Boolean)*
HK	*Home Economics (Boolean)*
EN	*English Language (Boolean)*
SP	*Spanish Language (Boolean)*
FR	*French Language (Boolean)*
TY	*German Language (Boolean)*
IDHP	*Sports and Health for Boys (Boolean)*
IDHF	*Sports and Health for Girls (Boolean)*

Table 6.3 Class Enrolment Credential Structure

CredClass	
Attribute	*Comment*
classNumber	*Represents the class name, e.g. 9A*
classGroup	Group: A, B, C, D. The following 12 classes were involved: 7A, 7B, 7C, 7D, 8A, 8B, 8C, 8D, 9A, 9B, 9C, 9D.
classYear	*This attribute indicates the year of the class to distinguish between the students who have been in the same class in different years (e.g. 9A of 2013 and 9A of 2014)*

Table 6.4 Role Credential Structure

CredRole	
Attribute	*Comment*
Pupil	*(Boolean)*
Counselor	*(Boolean)*
Teacher	*(Boolean)*
Guardian	*(Boolean)*
Other Role 1	*Had been considered in the credential to be used on demand (Boolean)*
Other Role 2	*Had been considered in the credential to be used on demand (Boolean)*
Other Role 3	*Had been considered in the credential to be used on demand (Boolean)*
Other Role 4	*Had been considered in the credential to be used on demand (Boolean)*
Other Role 5	*Had been considered in the credential to be used on demand (Boolean)*

Similar to the case of *credSubject*, it would have been possible to consider one credential per each role a person had, but due to the storage limitations all the roles were integrated into one credential with Boolean attributes for each role. Table 6.4 represents the design of this credential.

The relationship between the pupils and their guardians were modelled using *CredGuardian* (see Table 6.5) and *CredChild* (see Table 6.6). Each pupil received one or more *CredGuardian* containing the Pilot User Number of their parents/-guardians, and identically, each guardian would obtain one *CredChild* for each child who participated in the pilot as a pupil.

Table 6.5 Guardian Credential Structure

CredGuardian	
Attribute	*Comment*
Guardian	*Pilot User Number of one Guardian*

Table 6.6 Child Credential Structure

CredChild	
Attribute	*Comment*
Child	*Pilot User Number of one Child*

6.1.3.3 The concept of Restricted Area

The Community Interaction Platform used an abstract model called *Restricted Area* (RA) that provided the virtual environment for several types of activities. Restricted Areas were the functionality building blocks in the Community Interaction Platform and all the scenarios we describe in this chapter were conducted within the RAs.

Upon logging into the system the user would see a so-called *Dashboard* , essentially a personalised view of the existing RAs in the system, categorised into favourited areas, previously accessed areas, new conversations, etc. Every user in the pilot could initiate an RA and define access policies in order to restrict the participation to their desired target group. More specifically, the access policies were defined with the help of a Graphical User Interface (GUI) that offered the possibility to specify rules based on the attributes and the credentials that existed in the pilot. For example, a teacher could create an RA with "Chat" functionality to collect the opinions of the pupils about his teaching methods and limit the access to this chat room to participants of a specific class. In this case the pupils of that class could join the discussion and stay anonymous under an *Alias* (read more in Section 6.1.3.4) while the other students from the school were prohibited from entering this chat room.

6.1.3.4 Partial identity with "Alias"

The participants were provided the opportunity to choose how they wanted to appear in the system under different aliases. They could use the same alias to visit and post within multiple RAs in order to build a reputation based on their contributions. At the same time, they had the possibility to create another alias whenever they wanted, which made them unlinkable to all of their previous activities.

The aliases were human-readable, globally unique names in the system that were mapped to cryptographic pseudonym values behind the scenes. Therefore, nobody could impersonate another alias without having the smart card (the secret key) of the person who first picked the alias, as the mapping of the aliases and the cryptographic pseudonyms were stored on the server. Furthermore, binding the aliases to cryptographic pseudonyms made it possible to specify an alias in the access policies in order to address a specific person.

In addition to the user-selected alias names, every user received a *Default Alias* that was the full name of the user which was generated during the first login to the system. Consequently, the platform also supported the cases where the identification of users was desired so they could interact with the system using their real identity when the Default Alias was selected.

6.1.4 Security and Privacy Highlights

In summary, the School Community Interaction Platform supported a set of security and privacy features through its design, which made it different than any other existing platform. In this section, we will provide an overview of these features:

- *Strong authentication:* Employing hardware tokens improved the level of security in the authentication phase and relieved the burden of memorising usernames and passwords that are more easily compromised.

- *Unlinkable partial identities:* The platform allowed the users to appear in the activities using as many different identifiers (aliases) as they wished without having any linkage between them.
- *Resilience against identity theft:* As mentioned previously, the aliases were bound to cryptographic pseudonyms that were derived from the secret keys of the users. Therefore, without having the smart card, no one could take over an alias and impersonate another user.
- *Credential Binding:* All the credentials issued to a user were bound to the secret key of the user in order to prevent the user from credential pooling. Therefore, the credentials could not have been transferred or shared.
- *Privacy-respecting Access Control:* In order to access an RA, the users needed to disclose only the required information from their credentials and keep the other attribute values secret. Therefore, they could avoid over-identification towards both the system and the other participants, while assuring their eligibility to join the activity.
- *Accountability:* The School Community Interaction Platform was compliance with the requirement of the school concerning accountability and the capability of dealing with extraordinary situations where anonymity introduced a threat.

6.2 Deployment and Operation of the Pilot

6.2.1 The Deployment Architecture

In this section, we provide an overview of the deployment architecture in the Söderhamn pilot and briefly introduce its subsystems. One of the design goals was to let the users access the Community Interaction Platform using the school workstations as well as their private devices at home. Therefore, the distribution of the client machines were not bound to the school's internal network. Either way, the servers were hosted on the school premises to benefit from the existing secure infrastructure. Figure 6.2 depicts an overview of the components within the pilot deployment architecture.

6.2.1.1 ABC System

The reference implementation of the ABC4Trust project delivered the modules to support operations by each of the entities in the Privacy-ABCs' ecosystem. The so-called ABC System component representing these modules was integrated into the corresponding applications in the pilot either as libraries or via webservice wrappers. As demonstrated in Figure 6.2, the ABC System existed in every subsystem of the deployed architecture.

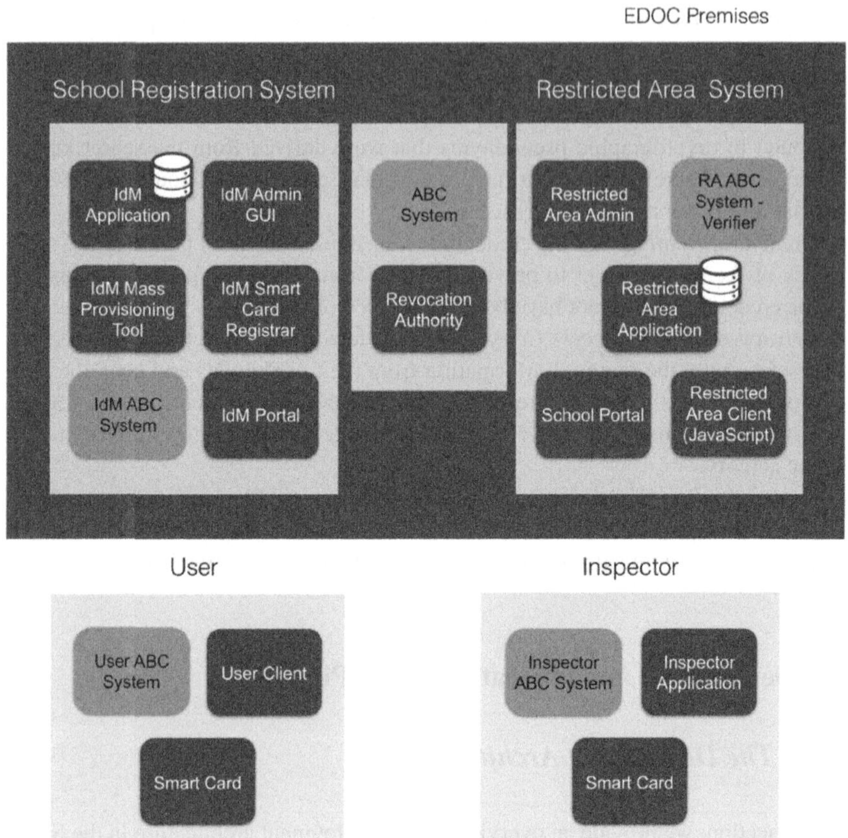

Fig. 6.2 Söderhamn pilot deployment architecture

6.2.1.2 School Registration System

The School Registration System performed as the Identity Service Provider in the pilot scenarios. It was responsible for the provisioning of the participants, managing their attributes and issuing credentials. The School Registration System also provided the administrators with tools that facilitated the initialization and roll-out processes. Most of the components were developed using Java and run in a Servlet container such as Apache Tomcat. Below, we briefly introduce the main components of the School Registration System:

IdM Application: The core of the Identity Manager (IdM) deployed in the Söderhamn pilot was the IdM Application. It provided the back-end database for storing users' profiles and additional information. The IdM Application was accessible via SAML from the other subsystems or via the front-end portal by the users.

IdM Portal: The front-end of the Identity Service Provider was called the IdM Portal. It essentially provided the user interface for the IdM Application. In order to access their profiles or obtain credentials, the users had to visit the IdM Portal.

IdM Smart Card Registrar: In the context of the pilot, the authorised smart cards had to be registered in the database before being distributed to the participants in order to stop the users from utilizing additional smart cards. The supplementary tool helped the administrators to extract scope-exclusive pseudonyms from the cards and store them in the database along with the smart card identifier and the cryptoengine type (Idemix or U-Prove) during the initialization process.

IdM Admin GUI: This was the administrative interface of the IdM that allowed the pilot administrators to manage the users' records and perform operations such as changing attribute values or requesting revocation of the credentials.

IdM Mass Provisioning Tool: In in order to speed up the user provisioning process, IdM Mass Provisioning Tool was developed to load the list of the users and their attributes from the input csv files and store them in the IdM database.

6.2.1.3 Restricted Area System

The actual functionalities of the School Community Platform were integrated within the Restricted Area System. It was a web-based application built using .NET Framework 4.0 and the C# programming language and deployed on a Windows 2008 Server. It used a Microsoft Internet Information Server (IIS) 7.5 as the web server to run the web application. More specifically, the Restricted Area System was comprised of:

School Portal: In a nutshell, the School Portal was the entry point to the pilot system. It guided the users as they found their way to different parts of the system such as the IdM Portal, the software download repository, the Restricted Area Application and the help materials.

Restricted Area Application: The RA Application is where the designed scenarios of the pilot were implemented. Once logged into the RA Application, the users saw the existing Restricted Areas created for various purposes such as counselling, document sharing, chat rooms, etc. The participants could act anonymously, under an *Alias* or use their real identities to interact with others. They also could create their own RAs and define the access policy for them or join activities in the existing RAs, if they could satisfy the corresponding policies.

Restricted Area Admin: The RA Admin was a web application with a deployment similar to the deployment of the School Portal, with its own separate URL to a server with an IIS 7.5 web server and ASP.NET installed. The RA Admin allowed for database manipulation (first name, last name, gender, age, class, role, etc.) to be made for testing. Since all attributes relating to the users were stored on the user's smart card as Privacy-ABCs, the RA Admin was utilized to enter default aliases (the real name of the user), create lists of aliases and append inappropriate words that were not possible to select as an alias.

Restricted Area Client: To enhance the user experience, the functionality of an *Alias Selector* and a *Dashboard* were developed. However, in order to avoid any privacy risk, these functions were implemented as JavaScript modules that ran locally in the users' browsers instead of on the server. Theoretically, these modules had to be part of the client-side deployment, as a malicious service provider would have had the freedom to perform privacy invasive operations in such a setting. But due to the fact that the client software of this pilot was developed as part of the ABC4Trust reference implementation, it could not cope with the pilot specific requirements alone and some extra implementation were needed.

- The Alias Selector handled the list of aliases owned by the user. It was designed to create new aliases, delete old ones, order existing aliases and switch between them. Alias information was stored on the user's smart card so that the server could not correlated them. When the Alias Selector had to be rendered, it contacted the ABC System installed on the client through the API of the browser plug-in provided by the reference implementation. After the list of aliases was retrieved, they were rendered as UI elements on the screen. Whenever an alias operation was performed, e.g. a switch between aliases, a presentation proof had to be performed towards the RA application in order to demonstrate the ownership of the alias.
- The Dashboard was the part of the client that allowed a user to see the Restricted Areas they had recently accessed or marked as favourites, as well as their private Restricted Areas. To avoid linkability, this had to be done in separate requests to the database for each alias. First, the Dashboard loaded alias IDs and made calls to the RA server to retrieve the list of Restricted Areas for the active alias and then the Restricted Areas were rendered on Dashboard as UI elements. Thus, the Dashboard created the dynamic type of output which let the user have a personalised start page view.

6.2.1.4 Revocation Authority

For various reasons, the validity of issued credentials might have to end prior the initial set time and, in general, it would often be necessary to be able to revoke credentials. For example, a user might lose control over their smart card, the role or attribute values of a user could have changed, a user was no longer part of the system, or a user had not followed certain rules associated with a credential. In any of these cases the authority (the school administration) that issued the credential was be able to revoke it in a way that did not interfere with the privacy properties of the

ABC technology. Revocation of credentials was performed by the school administrator using the IdM Admin GUI to select which user and which credential to revoke. The IdM Admin GUI sent the revocation handle of the credential to the revocation authority, which removed the revocation handle from the list of valid revocation handles and updated the non-revocation evidences for all users. When the school administrator used the IdM Admin GUI to change the value of one attribute, the IdM automatically performed a revocation of the corresponding credential containing the old attribute value. This ensured that any valid credential always contained the same attribute value as the IdM.

6.2.1.5 Identity Selector

The Identity Selector component provided by the reference implementation was used in the pilot to enable the users to manage their credentials and interact with the ABC System during the issuance and presentation sessions. On the one hand, the Identity Selector communicated with the Restricted Area System via the browser plug-in, and on the other hand, it called the API of the ABC System installed on the client machine. For example, when a user requested to enter a Restricted Area, it was the Identity Selector that popped up and guided the user through the steps of the protocol. The steps included the ability to view the different possible policies, select the preferred one, retrieve the cryptographic proof from ABC System and deliver it to the Restricted Area System.

6.2.1.6 Inspector Application

The inspection tokens were encrypted with the inspector's public key. They were retrieved from the database by the RA administrators and transferred to the Inspector. After receiving the decrypted reply from the application, the inspector forwarded the output to the Inspection Board.

6.2.2 Initialization and the Roll-out Process

The pilot administrators went through several steps in order to reach the state where they could deliver the smart cards to the pilot participants. Prior to the initialization of the cards, the following steps had to be taken:

- Defining the credential specifications
- Generating the system parameters (trusted groups, generators for commitments, pseudonyms, etc.)
- Generating the issuer parameters and the secret key for each of the issuers
- Generating Revocation Authority parameters

- Generating Inspector public and secret keys

When all the global parameters were fixed, the administrators initialized the smart cards for all the pilot participants and downloaded the configuration settings to the cards. The initialization process consisted of the following steps:

- Personalising the card by printing name, logotype, etc.
- Generating the user secret key on the smart card
- Retrieving the PIN and the PUK from the smart card
- Downloading either U-Prove or Idemix cryptographic parameters to the smart card.
- Requesting the card to generate a scope-exclusive pseudonym for the scope "`urn:soderhamn:registration`"
- Storing the scope-exclusive pseudonym along with the smart card ID and the cryptoengine type (Idemix vs U-Prove) in order to hinder the use of unauthorised smart cards in the pilot

In the first round of the pilot, when the cards were ready, the administrators distributed them randomly to the users along with the PIN and the PUK. To bootstrap the process of using the cards, the users received a One-Time Password (OTP) to access their records in the IdM Portal and obtain their credentials on the smart cards. Due to the large number of participants in the second round, nearly 400 total users, a decision was made that all of the relevant credentials would be loaded onto PIN protected smart cards before handing out the cards to the respective users. Following the initial use of the card and reader to login to their respective user default alias account, the user was able to create additional aliases and access areas where all of the access-protected information was located. The administrator also handed over the inspector's card to the responsible person. Finally, the client software packages needed to be configured with all the generated parameters before being delivered to the users.

6.2.3 Specification of the Key Use Cases

6.2.3.1 Smart Card Registration

This use-case mainly existed in the first round of the pilot, as the smart cards were personalised for the second round. Before being able to use the non-personalised smart cards, the users had to register their smart cards in the IdM Portal. All the smart cards initialized by the administrators were known to the system, so nobody could bring an extra smart card to the pilot and have double identity.

In this step, the users authenticated to the IdM Portal using their OTP. Then, they needed to prove the authenticity of their smart cards and link them to their profile records . The IdM had a list of scope-exclusive pseudonyms generated by the valid cards during the initialization phase for the scope string

```
1 <abc:PresentationPolicyAlternatives xmlns:abc="http://abc4trust.eu/wp2/abcschemav1.0" Version="1.0">
2  <abc:PresentationPolicy PolicyUID="urn:soderhamn:policies:loginPseudonym">
3   <abc:Message>
4     <abc:Nonce>some fresh nonce</abc:Nonce>
5   </abc:Message>
6   <abc:Pseudonym Exclusive="true" Scope="urn:soderhamn:registration"/>
7  </abc:PresentationPolicy>
8 </abc:PresentationPolicyAlternatives>
```

Fig. 6.3 Söderhamn Pilot - Presentation policy for smart card registration

`urn:soderhamn:registration`. The process required the user to present such a pseudonym. It was enforced by Line 6 of the presentation policy in Figure 6.3. If the pseudonym value existed in the records of the IdM and was not in use by another person, the IdM bound this smart card to the profile of the logged in user. After this step was completed, the users could use their smart cards to login to the IdM and later obtain their credentials.

6.2.3.2 Obtaining credentials

In the first round of the pilot, the participants had to obtain their credentials from the IdM Portal before being able to access the Schoool Community Interaction Platform. As the smart cards were personalised for the second round and ready to use, this step was not needed unless the credential had to be reissued. Once logged in to the IdM Portal, users could request to start the issuance protocol for every credential they were eligible for. The XML issuance policy of the school registration credential is provided in Figure 6.4. During the issuance phase, the issuer forced (Line 7) the user to present the same scope-exclusive pseudonym that was stored along with the user's record (scope string: `urn:soderhamn:registration`) in order to

```
1  <abc:IssuancePolicy Version="1.0" xmlns:abc="http://abc4trust.eu/wp2/abcschemav1.0">
2      <abc:PresentationPolicy PolicyUID="urn:soderhamn:policies:issuance">
3          <abc:Message>
4              <abc:FriendlyPolicyName lang="en">Policy: Authorized Users only</abc:FriendlyPolicyName>
5              <abc:FriendlyPolicyDescription lang="en">This policy will request the pupil to present the established
                       scope−exclusive Pseudonym with the scope "urn:soderhamn:registration".No Privacy ABCs are
                       required for this step.</abc:FriendlyPolicyDescription>
6          </abc:Message>
7          <abc:Pseudonym Exclusive="true" Scope="urn:soderhamn:registration" Established="false" Alias="#nym"/
               >
8      </abc:PresentationPolicy>
9      <abc:CredentialTemplate SameKeyBindingAs="#nym">
10         <abc:CredentialSpecUID>urn:soderhamn:credspec:credSchool</abc:CredentialSpecUID>
11         <abc:IssuerParametersUID>urn:soderhamn:issuer:credSchool</abc:IssuerParametersUID>
12     </abc:CredentialTemplate>
13 </abc:IssuancePolicy>
```

Fig. 6.4 Söderhamn Pilot - Presentation policy for obtaining school registration credential

ensure that the smart card in use belonged to the logged in user. Furthermore, the issued credential was bound to the same secret key as the one behind the presented pseudonym (Line 9).

6.2.3.3 Login to the Platform / Choose or Create an Alias

The users could choose to act anonymously or establish a partial identity. In the former case, users would have been assigned a temporary, one-time use, random alias that was usable only during that session, while in the latter case users could later claim the aliases again and resume their activities under that name. The aliases were globally unique in the system and bound to cryptographic pseudonyms. The users kept a list of their aliases (not the temporary ones) on their smart cards. Therefore, after they logged in to the platform, they were able to choose from the list of their previously created aliases or create a new one. The XML example in Figure 6.5 demonstrates the creation of a new alias and the relevant presentation policy. First, the system checked whether the given alias name was already taken or not. If the alias was free, the system requested the user (Line 6) to present a scope-exclusive pseudonym for the scope string`urn:soderhamn:alias:AliasID` (i.e. `urn:soderhamn:alias:superman`) in addition to the possession a valid school registration (Lines 7-16) credential for "Norrtullskolan" (Lines 17-19). The system then stored the provided pseudonym along with the alias name for future authentications. It is worth noting that when the users decided to use one of their previously established aliases, they had to present the same scope-exclusive pseudonym

```
1  <PresentationPolicyAlternatives Version="1.0" xmlns="http://abc4trust.eu/wp2/abcschemav1.0">
2    <PresentationPolicy PolicyUID="urn:soderhamn:policies:aliasAliasID">
3      <Message>
4        <Nonce>some fresh nonce</Nonce>
5      </Message>
6      <Pseudonym Exclusive="true" Scope="urn:soderhamn:alias:AliasID" />
7      <Credential Alias="#credSchool">
8        <CredentialSpecAlternatives>
9          <CredentialSpecUID>urn:soderhamn:credspec:credSchool</CredentialSpecUID>
10       </CredentialSpecAlternatives>
11       <IssuerAlternatives>
12         <IssuerParametersUID>urn:soderhamn:issuer:credSchool:idemix</IssuerParametersUID>
13         <IssuerParametersUID>urn:soderhamn:issuer:credSchool:uprove</IssuerParametersUID>
14       </IssuerAlternatives>
15     </Credential>
16     <AttributePredicate Function="urn:oasis:names:tc:xacml:1.0:function:string-equal">
17       <ConstantValue>Norrtullskolan</ConstantValue>
18       <Attribute CredentialAlias="#credSchool" AttributeType="urn:soderhamn:credspec:credSchool:schoolname"
             />
19     </AttributePredicate>
20   </PresentationPolicy>
21 </PresentationPolicyAlternatives>
```

Fig. 6.5 Söderhamn Pilot - Presentation policy for new alias creation

that was stored in the system when creating the alias. This presentation policy would look the same as the previous example.

6.2.3.4 Instantiate / Access a restricted area

When the users were logged in, they were able to create new RAs with their desired functionalities, i.e. discussion board, if they had an active alias (not anonymous). The users needed to specify the access policy of the new RA using the provided GUI. The interfaces made it possible to introduce various policy alternatives based on the credentials and attributes that existed in the system. The system then converted the defined policies into the XML format consumable by the client applications. Figure 6.6 shows a policy allowing "male" participants (Lines 21-24) to enter an inspectable RA. It means that the pupils had to deliver an encrypted version of their unique identifiers in the presentation token (Lines 14-19).

```
1  <PresentationPolicyAlternatives Version="1.0" xmlns="http://abc4trust.eu/wp2/abcschemav1.0">
2    <PresentationPolicy PolicyUID="urn:soderhamn:policies:area44p1">
3      <Message>
4        <Nonce>+SNFS6TGgmw=</Nonce>
5      </Message>
6      <Credential Alias="#credSchool">
7        <CredentialSpecAlternatives>
8          <CredentialSpecUID>urn:soderhamn:credspec:credSchool</CredentialSpecUID>
9        </CredentialSpecAlternatives>
10       <IssuerAlternatives>
11         <IssuerParametersUID>urn:soderhamn:issuer:credSchool:idemix</IssuerParametersUID>
12         <IssuerParametersUID>urn:soderhamn:issuer:credSchool:uprove</IssuerParametersUID>
13       </IssuerAlternatives>
14       <DisclosedAttribute AttributeType="urn:soderhamn:credspec:credSchool:civicRegistrationNumber">
15         <InspectorAlternatives>
16           <InspectorPublicKeyUID>urn:soderhamn:inspectorpk</InspectorPublicKeyUID>
17         </InspectorAlternatives>
18         <InspectionGrounds>Description of circumstances and process under which token may be inspected</
               InspectionGrounds>
19       </DisclosedAttribute>
20     </Credential>
21     <AttributePredicate Function="urn:oasis:names:tc:xacml:1.0:function:string-equal">
22       <ConstantValue>male</ConstantValue>
23       <Attribute CredentialAlias="credSchool" AttributeType="urn:soderhamn:credspec:credSchool:gender" />
24     </AttributePredicate>
25   </PresentationPolicy>
26 </PresentationPolicyAlternatives>
```

Fig. 6.6 Söderhamn Pilot - Presentation policy for accessing a Restricted Area

6.3 Evaluation of the School Pilot

6.3.1 Evaluation of the Deployment

The Söderhamn school pilot allowed for a successful demonstration of the strengths that underpin the Privacy-ABC technology. End users were introduced to a wide range of options for anonymously interacting within multiple communities for various purposes. This section evaluates the specific issues, experiences and outcomes within the ABC4Trust pilot deployment.

6.3.1.1 School Registration System

Over the course of the ABC4Trust project, it became clear that the School Registration System needed additional tools/applications in order to support the administrators of this system in their daily tasks. Due to the large number of participants, a tool for registering authorised smart cards (IdM Smart Card Registrar) and a tool for filling in the IdM Database (IdM Mass Provisioning Tool) were identified as being necessary enhancements even though they were not originally taken into account. Eventually, the IdM Admin GUI was added to the architecture enabling the administrators to modify attribute values of users during the second operational phase of the pilot.

6.3.1.2 Restricted Area Systems

The Restricted Area System added functionality to the pilot and provided the opportunity to demonstrate a real life application of the Privacy-ABC technologies. The RA System consisted of the School Portal, Restricted Area Application, Restricted Area Admin, RA ABC System Verifier and Restricted Area Client. The interfaces within all areas were user-friendly so that users with varying levels of computer experience could easily navigate their way through the system and perform the task(s) that they desired. A brief evaluation of the RA System's respective deployments are described below:

School Portal: The School Portal was filled with links to needed software such as the User Application Installer and the smart card reader installer. The School Portal was continuously updated with different types of user-friendly support materials for the users, such as: User Manuals, instructional videos, FAQs, inspection grounds document and links to the ABC4Trust official webpage.

Restricted Area Application: The Restricted Area Application was deployed on one of the virtual machines running on secured servers located within the school on the same sub network as the School Registration System and the Revocation Authority.

Table 6.7 Restricted Areas Created in the Second Round

Restricted Areas	Value for the 2 nd round	Description
Total Areas	115	Total number of Restricted Areas created by users, including Private Restricted Areas
Private Areas	40	Number of default RAs created automatically the first time a User signs in successfully using a default alias
Pupil Private Areas	29	Number of Restricted Areas created by pupils and/or guardians
Official Areas	29	Number of Restricted Areas created by school personnel using the default alias and marked as official for users
Counselling Areas	10	Number of Restricted Areas created for counselling sessions by request of the user
Private Chat Areas	7	Number of instances where the user requested one-to-one communication with another user by alias

Table 6.8 Aliases Used in the Second Round

User Aliases	Value for the 2 nd round
Default Aliases Available	381
Used Default Aliases	40
Anonymous Logins	62
Manually Created Aliases	108

Table 6.9 Content of the Restricted Areas in the Second Round

Participation Method	Value for the 2 nd round
Chat Messages	850
Wall Posts/ Document Uploads	52

Before the second round of the pilot the logging functionality of the User Application and the Restricted Area Application were significantly improved and debugging became more efficient. During operation of the second round the Restricted Area Application served the users well and no issues nor problems were documented.

Table 6.7 provides statistics about the many different Restricted Areas created either by the school or by other users (pupils and guardians) for different purposes with anonymity protection built-in for the second round of the pilot. It is worth noting that the only method that was in place for tracking the levels of participation with the RA was when a user posted something or created a new area. Users that logged in and browsed/lurked the areas were not counted as this was not built into the system.

All users were able to sign in to different RAs in a very secure manner to take advantage of the Privacy-ABC technologies, while maintaining the possibility to prove their gender, age, class, etc. When anonymity was desired, a user could choose to anonymously/pseudonymously sign in and participate in political discussion groups or counselling sessions without revealing any personal data. Table 6.8 represents the distribution of the various aliases accessed during the Pilot. Additional functionalities provided by the RA Application were the dashboard, search and browse functions for lists of Restricted Areas. Also, once inside a Restricted Area users could chat, upload files and leave messages on the wall (See Table 6.9).

Each RA was protected by one or several access policies that defined who may enter the RA and use its functionality (chat, wall, document sharing, political discussions, counselling, etc.) to see its content. To provide security and avoid linkability during anonymous sessions the dashboard made separate requests to the database for each alias. Additional layers of security within the structure included the issuance of session tokens and the use of the non-replayable https.

Restricted Area Admin: During the testing phase, all Privacy-ABC technologies were simulated and all test data (attributes) about the users were pre-loaded into the database using the RA Admin. During the 2nd round this was used to enter default aliases (the real name of the user) as well as to create a list of aliases and other inappropriate words that were not possible to select as an alias. The functionality of the RA Admin was continuously improved and tested during all phases of the pilot.

Restricted Area Verifier: The RA Verifier was deployed manually and configured to launch automatically on system start at the production server where all other Restricted Area System components resided. The old version of the RA ABC System that was emulating the Privacy-ABC technologies was replaced with a new version of the application that could verify Privacy-ABC presentation tokens. This allowed users to include specific pseudonyms in their presentation and issuance tokens in addition to the ability to authenticate themselves under previously established pseudonyms as well as prevent the possibility of users potentially hijacking the identity of another user.

The deployment of the RA Verifier in the ABC System in the Söderhamn pilot was different from the deployment in the Patras pilot in how the presentation policy alternatives were generated. The presentation policy alternatives, which in the Söderhamn pilot were based on the access policies associated with each Restricted Area, had to be generated dynamically. The reasoning behind this was that each Restricted Area was associated with one or more access policies, e.g. a RA for girls in class 9A would have had two different policies combined. Since those access policies could not be known in advance, the RA Application had to deal with this matter in a different way from what was the case in the Patras pilot. Thus, the Restricted Area Application had to be deployed so that it generated different presentation policy alternatives dynamically after retrieving the access policies that were applied to the Restricted Area.

Restricted Area Client: The Restricted Area Application hosted a JavaScript client that was executed locally in the user's browser to prevent transferring data from the user's computer and to avoid linkability between the different aliases/logins of the same user. Aliases were used as a mechanism to track returning users.

6.3.1.3 Revocation Authority

The Revocation Authority (RevAuth) of the Söderhamn pilot was a custom-developed web application installed on the target site. In order to speed up the installation, maps of the tasks of issuer parameter generation and RevAuth parameter generation went to the same team. In order to improve performance, revocation (the revocation handle) was removed from all credentials except for the main credential, *credSchool*. To make sure that revocation control could still take place, a default access policy was added to all Restricted Areas requiring the school name to be equal to "Nortullskolan". This access policy guaranteed that a revocation check was performed whenever a user was trying to login to any Restricted Area.

6.3.1.4 Inspector Application

The Inspector key was written to the Inspector's smart card using the Inspector Setup Tool before the smart card was handed over to the Inspector who, in the case of the Söderhamn pilot, was the schoolmaster. Should content be reported and confirmed for inspection by the School Inspection Board, a line would appear in the Inspector Wrapper and the Inspector would be able to inspect the targeted token to reveal the identity of the person who posted the content. The Inspect Tool and the Inspector Wrapper was deployed to the school Inspector's computer and the Inspector smart card was handed over with a pre-generated secret key on it so that the relevant information could be decrypted. No instances of inspection occurred during the Söderhamn pilot, however.

6.3.1.5 Smart cards and readers

Due to the large number of participants in the second round of the Söderhamn pilot a decision was made that credentials would be loaded onto their PIN protected smart cards before handing out the cards to the respective users, unlike the first round where the users were responsible for the download. This required more functionality to be added to the School Registration System. Finally, all users were provided the necessary tools so that they could easily browse the information that had been loaded onto their respective smart card, like the content of the credentials and aliases, while the secret key remained hidden and could not be manipulated.

The teachers were the first group to receive their smart cards and card readers at the school in order to have time to become familiar with the RA System and to prepare some Restricted Areas to be used by the pupils. The pupils were the next group to receive their smart cards, PIN/PUK codes and smart card readers. The last group to receive their cards were the guardians via the pupils taking them home to give to their parents. The guardians received their PIN/PUK codes within a letter sent directly to their home addresses. This entire distribution process was completed within 2 weeks. PIN Codes were able to be changed by the user as long as their PUK was successfully verified.

Even though there was a limit in the card's memory space where the aliases were stored, there were no reported problems from any users regarding the lack of space on the card. Also, during the first and the second rounds of the pilot the smart cards worked without any failure reports. The only reports that came from the users during the operation phase were related to problems such as resetting of the PIN code and other functions not classified as failures of the smart cards.

6.3.1.6 Legal grounds

The Swedish Personal Data Act was applicable since Norrtullskolan was located in Sweden and the data was also collected in Sweden and upon completion of the pilot all collected personal data was deleted. Additional legal agreements were in place between partner institutions and the local authorities. Finally, since the major target group of the pilot constituted minors, consent forms had to be signed by the minors' legal guardians prior to their participation within the pilot.

6.3.2 Evaluation of User Experience

6.3.2.1 Second round questionnaire

After the second round of the school pilot, each participant was asked to complete an evaluation questionnaire. This questionnaire functioned as a complement to the statistics of the communication system. This section will refer to the numbered questions of the questionnaire and provide a brief overview of the main results relevant to the evaluation of the pilot. The complete questionnaire can be found in the annex A, A.3 of deliverable D6.3 of the ABC4Trust project. Altogether, 91 persons completed the questionnaire, with a gender ratio of 55% male participants to 45% female participants. Of the whole participants group, 69% were pupils of the school, 19% were their legal guardians, and 12% were teachers.

Since the majority of the participants (71%) were minors, the questionnaire handed out was carefully drafted to meet their cognitive capabilities. This included a simple phrasing of questions with a limited amount of twenty questions. Moreover, taking the complexity of the ABC technology and the correlating concepts of privacy, anonymity and pseudonymity into account, these subjects were partially addressed in a rather general way to avoid overburdening the pupils. The questionnaire consisted of two parts, where the first part focused on questions directly relating to the Privacy-ABC system used in the pilot, while the second part addressed the users' general conceptual understanding of Privacy-ABCs. The first part of the questionnaire addressed several aspects of the Privacy-ABC that participants were given the opportunity to try. Some questions focused on the functionalities of the system and their utilisation, while other questions addressed system transparency and usability. Another set of questions addressed how understandable the system was for the users. Finally, some questions relating to the users' trust in the system and the general acceptance of Privacy-ABCs were integrated into the first part.

To establish a statistical foundation for future Privacy-ABC research work and for other developers implementing ABC technologies, the responses to the first group of questions provided some information about which functionalities provided in the pilot system were actually used and at what frequency. The opportunity of using several aliases depending on desired context is a core privacy protecting feature of the Privacy-ABC technology. Thereby, the questionnaire revealed that 53% of the users used more than one alias with the provided Privacy-ABC system, while 47% used the default alias only (see results of Q1 of the questionnaire). However, the statistics indicate that the participants who took advantage of this option used it quite frequently. While 40 default aliases were used (which is the real name of the participant), 108 further aliases were created. More specifically, users interacted under anonymous aliases a total of 62 times. As for those using only the default, the results showed that 31% of the participants were teachers or parents mainly using the PC capacities provided in the school. It can be assumed that these participants felt no need to operate under a different alias than their real name. Moreover, the concept of being able to use a system under different aliases was new and unknown to participants. Given the short time of the pilot, it can be assumed that getting accustomed to such possibilities required more time. It can be concluded that in future cases of development and implementation focused on similar systems, a stronger focus on advertising the system's functionalities and opportunities is advisable, for example by a pop-up window offering the usage of different aliases.

Fifty-five percent of the participants said they had interacted in inspectable areas, but only 35% were undoubtedly aware of it at the time (see results of Q6 + Q7). These Restricted Areas were inspectable due to strict legal responsibilities and oversight obligations of the school for its pupils. The main exception was the Restricted Area for political discussions. However, all chat rooms within the pilot system were inspectable and also used by nearly two thirds (69%) of the participants (Q9). Drawing from the fact that 69% of the overall number of participants were pupils, it can be presumed that nearly each pupil entered a chat room at least once. So the deployment of Restricted Areas for a specifically pre-defined group of people (and providing wall, share, and chat functions) can be considered a considerable success, which is underlined by the fact that 40% of the participants did not only enter a Restricted Area with limited access for a certain group but even created such an RA on their own (Q11). With relation to data protection aspects, this indicates that the users had the clear intention of limiting the access to content they posted. This awareness also became apparent through the fact that 26% of the participants checked which data was stored about them on their smart card (Q4). This is in fact a very considerable result, since a proactive check of their own data stored is not a common user behaviour. The browser plugin tool also offered a simplified procedure to realise the participant's right to access.

Regarding the transparency and usability addressed within the questionnaire, a focus was laid on crucial elements necessary for privacy enhancing technologies such as Privacy-ABCs. Since transparency means the comprehension of all privacy-relevant aspects of the data processing, including the legal, technical and organisational conditions setting the scope for this processing, it is closely connected to

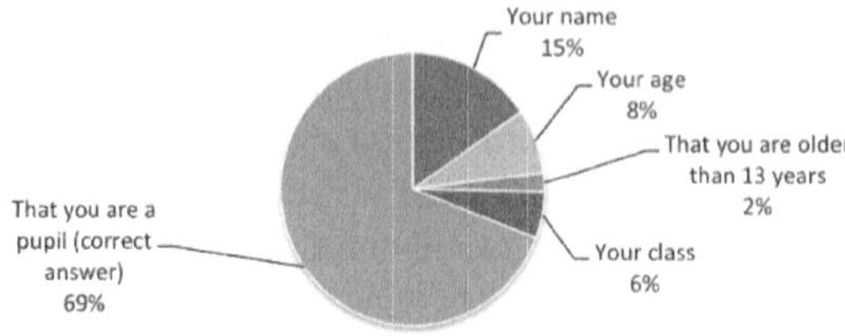

Fig. 6.7 Distribution of the answers to *Q3. Which information about yourself is disclosed in this presentation token?*

the usability of the system. Only users fully understanding their interactions with the provided Privacy-ABC systems can effectively determine the individual benefits and disadvantages of disclosing their own personal information. This applies all the more for a system based on Privacy-ABC technologies which aims at achieving minimal information disclosure based merely on necessity.

To achieve and foster transparency for the users, a new feature was implemented showing the current alias in the top right corner of the User Interface. This led to an enhanced awareness by the users, to the satisfactory result of 96% of the participants, using several aliases and thereby always being aware of their currently chosen alias (Q2). However, regarding system functionality transparency, there is still be room for improvement in future realisation of similar Privacy-ABC deployment settings. For example, 65% of the participants were aware of the fact that they were interacting in an inspectable area (Q7). Even though its execution is allowed only under specific pre-defined conditions, inspection is a feature which potentially enables the revelation of the user's identity. This makes it even more important to implement better and more comprehensive and prominent transparency features within such Privacy-ABC systems in future.

Going beyond the transparency issue, it is also necessary that the users are able to understand the concepts of the Privacy-ABC technology and the advantages it offers to them. Therefore, the questionnaire included two questions that addressed two core features of the ABC-system. These were the presentation token request (Q3) and access to a Restricted Area in compliance with its access policy (Q5). The first question was accompanied with a screenshot from the live system, simulating the process of requesting a presentation token in the Identity Selector. Thereby, the system shows which attributes are going to be revealed in the requested token. With the help of the given screenshot, 69% of the participants chose the correct answer (see the results in Figure 6.7).

So seemingly, the majority of users understood what information was required of them to disclose for accessing the Restricted Area. Still, it would be desirable to receive less than respondents' 31% false answers. However, it is difficult to determine what led to this number since it demonstrates that nearly one third of the participants did not fully comprehend which information was required from them. Since the Identity Selector was a central part of the Privacy-ABC technology used in the pilot, this shows the need to explore different ways of user comprehension

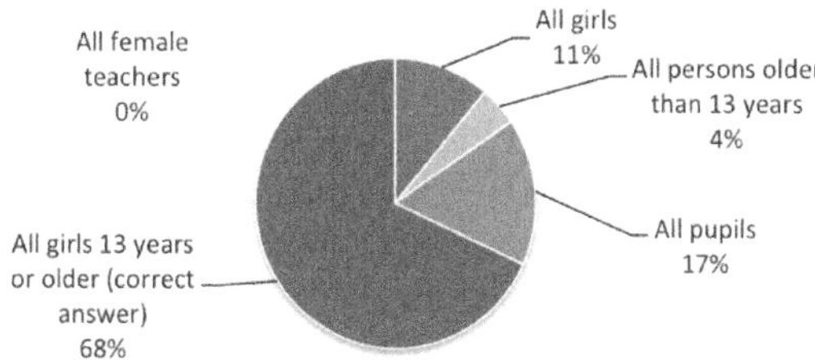

Fig. 6.8 Distribution of the answers to *Q5. Who is allowed to enter this Restricted Area?*

enhancement, e.g. by providing further information in the user interface or interactive tutorial features in future. The second question (Q5) was accompanied by a screenshot showing the access policy of a Restricted Area with limited access for a predefined group of all girls 13 years or older. Sixty-eight percent of the participants were able to determine who was allowed to access this Restricted Area with the help of this screenshot see the results in Figure 6.8).

Additionally, 15% of the other answers were at least half-correct by selecting a partially correct answer (either just "all girls", or "all persons older than 13 years"). Since a comprehensive perception of access policies correlates directly with being able to enter certain areas, this underscores the need for even more effort to support adequate dissemination user information for improved conceptual understanding.

A number of questions (Q8, Q10, Q12, Q13, and Q14) in the first part of the questionnaire were focused on the users trust in and acceptance of the ABC technology. Q8 revealed 79% of the participants who used inspectable areas felt safer because of the fact that this sphere of interaction was inspectable and they appreciated the knowledge of possible assistance and/or oversight if the need arose. This encompasses general trust in the school and its system administrator on the basis of the predefined inspection conditions as communicated to the users prior to the beginning of the pilot. However, this result is also owed to the increased need of oversight over a group of minors, so it may be possible that in different Privacy-ABC deployment settings, e. g. with participants being older or equipped with different national backgrounds, the acceptance of the inspection feature might be lower, depending on the privacy concerns of the involved user group. Q10 addressed the trust in the technology itself, with 96% of the participant respondents who entered a chat room with limited access for a certain group being confident that the access restriction worked. This unambiguous result shows that the majority of the users believed in the system working without fault.

Similarly, follow-up questions asked the users if they had ever tried to access a chat room they were not authorised for (Q12) and if they succeeded (Q13). These two questions were meant to explore the participant's attempts to test the system. They also had the side effect of elevating user trust since the participants were triggered to reflect over their failed attempts of accessing Restricted Area unauthorised.

The final question of the questionnaire's first part (Q14) derived insight regarding the general acceptance of the login possibility with the help of Privacy-ABCs compared to classical logins with password/username. Overall, 56% of the respondents stated they would prefer a login with the ABC system while 28% were undecided and 16% rejected the idea of using Privacy-ABCs for login activity. Taking into account the short time of the pilot and its factual, organisational and legal limitations, it could not adequately demonstrate the full range of opportunities Privacy-ABCs can provide. Nonetheless, it appears likely that under improved circumstances, the majority of the undecided users could still be convinced of the benefits of a Privacy-ABC system.

6.3.2.2 User Acceptance of Privacy-ABCs

Understanding why people accept or reject a certain information technology solution is an interesting field of research in information systems. Investigations started by understanding how the user's beliefs and attitudes on the importance of the provided technology impact the final use. These attitudes and beliefs could also be influenced by other external and less determinant factors.

Different user acceptance models of technology have been proposed in the last decade most of which originate from theories in sociology and psychology. Out of all, the Technology Acceptance Model (TAM) proposed by [Dav85] maintains a major dominance in the information science society. The TAM was built based on a sociocognitive theory called the Theory of Reasoned Action (TRA). The TRA suggests that a person's behaviour is determined by their intention to perform the behaviour and that this intention is, in turn, a function of their attitude toward the behaviour and their subjective norm. Intention, often regarded as the best predictor for behaviour, is the cognitive representation of a person's readiness to perform a given behaviour. The theory posits that a person's attitude towards behaviour consists of a belief that particular behaviour leads to a certain outcome and an evaluation of the outcome of that behaviour. If the outcome seems beneficial to the individual they may then intend to or even actually do this behaviour.

The TAM, as an information systems theory concept based on the TRA, tries to model how users come to accept and use a technology. The model suggests that when users are presented with a new technology, a number of factors influence their decision about how and when they will use it. In what follows, we will present the determinant factors affecting technology acceptance of Privacy-ABCs that were incorporated into the final questionnaire distributed to the pupils participating in the Söderhamn pilot.

Summary of Concepts

We utilized the basic concepts of the TAM for analysing how the intention to use was influenced by other factors such as usability, trust, and perception of anonymity. We used six constructs to help us understand the acceptance of Privacy-ABC based School Community Interaction Platform by the pupils. The constructs included Perceived Usefulness for Privacy Protection, Perceived Ease of Use, Perceived

Anonymity, Privacy-ABCs Trustworthiness, Subjective Norm, and Behavioural Intention to Use.

Before explaining the acceptance constructs separately, we analysed the correlations among themselves. We found out that most of the concepts were significantly correlated. For example: there was a high correlation between Trust and Perceived Anonymity which goes inline with the assumption that the pupils who trust the system will perceive better feeling of anonymity. However, we observed that Subjective Norm and Perceived Ease of Use were less correlated. The pupils actually found the School Community Interaction Platform easy to use, however, the weak correlation between Subjective Norm and Perceived Ease of Use could be due to the fact that the perception of pupils about the system's easiness was not influenced by their peers or elders.

Table 6.10 Correlations of the Perceived Anonymity *(PA)*, Perceived Ease of Use *(PEU)*, Perceived Usefulness *(PU)*, Subjective Norm *(SN)*, Trust *(Tr)*, and Intention to Use *(ItU)*.

	PA	*PEU*	*PU*	*SN*	*Tr*	*ItU*
PA	1	-	-	-	-	-
PEU	0,7072	1	-	-	-	-
PU	0,7406	0,9257	1	-	-	-
SN	0,6117	0,4901	0,5676	1	-	-
Tr	0,9508	0,7593	0,7947	0,6373	1	-
I*tU*	0,8948	0,7646	0,7995	0,6733	0,9642	1

Perceived usefulness for privacy protection

The perceived usefulness scale was originally constructed by [DBW89] with 14 scale items that were ultimately narrowed down to four items. The last four scale items were adapted to evaluate the perceived usefulness of Privacy-ABCs as privacy enhancing tools. The items were used to analyse the extent to which the pilot participants believed that the Privacy-ABC system would be useful in enhancing their privacy during their participation in the Privacy-ABC based school communication for different purposes, such as anonymous private chat. After evaluating the questionnaire, it turned out that most participants found the system useful for protecting their privacy while using the Restricted Area chat rooms (mean=3.373 σ=1.03 on a 5-point Lickert scale).

Perceived ease of use

The perceived ease of use scale has also gone through similar model maturity as that of perceived usefulness scale since it first appeared in [DBW89]. This concept is defined as the degree to which the technology (information technology system) is regarded as easy to understand and operate without having to exert extra efforts to learn from the user. The perceived ease of use of the system has an impact on the final technology adoption phase. In addition, it has been noted in technology acceptance research that perceived ease of use has direct and indirect effects towards behavioural intention. The learnability and simplicity to use the Privacy-ABC system was, therefore, analysed by adapting the constructs from the last scales in [DBW89]. The empirical results showed that most participants (m=3.27, σ=1.03 on a 5-point Lickert scale) found the system easy to use.

Perceived anonymity

At the core of ABC4Trust project is the provision of anonymity to the pupils when using the school online communication to exchange information such as chats, discussion rooms, counselling sessions and documents sharing. Absolute user anonymity in online services can easily lead to fraud. Whether users should be allowed to stay anonymous online and to what degree of anonymity is even debatable as mentioned in the works in [KBK13]. Nonetheless, researcher has been undertaken to provide anonymity in integration with accountability. Privacy-ABCs, therefore, provides a balance of anonymity for honest users and accountability for misbehaving users through a feature called Inspection. Whenever a pupil has a problem, be it physical, psychological, mental, financial, etc., they can anonymously discuss it with a counsellor or the school nurse. While pupils can feel assured that their anonymity is well protected, the counsellor can make sure that the user is indeed a pupil of the school and entitled to access the service.

The inclusion of the perceived anonymity concept to our user study allowed us to empirically evaluate the sense of anonymity the pupils perceived while communicating in the Restricted Area and other features of the system. The feeling of a sense anonymity helped pupils to be more willing to talk about the real issues they encountered, which they would otherwise feel reluctant, shy or scared to talk about if using their real identities.

Understanding how anonymity was perceived by the participants, and how they felt about it was a vital issue that affected the final adoption of a privacy enhancing technology such as Privacy-ABC system. We adapted scales from [BB05] to measure the strength of the psychometric feeling of anonymity of the pupils during Restricted Area chat. The statistical analysis shows that most of the pupils (mean = 3.59, σ = 0.0966) strongly felt a sense of anonymity and the feeling that Privacy-ABC system was able to protect their anonymity when they used the Restricted Area.

Privacy-ABCs trustworthiness

Trust, commonly defined as an individuals willingness to depend on another party because of the characteristics of the other party as defined in [RSBC98], plays an important role in further adoption of technologies. It also plays a central role in helping information technology users overcome perceptions of risk and insecurity by making them comfortable sharing personal information and interacting with the system. In our case, how much the pupils trusted the Privacy-ABC system was primarily investigated by incorporating trust measurement psychometric scales adapted from scales in [Pav03]. The analysis demonstrated that a majority of the pupils (mean=3.68, σ = 0.879 on a 5-point Lickert scale) believed that the Privacy-ABC system was trustworthy.

Subjective Norm

Subjective Norm (SN) as defined in [Ajz91] is an individual's perception of whether people important to the individual think the behaviour should be performed or not. In its purest essence, subjective norm is a kind of peer pressure. Whether or not a person participates or intends to participate in any behaviour is influenced strongly by the people around them. People are also inclined (or not inclined) to participate in a behaviour based upon their desire to comply with others. The contribution of the opinion of any given referent is weighted by the motivation that an individual has to comply with the wishes of that referent. Thus, it is a concept that looks at the influence of people in one's social environment on their behavioural intentions.

In our scenario, the beliefs of the pupils, weighted by the importance they attributed to the opinions of the teachers, school principal, parents and peers would be influenced by the behavioural intention to use the Privacy-ABC system. Accordingly, we found out that the pupils were influenced by the people around them to a considerable degree (mean = 3.04, $\sigma = 0.909$) of accepting the privacy enhanced school communication system.

Behavioural intention to use

The behavioural intention to use is the other psychological construct mainly utilized to estimate if the users would like to continue using the system. It was first posited by Davis as a construct mainly affected by the determinant concepts of perceived usefulness and perceived ease of use. Behavioural intention to use also mediates the perceived usefulness and actual system use. As the pupils perceived the Privacy-ABC system to be useful, this consequently influenced their behavioural intention to use the system. Further their perceived ease of use influences perceived usefulness leading to behavioural intention to use and ultimately led to actual system usage.

We adapted the last TAM scales to measure if the pupils would like to continue the using the Privacy-ABC system if it were to continue in the school. The empirical analysis showed that many of the pupils (mean = 3.27, σ= 1.04) would like to continue using the Privacy-ABC system in the future.

6.3.3 Conclusion

This pilot successfully offered a privacy-respecting social platform, Restricted Areas, to the pupils so that they could have a flexible means of not only communicating with each other, but with key adults who had an interest in their education and lives. By utilizing the Privacy-ABC technologies, the users of the Söderhamn pilot remained in full control of what level of personal information they disclosed, if any at all, to whomever and whenever. In hindsight, we can see that the users were able to utilize the Restricted Area Application in the way it was intended to be used with teachers creating Restricted Areas and defining access policies while the pupils and their guardians could enter defined Restricted Areas and post and receive messages and documents, etc.

On the whole, the users had a good level of understanding and appreciated the overall concept of the Privacy-ABC technology. At the conclusion of the pilot, as a part of the pilot's evaluation, we introduced twenty methodological survey questions to determine how the pupils reacted to the importance of the Privacy-ABC system in enhancing their privacy. A well-established model called the Technology Acceptance Model (TAM) was used as a basis to build the questionnaire concepts. The overall statistical analysis revealed that the pupils understood and trusted the system to improve their privacy when performing different activities such as anonymous chatting with other peers, parents or school teachers. Other measurement concepts also showed that many pupils would use the system if it were to continue operating.

The technological considerations were many, however all of the processes in place allowed for a relatively smooth implementation, deployment and operation within all the areas we had intended to address. This does not mean that there were not any bumps in the road along the way, but that the processes in place for isolation and debugging allowed for quick turnaround for solutions. The Söderhamn Pilot rigorously and successfully tested and improved the technologies into an overall solid system. A successful commercial version of these technologies in the future would require enhancements to be made with regard to the overall performance. While these technologies were successful within the contained scenarios of the test pilots, how these privacy-preserving tools can be implemented in a more multifaceted situation may not be as straightforward. Assuming the implementation of this technology will be complex and specific to each installation, the solutions will likewise be unique and without specific directions. Additionally it will require service providers to rethink the way they give access and identify their customers, while the users need to be informed about what personal information they are sharing and whether inspection is on or off for a particular service/section.

References

[Ajz91] Icek Ajzen. The theory of planned behavior. *Organizational behavior and human decision processes*, 50(2):179–211, 1991.

[BB05] Anick Bosmans and Hans Baumgartner. Goal-Relevant Emotional Information: When Extraneous Affect Leads to Persuasion and When It Does Not. *Journal of Consumer Research*, pages 424–434, 2005.

[Dav85] Fred D Davis. *A technology acceptance model for empirically testing new end-user information systems: Theory and results*. PhD thesis, Massachusetts Institute of Technology, 1985.

[DBW89] Fred D Davis, Richard P Bagozzi, and Paul R Warshaw. User acceptance of computer technology: a comparison of two theoretical models. *Management science*, 35(8):982–1003, 1989.

[Fin13] Olle Findahl. Swedes and the Internet. `https://www.iis.se/docs/Swedes_and_the_internet-2013.pdf`, 2013.

[KBK13] Ruogu Kang, Stephanie Brown, and Sara Kiesler. Why do people seek anonymity on the internet?: informing policy and design. *In Proceedings of the SIGCHI Conference on Human Factors in Computing Systems*, pages 2657–2666, 2013.

[Pav03] Paul A Pavlou. Consumer acceptance of electronic commerce: integrating trust and risk with the technology acceptance model. *International journal of electronic commerce*, 50(2),:101–134, 2003.

[RSBC98] Denise M Rousseau, Sim B Sitkin, Ronald S Burt, and Colin Camerer. Not so different after all: a cross-discipline view of trust. *Academy of Management Review*, 23:393–404, 1998.

Chapter 7
Course Evaluation in Higher Education: the Patras Pilot of ABC4Trust

Yannis Stamatiou, Zinaida Benenson, Anna Girard, Ioannis Krontiris, Vasiliki Liagkou, Apostolos Pyrgelis, and Welderufael Tesfay

Abstract In this chapter we describe one of the pilots of the ABC4Trust project that we developed in order to offer privacy-preserving course evaluations at universities. The distinctive feature of this application is that the pilot system can authenticate students, with respect to their eligibility to evaluate a course, without requiring from them any identifying information. Thus, it is impossible for the system to link participants with their evaluations and, therefore, participants' privacy is protected while the system is certain to receive evaluations only from eligible participants. In this chapter we describe the pilot context, the high level architecture of the pilot system as well as a questionnaire-based evaluation process for user acceptance. Along with a usability evaluation of the pilot prototype, we considered possible user acceptance factors for Privacy-ABCs and developed a novel model of user acceptance in a privacy critical setting.

This chapter describes one of the two pilots of the ABC4Trust project. The goal of the pilot was to implement a university course evaluation system using the Privacy-ABC technology that allows the students to participate in a privacy preserving, remote course evaluations at the University.

The objectives of the pilot were the following:

1. Develop a pilot system for supporting remote, privacy preserving course evaluations of university courses.

Yannis Stamatiou, Vasiliki Liagkou, and Apostolos Pyrgelis
Computer Technology Institute and Press "Diophantus", University Campus of Patras, Greece, e-mail: stamatiu@ceid.upatras.gr, liagkou@cti.gr, pyrgelis@ceid.upatras.gr

Zinaida Benenson and Anna Girard
Friedrich-Alexander-University Erlangen-Nuremberg, Germany, e-mail: {zinaida.benenson, anna.girard}@fau.de

Ioannis Krontiris and Welderufael Tesfay
Goethe University Frankfurt, Germany, e-mail: welderufael.tesfay@m-chair.de

K. Rannenberg et al. (eds.), *Attribute-based Credentials for Trust*,
DOI 10.1007/978-3-319-14439-9_7

2. Provide feedback to the partners developing the Privacy-ABC technology and the Privacy-ABC reference implementation.
3. Evaluate usability of the developed prototype and investigate user acceptance factors for the Privacy-ABC technology.

The pilot addressed the special challenge that for the results of an evaluation process to be as fair and impartial as possible, the participants should not be forced to reveal identifying information to the evaluation system. However, at the same time, the system should be in position to verify that the user that contacts it is *eligible* to participate in the evaluation process. The Privacy-ABC technology was able to handle these important requirements by guaranteeing than no information is sent to the course evaluation system which can later be used to identify the students. At the same time, it was ensured that only eligible students could access the course evaluation questionnaire and submit their evaluation.

To satisfy these requirements, each participating student was given a smart card on which credentials based on the Privacy-ABC technology were stored, issued by the University Registration System. These credentials were used by the students at the end of the semester to prove, without submitting any identifying information, the required eligibility criteria, i.e. that they are students of the university, they are registered to the course under evaluation and have attended the course sufficiently many times (above a preset threshold). With respect to the last eligibility criterion the students used their smart cards in order to collect attendance credits throughout the semester by waving their cards in front of a contactless smart card reader installed in the lecture room under the lecturer's supervision.

This chapter gives the salient information behind the pilot set-up and operation as well as a brief account on the acceptance of Privacy-ABCs by the students. In Section 7.1 we describe the pilot use case and scenarios as well as how it was organized and conducted. In Section 7.2 we discuss the deployment of the pilot system and some implementation related information. Furthermore, in Section 7.3 we present the usability and user acceptance results and develop an innovative user acceptance model for Privacy-ABCs. Finally, we summarize our work and findings in Section 7.4.

For more detailed information the reader is directed to Deliverables D5.1 (pilot scenario definition, see [BGL+12]), D7.1 (pilot application description, see [ALP+12]), D7.2 (pilot system deployment and operation, see [DGG+12]), and D7.3 (user acceptance results, see [DEK+14]).

7.1 Application Description

Course and instructor evaluations have become standard practice in most higher education institute. Most commonly, at least in Greece, they are conducted in the lecture room where the course takes place with paper based questionnaires that the students fill in *anonymously*.

The course evaluations in each department are performed by the members of the internal evaluation committee, which is composed by a number (usually four) instructors of the department. The evaluations are organized and monitored by the Quality Assurance Unit of the university. This unit designs and analyzes the questionnaires that are handed to students in order to evaluate courses and instructors.

The internal evaluation committee decides on the courses and lecture dates at which one of their members will conduct the evaluation. The assigned committee member goes in the lecture room (usually before the lecture starts or during the break) and explains to the students the evaluation process, in the presence of the instructor. Then three strudents are selected from the audience which will help with the process. Then the committee member gives the questionnaires to the three students, who will distribute them to the students after the committee member and the instructor leave the lecture room.

After the completion of the questionnaires, the three students enclose the questionnaires in a sealed envelope, signed by all of them, which they hand over to the internal evaluation committee member who is waiting, with the instructor of the course, outside the lecture room. Then the questionnaire is delivered, still sealed, to the Quality Assurance Unit of the university for further processing and analysis of results.

The process described above is followed by all university departments in Greece. However, conducting evaluations that require the physical presence of the students within the lecture room in order to fill in paper based questionnaires has a number of disadvantages. An obvious privacy violation is that the course instructor knows, exactly, who has participated in the evaluation. If there are few students in the lecture room and the instructor receives negative evaluations, then the instructor knows the students who gave these evaluations. Then, students may see, inadvertently or purposely, the evaluations of each other. Moreover, due to the anonymity requirement, it is not possible to prevent outsiders from participation, i.e. non-students or students who are not registered to the course under evaluation. This is not fair for the instructor and, in addition, "contaminates" the evaluation results. Finally, it may be possible that some students who participate in the evaluation have not, actually, attended the lectures sufficiently many times (they may, actually, have never seen the instructor before) to be able to give a fair opinion.

One way to handle these privacy and fairness issues with the added value of fast electronic archiving and processing of the evaluation results, is to offer to the students the possibility of evaluating the course remotely, from their computers. In doing so, however, we should ensure that the students stay anonymous but they are still partially authenticated by the evaluation system as eligible to evaluate the course. Thus, the pilot system verified, before giving access to the evaluation questionnaire, that the user (1) is, actually, enrolled at the university, (2) is registered to the course, and (3) has attended the lectures sufficiently many times to be able to give a fair and impartial opinion.

7.1.1 The Basic Requirements and Functionalities of the Pilot

The pilot was conducted in two consecutive rounds. The division of the pilot into two rounds helped reduce the complexity and difficulties in its realization. Moreover, it assured that the second round took advantage of the experiences from the first round while it, also, included a number of important advanced features and functionalities that would be difficult to introduce in the first round.

In what follows, we state the basic requirements and features of the first and the second round of the pilot:

1. The pilot participants need to be equipped with smart cards, as the hardware tokens for the storage of their secret keys and credentials, as well as smart card readers.
2. Use of smart cards to obtain or present credentials must be protected by a PIN.
3. Except from the secret keys, which remain inaccessible, the users must be provided with tools to browse the information stored on their smart cards.
4. The users must be able to change the PIN of their smart cards.
5. Upon continuous use of the smart card during a session, the PIN must be cached to improve the usability.
6. Personal Unlock Key (PUK) is needed to avoid losing control of the smart cards in case the PIN is forgotten.
7. User-friendly administrative and user interfaces are required in the system as well as fast response times.
8. Log files must be generated by the reference implementation libraries, which will provide input for debugging sessions.
9. The users must not be able to share or exchange their credentials.
10. Combining attributes from different credentials in the same presentation token must be possible.
11. It must be possible to request users to include specific pseudonyms in their presentation and issuance tokens.
12. Users should be able to authenticate under previously established pseudonyms.
13. All processing of personal data requires a legal ground. Such a legal ground may be stipulated by the applicable national law. Further grounds for lawful data processing can be e.g. consent or contract.
14. In an anonymous session, the Privacy-ABC presentation token must be unlinkable to the credentials' issuance.
15. A mechanism to identify a returning user in a specific context (scope) must be in place.
16. Personal data stored in the system must be deleted once it is not needed anymore (e.g. when the pilot is over). For this, a data retention period and a deletion process must be defined prior to the processing. Furthermore, if smart cards are given back, the data stored on them must be erased as well.
17. The system should allow secure authentication and the issuance and presentation processes must be resilient against replay attacks. Therefore the credentials,

Privacy-ABC presentation and issuance tokens must be resilient against unauthorized manipulation.

18. (Second round) A mechanism to revoke the credentials must be in place (*credentials revocation* feature).
19. (Second round) During the issuance of new credentials, these can contain attributes from credentials already owned by the user without the credentials Issuer knowing the value of these attributes (*carry-over attribute* feature).
20. (Second round) It is possible to issue credentials with inspectable attributes, i.e. attributes which can be revealed by an authorized entity (*attribute inspection* feature) called *Inspector*.

Both rounds of the pilot took place at the Computer Engineering and Informatics Department of the University of Patras in Greece (CEID). This is one of the most highly esteemed departments related to computer science in Greece. It is located very near to CTI's premises in the city of Patras.

All the participating students of the first and the second round of Student Pilot used the Privacy-ABCs for the evaluation of the "Distributed Systems I" course. This course is a non-compulsory course that takes place at the 7th semester and the number of students that attended it was approximately 60 in both pilot rounds.

The first round was run with the first version of the reference implementation, while the second round (which began on the 15th of October 2013) tested an enhanced version with additional functionality. All the students were able to access the pilot systems at any time from their homes, as well as (if necessary) from a specific personal computer located at CTI's premises which was equipped with smart card readers and the User Client Application.

The second round of the Student Pilot started in the first month of the fall semester of 2013 targeting again the evaluation of the course "Distributed Systems I", whose final examination was scheduled for the 15th of January 2014. The second round of Student Pilot took place between 15th of October 2013 and February 2014. However, the Second Round of the Course Evaluation Pilot included some additional features (listed from 18 to 20 above). For the second round of Student Pilot a group of 45 students took part in the evaluation. All the participating students could evaluate the course by using both the Idemix and U-Prove technologies.

All of the 45 participating students had in their possession a MultOS smart card, which was compatible with Idemix and U-Prove technologies and they were able to take sequentially the following actions in order to evaluate the course in a way that both ensures the credibility of results and preserves the privacy of the students expressing their opinion:

1. They could register their smart card.
2. After this registration step, the students were able to obtain their credentials from the University Registration System.
3. All the students collected their attendance information at each lecture upon entering the lecture room.

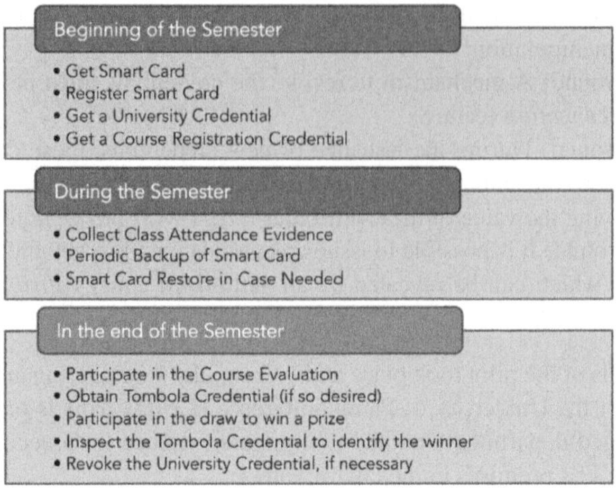

Fig. 7.1 The steps that the students followed during the semester.

4. Each student could make a backup of her attendance information as well as restore the backed up data on a new smart card (e.g. in the case of smart card loss).
5. In order to submit their course evaluation they had to prove that: i) they are indeed students of the department offering the course, ii) they are registered to the course under evaluation, and iii) they have attended a sufficient number of lectures.
6. (Second round) After the evaluation step, the students could obtain (if they wished) a tombola credential in order to participate in a tombola game. Also, after the whole process was over, the students' credentials were revoked. This use-case was based on the features 18 to 20 in the requirements lists above.

The steps that the students followed during the semester are shown in Figure 7.1 and in Figure 7.2 we can see the credentials obtained by the students. The little keys in the credentials figure signifies that the credentials are key-bound.

7.1.2 Advanced Features and Functionalities

For the second round of the pilot, we enhanced the scenarios that were used in the first one in order to demonstrate a set of advanced functionalities and features of Privacy-ABCs. Thus, during the second round a number of additional modules, entities and use-cases were introduced to demonstrate and test the advanced features of Privacy-ABCs, i.e. revocation, carry-over attributes, and inspection.

The first feature that we introduced was the capability of revocation of the University credential. This feature is required in the cases where a student leaves the

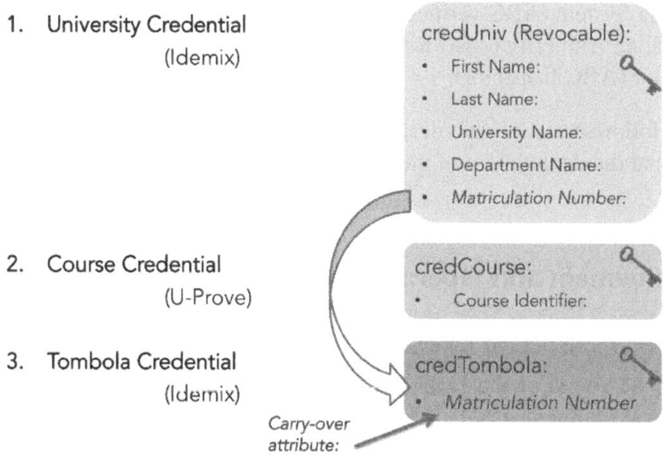

Fig. 7.2 The credentials obtained by the students

University or loses her smart card. A CTI administrator had the authority to revoke a student's University credential using the University Registration System.

With respect to the Course Evaluation System, we made two basic modifications. First, in order to log in the Course Evaluation System, the student was required to possess a non-revoked University credential and a Course credential. He was, additionally, required to present a scope-exclusive pseudonym for the scope "*urn:patras:evaluation*", bound to the same secret key as the University credential. Moreover, after submitting the course evaluation, the student was engaged in an "issuance with carry-over" protocol. During use of this protocol, the student had to prove possession of the scope-exclusive pseudonym that he had previously sent to the Course Evaluation System, upon which her matriculation number was carried over (blindly) from her University credential to a newly issued Tombola credential. In this way, the students' anonymity towards the Course Evaluation System was preserved.

After obtaining the Tombola credential, the students accessed the Tombola System in order to register for the contest. The Tombola System requested from the students to use their Tombola credential and embed their matriculation number verifiably encrypted (with the Inspector's public key), into the presentation token. When the Tombola ended, the winning presentation token was communicated to the Inspector who decrypted the matriculation number out of it, announcing the winner.

In summary, the entities that were involved in the second round of the pilot and their corresponding ABC roles were the following (see Section 7.2 for more details):

- University Registration System (ABC Issuer & verifier).
- Class Attendance System (No ABC role).
- Course Evaluation System (ABC verifier & ABC Issuer).
- Students (ABC user).

- Tombola System (ABC verifier).
- Revocation Authority (ABC Revocation Authority).
- Inspector (ABC Inspector).

In the followin section, we describe in more detail the architectural elements of the pilot and the deployment of the entities listed above.

7.2 Deployment and Operation of the Pilot

In this section we provide a high level description of the systems that were deployed in the second round of the University pilot. In Figure 7.3 we show the sequence in which the components of the pilot were accessed by the student participants, following the steps that were defined in the pilot use cases. Figure 7.4 provides an overview of the pilot system architecture as it was, actually, deployed to facilitate the pilot run.

In the sections that follow, we describe the functionality and the characteristics of each pilotl component that is shown on the high level architecture figure.

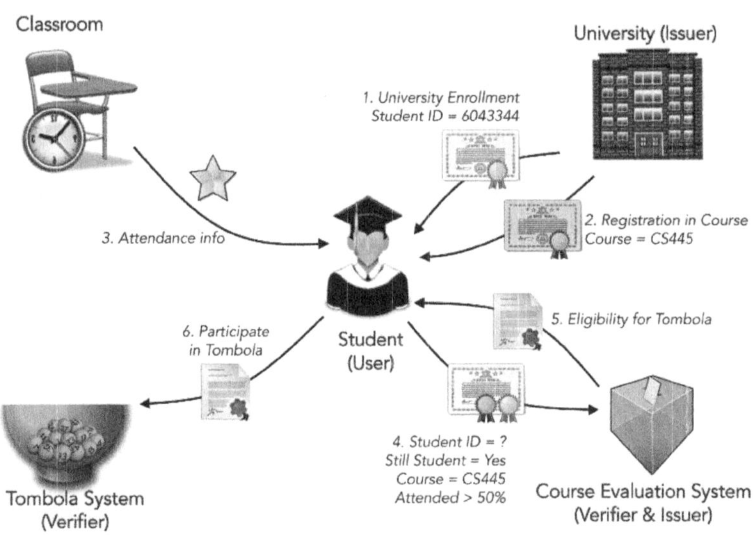

Fig. 7.3 Information flow for the student activities

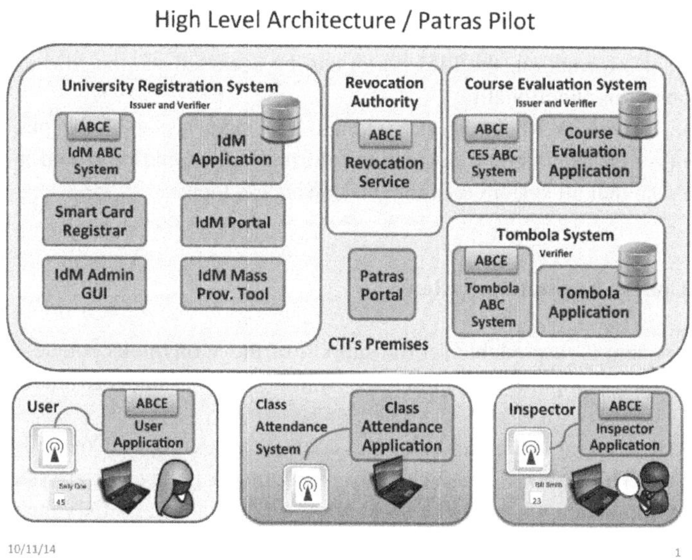

Fig. 7.4 The architecture diagram of Patras Pilot

7.2.1 The Deployment Architecture

7.2.1.1 University Registration System

The University Registration System is mainly used for issuing Privacy-ABCs to the users of the system. Its main sub-components are the Privacy-ABC System, the IdM (Identity Management) Application, and the IdM portal. The IdM application is a web application whose users are students and administrators.

In particular, through the University Registration System the following functionalities are offered:

1. The administrator can insert into the database of the University Registration System the personal information of the participating students.
2. The administrator can register the smart cards that were distributed to the students.
3. The administrator can issue a request to the revocation authority in order to revoke a student credential. This may be necessary when, for instance, a student graduates from the university or upon the student's request (e.g. due to smart card loss).
4. Students can collect their Privacy-ABCs certifying that they are students of the university as well as registered to the course under evaluation.
5. Students can browse their personal information that is stored in the IdM database.

When the IdM application is required to issue Privacy-ABCs to users invokes the ABC System which performs the issuance protocols. When a user needs to browse her personal information, the IdM portal can be accessed via the IdM application that supports this functionality.

As the University Registration System is the main issuer of the pilot, its parameters (system parameters, revocation information) should be stored in a public repository, so that all system components can access them.

7.2.1.2 Course Evaluation System

This component is responsible for the support of the anonymous course evaluation process. Its sub-components are the ABC System and the Course Evaluation Application.

The ABC System is a component that controls access to the Course Evaluation Application. This control is achieved by presenting a policy to the system users. Only users (students) who own the appropriate credentials that satisfy the policy are allowed to access the Course Evaluation Application and fill in the course evaluation questionnaires. The system, thus, acts as a verifier. After the student has submitted the questionnaire, the system asks her if she wishes to participate in the Tombola draw. If the student agrees, the system issues the Tombola credential using the carry-over mechanism of Privacy-ABCs. This mechanism was employed in order to issue the Tombola credential to contain the students' matriculation number taken from her University credential without being revealed. After obtaining the Tombola credential on her card, the student is directed to the Tombola system to register for the draw.

The other component of the course evaluation system is the Course Evaluation Application. This is a web application that implements the requirements of the course evaluation procedure set by the university. Users of this application are the students, the university lecturers and the university evaluation committee.

In particular:

- Course lecturers or the university evaluation committee can upload questionnaires for the courses under evaluation.
- Students are able to evaluate courses, anonymously, after proving their eligibility using their Privacy-ABCs.
- When the evaluation period has ended, the evaluation results can be electronically archived and subjected to automatic analysis in order to produce useful evaluation results about the courses and the lecturers.

7.2.1.3 Class Attendance System

The Class Attendance System is a system that is located in the lecture room of the course under evaluation and is responsible for giving lecture attendance credits to the participating students. More specifically, when a student comes into the lecture room, waves her smart card near a contactless smart card reader in order to obtain one attendance unit (actually, a counter in the smart card is incremented). These units will be used, later, in order to satisfy the policy of the course evaluation system along with the university and course credentials.

The Class Attendance System consists of a laptop and a contactless smart card reader attached to it. The reader is able to communicate with the contactless smart cards that the students have with them when they enter the lecture room. The Class Attendance System is brought into the lecture room 15 minutes before the start of the lecture and taken out 15 minutes before the end of the lecture. The laptop was supervised, during the lecture, by the lecturer.

The Class Attendance Application needed to be configured prior to each course lecture with the course identifier and the lecture identifier. This configuration was set by CTI engineers.

7.2.1.4 Revocation Authority

In certain cases, a student's credential needs to be revoked. As an example, when a student has lost her smart card, there is the danger of another student that found the card to impersonate the original card owner. In this case, the student must declare her smart card loss to the University Registration Office. The University Registration System Administrator, then, must revoke the student's University credential and delete the student's private information from the ABC system. Then she can get a new envelope (containing PIN, PUK) and a smart card and obtain, again, her credentials. As a second example, when a student graduates, the University Registration Office should revoke her credentials. The University Registration System Administrator revokes the student University credential and deletes the student's personal information from the ABC system

The Revocation Authority is the entity responsible for revoking Privacy-ABCs. The revocation authority has contractual and technical relationship with the Issuer (University Registration System), to know about invalid (and valid) credentials. The Revocation Authority publishes its revocation parameters, which contain information about where the verifier (Course Evaluation System) can check about the latest revocation information and what mechanism to use for this. Revocation information is a set of certified data about the revoked credentials published by the Revocation Authority, which the verifier uses to check that a certain presentation token presented by a user is not produced by a revoked credential or a combination of them. Users also maintain some information about the validity of their credentials, known as non-revocation evidence, which they must update for every credential they possess and against every Revocation Authority listed for that credential.

7.2.1.5 Tombola System

The Tombola System is responsible for conducting an online raffle for the students that participate in the Patras pilot. The students can interact with this system and register for the Tombola, after they submit their evaluation for the pilot course and obtain the Tombola Credential from the Course Evaluation System.

The Tombola System consists of the Tombola Application and the Tombola ABC System. The Tombola Application simply presents to the student the rules of the draw as well as information about the prize and the draw deadline. The Tombola ABC system acts as a verifier. Its goal it to verify that the student has submitted the course evaluation questionnaire by checking that she has the Tombola credential.

7.2.1.6 Inspector

One of the most important functionalities added in the second round of the Student Pilot was the introduction of inspection. In inspection, the most important issues are the legal considerations regarding the implementation of this feature, which will be covered in the following subsections.

Inspection grounds

Inspection grounds can be defined as the reasons for revealing the real identity of a pseudonymous user by decrypting the inspectable presentation token which includes the identity cryptographically hidden. Consequently, during the inspection the request for inspection and the correlating scenario have to be reviewed in regards to their accordance with the inspection grounds. Different Privacy-ABCs systems will include different inspection grounds, since they have to be adapted to the relevant use-case. However, in most cases a common inspection ground will be a legally justified demand of a third party such as a law enforcement authority. Any additional grounds will be dependent on the purpose of the inspection in the relevant use case. The second round of the Student Pilot on the other hand is an example of a use case with a very limited scope for inspection. The only reason for including the inspection feature was to reveal the identity of a single person – the winner of the tombola. Consequently, the inspection ground for the Student Pilot was: "Inspection is permitted to identify the winner of a prize and if the prize cannot be awarded to this person for the identification of an alternate winner of the prize."

Besides identifying the winner of the tombola prize, there was no reason imaginable for CTI that would justify an inspection. Even the generic reason of a legally justified demand of a third party such as a law enforcement authority did not appear possible. While it was very unlikely that the evaluation was used as a criminal mean, it was not completely impossible. Nevertheless, even if law enforcement entities would have requested the identification of one or all participants, the inspection of the tombola tokens would have only revealed that a user evaluated the course and used her tombola token for the tombola. Inspection of the tombola token would not have revealed the content of the evaluation sent by a user. On top of that the scope-exclusive pseudonyms of the evaluation systems and the tombola system were not linkable and the course evaluation itself system did never obtain the matriculation number or any other linkable information from the students. Furthermore, the course evaluation system did not store any information about the students IP-addresses. Moreover, in the case that only a very limited number of students would have evaluated the course at all, the whole set of collected evaluation data would have been deleted from the course evaluation system. Consequently, the inspection itself would not have helped to identify a user beyond the inspection ground and seemed therefore useless for any official investigation.

However, since the inspection feature allows to identify the user and inspectable presentation tokens restrict users to pseudonymous interactions, instead of anonymous ones, the feature itself interferes with the right to privacy. Consequently, providing information to the user is of upmost importance. This information should include a detailed description of the inspection grounds, the procedure of inspection and whether additional parties will be involved as a safeguard against abuse of inspection. Nevertheless, the exact scope and how the information is provided to the users is dependent on the inspection grounds, because they determine how intensely the right to privacy is constrained.

The second round of the Student Pilot was a less complex case of inspection with a very limited inspection ground. Furthermore, the participation in the tombola was voluntarily and the utilisation of the inspectable presentation token provided the users only with an additional benefit – the chance of winning the tombola. Not using the token, however, did not result in any disadvantage, since the participation in the test pilot was still possible. Therefore it was sufficient to stipulate the sole reason for inspection in the consent form.

Description of Inspection process

As mentioned before, it is necessary to describe the process of the inspection to the users in addition to informing them about the specific inspection grounds. In the Patras case it made sense to indicate which system is having which type of information and how they interact with each other. In detail there were three phases which had to be elaborated on - starting at obtaining the information through the Course Evaluation System and ending with the inspection for the tombola. While these phases will be explained here all previous steps of the pilot such as initialization of cards or obtaining credentials etc. will not be discussed in this section:

1. Evaluation phase: Students use the university credential to verify their status as an enrolled student towards the system and provide the evaluation data in form of answers to the question provided about the quality of the lecture. The evaluation data is stored on the Course Evaluation System. To ensure that participants may resume the evaluation or change their replies until the end of the evaluation period the user can re-authenticate on basis of a scope exclusive pseudonym reliably proving that the same user interacts with the system. The scope for this purpose is “urn:patras:evaluation”. A check for the minimum participation is

done. If the size of the sample does not reach the size of the previously defined minimum anonymity set, it was foreseen that the evaluation data will be deleted. In this case, this particular lecture cannot be evaluated due to lack of data material. After finishing the evaluation, the users had the possibility to obtain a tombola credential for a voluntary participation in the Tombola.

2. Join Tombola: The user joins the tombola by providing proof of participation in the evaluation with her tombola credential. In addition, the inspectable part of the token provided containing the matriculation number is produced on basis of the university credential. To ensure that a user may only join the tombola once, a scope exclusive pseudonym is obtained allowing the re-identification of a user accessing the system more than once. The scope for this purpose is "urn:patras:tombola". Since the tombola credential is stored on the smart card and cannot be obtained after the course evaluation period is over, it may be possible to lose the smartcard after the end of the evaluation period and before using the tombola credential. In this case, it is not possible to regain the lost tombola credential since it is no longer issued by the course evaluation system. This risk was labelled as acceptable within the limited scope of this pilot.
3. Tombola execution:

    a. Once the timeline for joining the tombola is closed, the list of valid tokens is produced. Under supervision of one or more students, the winner is drawn. This may happen e.g. on basis of a numbered list with the hash-values of the tokens where a random number decides about the winner. The presentation policy of the Tombola System demands from the user to prove the possession of a scope-exclusive pseudonym for the scope "urn:patras:tombola". The Tombola system checks if the pseudonym has already been registered and if so the registration process is terminated.
    b. Inspection: The winning presentation token is submitted to the designated Inspector. For the second round of the pilot, a randomly selected student from within the class takes this role and proclaims the winner using a special Inspector smart card to decrypt the winner's matriculation number. In case the winner does not claim the prize within the previously defined timeframe, step 3 is repeated. Even students who are no longer a member of the university are eligible to win the price since the prize is not bound to still being a student at the university, but taking part in the course evaluation during the pilot runtime.
    c. Deletion of data: Once the prize has been awarded, the tokens submitted for the tombola are deleted as the sole purpose of the processing has been achieved.

7.2.1.7 User

The user has to install a software module on her computer in order to interact with her smart card using a smart card reader. The main sub-component of this module is an ABC System. This software module is triggered every time a user is required to provide data stored on her card and asks for her consent. The ABC System provides to the user an interface between the browser and her smart card. For this reason, it employs a software component called "User Client" that runs locally on her PC.

7.2.1.8 Patras Portal

This component is an information web portal. Through this portal, the users can be informed about the "Course Evaluation by Certified Students" pilot. Thus, the portal provides to the users the necessary links to the components of the system (e.g. University Registration System, Course Evaluation System) that are responsible for specific functionalities. Every time a user wants to interact with the system, her first action is to visit this portal and by following the instructions she can perform various pilot operations (e.g. register to a course, evaluate a course).

7.2.2 *Policy Specifications for the Main Use Cases*

In the following sections we provide the technical specifications of the policies for the various use case scenarios pertaining to the pilot that were presented in Section 7.1. We begin by describing the specification of smart card registration then we present the technical specification for obtaining credentials for the University/-Course registration and course evaluation. We also describe the details for obtaining and registering the Tombola credential.

7.2.2.1 Smart card registration

As a first step, the users authenticate to the IdM Portal using a One-Time Password (OTP). Then, they need to prove the authenticity of their smart card by presenting a pseudonym for the scope string `urn:patras:registration`. If the pseudonym value exists in the records of the IdM, the IdM will bind this smart card to the profile of the logged in user. After this step is completed, the users do not need their OTP anymore and can use their smart cards in order to login to the IdM. Figure 7.5 provides the presentation policy used in this scenario.

7.2.2.2 Obtain University and Course credentials

The pilot students need to obtain their University and Course credentials from the IdM Portal before being able to use the Course Evaluation System. When logged in to the IdM Portal, they can request to start the issuance protocol for every credential they are eligible for. In Figure 7.6, the XML issuance policy of the University cre-

```
<abc:PresentationPolicyAlternatives xmlns:abc="http://abc4trust.eu/wp2/abcschemav1.0" Version="1.0"
xmlns:xsi="http://www.w3.org/2001/XMLSchema-instance"
    xsi:schemaLocation="http://abc4trust.eu/wp2/abcschemav1.0 ../../../../../../../abc4trust-xml/src/main/resources/
        xsd/schema.xsd">
  <abc:PresentationPolicy PolicyUID="urn:patras:policies:loginPseudonym">
    <abc:Message>
      <abc:Nonce>bkQydHBQWDR4TUZzbXJKYUphdVM=</abc:Nonce>
    </abc:Message>
    <abc:Pseudonym Exclusive="true" Scope="urn:patras:registration"/>
  </abc:PresentationPolicy>
</abc:PresentationPolicyAlternatives>
```

Fig. 7.5 Patras Pilot - Presentation policy for smart card registration

```
<?xml version="1.0" encoding="UTF-8" standalone="yes"?>
<abc:IssuancePolicy Version="1.0" xmlns:abc="http://abc4trust.eu/wp2/abcschemav1.0"
xmlns:xsi="http://www.w3.org/2001/XMLSchema-instance"
    xsi:schemaLocation="http://abc4trust.eu/wp2/abcschemav1.0 ../../../../../../../abc4trust-xml/src/main/resources/
        xsd/schema.xsd">
  <abc:PresentationPolicy PolicyUID="urn:patras:policies:issuance:credUniv">
    <abc:Pseudonym Exclusive="true" Scope="urn:patras:registration" Established="true" Alias="#nym"/>
  </abc:PresentationPolicy>
  <abc:CredentialTemplate SameKeyBindingAs="#nym">
    <abc:CredentialSpecUID>urn:patras:credspec:credUniv</abc:CredentialSpecUID>
    <abc:IssuerParametersUID>urn:patras:issuer:credUniv</abc:IssuerParametersUID>
  </abc:CredentialTemplate>
</abc:IssuancePolicy>
```

Fig. 7.6 Patras Pilot - Presentation policy for obtaining university registration credential

dential is provided. During the issuance phase, the issuer forces the user to present the same scope-exclusive pseudonym that is stored along with the user's record (scope string: `urn:patras:registration`) in order to ensure that the smart card in use belongs to the logged in user.

7.2.2.3 Evaluating the course

In order to enter the Course Evaluation System the user has to prove that she has a valid University credential as well as a Course credential for the course that is under evaluation. Moreover, in order to perform consumption control (i.e. users feedback should not be counted more than once when computing the evaluation results) a pseudonym for the scope string `urn:patras:evaluation` is required. When logging into the Course Evaluation System the user gets access to a questionnaire for the course and is able to provide her feedback. The student will be able to fill in the uploaded questionnaire if she satisfies the following requirements:

- The student is a Patras University student (i.e. she possesses a Patras University Credential)
- The student is indeed registered to the course (i.e. she possesses the Course Credential)

```
<?xml version="1.0" encoding="UTF-8" standalone="yes"?>
<abc:PresentationPolicyAlternatives xmlns:abc="http://abc4trust.eu/wp2/abcschemav1.0" Version="1.0"
xmlns:xsi="http://www.w3.org/2001/XMLSchema-instance"
    xsi:schemaLocation="http://abc4trust.eu/wp2/abcschemav1.0 ../../../../../../../../abc4trust-xml/src/main/resources/xsd/schema.xsd">
  <abc:PresentationPolicy PolicyUID="urn:patras:policies:courseEvaluation">
    <abc:Message>
      <abc:Nonce>zlMigWDIJGDkmPLGPLlhsCQ=</abc:Nonce>
      <abc:FriendlyPolicyName lang="en">Log-in to Course Evaluation System</abc:FriendlyPolicyName>
      <abc:FriendlyPolicyDescription lang="en">This policy demands from the user to prove possession of a University and a Course credential.</abc:FriendlyPolicyDescription>
    </abc:Message>
    <abc:Pseudonym Exclusive="true" Scope="urn:patras:evaluation" SameKeyBindingAs="#credCourse"/>
    <abc:Credential Alias="#credCourse">
      <abc:CredentialSpecAlternatives>
        <abc:CredentialSpecUID>urn:patras:credspec:credCourse</abc:CredentialSpecUID>
      </abc:CredentialSpecAlternatives>
      <abc:IssuerAlternatives>
        <abc:IssuerParametersUID>urn:patras:issuer</abc:IssuerParametersUID>
        <abc:IssuerParametersUID>urn:patras:issuer:uprove</abc:IssuerParametersUID>
      </abc:IssuerAlternatives>
    </abc:Credential>
    <abc:Credential Alias="#credUniv" SameKeyBindingAs="#credCourse">
      <abc:CredentialSpecAlternatives>
        <abc:CredentialSpecUID>urn:patras:credspec:credUniv:revocable</abc:CredentialSpecUID>
      </abc:CredentialSpecAlternatives>
      <abc:IssuerAlternatives>
        <abc:IssuerParametersUID>urn:patras:issuer</abc:IssuerParametersUID>
        <abc:IssuerParametersUID>urn:patras:issuer:idemix</abc:IssuerParametersUID>
      </abc:IssuerAlternatives>
    </abc:Credential>
    </abc:PresentationPolicy>
 </abc:PresentationPolicyAlternatives>
```


Fig. 7.7 Patras Pilot - Presentation policy for accessing the Course Evaluation System

- The student has collected sufficient attendance credits during the semester (i.e. the counter value in her smart card is above a preset threshold value, meaning that she has attended the course lectures sufficiently many times to be able to give a fair evaluation)

These authentication requirements of this use case are described in the presentation policy of Figure 7.7, except the counter value requirements which is simply checked by the smart card software itself. When a student satisfies these requirements, the Course Evaluation System prompts her to fill in the evaluation form and stores the result of the *last* submitted course evaluation so that the student can change her evaluation any number of times she wishes. If the student does not satisfy all the above three policies, she will receive a notification and the evaluation process will be terminated.

7.2.2.4 Obtaining the Tombola credential

As soon as a student has submitted her evaluation for the course, she has the chance to get issued a credential (called Tombola credential) that allows her to participate

```
<?xml version="1.0" encoding="UTF-8" standalone="yes"?>
<abc:IssuancePolicy xmlns:abc="http://abc4trust.eu/wp2/abcschemav1.0" Version="1.0">
  <abc:PresentationPolicy PolicyUID="urn:patras:policies:issuance:credTombola">
    <abc:Message>
      <abc:FriendlyPolicyName lang="en">Issuance of Tombola Credential</abc:FriendlyPolicyName>
      <abc:FriendlyPolicyDescription lang="en">This policy will blindly carry over the matriculation number for
          users uninversity credential to the tombola credential</abc:FriendlyPolicyDescription>
    </abc:Message>
    <abc:Nonce>geWthPERTBSfdQDCPKtevPL=</abc:Nonce>
    <abc:Pseudonym Exclusive="true" Scope="urn:patras:evaluation" Alias="#nym">
          <abc:PseudonymValue>UDHlYk3VOuN5nYCnllUnguUINXOYdrxmUCvO/1QNARNbDpv/9
              KC3fRNbvX7i9PcpM38T0sTvjzDAyUrtm28AZsRIfQxyfqH7HI0+JA==</abc:PseudonymValue
              >
    </abc:Pseudonym>
    <abc:Credential Alias="#credUniv" SameKeyBindingAs="#nym">
      <abc:CredentialSpecAlternatives>
        <abc:CredentialSpecUID>urn:patras:credspec:credUniv</abc:CredentialSpecUID>
      </abc:CredentialSpecAlternatives>
      <abc:IssuerAlternatives>
        <abc:IssuerParametersUID>urn:patras:issuer:idemix</abc:IssuerParametersUID>
      </abc:IssuerAlternatives>
    </abc:Credential>
  </abc:PresentationPolicy>
  <abc:CredentialTemplate>
    <abc:CredentialSpecUID>urn:patras:credspec:credTombola</abc:CredentialSpecUID>
    <abc:IssuerParametersUID>urn:patras:issuer:idemix</abc:IssuerParametersUID>
     <abc:UnknownAttributes>
      <abc:CarriedOverAttribute TargetAttributeType="urn:patras:credspec:credTombola:matriculationnr">
        <abc:SourceCredentialInfo Alias="#credUniv" AttributeType="urn:patras:credspec:credUniv:
            matriculationnr"/>
      </abc:CarriedOverAttribute>
    </abc:UnknownAttributes>
  </abc:CredentialTemplate>
</abc:IssuancePolicy>
```

Fig. 7.8 Patras Pilot - Issuance policy for tombola credential

in an on-line Tombola game and have the chance to win a prize. The Tombola credential should contain the student's matriculation number as a means to identify the winner at the end of the Tombola. As the Course Evaluation System does not know the student's matriculation number, an advanced issuance protocol with carry-over attribute is used. More precisely, the matriculation number is "blindly" carried over from the student's University credential to the newly issued Tombola credential. Moreover, the presentation policy (shown in Figure 7.8) requests from the student to present that she possesses the scope exclusive pseudonym for scope `urn:patras:evaluation`, that she has logged-in with at the Course Evaluation System.

7.2.2.5 Registering at the Tombola

After the student has obtained her Tombola credential from the Course Evaluation System, she is able to register for the online Tombola game. The Tombola System requires from the users in its policy to present a pseudonym for the scope string `urn:patras:tombola` (again for consumption control) as well as prove that

```
<abc:PresentationPolicyAlternatives xmlns:abc="http://abc4trust.eu/wp2/abcschemav1.0" Version="1.0">
  <abc:PresentationPolicy PolicyUID="urn:patras:policies:Tombola">
    <abc:Message>
      <abc:Nonce>bkQydHBQWDR4TUZzbXJKYUphdVM=</abc:Nonce>
      <abc:FriendlyPolicyName lang="en">Presentation Policy for Tombola</abc:FriendlyPolicyName>
      <abc:FriendlyPolicyDescription lang="en">Register for the Tombola game – your matriculation number will
          be encrypted with the Inspector's public key</abc:FriendlyPolicyDescription>
    </abc:Message>
    <abc:Pseudonym Exclusive="true" Scope="urn:patras:tombola" SameKeyBindingAs="#credTombola"/>
      <abc:Credential Alias="#credTombola">
      <abc:CredentialSpecAlternatives>
        <abc:CredentialSpecUID>urn:patras:credspec:credTombola</abc:CredentialSpecUID>
      </abc:CredentialSpecAlternatives>
      <abc:IssuerAlternatives>
        <abc:IssuerParametersUID>urn:patras:issuer:credTombola</abc:IssuerParametersUID>
        <abc:IssuerParametersUID>urn:patras:issuer:idemix</abc:IssuerParametersUID>
      </abc:IssuerAlternatives>
          <abc:DisclosedAttribute AttributeType="urn:patras:credspec:credTombola:matriculationnr">
        <abc:InspectorAlternatives>
          <abc:InspectorPublicKeyUID>urn:patras:inspector:tombola</abc:InspectorPublicKeyUID>
        </abc:InspectorAlternatives>
        <abc:InspectionGrounds>
          Only the winner of the tombola will have his/her matriculation number revealed.
        </abc:InspectionGrounds>
      </abc:DisclosedAttribute>
    </abc:Credential>
  </abc:PresentationPolicy>
</abc:PresentationPolicyAlternatives>
  </abc:PresentationPolicy>
</abc:PresentationPolicyAlternatives>
```


Fig. 7.9 Patras Pilot - Presentation policy for participating in tombola

they own a Tombola credential. Moreover, it demands the user's matriculation number contained in the Tombola credential to be encrypted with the Inspector's public key. This way in the end of the Tombola, only the matriculation number of the winner will be known and the anonymity of the rest of the participants will be preserved. The presentation policy can be seen in Figure 7.9.

7.3 Evaluation of Usability and User Acceptance of Privacy-ABCs

User adoption of privacy-enhancing technologies poses an important open research question, as despite the continued research and development efforts, the privacy-enhancing technologies are still not widely used [SC09]. Therefore, along with providing a reference implementation and considering technical issues of Privacy-ABCs' deployment, the Patras Pilot aimed at gathering the subjective view of the users at the Privacy-ABC technology and at understanding the factors that lead to user adoption or rejection of Privacy-ABCs.

In this section, we present the results of a usability evaluation and also develop and test the first (to our knowledge) user acceptance model for Privacy-ABCs. We hope that the results of this research will facilitate a better understanding of user adoption of privacy-enhancing technologies in general.

Roadmap. This section is organized as follows. We first present our research questions in Section 7.3.1. Theoretical background, a research model for user acceptance factors and corresponding hypotheses are developed in Section 7.3.2. Next, we present theoretical background for some additional user acceptance factors in Section 7.3.3. The corresponding quantitative questionnaire and the demographic characteristics of the participants are described in Section 7.3.4. The following sections are dedicated to the results of our study: Section 7.3.5 presents usability evaluation results, Section 7.3.6 evaluates factors for the user acceptance of Privacy-ABCs, and finally Section 7.3.7 discusses the participants' understanding of Privacy-ABCs. We summarize the results in Section 7.3.8 and discuss limitations and future work in Section 7.3.9.

7.3.1 Research Questions: Usability and User Acceptance

The implementation of the Course Evaluation System using Privacy-ABCs and the setting up of the finally implemented system necessarily involved decisions concerning different aspects of the technology. The corresponding research question is formulated as follows:

- What can be learned from the user feedback about the key aspects of the design decisions and of the implementation of the pilot system?

Usability is defined as "the extent to which a product can be used by specified users to achieve specified goals with *effectiveness*, *efficiency* and *satisfaction* in a specified context of use" according to the ISO 9241-11 standard [ISO]. Usability can be measured objectively (for example, using the data from the system logs) or subjectively, which means asking the users about their impressions from the system usage. Here, we consider subjective usability. According to the above definition, usability evaluation of the Privacy-ABC System should answer the following research questions:

- *Effectiveness:* Do the participants think that the system enables them to reach their goal? In our case, the goal is to conduct course evaluations. For example, were all participants able to evaluate the course? Would they like to use the system for course evaluation in the future?
- *Efficiency:* Do the participants perceive the system usage as efficient? For example, was it possible to learn the system usage quickly? Is the usage perceived as too cumbersome or taking too much time?
- *Satisfaction:* Do the participants report that they are satisfied with the system usage? For example, is the user interface perceived as pleasant? Do users like the system?

Although subjective usability is a very important indicator of user adoption, some other factors may influence the intention to use the system in the future. In order to find these possible factors, we considered the following research questions:

- Which factors influence user acceptance of Privacy-ABCs?
- Can we combine these factors into a predictive model for user acceptance of Privacy-ABCs and other privacy-enhancing technologies?

In the next section we present conceptual development of a user acceptance model for Privacy-ABCs.

7.3.2 *Conceptual Development of a User Acceptance Model*

In this section, we gradually adapt the Technology Acceptance Model to the Privacy-ABC technology in Sections 7.3.2.1-7.3.2.3 and develop a model for user acceptance with the corresponding research hypotheses (Section 7.3.2.4).

7.3.2.1 Technology Acceptance Model

We decided to investigate user acceptance of Privacy-ABCs within the scope of the *Technology Acceptance Model (TAM)*, a successful predictive model for user acceptance of information technology [Dav93, VB08]. TAM was developed in the 1980-ties [Dav89] and extended and validated since for a wide range of technologies, from email and spreadsheet software to adoption of e-commerce [Pav03], online games [HL04] and ubiquitous computing [Spi08]. However, an extension of the TAM for the adoption of privacy-enhancing technologies is lacking so far.

The overall TAM framework is depicted in Figure 7.10. TAM considers *Perceived Ease of Use* and *Perceived Usefulness* of a technology as main factors in user adoption [Dav89, Dav93, VD00, VB08]. These two factors positively influence *Intention to Use* the technology, which in turn positively influences the actual

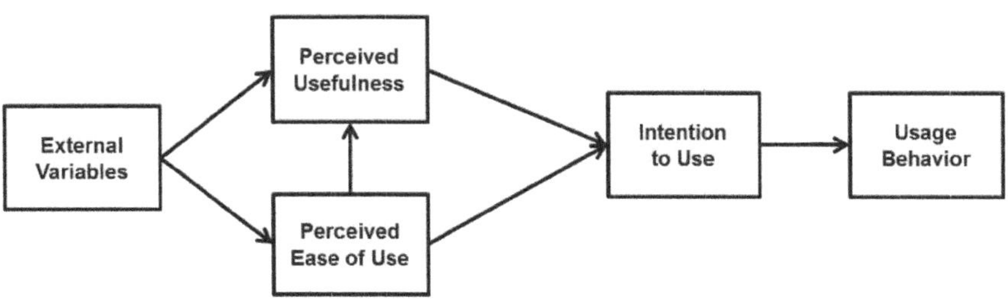

Fig. 7.10 The general framework of the Technology Acceptance Model

Usage Behavior.[1] Additionally, Perceived Ease of Use directly influences Perceived Usefulness.

The TAM factors are defined as follows:

- *Perceived Ease of Use* is "the degree to which a person believes that using a particular system would be free of effort" [Dav89][p. 320].
- *Perceived Usefulness* is "the degree to which a person believes that using a particular system would enhance his or her job performance" [Dav89][p. 320]. Depending on the system being evaluated, performance of tasks corresponding to the particular context is considered instead of job performance.
- *Intention to Use*, also called Behavioral Intention in the literature, refers to the "degree to which a person has formulated conscious plans" to use or not to use a specific technology [WD85][p. 214].
- *Usage Behavior* is the actually observed and measured usage, for example frequency and duration of the usage.

TAM research also considered external variables that may influence Perceived Usefulness and Perceived Ease of Use [VD00, VB08], such as characteristics of the system (e.g., relevance of the system for the task, perceived quality of system's results), individual differences between the users (e.g., age, gender, experience, computer proficiency) or characteristics of the user's environment (e.g., technical and managerial support, influence of other users).

We do not consider the above factors here, as we are primarily interested in the adaptation of the core TAM constructs to the new scenario of the Privacy-ABC technology. Nevertheless, we believe that the two following factors should be considered when investigating any security- or privacy-related technology: trust into the system and perceived risk of system usage.

7.3.2.2 Trust and Risk

Security- and privacy-sensitive scenarios usually involve perceived risk and trust as factors of user participation. User's assets (such as data, money or reputation) can be put at risk, and the decision to participate in such a scenario involves risk assessment and depends on the trust of the participant in other participating parties and in the underlying technology [Pav03, MCTC11]. *Perceived Risk* is defined as "subjective belief of suffering a loss in pursuit of a desired outcome" [Pav03][p. 77]. *Trust* in the context of the Privacy-ABC technology is defined as a belief that this technology "has the attributes necessary to perform as expected in a given situation in which negative consequences are possible" [MCTC11][p. 7].

To investigate the role of trust and risk in the user adoption of Privacy-ABCs, we decided to adapt the framework of Pavlou [Pav03] that integrates Trust and Per-

[1] The original TAM [Dav89, Dav93] also considered *Attitude Towards Using* the technology as a factor affecting Intention to Use. However, this factor was excluded from the model later [VD00, VB08].

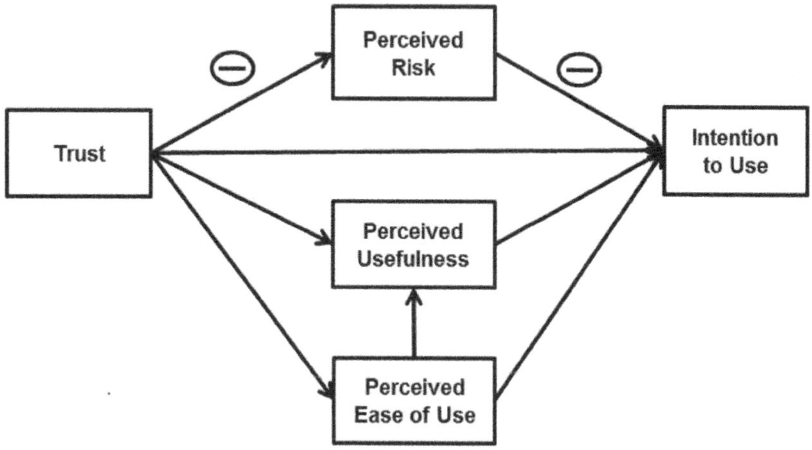

Fig. 7.11 Integration of Trust and Perceived Risk into the Technology Acceptance Model [Pav03]. Negative influence is labeled as (-), non-labeled arrows depict positive influence.

ceived Risk into the TAM in the context of online shopping, see Figure 7.11. According to this framework, Trust into the web retailer positively influences all three TAM variables: Perceived Usefulness, Perceived Ease of Use and Intention to Use. Moreover, there is a negative relationship between the Trust and the Perceived Risk associated with the web retailer: the more trustworthy a retailer is perceived to be, the less risky seems the purchase action. Perceived Risk is also considered to have a direct negative influence on the Intention to Use. Pavlou did not consider actual system usage in his framework. Similarly, actual usage behavior cannot be considered in the context of this pilot, as the trial participants will not have the opportunity to use the Privacy-ABC System in the near future.

7.3.2.3 Adapting the TAM: Perceived Usefulness for the Primary and for the Secondary Task

Whereas Perceived Ease of Use can be applied to each system without restrictions, the definition of Perceived Usefulness is not always directly applicable. Firstly, TAM was initially developed in the context of the introduction of new information systems at the workplace, hence the definition of Perceived Usefulness is usually adapted to the studied concepts when TAM is applied in other contexts, for example "the degree to which consumers believe that a particular technology will facilitate the transaction process" for online shopping [Pav03].

Secondly and most importantly, security- and privacy-enhancing technologies rarely serve *primary* user goals. That is, the primary goal of the user may be writing an article, preparing a presentation, communicating with peers or colleagues via email or social networks, exchanging files, making purchases or managing a banking account, whereas security- and privacy-enhancing tools such as anti-virus software, firewalls and anonymizers are expected to work in the background, protecting the user and thus facilitating the successful execution of the primary goal [WT99, CG05].

Interestingly, although some researchers examined TAM in security and privacy contexts, such as single sign-on [SPM+11], or privacy-enhancing technologies for RFID [Spi07], the "secondary goal" property has not been considered so far to our best knowledge. In the Patras Plilot, the primary goal of the participants was course evaluation, and the secondary goal was privacy protection during the course evaluation. Therefore, we define two types of Perceived Usefulness as factors of user acceptance:

- *Perceived Usefulness for Course Evaluation* is the degree to which a person believes that using the Privacy-ABC System for course evaluation is useful.
- *Perceived Usefulness for Privacy Protection* is the degree to which a person believes Privacy-ABCs to be useful for his/her privacy protection.

An interesting question is whether usefulness for privacy protection should be defined with respect to the course evaluation scenario. We decided against this option, because we think that the belief in the ability of a particular technology to protect one's privacy is independent from the particular scenario, as long as this scenario fits the purpose of the technology.

7.3.2.4 Acceptance of Privacy-ABCs: Hypotheses

According to the TAM framework with the integrated trust and perceived risk, we developed a set of hypotheses for user acceptance of Privacy-ABCs for the course evaluation. We note that the TAM framework is meant to be applied to concrete situations of the technology usage, such that we cannot apply it to the general adoption of Privacy-ABCs for other scenarios than course evaluation.

The main research model is depicted in Figure 7.12. We formulate the following hypotheses:

- H1: Perceived Usefulness for Course Evaluation is positively related to the Intention to Use Privacy-ABCs for Course Evaluation.
- H2: Perceived Usefulness for Privacy Protection is positively related to the Intention to Use Privacy-ABCs for Course Evaluation.
- H3: Perceived Ease of Use is positively related to the Intention to Use Privacy-ABCs for Course Evaluation.
- H4: Trust in the Privacy-ABC System is positively related to the Intention to Use Privacy-ABCs for Course Evaluation.
- H5: Perceived Risk is negatively related to the Intention to Use Privacy-ABCs for Course Evaluation.
- H6: Perceived Risk is negatively related to the Intention to Use Privacy-ABCs for Course Evaluation.

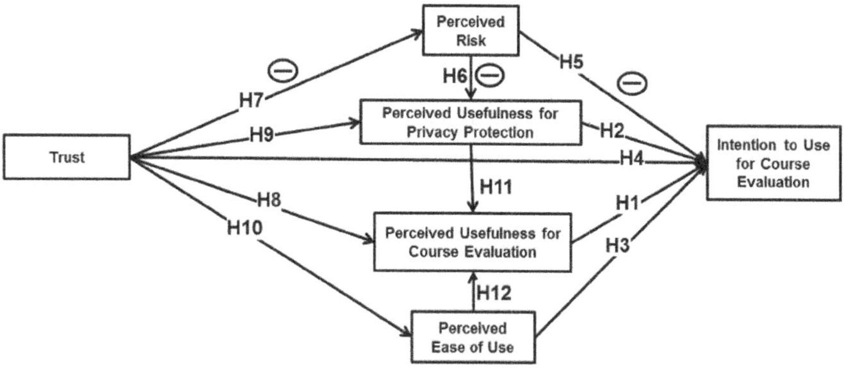

Fig. 7.12 Research model for user acceptance of Privacy-ABCs for course evaluation. Negative relations are labeled with (–).

- H7: Trust in the Privacy-ABC System is negatively related to Perceived Risk.
- H8: Trust in the Privacy-ABC System is positively related to Perceived Usefulness for Course Evaluation.
- H9: Trust in the Privacy-ABC System is positively related to Perceived Usefulness for Privacy Protection.
- H10: Trust in the Privacy-ABC System is positively related to Perceived Ease of Use.
- H11: Perceived Usefulness for Privacy Protection is positively related to Perceived Usefulness for Course Evaluation.
- H12: Perceived Ease of Use is positively related to Perceived Usefulness for Course Evaluation.

Apart from the TAM-specific factors of user acceptance, some other factors may be important according to the available literature and to our understanding of the nature of the Privacy-ABC technology. We present these factors in the next section.

7.3.3 *Additional Factors of User Acceptance*

In this section we consider some additional factors that may play a role in the user acceptance of Privacy-ABCs: Understanding of the Technology (Section 7.3.3.1), Perceived Anonymity (Section 7.3.3.2) and Situation Awareness (Section 7.3.3.3).

We reason why these factors might be important and show that there is not enough evidence from previous research for their integration into the TAM for Privacy-ABCs. Therefore, we conduct an exploratory study with the following research question:

What is the role of Understanding of the Technology, Perceived Anonymity and Situation Awareness in the user acceptance of the Privacy-ABC technology?

7.3.3.1 Understanding of the Technology

It is common knowledge that people do not have to understand exactly how a technology works in order to be able to use it. Much more important than the exact understanding is the development of a *mental model* of the technology that enables the user to use it correctly [WR11]. Mental models are representations of reality in people's minds, their conceptions about how things work. Right mental models of anonymous credentials seem to be especially difficult to convey [WAFH12].

Although the exact technical knowledge may not play an important role in user adoption of privacy- and security-enhancing technologies, users' *misunderstanding* of some key concepts may result in poor adoption. For example, Sun et al. [SPM+11] discovered that some users think that their login credentials are given to every participating party when they use single sign-on, which lead to (wrongly) perceived additional insecurity. Therefore, we investigate Understanding of Privacy-ABCs as a possible factor of user adoption.

7.3.3.2 Perceived Anonymity

In the framework of the Patras Pilot, the Privacy-ABC technology was used to provide anonymous (or, more exactly, pseudonymous) authentication for the Course Evaluation System. Therefore, users' perception of their anonymity should play an important role in the user acceptance. Although to our best knowledge there is no related work that investigates perceived anonymity for privacy-enhancing technologies, we rely in this argumentation on related research from the security area. For example, Sun et al. [SPM+11] in their investigation of the acceptance of single sign-on conclude that the perceived security protection seems to play an important role in user adoption, as it mitigates the perceived risk of the technology. Also Regal et al. [RBD+13] found that perceived security of the technology makes a difference in user acceptance of the ATM interactions via mobile phone.

As there is not enough evidence in the literature for the more precise connections of the Perceived Anonymity to the TAM variables, we consider it as a additional factor of user adoption.

7.3.3.3 Situation Awareness

Spiekermann [Spi08] investigates Perceived Control as one of possible factors that drive adoption of privacy-enhancing technologies for RFID. Perceived Control is defined as "extent to which an agent can intentionally produce desired outcomes and prevent undesired ones" [Spi08][p. 32]. She found only partial support for the hypothesis that Perceived Control plays an important role in user adoption, so the integration of this factor into the TAM is not clear and needs additional investigation.

We note that although the goal of the Privacy-ABC technology is to give the users more control over their personal data, the Patras Pilot did not give the students a possibility to exercise this control, apart from the choice to participate or not to participate in the trial. The reason for this is that all information that the students revealed about themselves during the pilot was determined in advance. Thus, we do not have the possibility to investigate Perceived Control as a factor of user adoption.

However, Spiekermann also describes a sub-category of Perceived Control that fits the Patras Pilot quite well. *Situation Awareness* is defined as "personal perception to be informed about what is going on" [Spi08][p. 134]. In connection with Privacy-ABCs, Situation Awareness includes knowing which information will be disclosed in order to get a credential, who receives the data, which data is stored on the smart card, etc. Hence, we consider Situation Awareness as a user acceptance factor for Privacy-ABCs.

7.3.4 Research Methodology

We developed a quantitative standardized questionnaire that the participants of the Patras Pilot filled in after the end of the pilot. In the first pilot round, a preliminary version of the questionnaire was developed and tested (the results are published in Benenson et al. [BGK$^+$14]). In the second round, a revised questionnaire was developed using the experience from the first round. In this section we present measurement scales that we used in the questionnaire (Section 7.3.4.1) and the demographic characteristics of the participants (Section 7.3.4.2).

7.3.4.1 Measurement scales

In social sciences, the complex latent constructs such as Perceived Usefulness or Situation Awareness are measured using so-called Likert scales [Lik32] consisting of several statements, called items. The users have to rate these statements using a rating scheme, for example using five rating possibilities from 1 = "strongly disagree" to 5 = "strongly agree". The development of the scales is a complex process, as the scales have to fulfill strict statistical criteria that are tested through the deployment of the scales in several adaptation cycles. Therefore, it is considered a good practice to use already existing scales that were extensively tested and are known to fulfill all relevant criteria. In case no scales are available, a common practice is to adapt a similar existing scale. In any case, the scales have to be tested against the statistical criteria in every deployment, as presented in the end of this section.

The constructs considered in this research were measured on a 5-point Likert scale ranging from "strongly disagree" to "strongly agree", see also Table 7.1. Perceived Ease of Use, Perceived Usefulness for Course Evaluation, Perceived Usefulness for Privacy Protection and Intention to Use for Course Evaluation closely follow the scales by Venkatesh et al. [VD00, VB08], whereas Trust and Perceived Risk are measured using a single item respectively, adapted from Pavlou [Pav03].

We do not employ subjective usability scales such as System Usability Scale (SUS) [Bro96], because we already measure Perceived Ease of Use which is sufficiently close to SUS [LUM13]. However, we separately ask about Ease of Learning, Error Recovery and Interface Usability following the concepts of the PET-USES questionnaire [WWK10] as well as the IBM Computer System Usability Questionnaire CSUQ [Lew95]. The questions from CSUQ concerning quality of help provided by the system were combined with the Helpfulness scale by McKnight et al. [MCTC11].

Table 7.1: Measurement Scales for the Adapted TAM, Additional User Acceptance Factors and Usability Aspects; All items are measured on a 5-point scale ranging from 1 = "strongly disagree" to 5 = "strongly agree"

Intention to Use for Course Evaluation (adapted from [VD00, VB08])
Assuming that the Privacy-ABC system is available for course evaluations, I intend to use it. I would use the Privacy-ABC system for course evaluations in the next semester if it is available. Given that the Privacy-ABC system is available for course evaluations, I would use it.
Perceived Usefulness for Privacy Protection (adapted from [VD00, VB08])
Using Privacy-ABCs improves my privacy protection. Using Privacy-ABCs enhances the effectiveness of my privacy protection. I find Privacy-ABCs to be useful in protecting my privacy.
Perceived Usefulness for Course Evaluation (adapted from [VD00, VB08])
Using Privacy-ABCs improves the performance of course evaluation. Using Privacy-ABCs enhances the effectiveness of course evaluation. I find Privacy-ABCs to be useful for course evaluation. The Privacy-ABC System meets my requirements for a course evaluation.
Perceived Ease of Use (adapted from [VD00, VB08])
My interaction with the Privacy-ABC System is clear and understandable. Interacting with the Privacy-ABC System does not require a lot of my mental effort. The Privacy-ABC System is easy to use. I find it easy to get the Privacy-ABC System to do what I want to do.
Perceived risk (adapted from [Pav03])
I would see the decision to evaluate the course with the Privacy-ABC System as a risky action.
Trust into the Privacy-ABC technology (adapted from [Pav03])
The Privacy-ABC System is trustworthy.
Perceived Anonymity (adapted from [BB05])
Privacy-ABCs are able to protect my anonymity in course evaluation. With Privacy-ABCs I obtain a sense of anonymity in course evaluation. Privacy-ABCs can prevent threats to my anonymity in course evaluation.
Situation Awareness (adapted from [WWK10])

Continued on next page

Continued from previous page

With Privacy-ABCs, I always know which personal information I am disclosing. I find it easy to see which information will be disclosed in order to get a credential. Privacy-ABCs let me know who receives my data. The Privacy-ABC system gives me a good overview of my personal data stored on my Smart Card. I can easily find out when (e.g., at which date) I have received a credential via the University Registration System. I get a good overview of who knows what about my private information from the Privacy-ABC System. I can easily see which and how many Privacy-ABC credentials I have been issued.
Helpfulness (adapted from [Lew95, MCTC11])
The help information (such as on-line help, on-screen messages and other documentation) provided with the Privacy-ABC System is clear and understandable. It is easy to find the help information I need. The Privacy-ABC System provides very sensible and effective advice through the help information, if needed. The Privacy-ABC System provides competent guidance (as needed) through the help information.
Ease of Learning (does not fulfill scale quality criteria, adapted from [Lew95, WWK10])
I found it easy to learn how to use the Privacy-ABC System. Often I could not remember how to interact with the Privacy-ABC System.
Error Recovery (does not fulfill scale quality criteria, adapted from [Lew95])
The Privacy-ABC System provides error messages that clearly tell me how to fix problems. Whenever I make a mistake using the Privacy-ABC System, I recover easily and quickly.
Interface Usability (adapted from [Lew95])
The interface of the Privacy-ABC System is pleasant. I like using the interface of the Privacy-ABC System.

The scale for Perceived Anonymity was adapted from the "Sense of Security" construct by Bosmans et al. [BB05]. Situation Awareness was constructed using different (slightly changed) items from the PET-USES questionnaire [WWK10]. Understanding of Privacy-ABCs is a newly developed knowledge index that is presented in Section 7.3.7.

We run an exploratory factor analysis with a Varimax rotation to ensure the one-dimensionality and hence the validity of the measured constructs. We also conducted several reliability tests to assure the quality of each measurement scale. All reported multi-item scales fulfill the following quality criteria: one-dimensionality (e.g., Kaiser-Meyer-Olkin criterion > 0.5, total variance explained $> 50\%$) and reliability (Cronbach's $\alpha > 0.7$) [Fie13].

The Ease of Learning and Error Recovery scales did not fulfill the quality criteria and their statistical properties also could not be improved by removing items, as they both consist of two items. Hence we used the answers provided to the corresponding questions for descriptive data analysis only.

7.3.4.2 Sample characteristics

60 computer science students enrolled in the course "Distributed Systems I" were given an introductory lecture on Privacy-ABCs and 45 of them decided to take part in the trial. They were given smart cards and corresponding readers, as well as supporting material (manual and videos). The printouts of the questionnaire were distributed to the pilot participants at the end of the semester. We received 30 filled out questionnaires. Thus, all further descriptions relate to the sample size of 30 subjects (23 male, 7 female, 23 years old on average).

Apart from the usual demographic questions concerning age and gender, some other characteristics of the trial participants are important in order to consider external validity of the study. For example, computer science students might have a much higher computer proficiency than an average user, and thus we may expect the participants to make an intensive usage of security- and privacy-related online services, such as online shopping and banking, online social networks and cloud storage.

Important user attributes are also privacy concerns and privacy-aware behavior in general, and especially usage of privacy-enhancing technologies. We expect the trial participants to exhibit more privacy-aware behavior than an average Internet user. A high level of privacy concerns may influence student's interest in the trial participation.

Most participants are active users of Internet services. Almost all students (93%) use online storage services such as Dropbox, 83% participate in online social networks, 73% shop online, and 57% use online banking. They expressed a middle to high level of Internet privacy concerns ($m = 4.03$, $\sigma = 0.86$)[2] on a 5-point Likert scale developed by Dinev and Hart [DH06].

Only three participants said that they have used a privacy protection tool before the Patras trial. All three of them use TOR, and one additionally mentioned adblock plug-ins. However, most participants exhibit some other kinds of privacy-aware behavior: 29 out of 30 said that they sometimes delete cookies, 27 sometimes or often clean browser history and 23 sometimes or often use their browser in the private mode. 26 participants said that they sometimes provide fake information when creating a web account.

20 students reported that they participated in paper-based course evaluation before, and seven students already participated in an electronic course evaluation. Most students (21) agreed or strongly agreed that participating in course evaluations is important to them ($m = 3.87$, $\sigma = 0.78$), and also most (19) participants reported that protecting their anonymity in course evaluations is very important to them ($m = 4.57$, $\sigma = 0.63$).

[2] m denotes mean value, σ denotes standard deviation

In the following two sections we first present the results of user feedback and usability evaluation (Section 7.3.5) and then the results on user acceptance factors for Privacy-ABCs (Section 7.3.6).

7.3.5 Results of User Feedback and Usability Evaluation

The user feedback part of the questionnaire was designed to provide information to the developers and the deployment team about positive and negative sides of the trial with the goal to learn how to improve the future implementations and deployments of Privacy-ABCs.

7.3.5.1 System usage

All 30 participants used the provided Privacy-ABC system for course evaluation, and 26 of them participated in the Tombola. From the four that did not participate in the Tombola, one said that he/she did not have time for it, and two said that they were not interested.

As described in Section 7.2.1.6 on page 208, the role of the Tombola Inspector was given to a student chosen randomly at the beginning of the trial. An alternative would have been to pick a CTI member. When asked which variant they prefer, 10 participants preferred a student to be the Inspector, whereas 7 participants would have liked a CTI member to be the Inspector, and 11 participants do not care who plays this role. None of the students believed that the Inspector would use his/her position for getting more information about the Tombola participants.

7.3.5.2 Usability

Most users reported quite a good Ease of Use (mean value $m = 3.83$, standard deviation $\sigma = 0.65$) on a 5-points Likert scale. The reported Interface Usability was lower than the overall usability ($m = 3.58$, $\sigma = 0.74$).

Privacy-ABCs required usage of the Firefox browser and setting up a PKI certificate. Most participants (25) found setting up Firefox for the system usage easy or very easy, although 16 participants did not use Firefox as their default browser prior to the trial.

We also asked whether using the Privacy-ABC system takes too much time doing manual operations (for example clicks, data input, handling the smart card). Only 5 participants agreed or strongly agreed with this statement.

7.3.5.3 Situation Awareness and Credential Management

Situation Awareness (user's perception of being well informed about what is going on in the system) can be considered as a usability property. It was computed as an index consisting of seven items and got quite a good grade ($m = 3.87$, $\sigma = 0.63$) on a 5-point Likert scale.

Also the management of Privacy-ABC credentials should be transparent and easy to use. We adapted two Credential Management questions from PET-USES questionnaire [WWK10] :

- Obtaining a valid credential with the Privacy-ABC system is easy.
- I find it easy to manage (delete, restore, backup) my personal information on my smart card with the Privacy-ABCs.

Most users said that obtaining credentials was easy ($m = 4.10$, $\sigma = 0.61$), whereas managing of personal information on the smart card was ranked as less easy ($m = 3.70$, $\sigma = 0.75$).

7.3.5.4 Smart card usage and concerns

Most of the participants (19) did not worry that they might lose their smart card, however 6 participants said that they worried about this. Only two participants felt uncomfortable knowing that their personal data is stored on the smart card. We note that the high percent of the people unconcerned about the smart card could also result from the pre-selection bias, as people who find smart cards inconvenient or otherwise undesirable to use probably did not enroll in the trial.

12 participants used the backup function of the smart card, with 7 of them saying that the usage was easy or very easy, and two saying that the usage was difficult. Out of the remaining 18 students, two said that they did not know about the backup function, and one explicitly said that he/she considered the backup to be unnecessary.

7.3.5.5 Ease of learning, helpfulness and error recovery

More than half of the participants (18) agreed or strongly agreed with the statement that the Privacy-ABC system was easy to learn. However, half of the participants (15) agreed or strongly agreed that they often could not remember how to interact with the system. These contradictory results show that ease of learning requires further investigation.

Participants reported a rather high system helpfulness ($m = 3.88$, $\sigma = 0.73$). Moreover, 28 out of 30 participants agreed or strongly agreed that the user manual was very helpful with median being 4 out of 5. CTI members as support team received the highest rating: 28 out of 30 participants agreed or strongly agreed that the CTI support was very helpful, with median 5.

When people use a new system, they are quite likely to make mistakes, and in this case successful and easy error recovery is very important. The answers of the participants did not provide a very conclusive evidence to the helpfulness of the system's error messages: 6 users found the error messages unhelpful, 14 found them whether helpful nor unhelpful (probably some of them did not encounter any errors), and 10 users found the error messages helpful ($m = 3.23$, $\sigma = 0.9$ on a 5-points Likert scale). Half of the users agreed or strongly agreed that they easily and quickly recovered from the mistakes ($m = 3.43$, $\sigma = 0.97$). The issue of error messages thus requires further investigation.

7.3.5.6 Satisfaction and overall attitude to the usage

23 out of 30 participants agreed or strongly agreed with the statement that the benefits of using the system are bigger than the effort to use it, which shows a high user acceptance of the prototype. 28 participants said that they prefer using a Privacy-ABCs-based system for course evaluation over a paper-based system.

When asked if they would use Privacy-ABCs in other scenarios (apart form the course evaluation), 24 participants answered in the affirmative and 5 participants said that they would not use the technology (one answer is missing). When asked to name alternative usage scenarios, the participants suggested online marketing, online voting, online private discussions and bank transactions.

7.3.6 Results on User Acceptance Factors

In this section we explore the relations between the measured constructs and their role in the user acceptance of Privacy ABCs. We conducted bivariate non-parametric correlations (two-tailed) using Kendalls correlation coefficient (τ), because this test does not require normal data distribution and works for ordinal data and small sample sizes [Fie13]. Correlation coefficients can also interpreted as effect sizes: $0.1 < \tau \leq 0.3$ indicates a small effect size, $0.3 < \tau \leq 0.5$ a medium and $\tau > 0.5$ a large effect size [Coh88].

Apart from the correlation coefficient τ we report the significance level p of the correlations. The highest significance level is indicated by $p < 0.01$, which means that the probability of the corresponding correlation to occur by chance is less than 1%. We also consider significance levels $p < 0.05$ and $p < 0.1$. Significance level $p \geq 0.1$ is considered non-significant.

Unfortunately, we did not have enough data for a deeper analysis, such as multiple regressions or structural equation modeling, as the sample size of 30 participants is too small.

We present the hypotheses testing results in Section 7.3.6.1 and consider additional user acceptance factors and their possible integration into the user acceptance model in Section 7.3.6.2.

7.3.6.1 Results of hypotheses testing

According to the hypotheses from the Section 7.3.2.4, we looked into the correlations between the constructs as depicted in Figure 7.12 on page 220. We found statistically significant correlations at $p < 0.05$ or at $p < 0.01$ significance level between the constructs for all hypotheses but H7 (negative relation between perceived risk and trust into the system). However, for H7 we found a a significant negative relationship with medium effect size at the $p < 0.1$ level ($\tau = -.308$, p=.063), see Figure 7.13.

We also found a number of other interesting correlations between the constructs. Especially, perceived risk is correlated to the same constructs to which trust is correlated. This means that trust and perceived risk both play an important role in user acceptance of Privacy-ABCs, but they seem to be more decoupled from each other in the course evaluation situation than in the web shopping situations considered by Pavlou [Pav03]. One possible reason for the low significance might be that the participants did not consider course evaluation as a risky situation at all, independently of the technology that is used for this task.

Considering the results on trust and perceived risk in more detail as depicted in Fig 7.14, we can see that cumulatively, 80% of the participants consider the situation as not risky, and that 80% of the participants trust the system.

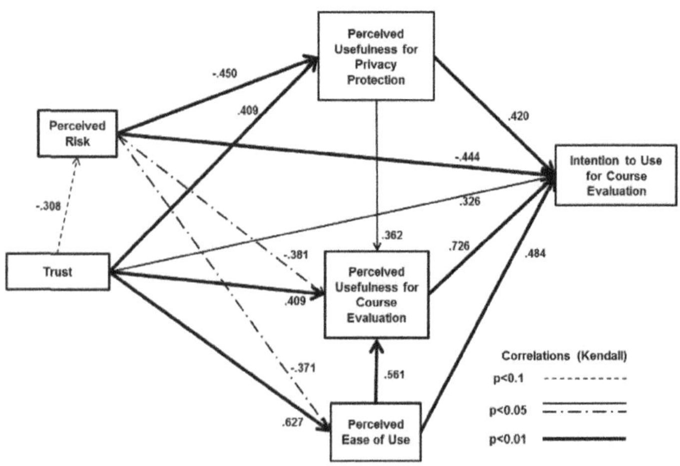

Fig. 7.13 Correlations between the constructs of the adapted TAM (Section 7.3.2.4). Additional (not present in the initial model) correlations are depicted with dot and dash lines. Effect sizes (Kendall's τ) are depicted near the corresponding arrows.

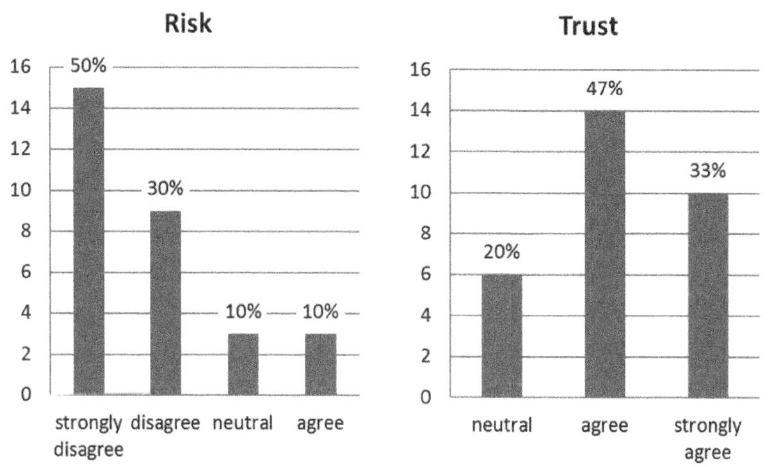

Fig. 7.14 Descriptive data for user perception of the risk connected to the participation in the trial and the trustworthiness of the Privacy-ABC system. Most users disagreed with the statement that course evaluation using Privacy-ABCs is a risky situation, and agreed with the statement that the Privacy-ABC System is trustworthy.

7.3.6.2 Results on additional User Acceptance Factors

In Section 7.3.3 we asked the question what is the role of Perceived Anonymity, Situation Awareness and Understanding of Technology in the user acceptance of the Privacy-ABC technology. To answer this question, we looked at the correlations between these constructs and the TAM constructs that are depicted in Figure 7.13. The corresponding correlation matrix is presented in Table 7.2.

Table 7.2 Statistically significant correlations between the TAM constructs (Perceived Risk *"PRisk"*, Trust, Perceived Usefulness for Privacy Protection *"PU for PP"*, Perceived Usefulness for Course Evaluation *"PU for CE"*, Perceived Ease of Use *"PEoU"*, Intention to Use *"IntUse"*) and additional factors (Understanding of Privacy-ABCs *"Under"*, Situation Awareness *"SitAw"* and Perceived Anonymity *"PAnon"*. Significance levels are indicated as follows: * means $p < 0.05$, ** means $p < 0.01$.

	Under	SitAw	PAnon	PRisk	Trust	PU for PP	PU for CE	PEoU	IntUse
Under	x	.317*	.404**	–	–	–	–	–	–
SitAw	.317*	x	.403**	–	–	.309*	.317*	.361**	.319*
PAnon	.404**	.403**	x	-.383*	.444**	.455**	–	–	–

Some interesting connections can be discovered from the correlation matrix. For example, Perceived Anonymity is significantly correlated to Perceived Risk, Trust and Usefulness for Privacy Protection, but is not correlated to other TAM constructs. This indicates that Perceived Anonymity plays an important role in risk perception and perception of the trustworthiness of the system.

Situation Awareness, on the other hand, significantly correlates with the TAM constructs Perceived Usefulness for Privacy Protection, Perceived Usefulness for Course Evaluation, Perceived Ease of Use and Intention to Use. These connections may indicate that Situation Awareness is a direct influencing factor for user acceptance (users should be able to understand "what is going on"). A significant correlation between Situation Awareness and Perceived Anonymity shows that users may feel more anonymous if they have a clear picture of the data flow in the system.

Understanding of the technology seems not to play an important direct role in user acceptance, but may influence it indirectly through its significant correlations to Situation Awareness and Perceived Anonymity. The resulting extended TAM is depicted in Figure 7.15.

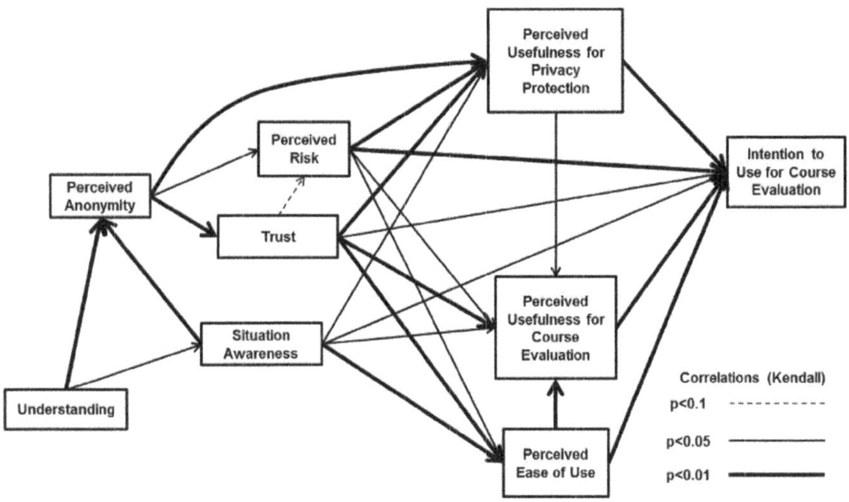

Fig. 7.15 Extended Technology Acceptance Model for Prvacy-ABCs derived from the correlations between the constructs of the adapted TAM and the additional factors of user acceptance.

7.3.7 Insights into the Understanding of Privacy-ABCs

Understanding of the principles behind the Privacy-ABC technology is of independent interest. For example, it might provide an upper bound on the ability of non-specialists to understand Privacy-ABCs, as the participants in the Patras trial have high technical literacy and were given an introductory lecture on the topic. Moreover, knowing which concepts are understandable and which are not may inform the future interface design, such that more emphasis should be placed on clear communication of the less understandable features of the Privacy-ABC technology.

We measured how well the participants understand the concepts behind the Privacy-ABCs by means of a new index consisting of eight statements that could be rated as true or false, with the "don't know" answer option also available:

1. When I authenticate to the Course Evaluation System (called CES in the following), the smart card transmits my matriculation number to the CES. **(false)**
2. When I authenticate to the CES, the smart card transmits the number of my class attendances to the CES. **(false)**
3. When I evaluate the same course for the second time, the CES does not recognize that I have already evaluated the course. My first evaluation and my second evaluation are seen as evaluations by different students by the CES. **(false)**
4. When I evaluate the same course for the second time, the CES knows that I have already evaluated the course, but it is still not able to identify me. **(true)**
5. When I access the CES from a PC, Privacy-ABCs anonymize my IP address. **(false)**
6. My Tombola credential contains my matriculation number. **(true)**
7. The administrator of the Tombola system can decrypt my matriculation number if I am not the winner. **(false)**
8. The administrator of the Tombola system can decrypt the winner's matriculation number. **(false)**

Question 1 refers to the *pseudonymity* of the Privacy-ABC transactions: a matriculation number is an identifying piece of information, thus it cannot be transmitted during a course evaluation. Only half of the participants answered this question correctly (see Figure 7.16).

Only one third of the users correctly answered question 2. It refers to the *minimal disclosure* property: the number of class attendances is an unnecessarily detailed

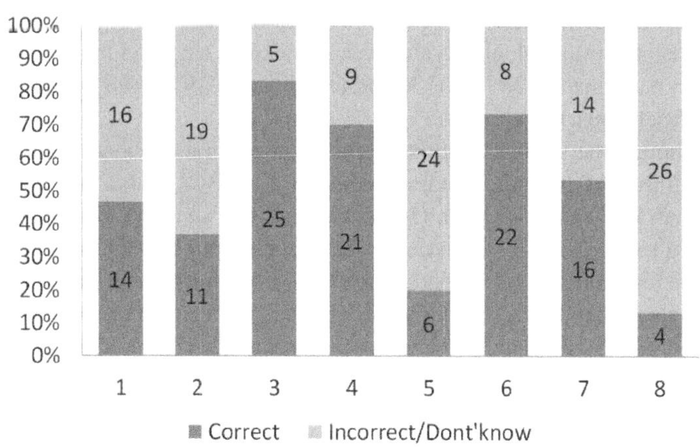

Fig. 7.16 Answers of the trial participants to the eight questions about the properties of Privacy-ABCs

information that can even be used for de-anonymization. Actually, only a boolean value is transmitted that indicates whether the student attended enough lectures in order to be entitled to course evaluation.

Questions 3 and 4 concern the *consumption control* and the *unlinkability* properties: on the one hand, the opinion of the same person cannot be counted twice, and on the other hand, two course evaluations by the same person cannot be used for de-anonymization of this person. Most students were able to understand these facts.

Question 5 refers to the property of network anonymity. This property should be guaranteed on the network layer, and thus, the Privacy-ABC System actually does not possess it. The fact that most of the students thought otherwise gives a clue for the future implementations of Privacy-ABCs: the network anonymity property should either be satisfied, or the implementation should make clear that the protection given by Privacy-ABCs has certain limits.

Finally, questions 6, 7 and 8 refer to the understanding of the *carry-over attributes*. Whereas most students understand that the Tombola credential should contain some identifying piece of information (question 6), most of them did not understand that the only entity that should be able to de-anonymize the winner is the Inspector (and not the system adminstrator).

On the whole, the understanding of Privacy-ABCs seems to be insufficient and difficult to achieve. Probably better understanding can be achieved by specially designed user interfaces, as suggested by Wästlund et al. [WAFH12].

7.3.8 Discussion of the Evaluation Results

We conducted a usability and user acceptance evaluation of the Privacy-ABC technology in the Patras trial. The system was generally perceived as easy to use, although the learnability and the communication of error messages should be improved. Also the usage of smart cards was reported as easy and mostly free of concern. Most participants (28 out of 30) prefer Privacy-ABC-based course evaluation over the usual paper-based form.

Even though the students had background in computer science, many of them showed difficulties in understanding how Privacy-ABCs work. For example, onlay less than half of the students (14) knew that their matriculation number is not transmitted to the Course Evaluation System during the course evaluation. Nevertheless, the reported anonymity perception was very strong, as 29 students agreed or strongly agreed that they feel anonymous and well protected during the course evaluation. Moreover, 24 participants agreed or strongly agreed that the Privacy-ABC System is trustworthy (the remaining 6 participants reported a neutral opinion on this topic). These results raise the question whether the understanding of the technology is really important for user acceptance and trust.

Our adaptation of the Technology Acceptance Model (TAM) to the usage of Privacy-ABCs seems quite promising. The division of Perceived Usefulness of the technology into the usefulness for primary and for secondary goals may help to understand user acceptance in more depth. A new and important factor of user acceptance that we discovered is Situation Awareness that represents user's perception of data and information flow in the system.

7.3.9 *Limitations and Future Work*

This study has a set of limitations that do not allow for a broad generalization of the results. Firstly, 45 out of 60 possible participants (all students that enrolled in the considered university course) decided to participate in the trial. Thus, probably people that were concerned about the Privacy-ABC technology decided not to participate (self-selection bias).

Moreover, out of 45 students that decided to participate in the trial, only 30 finished the trial. However, this is most probably not due to the Privacy-ABC technology, as the remaining 15 students actually dropped the course and did not take the final examination. Unfortunately, the small sample size only allowed statistical analysis of correlations, without the possibility to find out the causal relationships between the user acceptance factors.

Furthermore, our participants were computer science students that are probably used to getting in contact with new technologies and enjoy this. They also have high skills in computer and Internet literacy. These characteristics may have strongly affected the usability results.

The above limitations call for investigations of other scenarios, for example online elections or web shopping, where the anonymity may be more important for the participants, or their risk perception higher. Future studies should be conducted with larger and more heterogeneous samples, and with more sophisticated statistical means, such as multiple regressions or structural equation modeling.

7.4 Conclusion

The Privacy-ABCs technology offers cryptographic primitives and tools for eIdentity management that allow users to take more control over their privacy. They can choose to reveal towards services only personal information that is really required in order to use the services. In this context, we organized and run a pilot where students of the University of Patras performed remote course evaluations after providing evidence of their eligibility using the Privacy-ABCs technology.

The pilot system was built using the Reference Implementation of Privacy ABCs and implemented all the Privacy-ABCs entities required to implement the chosen scenarios. This pilot system offered a course evaluation service to the students such that they could evaluate their course electronically from their homes. The Privacy-ABCs technology guaranteed that no information is sent to the course evaluation system which can later be used to identify the students who participated as well as linke them with their evaluations. Moreover by utilizing the Privacy-ABC technologies, the users of the pilot remained in full control of what level of personal information they disclosed.

With respect to the acceptance of the system and the technology by the pilot participants, we conducted an evaluation using a quantitative standardized questionnaire. Overall, the evaluation results showed that the participants found the pilot system useful and quite easy to use, although some usability problems were encountered. The students also had a high level of trust into the system. They expressed a high preference for the Privacy-ABC-based course evaluation compared to the paper-based evaluation. The majority of the students also reported that they would use Privacy-ABCs for other tasks than course evaluation, such as online voting, online private discussions and bank transactions.

The developed user acceptance model for Privacy-ABCs based on the Technology Acceptance Model was successfully tested. Moreover, investigation of additional user acceptance factors showed that a clear view of the data and information flow in the system plays an important role in user acceptance, whereas detailed understanding of the technology is less important.

We would like to conclude this chapter with some lessons learned through our experiences with the pilot as well as with the analysis of the evaluation questionnaires:

1. Modern cryptography and ICT security techniques can provide all the necessary primitives and tools for building trustworthy systems based on Privacy-ABCs.
2. Security sensitive services and systems should be built using the "privacy-by-design" approach where privacy is a feature of the target system incorporated from the beginning and not simply added after a first privacy breach incidence.
3. A positive attitude towards privacy and Privacy-ABCs can be potentially shaped early by raising awareness in privacy issues through courses that acquaint people, from their school and university years, with the basics of the Internet, its services as its privacy issues.

Finally, given the successful operation of the pilot, our plan is to introduce the Privacy-ABC technology in more services targeted at the educational community of Greece at all education levels. The Privacy-ABC technology can be used as means for educating young people about privacy in the evolving Internet society as well as raising awareness about privacy risks.

References

[ALP+12] Joerg Abendroth, Vasiliki Liagkou, Apostolos Pyrgelis, Christoforos Raptopoulos, Ahmad Sabouri, Eva Schlehahn, Yannis Stamatiou, and Harald Zwingelberg. D7.1 application description for students, 2012. https://abc4trust.eu/download/ABC4Trust-D7.1-Application-Description-Students.pdf.

[BB05] Anick Bosmans and Hans Baumgartner. Goal-relevant emotional information: When extraneous affect leads to persuasion and when it does not. *Journal of Consumer Research*, 32(3):424–434, 2005.

[BGK+14] Zinaida Benenson, Anna Girard, Ioannis Krontiris, Vassia Liagkou, Kai Rannenberg, and Yannis Stamatiou. User acceptance of privacy-abcs: An exploratory study. In *HCI International: Human Aspects of Information Security, Privacy and Trust*, 2014. (to appear).

[BGL+12] Souheil Bcheri, Norbert Götze, Vasiliki Liagkou, Apostolos Pyrgelis, Christoforos Raptopoulos, Yannis Stamatiou, Katalin Storf, Peder Wängmark, and Harald Zwingelberg. D5.1 scenario definition for both pilots, 2012. https://abc4trust.eu/download/ABC4Trust-D5.1-Scenario-Definition.pdf.

[Bro96] John Brooke. SUS - A quick and dirty usability scale. *Usability evaluation in industry*, 189:194, 1996.

[CG05] Lorrie Faith Cranor and Simson Garfinkel. *Security and Usability: Designing Secure Systems that People Can Use*. O'Reilly, 2005.

[Coh88] Jacob Cohen. *Statistical power analysis for the behavioral sciences*. Lawrence Erlbaum Associates, Inc, 1988.

[Dav89] Fred D. Davis. Perceived usefulness, perceived ease of use, and user acceptance of information technology. *MIS quarterly*, pages 319–340, 1989.

[Dav93] Fred D. Davis. User acceptance of information technology: system characteristics, user perceptions and behavioral impacts. *International Journal of Man-Machine Studies*, 38(3):475–487, 1993.

[DEK+14] Daniel Deibler, Malte Engeler, Ioannis Krontiris, Vasiliki Liagkou, Apostolos Pyrgelis, Eva Schlehahn, Yannis Stamatiou, Welderufaelr Tesfay, and Harald Zwingelberg. D7.3 evaluation of the student pilot, 2014. https://abc4trust.eu/index.php/pub/deliverables.

[DGG+12] Kasper Damgaard, Hamza Ghani, Norbert Götze, Anja Lehmann, Vasiliki Liagkou, Jesus Luna, Gert Læssøe Mikkelsen, Apostolos Pyrgelis, and Yannis Stamatiou. D7.2 necessary hardware and software package for the student pilot deployment, 2012. https://abc4trust.eu/download/ABC4Trust-D7.2.Hard-and-Software-Package-for-Student-Pilot.pdf.

[DH06] Tamara Dinev and Paul Hart. Internet privacy concerns and social awareness as determinants of intention to transact. *International Journal of Electronic Commerce*, 10(2):7–29, 2006.

[Fie13] Andy Field. *Discovering statistics using IBM SPSS statistics*. Sage, 2013.

[HL04] Chin-Lung Hsu and Hsi-Peng Lu. Why do people play on-line games? An extended tam with social influences and flow experience. *Information & Management*, 41(7):853–868, 2004.

[ISO] ISO/IEC. 9241-11 Ergonomic requirements for office work with visual display terminals (VDT)s - Part 11 Guidance on usability. 1998: ISO/IEC 9241-11: 1998 (E).

[Lew95] James R. Lewis. IBM computer usability satisfaction questionnaires: psychometric evaluation and instructions for use. *International Journal of Human-Computer Interaction*, 7(1):57–78, 1995.

[Lik32] Rensis Likert. A technique for the measurement of attitudes. *Archives of psychology*, 1932.

[LUM13] James R. Lewis, Brian S. Utesch, and Deborah E. Maher. UMUX-LITE: when there's no time for the SUS. In *Proceedings of the SIGCHI Conference on Human Factors in Computing Systems*, pages 2099–2102. ACM, 2013.

[MCTC11] D. Harrison McKnight, Michelle Carter, Jason Bennett Thatcher, and Paul F. Clay. Trust in a specific technology: An investigation of its components and measures. *ACM Transactions on Management Information Systems (TMIS)*, 2(2):12, 2011.

[Pav03] Paul A. Pavlou. Consumer acceptance of electronic commerce: integrating trust and risk with the technology acceptance model. *International journal of electronic commerce*, 7(3):101–134, 2003.

[RBD+13] Georg Regal, Marc Busch, Stephanie Deutsch, Christina Hochleitner, Martin Lugmayr, and Manfred Tscheligi. Money on the move workload, usability and technology acceptance of second-screen atm-interactions. In *Proceedings of the 15th international conference on Human-computer interaction with mobile devices and services*, pages 281–284. ACM, 2013.

[SC09] Sarah Spiekermann and Lorrie Faith Cranor. Engineering privacy. *Software Engineering, IEEE Transactions on*, 35(1), 2009.

[Spi07] Sarah Spiekermann. Privacy enhancing technologies for RFID in retail – an empirical investigation. In *UbiComp 2007: Ubiquitous Computing*, pages 56–72. Springer, 2007.

[Spi08] Sarah Spiekermann. *User control in ubiquitous computing: design alternatives and user acceptance*. Shaker, 2008.

[SPM+11] San-Tsai Sun, Eric Pospisil, Ildar Muslukhov, Nuray Dindar, Kirstie Hawkey, and Konstantin Beznosov. What makes users refuse web single sign-on?: an empirical investigation of OpenID. In *Proceedings of the Seventh Symposium on Usable Privacy and Security*, page 4. ACM, 2011.

[VB08] Viswanath Venkatesh and Hillol Bala. Technology acceptance model 3 and a research agenda on interventions. *Decision sciences*, 39(2):273–315, 2008.

[VD00] Viswanath Venkatesh and Fred D. Davis. A theoretical extension of the technology acceptance model: four longitudinal field studies. *Management science*, 46(2):186–204, 2000.

[WAFH12] Erik Wästlund, Julio Angulo, and Simone Fischer-Hübner. Evoking comprehensive mental models of anonymous credentials. In *Open Problems in Network Security*, pages 1–14. Springer, 2012.

[WD85] Paul R. Warshaw and Fred D. Davis. Disentangling behavioral intention and behavioral expectation. *Journal of experimental social psychology*, 21(3):213–228, 1985.

[WR11] Rick Wash and Emilee Rader. Influencing mental models of security: a research agenda. In *New security paradigms workshop*, pages 57–66. ACM, 2011.

[WT99] Alma Whitten and J. Doug Tygar. Why Johnny cant encrypt: A usability evaluation of PGP 5.0. In *Proceedings of the 8th USENIX Security Symposium*, volume 99, page 16, 1999.

[WWK10] Erik Wästlund, Peter Wolkerstorfer, and Christina Köffel. PET-USES: Privacy-enhancing technology–users self-estimation scale. In *Privacy and Identity Management for Life*, pages 266–274. Springer, 2010.

Chapter 8
Experiences and Feedback from the Pilots

Norbert Götze, Daniel Deibler, and Robert Seidl

Abstract This chapter focuses on the experiences gained during the development and operation of the pilot applications molten down to give both technical and legal feedback to future adopters of Privacy-ABC technologies.

Both the Söderhamn and Patras pilots made use of predecessors of the current "Reference Implementation", a set of libraries and ready-to-use services which enable deployment of Privacy-ABC technologies (see Chapter 9). As each pilot was split into two rounds and as every round comprised all development stages, the first adopters of the Privacy-ABC technologies were able to provide their feedback about former versions of the Reference Implementation on many occasions. The outcome of these improvement cycles is the "Final Reference Implementation" (see [BBE$^+$14]).

This chapter will focus on experiences and feedback which are still relevant in the light of this "Final Reference Implementation" and which are of interest for new projects planning to adopt Privacy-ABC technologies. Contrary to this, issues that have been identified and solved during the course of the ABC4Trust project are excluded from this chapter. Readers interested in those details can refer to D5.3 (see [BDD$^+$14]) instead.

Norbert Götze and Robert Seidl
Nokia, Sankt-Martin-Straße 76, D-81541 Munich, e-mail: {norbert.goetze, robert.seidl}@nsn.com

Daniel Deibler
Unabhängiges Landeszentrum für Datenschutz Schleswig-Holstein, Germany, e-mail: uld68@datenschutzzentrum.de

K. Rannenberg et al. (eds.), *Attribute-based Credentials for Trust*,
DOI 10.1007/978-3-319-14439-9_8

8.1 The Project Setup

In order to understand how the experiences and feedback were provided, a closer look at the work-split, the processing contracts and the to-be-developed applications needs to be taken.

8.1.1 Development and Operational Work-Split

Four teams were involved in the development phases of the pilot applications: the Reference Implementation team, the team responsible for the School and University Registration Systems and the two "pilot conductors" (see Chapters 6 and 7). However, only the two pilot conductors were involved in the operational phases of the systems.

The pilot developers are the primary group providing the experiences and feedback, i.e. the developers of both Registration Systems and both pilot conductors. Since some applications deployed in the pilots were developed by the Reference Implementation team, the experiences and feedback mapped to these applications are restricted to the operational phases only.

8.1.2 Processing Contracts between Developers and Operators

Next to development and operation topics, a third issue had to be considered in the very beginning of the pilots. As it seemed possible that the developers, in particular NSN as developer of the "Registration Systems", would come in touch with or even process personal data of the users of the pilots, certain privacy safeguards had to be established. In accordance with the different legal roles in a data processing operation, explained in Section 5.1.4 , the University of Patras and the school in Söderhamn had to be categorised as data controller, since they determined the purpose(s) and means of the personal data processing. NSN, however, was likely to process personal data on behalf of the controllers, since they were tasked with the administration, debugging and monitoring of the Registration Systems. Therefore, NSN had the role of a data processor for the pilot in Patras. Even more complicated was the situation in the Swedish pilot, as another entity Eurodocs was involved. As Eurodocs primarily operated the pilot system in Sweden while NSN only supported Eurodocs, Eurodocs was classified as data processor and NSN as sub-processor.

Since the data controller remains fully responsible for the data processing, the data processor has to be bound to the instructions of the controller by a processing contract. For the Söderhamn pilot, even a chain of processing contracts needed to be set up that subordinated Eurodocs to the instructions of the school and NSN to the instructions of Eurodocs. Therefore, two types of contracts (and 3 contracts in total) had to be drafted before the start of the pilots:

- The processing contract between CTI / University of Patras as controller and NSN as processor
- The processing contract between Norrtulskolan as controller and Eurodocs as processor
- The sub-processing contract between Eurodocs as processor and NSN as sub-processor

While more detailed explanations regarding the legally required content and the legal foundation of the processing contracts can be found in Section 5.2.2, the actual contracts can be found in appendices A.1, A.2 and A.3 of D5.3 (see [BDD$^+$14]).

Even though a basic contractual relationship would have fulfilled the minimum standards of European data protection law, it was decided to further strengthen privacy protection by strictly observing the principles of data avoidance and data minimisation. As mentioned above, NSN was tasked with the administration, debugging and monitoring of the pilot systems. To limit the contact of NSN with personal data as much as possible, a step-by-step procedure regarding the solving of technical problems was outlined in the contracts. The procedure entailed, amongst other safeguards, the obligation to anonymise log files or screenshots before forwarding them to NSN unless when such an anonymisation would have hindered NSN to perform the debugging or other mandatory contractual obligations. Only in these exceptional situations, NSN was authorised to receive and process log files or screenshots of the system still containing personal data. Additionally, certain obligations of keeping protocols and logging were integrated into the contracts. Thereby, the controller was able to check the documentation for cases of misuse, unauthorized access, or actions not in compliance with the given instruction. Last but not least, as NSN assisted in setting up the pilot application, once these preparations were finished, NSN's direct administrative access was deactivated to ensure that NSN would never have direct insight to the personal data of the pilot participants. Therefore, NSN knew in a very early phase of the project that its applications must be operable by the pilot conductors themselves, thus remote debugging must be facilitated. However, while the Reference Implementation developers faced a similar problem, no additional contracts or other privacy safeguards were necessary, since it could be ruled out that they would come into contact with any personal information of the pilot users.

8.1.3 Pilot Applications

Tables 8.1 and 8.2 give an overview of the applications developed for the pilots. The left column shows a list of the applications. Please refer to Chapters 6 and 7 for further information about these components. In the case that the applications adopted Privacy-ABC technologies, the column "Privacy-ABC Role" shows which role the application had to play. The column "Implemented by" indicates who implemented the applications. The last column "Public Code Location" points to where the sources and/or binaries can be found on the Internet.

Table 8.1 Söderhamn Pilot Applications

Söderhamn Pilot		**Privacy-ABC Roles**	**Implemented by**	**Public Code Location**
Restricted Area Systems	RA Application		e	
	RA Admin		e	
	RA Client Alias Selector		e	
	RA Client Dashboard		e	
	School Portal		e	
	RA ABC System	Verifier	r	
User	Browser Plugins		r	1
	Identity Selector		r	1
	User ABC System	User	r	1
	Tray Application		e	
Smart Card	MUtil.exe Tool			2
	Smart Card Initialization Tool		r	3
Revocation Authority	Revocation Service	Revocation Authority	r	
School Registration System	IdM Application		n	
	IdM Admin GUI		n	
	IdM Smart Card Registrar		n	
	IdM Mass Provisioning Tool		n	
	IdM Portal		n	
	IdM ABC System	Issuer and Verifier	n	
Inspector	Inspector Setup Tool		r	
	Inspect Tool	Inspector	r	
	Inspector Wrapper		e	

1) See Reference Implementation: Installer
2) See MULTOS website
3) See Reference Implementation: abce-components
4) See Reference Implementation: abce-services
e) Pilot Developers: Eurodocs
n) Pilot Developers: NSN
r) Reference Implementation Developers

As it is presented in the tables, not all applications were developed by the pilot developers. It must also be noted, that most of the applications are not publicly available. This even applies for some applications provided by the developers of the Reference Implementation. One example of such an application is the "Inspect Tool".

It is worth noting that all applications mapped to a Privacy-ABC role deployed methods from the "service-helper" library of the Reference Implementation (see Chapter 9). Furthermore, the Revocation Authority of Patras is an unchanged copy of the generic RESTful Revocation Service provided in the "abce-services" directory of the Reference Implementation. Contrary to this, the Revocation Authority of Söderhamn is a customized Revocation Service based on an former version of the Reference Implementation, thus taking it out of focus of this chapter.

Table 8.2 Patras Pilot Applications

Patras Pilot		**Privacy-ABC Roles**	**Implemented by**	**Public Code Location**
Course Evaluation System	Course Evaluation Application		c	
	CES ABC System	Verifier and Issuer	c	
Tombola System	Tombola Application		c	
	Tombola ABC System	Verifier	c	
Patras Portal	Patras Portal		c	
Class Attendance System	Class Attendance Application		c	
User	Browser Plugins		r	1
	Identity Selector		r	1
	User ABC System	User	r	1
Smart Card	MUtil.exe Tool			2
	Smart Card Initialization Tool		r	3
Revocation Authority	Revocation Service	Revocation Authority	r	4
University Registration System	IdM Application		n	
	IdM Admin GUI		n	
	IdM Smart Card Registrar		n	
	IdM Mass Provisioning Tool		n	
	IdM Portal		n	
	IdM ABC System	Issuer and Verifier	n	
Inspector	Inspector Setup Tool		r	
	Inspect Tool	Inspector	r	

1) See Reference Implementation: Installer
2) See MULTOS website
3) See Reference Implementation: abce-components
4) See Reference Implementation: abce-services
c) Pilot Developers: CTI
n) Pilot Developers: NSN
r) Reference Implementation Developers

8.2 Lessons Learned from the Pilots

In the course of the project, the differences between the pilot architectures decreased. One reason for this is that whatever was required for one pilot was mostly regarded as being useful also for the other pilot and therefore was readily taken over. An example for this is the IdM Admin GUI, which was first introduced in the second round of the Söderhamn pilot, and was then adopted by the second round of the Patras pilot. The other reason was that the enhancements in libraries of the Reference Implementation were automatically propagated to all applications connecting to it. Therefore, a good starting point for identifying material for the "Lessons Learned" is to analyse the remaining differences between the pilots and to have a closer look at the history of the Reference Implementation.

8.2.1 Usability

As depicted in Table 8.1, the Söderhamn pilot was provided with an "RA Client Alias Selector" and an "RA Client Dashboard". On top of this, a "Tray Application" and an "Inspector Wrapper" were designed. These four applications were not available in the Patras pilot. But both pilots used an "Installer" that encapsulated the user applications and enabled easy installation on the user's PC in one go. What all of these applications targeted was a raise in usability. Since mostly non IT-savvy users were involved in the Söderhamn pilot, the requirement for a better usability became increasingly important during the project. Contrary to this, the pilot participants at the Patras university pilot were computer science students. In that case, the users were IT-savvy, therefore the requirement for easy-to-use GUIs was not crucial.

Usability is also among the key factors determining the acceptance of a system. If the users do not find the GUIs self-explaining, attractive and modern, the services of the system will not be used even if the technologies under-the-hood would be highly beneficial for the users. This also applies for the language of the GUIs. Originally, all GUIs were rendered in English. But in order to ensure that the GUIs would be understandable by all users, the Söderhamn pilot conductors requested to change the IdM Portal, the IdM Application, the Browser Plugins and the Identity Selector to render in Swedish language. This resulted in significant impacts not only in the mentioned applications but also in the credential specifications, in the issuance and the presentation policies, in the IdM ABC System and in the IdM Database. Before the operational phase of the Söderhamn pilot, the pilot conductors came to the decision, that in order to reduce the complexity in the initialization phase, they may need to distribute "RA-ready" smart cards to the pupils. This means that the pupils obtained personalized smart cards containing all the credentials they were authorized to obtain. So in the second round, the pupils did not need to visit the IdM Portal in the beginning. As a result, the usability of the system was improved at the cost of trust.

Even administrators regard usability as an important aspect. Because of the large number of smart cards that had to be prepared, the Söderhamn pilot conductors requested for a tool to speed up the registration of the smart cards. The original work flow was to use the Smart Card Registrar to manually input the smart card ID and the crypto engine type, and thereafter to extract the scope-exclusive pseudonym from the card. Finally, the Smart Card Registrar had to write this data into the IdM Database. The faster and less error-prone alternative work flow was to enhance the Smart Card Initialization Tool to output these parameters into a table and copy the contents of this table along with the personal data of the users into the IdM Database via the IdM Mass Provisioning Tool. In this way, the administrators did not need to visit the Smart Card Registrar. The Söderhamn pilot conductors chose the faster work flow, thereby significantly reducing the pilot preparation time.

An important aspect of acceptance is how the users feel if different services of a system have different designs. At a late point in time, the Söderhamn pilot identified that it would be advantageous if the designs of all GUIs, pop-up boxes and select menus, with which the pupils interact, have the same "look and feel". Unfortunately, this was not feasible any more. Not only because of a lack of time, but also because the developer teams used different visualization technologies for their applications.

In a nutshell, projects planning to adopt Privacy-ABC technologies must investigate the characteristics of their target users and analyze their GUI requirements before the development is launched. As the Söderhamn pilot has shown, the impacts of the GUIs on the back-end logic and in the administration might be significant.

Not mentioned so far in this chapter are the tolerated delay times. How long would a user wait for the system to respond during the issuance and presentation processes? Adopters of Privacy-ABC technologies must be aware that the operators of the applications can speed up the system by reducing the cryptographic key sizes, limiting the number of revocable credentials, or optimizing the presentation policies regarding the complexity of proofs. Nevertheless, measures such as reducing the key-size is a trade-off between security level and performance. Moreover, while the system is busy with Privacy-ABC issuance or presentation, feedback mechanisms such as progress bars or spinning wheels are helpful to keep impatient users from pressing too many buttons, as users tend to accept delays more if they see such indicators on the GUIs.

Both pilots used smart cards to protect the users' secret keys and store the credentials. The smart cards were PIN protected, therefore, every time the card was accessed the user had to enter the PIN code. In the Söderhamn pilot, it would have been very inconvenient to type the PIN every time accessing a "Restricted Area". So the developers of the Reference Implementation decided to modify the Browser Plugin so that it caches the PIN first time the user enters it. This approach enhanced the usability at the cost of security.

In summary, the users are the ones who determine if a product is successful or not. So the GUIs with which the users interact are of prime importance. These GUIs must be customized in such a way that they can easily be handled and give the feeling of full-control on the activities to the user. If long delays due to data processing are unavoidable, the user must not get the impression that her browser is frozen. And finally, if additional software has to be installed on the users' PCs, the installation should be simple and nearly automatic.

8.2.2 Strategy for Adopting Privacy-ABC Technologies

Developers planning to incorporate Privacy-ABC technologies into their applications should take the "abce-services" of the Reference Implementation as coding examples. Using Maven, one can build a dedicated RESTful web service for every Privacy-ABC Role (see Chapter 9 for details). As said before, the second round of the Patras pilot made use of this code for its Revocation Authority. Please note that the RESTful web services provide access to all features, including the features restricted for administration and maintenance. So the developers may need to adjust these coding examples and introduce a proxy service as gatekeeper to the abce-services. Alternatively, developers could separate the features and implement an administrator interface and a user interface. Thereafter the infrastructure of the network can be configured to prevent users from accessing the administrator interface. In both of the pilots, the Registration Systems introduced such measures. The IdM ABC System was not directly accessible by the users. Users logging in to the

Registration System via smart card were redirected from the IdM Portal to the IdM Application. The IdM Application acted as a proxy for verification. And users requesting for new credentials had to visit the IdM Portal which served as a proxy for issuance. The administrative applications and the non-administrative applications of the Registration Systems listened on different ports so that simple firewall rules were able to prevent users from accessing the former via the Internet.

Best practice development begins simple and gradually gets more and more complex. The same recommendation can be given when adopting Privacy-ABC technologies. Developers should begin with credential specifications containing only a small number of attributes and without revocation handles. The issuance and verification policies should be simple too. When the first credentials have been successfully issued and when the first presentation tokens have been successfully verified, the developers are provided with a good starting point for moving closer to their target use-cases.

The user, the issuer and the verifier are mandatory Privacy-ABC roles and have to be available in the very beginning of a project. The inspector and the revocation authority roles are optional. If projects require an inspector, it must be noted, that not all attributes are suitable for inspection purposes (e.g. hash values). Furthermore, the public key of the inspector must be made available to the users. Finally, if projects require a revocation authority, it is important to know that this service must always be online and that the generation of parameters becomes more complex.

8.2.3 Language Support

As already mentioned in Section 8.2.1, the user group typically defines which languages must be supported by the GUIs. In the Söderhamn pilot, the users were pupils of a primary school so the support of Swedish became a requirement. And in the Patras pilot, the users were students so English could be left as requirement. Based on the language settings in the browser, the GUIs display the corresponding "friendly name" of the XML documents. Both pilots made use of the parameters "FriendlyCredentialName" and "FriendlyAttributeName" in the credential specification, and "FriendlyPolicyName" as well as the "FriendlyPolicyDescription" in the policies. The decision which languages have to be supported must be made very early in the project as it impacts most of the applications.

8.2.4 Debugging

Typically the logs generated by the applications contain timestamps, log levels from INFO to SEVERE and some information on what the applications are currently doing. In most cases the applications using Privacy-ABC technologies are hosted in different web service containers (e.g. Apache-Tomcat) and each container generates its own log files. A hard requirement resulting from such distributed systems is to enable ordering the entries of all log files chronologically so that debugging is facilitated. Therefore, a general recommendation is to use a time-server that keeps the devices which host the applications in sync.

During the operational phases of the pilots, only the pilot conductors had direct access to the administrative interfaces of the applications. The reason for this was primarily that sensitive data of pupils and students had to be processed and stored. Consequently, the pilot developers who were not also the pilot conductors had to take special care when adding log method printouts to the code. These printouts had to be self-explaining, precise and concise so that the pilot conductors were able to perform the debugging on their own. In case they still needed support from the others, the logs had to provide enough information so that it was possible to solve the problem via a simple telephone call without leaking any sensitive data. Obviously, the pilots found enough information in the logs as only one case was reported in which it was necessary to forward an anonymized excerpt from a log file (in accordance with the processing contract) to identify and fix the issue. Projects handling personal data of users will encounter the same restrictions during the operational phases especially if the developers are not located in the same country which hosts the applications. The recommendation here is to enhance the logs so that these developers never need to access the administration interfaces of the applications.

8.2.5 Bootstrapping the System

The adopters of Privacy-ABC technologies must be aware that users can perform presentation without owning any credentials. Instead of using attributes extracted from the credentials, the secret key of the user can be used to generate a presentation token that includes a pseudonym but transports no other personal information. In the case of both pilots, the secret key was embedded securely into the user's smart card making it a "device secret". The presentation policy can request for a scope-exclusive pseudonym. This special pseudonym is mapped to a "scope" chosen by the verifier. When generating a pseudonym, the device secret needs to be engaged. What the reader must know is that if the verifier receives two identical scope-exclusive pseudonyms based on the same scope, he is certain that the same device secret has been used to generate them. The IdM Portals of both pilots made use of this feature in order to bootstrap the systems. The bootstrapping itself begins when the administrators extract the scope-exclusive pseudonyms from all the smart cards and store them in the whitelist of the IdM Database. After this, the personal data of the users along with a username and a unique one-time password is stored in a different area of the IdM Database. The user then receives a random smart card from the pilot conductor. When the user logs in to the registration system using her one-time password, the scope-exclusive pseudonym generated by her smart card can be mapped to her personal data set. From then on, the user can log in via Privacy-ABC technologies and obtain credentials based on her personal data set. Logging in "via

Privacy-ABC technologies" means in this case, that the user presents her scope-exclusive pseudonym. Unauthorized smart cards which generate scope-exclusive pseudonyms unknown to the IdM can therefore be excluded from participation in the pilots.

The above described bootstrapping solution impacts the handling possibilities when smart cards are lost or stolen. If the replacement card contains the same device secret as the old card, both cards will generate the same scope-exclusive pseudonyms making it impossible to block the old card from accessing services protected by Privacy-ABC technologies. Contrary to this, if the replacement card contains a new device secret, the old card can be effectively excluded from services by a) deleting the old scope-exclusive pseudonyms from the whitelist of the IdM Database and by b) revoking all credentials bound to the old device key.

8.2.6 The Smart Cards

The pilots introduced smart cards in order to provide a secure and tamperproof storage area for the users' secret keys. Furthermore, the smart cards provide flexibility to the users, as the user just needs to find a PC equipped with a smart card reader to perform issuance and presentation. And finally, the pleasant side effect was that the smart cards made participation in the pilots more attractive.

Credentials, pseudonyms, aliases and class attendance counter values were stored in the blob store of the smart cards. But the smart cards used in the pilots had only a very limited storage space. Since users of both pilots were able to apply for new credentials at any point in time, the card space turned out to be a problem that had to be solved. The Söderhamn pilot was impacted even more by this limitation of smart cards as a user could obtain up to 5 different credential types. The solution itself was fourfold.

(a) Special credential types were defined which made the need for having multiple credentials of the same kind obsolete. An example for this was the "Subject Credential". Instead of providing pupils with one credential per subject, the Subject Credential was modified to contain all possible subjects, each mapped to a Boolean value.
(b) Since users were able to launch issuance of a specific credential multiple times, the issuance itself would have failed if the card space was full. So the Browser Plugin was enhanced to include a menu that enabled the users to delete their old credentials.
(c) The User ABC System was enhanced to check periodically the blob store for revoked credentials. If a revoked credential was found, it was automatically deleted.
(d) The developers of the Reference Implementation reduced the footprints of the Idemix and U-Prove credentials to an absolute minimum.

Adopters of Privacy-ABC technologies planning to use smart cards must therefore estimate the required card space in a very early phase of their project. Impacts in the number of credential types and in the credential specifications are expected when adjusting the use-cases to what is physically available. In addition to that, even the code might be impacted, as it must be clarified which of the typical features offered by the smart cards are requested for the project.

Since every successful issuance leads to a new credential, future projects might consider adding additional functionality that either "deletes and revokes" the old credential or prevents the issuer from issuing a new credential if the old one is still valid. The latter would be challenging to implement in a water-proof way, as the issuer cannot be aware if the last issuance process was successful on the user side. Even if an acknowledge is sent to the issuer, there is no guarantee that this message reaches the recipient.

Users interacting with web services using smart cards expect a set of features to be implemented. As the smart cards are normally PIN protected, a possibility for changing the PIN must be given. On top of this, a PUK must be provided to unlock the card. In the ABC4Trust project, the Browser Plugin provided such features.

8.2.7 Inspector Application Enhancements

As can be seen in Table 8.1 and 8.2, the inspector applications are not publicly available. What is available is the "inspect service" located in the abce-services directory of the Reference Implementation. Adopters of Privacy-ABC technologies requiring an inspector would have to implement the inspector applications based on this "inspect service". One possible design approach could be to re-use the code in the Installer and to modify it to handle inspection.

8.2.8 Some Pitfalls

Presentation of tokens and their verification is performed in several steps. First, the user receives a presentation policy from the verifier. Then, the user selects which credentials she wants to use to satisfy the policy and then uses these to generate a presentation token. Next, the user sends both token and matching policy to the verifier who finally check whether the presentation token is cryptographically valid and whether it satisfies the policy.

The implementation of the communication between the user and the verifier is a task of the developer of the application that uses the ABC4Trust reference implementation. Thereby the following points need to be taken into account in order to prevent attacks that can be mounted if the user could directly connect to the ABC4Trust verification components. In particular, the user could just reply presentation tokens and policies, or even send a policy completely different from the one initially received. Thus, a stateful component must be positioned between the user and the ABC4Trust verification components. This components needs to store the original policy sent by the verifier in the session of the user before forwarding it to the user and to add this policy to the user's token before forwarding both to the verifier. Furthermore, to prevent replay attacks, the component needs to ensure that a) new policies always contain new nonces and b) old policies are deleted from the session after having received a token from the user.

Modifying credential specifications when the applications have been brought online should be avoided. If the project still insists on doing so, several aspects need to be taken into account. In the case that the impacted credentials contain revocation handles, the old credentials can be revoked. Prerequisite for this is that these revocation handles have been stored and can be mapped to the credential types. In the case that the impacted credentials do not contain revocation handles one cannot prevent the users from still using them. It would then be better to introduce a new credential type instead and to request all verifiers not to generate policies based on the old credential type. The down-side of both solutions is that new parameters need to be generated and distributed, along with the corresponding credential specification, not only to all verifiers and inspectors, but also to all users. On top of that, if the new credential contains a revocation handle, the revocation authority parameters need to be generated too. In the Reference Implementation, the credential specifications and the parameters are stored locally on each server hosting Privacy-ABC technologies. An alternative and more flexible solution would be, to introduce a new ABC4Trust component which stores this information centrally and which distributes it to all users, verifiers and inspectors. This new component could then also store the public keys of the inspectors and the global parameters thereby adding more flexibility and scalability to the system.

If a new project plans to use smart cards, it needs to focus on the latency times during issuance and presentation. In the ABC4Trust project the smart cards have been identified as the bottleneck. More than half the time was consumed during presentation for reading from the smart cards and for smart card operations. Caching the data from the smart cards for later re-use speeds up the system, but the remaining smart card operations time still cause significant delays.

In the Söderhamn pilot, the "RA Client Alias Selector" was a user interface that enabled controlling the aliases. With this functionality, the users were able to switch between aliases, to create new aliases or delete them with a few mouse clicks. Aliases were unique in the system and offered controlled linkability. So if "Superman" is chatting with "bigBoss" in different Restricted Areas, it is guaranteed that the same users are communicating with each other. As the "RA Client Alias Selector" was JavaScript hosted in the Restricted Area, downloaded and executed by the users' browsers, there is the security risk that a malicious server could request for all aliases of the user. This way, the server may even be able to identify the user if it combines the content that the user provided in different Restricted Areas using her aliases. This security risk can be avoided if the code of the "RA Client Alias Selector" were shifted into a user application, e.g. into the Browser Plugin. In general, JavaScript always bears security risks. Projects providing security and privacy should avoid using JavaScript wherever possible.

If U-Prove credentials are used in a Privacy-ABC enabled project, it must be noted that the users must apply for a batch of new tokens after having spent the old ones in order to avoid linkability due to the reuse of tokens. This process is called "re-issuance". However, re-issuance is not available in the Reference Implementation. If new projects plan to use U-Prove and need to guarantee unlinkability of presentations, they would either have to implement re-issuance themselves or define a sufficient number of tokens for the relevant credential during the setup phase of the issuer. If an adopter of Privacy-ABC technologies chooses to implement re-issuance himself, he must be aware that the issuer must always be online.

8.2.9 Data Transfer

As explained in Chapter 5, within the European Economic Area (EEA), the "place of business" of the data controller generally determines the applicable national law. However, the situation becomes more complicated if data should be transferred from one entity to another and both reside in different countries. Therefore, this section will focus on the issue of cross border data transfers and the transfer of data between data controllers and data processors.

Due to the common protection standards, as stipulated by the Directive 95/46/EC (see [Dir]), transferring data across borders is permitted within the EEA. Nonetheless, when the receiving party is established in a non-EEA state - normally referred to as "third country" - Article 25 Directive 95/46/EC generally prohibits such data transfers. Only if an adequate level of data protection can be ensured (i.e. a level of protection comparable to the one in the EEA), exemptions from this general prohibition can be granted. The adequate protection level can either be determined by a binding decision of the European Commission for an entire country or can result from other safeguards, such as appropriate contractual clauses.

Nevertheless, one must be aware that from a legal point of view, the factual transmission of data does not necessarily constitute a transfer of data in a legal sense. A transmission can only be categorised as data transfer in the meaning of the Directive 95/46/EC, if the recipient is a third party as well as located in a third country. The definition of "third party" in the directive shows, however, that data processors (such as NSN in the project pilots) are not a "third party". Therefore, according to European law, it does not constitute a data transfer if the recipient of the data is a data processor, even if located in a third country. While this result might seem odd on a first glance, it can easily be explained by the concept of a data processor and his dependency on the data controller. The processing activities of the processor are attributed to the controller, since the processor is only working on his behalf, and therefore the controller stays responsible for the data processing by the processor. Consequently, every exchange of data between those two parties has to be categorised as internal processing but not as an external data-transfer.

Therefore, transferring personal data to the pilot developers of NSN would generally not have been problematic, since they were only data processors/sub-processors and, moreover, located in Germany, in the EEA. Nonetheless, to adhere to the privacy principles of data avoidance and data minimisation it was agreed upon to include in the processing contracts the restrictions explained in Section 8.1.2 and thereby limit NSN's access to the personal data of the pupils and students.

References

[BBE+14] Thomas Baignères, Patrik Bichsel, Robert R Enderlein, Hans Knudsen, Kasper Damgård, Jonas Jensen, Gregory Neven, Janus Nielsen, Pascal Paillier, and Michael Stausholm. Final Reference Implementation. Deliverable D4.2, The ABC4Trust EU Project, 2014. Available at https://abc4trust.eu/download/D4.2%20Final%20Reference%20Implementation.pdf, Last accessed on 2014-11-08.

[BDD+14] Souheil Bcheri, Kasper L. Damgård, Daniel Deibler, Norbert Götze, Hans G. Knudsen, Maxim Moneta, Apostolos Pyrgelis, Eva Schlehahn, Michael B. Stausholm, and Harald Zwingelberg. Experiences and Feedback of the Pilots. Deliverable D5.3, The ABC4Trust EU Project, 2014. Available at https://abc4trust.eu/download/D5.3_ExperiencesAndFeedback_Final.pdf, Last accessed on 2014-11-08.

[Dir] Directive 95/46/EC of the European Parliament and of the Council of 24 October 1995 on the protection of individuals with regard to the processing of personal data and on the free movement of such data (1995).

Chapter 9
Technical Implementation and Feasibility

Gert Læssøe Mikkelsen, Kasper Damgård, Hans Guldager, Jonas Lindstrøm Jensen, Jesus Garcia Luna, Janus Dam Nielsen, Pascal Paillier, Giancarlo Pellegrino, Michael Bladt Stausholm, Neeraj Suri, and Heng Zhang

Abstract This chapter provides application developers with a presentation of the implemented reference implementation of the ABC4Trust architecture and protocols as well as a presentation on how to get started using the reference implementation. The reference implementation includes the ABC-Engines of the different entities, namely the User, Issuer, Verifier, Inspector, and Revocation Authority, and the smart card implementation for the User. This chapter also presents results of a perturbation analysis of the reference implementation. Even though the ABC4Trust focused on a server-desktop environment, we have done some proof of concept implementations and analysis of the feasibility of using smart phones for the user side of a Privacy-ABC setup; these results are also presented in this chapter.

This chapter will give an introduction and an overview of the reference implementation, including an introduction to a number of issues related to the reference implementation. It will however, not necessarily be exhaustive, i.e., in most of the cases further reading is required to get a complete understanding of the issue at hand. The presentation will start of by giving an explanation of the source code itself. This includes instructions on how to obtain and build the reference implementation, how

Gert Læssøe Mikkelsen, Kasper Damgård, Jonas Lindstrøm Jensen, Janus Dam Nielsen, and Michael Bladt Stausholm
Alexandra Institute, Aabogade 34, DK8200 Aarhus N., e-mail: {gert.l.mikkelsen, kasper.damgaard, jonas.l.jensen, janus.nielsen, michael.stausholm}@alexandra.dk

Hans Guldager
Miracle A/S, Skanderborgvej 232, DK8260 Viby J, e-mail: hgk@miracle.dk

Neeraj Suri, Jesus Garcia Luna, Giancarlo Pellegrino, and Heng Zhang
TU Darmstadt, Hochschulstraße 10, D-64289 Darmstadt, e-mail: suri@cs.tu-darmstadt.de, {jluna, gpellegrino, zhang}@deeds.informatik.tu-darmstadt.de

Pascal Paillier
Crypto Experts, 41 Boulevard des Capucines, 75002 Paris, e-mail: pascal.paillier@cryptoexperts.com

K. Rannenberg et al. (eds.), *Attribute-based Credentials for Trust*,
DOI 10.1007/978-3-319-14439-9_9

it should be deployed and how it can be integrated with custom applications. Introductions to tutorials and example applications are also given, to make the code easier to access for application developers.

The focus of the reference implementation is a typical server-desktop environment, where all computers involved are servers/PC's capable of running installed Java code. Additional security and mobility is added by the usage of smart cards, and the smart card implementation is also presented in this chapter.

Despite the focus on a server-desktop environment in the ABC4Trust project, some additional work has been done in an effort to study how feasible it would be to enable ABC4Trust on mobile platforms, i.e. tablets and smart phones. This work is based on some proof of concept implementations, and the result of this work is also covered in this chapter.

In addition to a series of functional tests, a perturbation analysis was also carried out. While the functional tests strives to prove correctness of the implemented code, the goal of the pertubation analysis is to to evaluate the robustness of the reference implementation. This analysis is also presented in this chapter.

9.1 The Reference Implementation

In the ABC4Trust project a reference implementation [BBE$^+$14] of a Privacy-ABC scheme has been implemented realizing the architecture demonstrated in Figure 9.1 and described in Chapter 2. The reference implementation has been used in the pilots of the ABC4Trust poject, and has been made public available for others to use, as described in the next section. The reader is also referred to [BBE$^+$14] for a description of the final reference implementation of the ABC4Trust project.

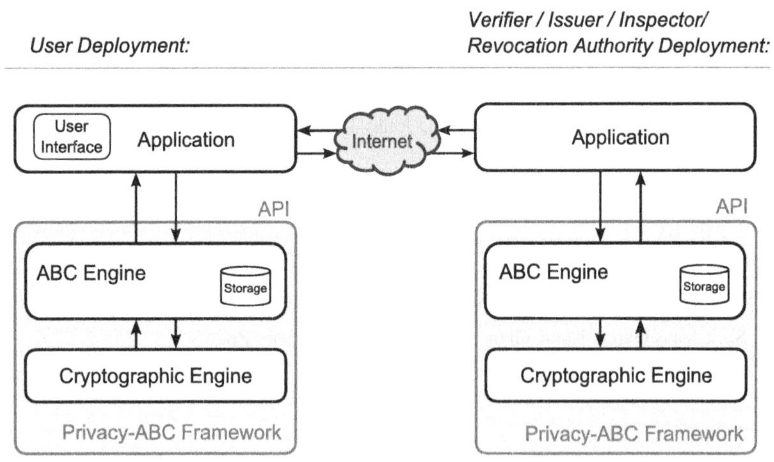

Fig. 9.1 Architecture of a Privacy-ABC System

The reference implementation has been implemented in Java and the target platform is a typical server-desktop environment with support for smart cards for security and mobility. In this section we describe the reference implementation of the ABC Engine (ABCE), the layers above the cryptographic engine (see Chapter 3) supporting the architecture and the interfaces described in Chapter 2.

9.1.1 *Obtaining and Compiling the Source Code*

The reference implementation can be obtained from the ABC4Trust source code page[1]. The reference implementation is done in Java, and the build tool Maven[2] is used. The reference implementation consists of a number of components, each serving a specific purpose and contained in a separate Maven project. These components can be split into two major groups, one responsible for the base Privacy-ABC functionality (the *core-abce*) and one responsible for providing a user interface (the *java-ui*). We explain these components in the next subsections.

As mentioned, all of the (sub-)projects are Maven based. Both the main *core-abce* and the *java-ui* projects can therefore be built using the command:

```
mvn clean install -DskipTests
```

In addition to this, any of the sub-projects of the *core-abce* and *java-ui* projects can be individually built in a similar fashion, provided that their dependencies are already built.

If you wish to import the projects into Eclipse, Eclipse projects files can be constructed using the command

```
mvn eclipse:eclipse
```

From Eclipse you can then choose *"Import"→"Existing Projects into Workspace"* to import the projects.

9.1.1.1 core-abce

The components contained in the *core-abce* project are responsible for the main Privacy-ABC functionality, i.e. these components can issue and revoke credentials, create and verify presentation proofs and other operations required to make a full Privacy-ABC system. These components are intended to be integrated in custom applications, which will be responsible for handling the various business logic involved in the overall Privacy-ABC system. For example, in order to be able to issue a

[1] https://github.com/p2abcengine/p2abcengine
[2] http://maven.apache.org/

passport credential, an issuer must implement some kind of user authentication and authorization mechanism ensuring that the credential is only issued to the right person and that the attributes contained in the credential does in fact reflect the claimed identity of the user.

The project contains a number of sub-projects for integration tests, utilities, helper classes, ui connectivity and the central ABC functionality. We will give a short explanation of the *abc4trust-xml, abce-interfaces, abce-components* and *abce-services* projects which are central for the ABC functionality and therefore most likely to be of interest to third party developers. The remaining projects can be looked at for inspiration and understanding.

abc4trust-xml

This project contains the xml schema definition (XSD) of the datatypes, such as presentation policies or credential specifications, used in the various ABC4trust protocols. The XSD will allow custom implementations of the ABC4Trust system to construct xml messages understandable by the reference implementation. The XSD also allows JAXB to automatically generate Java classes representing the XML datatypes. These Java classes can be instantiated using the ObjectFactory class.

abce-interfaces

This project contains interfaces for the classes in *abce-components*. A developer looking to integrate the reference implementation into a Java application, will most likely be interested in the interfaces in the eu.abce4trust.abce.external package, as they act as the API for the various ABC engines. Developers looking to modify the reference implementation or implement a custom ABC4Trust implementation themselves, may look at the interfaces for inspiration.

abce-components.

This project contains the classes that provide the functionality required for the complete Privacy-ABC system. This includes ABC engines for users, issuers, verifiers, inspectors and revocation authorities as well utility classes handling management of smartcards and storage of various parameters and keymaterial. The project makes extensive use of Guice for dependency injection. The configuration for the dependency injection is handled by Java classes in the package eu.abc4trust.guice. For further documentation on Guice[3], we refer to the Guice homepage.

[3] https://code.google.com/p/google-guice/

abce-services

This project contains a set of web services for the various ABC engines. This allows a developer wishing to integrate ABC4Trust into an application to use a REST API rather than using the Java classes directly. The services could in principle be exposed directly to the users, however since they expose all the methods of the ABCE engines, this might pose a security risk. For instance, if an inspector ABC web service was exposed to the public Internet, anybody knowing the URL could inspect presentation tokens. The web services should therefore be protected somehow. As we will describe later, we suggest wrapping them by some other web service, which can then provide access control in addition to implementing context specific business logic.

9.1.1.2 java-ui

The code provided in *core-abce* can perform the logic behind the various Privacy-ABC operations, e.g. performing a proof given a credential and a presentation policy. It is however assumed that all other entities in the system are potentially malicious. For the server side services this is partially handled by the Privacy-ABC protocols themselves and partially by the service specific application. On the user side, a trusted platform is required to manage credentials, i.e list and delete credentials as well as update revocation information at random intervals, and inform the user about what information will actually be revealed in order to satisfy some presentation or issuance policy.

The goal of the *java-ui* project is to provide an interface to a trusted platform, in a generic fashion, integrated with the common browsers Mozilla Firefox and Microsoft Internet Explorer. This will cover some common use-cases, where some browser based web-application needs to authenticate the user to some degree, such as webshops and internet forums.

The general architecture behind the user interface consists of 3 main components. An ABC user service, essentially the user service from *core-abce* with some minor additions, a browser plugin and a web application for displaying the graphical user interface. This architecture is used to allow for maximal reuse of code; In order to support a new browser, only a new browser specific plugin is required, both the ABC user service and the web application can be reused.

When some web application wishes to use an ABC4Trust protocol for either issuing a credential or performing a presentation proof, the following workflow is performed (an example of presentation is shown in Figure 9.2):

1. The initiating web application uses Javascript to create and trigger an event (containing certain resources).
2. The browser plugin listens for this event, so when the event is triggered, the plugin knows where the needed resources, i.e. the presentation policy, issuance policy or verification endpoint, can be located.
3. The plugin downloads the policy and passes this to the local ABC userservice.

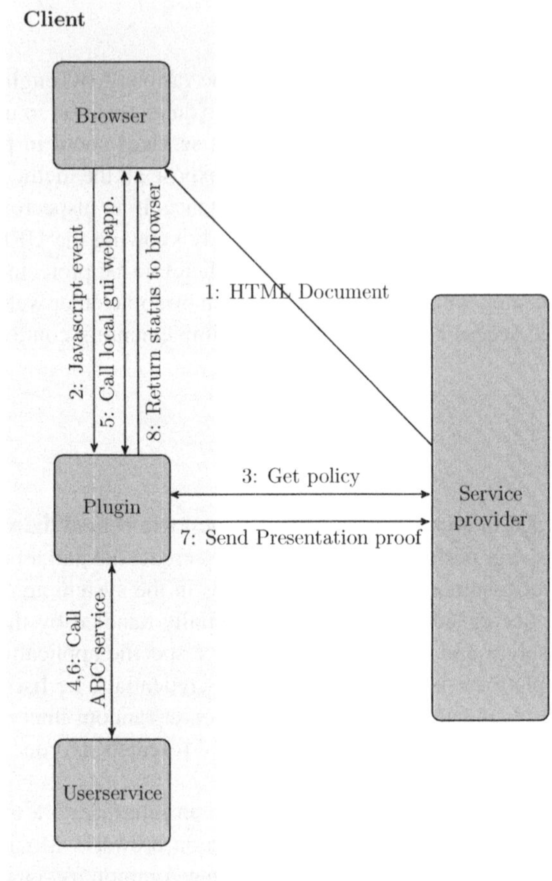

Fig. 9.2 The communication flow when performing a presentation

4. The ABC userservice computes the possible combinations of credentials that can be used to satisfy the policy and returns the list to the browser plugin.
5. The plugin passes this information to the local GUI web application which presents the choices to the user.
6. Once the user has made a selection, the choice is returned to the plugin.
7. The plugin passes the choice to the local ABC userservice.
8. The ABC service computes an ABC protocol message (a presentation token or issuance message), which is send to the plugin.
9. The plugin sends this protocol message to the initiating web application, which can then act accordingly, e.g. if the presentation token was valid, the user is taken to another webpage.

In case of issuance, there is most likely multiple steps in the protocol. In this case the browser plugin sends the protocol message produced in step 9 to an URL specified in the event from step 1. The response is passed on to the local ABC service and the workflow is restarted from step 7.

The browser plugin mainly acts as a communication layer between the ABC service and the graphical user interface, as the workflow above indicates.

In order to support other browsers or change the behaviour of the existing plugins, a custom browser plugin can be constructed. This plugin must only satisfy a few basic requirements in order to be functional, but should also offer certain additional functionality, in order to take advantage of all the possibilities provided by ABC4Trust. If the plugin is capable of listening for the javascript ABC4Trust events and can handle them meaningfully, i.e. pass data between the local ABCE userservice, the local GUI web application and the external Privacy-ABC service provider, the most basic functionality of Privacy-ABC is covered. However, the plugin should also offer functionality to administer (list, delete and request updated revocation information) for locally stored credentials and pseudonyms and as well as handle smart,cards, i.e. prompt the user for PIN codes.

9.1.2 Deployment of the ABCE as Web Services

The ABCE can be deployed as a number of RESTful web services as defined in the reference architecture [BCD+14] and Chapter 2. A web service interface allows the ABCE to be deployed using standard techniques and makes integration less time consuming by exposing a REST-based interface.

In this section we describe how to build, setup, and integrate the ABCE issuer, user, verifier, inspector, and revocation web services.

The web services act as wrappers for the respective ABCE roles, allowing for easy deployment and integration, and they expose a simple REST interface with resources mapping directly to the counterparts defines in the architecture. The web services and can either be deployed in any standard Java application server like Glassfish or Tomcat, or as standalone applications using a lightweight embedded Jetty servlet container. The reference implementation provides binaries for both deployment scenarios. A Java API is also provided by the reference implementation if a tighter integration is needed, see Section 9.1.3.

An example setup of an ABC4Trust issuer could be roughly as follows: The ABCE issuer web service would be located on an internal network or behind a firewall only accepting connections from whitelisted IP addresses. This prevents any external users to access the ABCE web service directly. The issuer web application would on the other hand be open for outside connections. This web application would, in addition to providing some webpage allowing user interaction, expose some of the same resources as the ABCE web service, namely the *initIssuanceProtocol* and *issuanceProtocolStep* resources. Although the two mentioned resources should be available to the public, the web application should still take measures to ensure that only authenticated users have access to them.

Similarly to the issuer case, a revocation service will have to expose certain resources, allowing clients to obtain revocation handles and revocation information, to the public while limiting access to other resources, such as the ability to revoke credentials. Both the inspector and user services should be inaccessible by external users.

Like the Java ABC engines, some of the web service ABC engines must be initialized, i.e. they must be given system parameters and various other public key information before they can be used. This should be done either manually using a tool such as Curl or could be done by a context specific application, such as a the (web) application utilizing the ABCE service, depending on the general Privacy-ABC system setup.

9.1.2.1 Building the ABCE web services

The ABCE web services are implemented using Java and Jersey, the JAX-RS reference implementation, is used as the foundation for exposing the service interface. The services can be compiled using a standard Java tool chain based on Maven. Each service can be compiled either as a standalone executable or a war-file ready for deployment in a standard application server/servlet container, e.g. Tomcat. The standalone executable is comprised of the service implementation bundled and an embedded Jetty servlet container, and allows for easier installation.

In this section we will show how to build the web services. The source code for the services is located in following path of the project repository:

```
Code/core-abce/abce-services
```

All commands are relative to this path. And assumes that a

```
mvn clean install -DskipTests
```

has been run in the parent directory. This will download dependencies and compile the ABCE for inclusion into the services. The standalone executable is created by instantiating the following command template with the proper value for "{service-name}" which can be: *issuance*, *verification*, *revocation*, *user*, or *inspection*.

```
mvn -P selfcontained-{service-name}-service install -DskipTests
```

The war-files suitable for deployment in a servlet container are compiled by instantiating the following command template with the proper value for "{service-name}" which is drawn from the set: issuance, verification, revocation, user, and inspection.

```
mvn -P {service-name}-service install -DskipTests
```

A bash script found in the abce-services directory has been created to generate both kinds of artefacts in an automated and reliable manner. The script is executed using the following command (remember to check permissions if the script fails) from the abce-services directory:

```
compileServices.sh
```

The artefacts can be found in the abce-services/target directory.

9.1.2.2 Setting up and running the ABCE web services

The standalone executable is executed as a standard Java jar file. The port number is an optional argument with the default value of 9500. The following command template can be used to make it run on a port defined by the value of "{port-number}":

```
java -jar selfcontained-{service-name}-service.war {port-number}
```

Each service will create storage directories as direct subfolders to the directory in which they are executed. The war-file can be deployed in the standard ways defined for the given servlet container. They will be available on the port number as configured in the servlet container.

9.1.2.3 Running the ABCE web services in debug mode

The standalone web services can easily be made available for a remote debugger. This is highly useful for identifying bugs during development of the ABCE web services. The following command template can be instantiated to enable a standard Java debugger to attach to the web service process on port 4000:

```
java -Xdebug -Xrunjdwp:transport=dt_socket,address=4000,server=y,
    suspend=n -jar target/selfcontained-{service-name}-service.
    war {port-number}
```

9.1.2.4 Deployment and integration of the services

As mentioned above, the issuance, verification, revocation, and inspection services can be deployed either as standalone or in a servlet container. This allows for the ABCE to be deployed and maintained in the same way as other Java servlet based infrastructure. Since the ABCE web services do not implement any kind of access control, they are not meant to be facing a network e.g. a corporate network or the Internet. A layer consisting of at least a firewall is required, and often also a layer containing some level of business logic.

An example is the issuer, which provides a wide range of resources. Some of them like *issuanceStep* should be available to users and others like *setupSystemParameters* or *setupIssuerParameters* should not be widely exposed. Also *initIssuanceProtocol* should not be directly exposed to the network, but rather only be exposed to some business application, which can do the initial validation of users, and lookup their attributes, which should be provided to the issuance service as input to the *initIssuanceProtocol*.

Because the web services do not currently provide any authentication mechanisms anybody who has network access to the services can send commands to the services. This does not threat the secret keys stored at each service, as the keys themselves are not exposed. However, service interrupts can easily be accomplished by e.g. requesting new revocation authority parameters with the same UID as the current parameters. This will overwrite the parameters at the revocation authority and result in requests being rejected or responses being malformed. In addition to service interrupts, anyone with network access to an issuer service, will be able to initiate an issuance with self provided attributes. Therefore we recommend that the ABCE web services are run behind a firewall and access only be allowed from outside to the necessary resources.

The user services also support the same flexible deployment options. The user service would most likely be deployed as a standalone executable, which can be installed on users machines. The project has created a Windows installer which downloads a precursor for user web service as part of the installation process and installs the user web service as a Windows services. And thus makes it available for the browser plugins which also have been developed and which provide the graphical user interface to the supported user actions.

9.1.2.5 Tutorial for interacting with the ABCE web services

The ABCE web services expose a REST over HTTP interface defined in [BCD$^+$14], which is a superset of the interface defined in [BBE$^+$14]. The main difference between [BCD$^+$14] and [BBE$^+$14] is the addition of endpoints for storing various resources such as system parameters and credential specifications on the relevant web services. We will give a brief introduction to the web services interface by presenting excerpts of a tutorial demonstrating the usage of the web services. The tutorial is available as part of the source code in the abce-services directory. In addition a bash script to automatically execute the tutorial given a setup of the web services is available.

The scenario of the tutorial is a soccer team selling tickets for their home matches using an external ticket handling company (e.g. like TicketMaster.com), which will issue tickets on behalf of the soccer team. The soccer team employees will then verify the tickets at the soccer arena on the day of the match to make sure that only paying customers are allowed in. Furthermore, the soccer team provides special treatment to VIP customers who will enter in a raffle if they show up. The scenario can naturally be extended to cover a wide range of situations where an organization e.g. a theatre or a museum sells tickets to one or more events.

The tutorial consists of the following steps:

Setup phase

1. Define credential specification and presentation policies
2. Setup system parameters
3. Generate inspector keys
4. Setup revocation authority parameters
5. Setup issuance parameters

Live phase

6. Issue ticket (credential)
7. Present ticket (generates a presentation token)

Remark that although inspector keys are generated and revocation parameters are setup, these are not used in the tutorial. The tutorial can be extended to include inspection and revocation by using the inspector key and the revocation parameters.

The first step is to define credential specifications. for a VIP ticket, which we use in this tutorial. The next step after we have defined the credential specification and presentation policies is to create the system parameters. An issuer, in our case the ticketing company, generates the system parameters. The issuer executes an HTTP request against the issuer web service. We show it here using curl, which is a program for executing HTTP requests.

```
curl -X POST --header 'Content-Type: text/xml' 'http://localhost
    :9100/issuer/setupSystemParameters/?securityLevel=80&
    cryptoMechanism=urn:abc4trust:1.0:algorithm:idemix' >
    systemparameters.xml
```

In this case curl is instructed to make an HTTP POST request against an issuance service running on port 9100 at localhost. We target the *setupSystemParameters* resource and provide the security level and crypto mechanism as arguments. The security level ultimately dictates the key size to be used in the deployment which uses the system parameters, e.g. 2048 bit. The crypto mechanism can be either Idemix or U-Prove or others. The resulting system parameters are written to a file called systemparameters.xml. This process, depending on the hardware, may take more than 15 seconds. Next the system parameters must be distributed among the other parties (users, verifier(s), revocation authority/ies, and inspector(s)). As an example, we here show the HTTP request for storing the system parameters at the revocation authority:

```
curl -X POST --header 'Content-Type: text/xml' -d
    @systemparameters.xml 'http://localhost:9500/revocation/
    storeSystemParameters/' >
    storeSystemParametersResponceAtRevocationAutority.xml
```

The revocation authority needs to generate revocation authority parameters before the issuer can generate issuer parameters.

```
curl -X POST --header 'Content-Type: text/xml' -d @tutorial-
    resources/revocationReferences.xml 'http://localhost:9500/
    revocation/setupRevocationAuthorityParameters?keyLength=1024&
    cryptoMechanism=urn:abc4trust:1.0:algorithm:idemix&uid=http%3
    A%2F%2Fticketcompany%2Frevocation' >
    revocationAuthorityParameters.xml
```

Here the key length, crypto mechanism, and revocation authority parameters UID are given as arguments. The UID is URL encoded. The revocation authority parameters and credential specification must be distributed among the issuer, users, and verifier. The commands are similar to the one for storing system parameters. The rest of the tutorial is available online at the ABC4Trust homepage.

9.1.3 Integrating the ABCE in Custom Solutions

During the process of developing the core-abce a 'service helper' were created for each ABCE engine to wrap the boilerplate code needed for setting up the engine. These helpers setup the ABCE engines by reading parameters from files, importing them, performing simple cross validations and automatically generating and exporting parameters if needed. These service helpers were mainly intended for internal use in integration test, but because of their simplicity also used in early demo applications, and ended up in the demo services created for the pilots. Integration tests and helpers are further described below.

As the pilots started to implement their systems they used these helpers instead of coding directly towards the ABC4Trust API, hereby saving the job to write the equivalent initialization code. It also spared them from having to update their applications as the ABCE API changed a bit during the run of the pilots. Therefore, the pilots could concentrate more on implementing their web applications.

For an implementer who wants to experiment with the ABC4Trust libraries, the service helpers would be a good start for learning the concepts of setting up an ABC system. Going further to a real world setup with heavy load, one may need to replace the simple file-based storage mechanism supplied with the reference implementation with database storage. To do this, it is necessary to implement the various storage interfaces of the ABC4Trust API and replace the default implementations. Overriding the default storage implementation is not supported, but the source code could be used as basis for creating their own helpers. Here the helper initialization methods should be updated, but everything else could be left unchanged, as all the other parts of the helpers would stay unaffected.

9.1.3.1 Integration tests

The motivation for creating the integration test was to make sure that the ABCE engines could run separately and reveal any side effects not detected in the normal unit test where all ABCE engines are running inside the same Java Virtual Machine. The integrations tests are also used to check if ABC4Trust xml messages are marshaled correctly when sent over wire.

In the integration tests, each ABCE engine role would be started in a web service running on its own Java Virtual Machine and the other required engines would then be combined in a test class running a test scenario. For example, when testing the issuer, the service generates the issuer parameters, and exports them so that they can be picked up by the user and the verifier. After the user and the verifier imported the parameters, credentials are issued to the user and then a presentation is made towards the verifier.

All the integration tests relies on the service helpers, and the web services in each integration tests also serve a small demo application.

9.1.3.2 IssuanceHelper

The helper for the issuer ABCE, the *IssuanceHelper*, can be use to setup the basis for a Privacy-ABC system.

On the startup, it reads a list of pairs of credential specification and issuance policies, runs through this list and checks if credential specifications are stored in the key manager, extracts the issuer parameter UID from the policy, and checks if an issuer parameter has been generated and stored for the UID. When checking the issuer parameters, it uses a simple convention of appending crypto engine names to the UID, e.g. for the course credential used in the Patras pilot the issuer parameters with UIDs *urn:patras:issuer:credCourse:idemix* and *urn:patras:issuer:credCourse:uprove* will be tested. In the case that the issuer parameters need to be generated, they will also be exported as a file resource so that it can be imported by the other ABCEs.

The *IssuanceHelper* also contains an alternative initialization method where issuer parameters from another issuer can be imported, if these are needed by the issuance policy. In the case that the issuer is dealing with revocable credentials the *IssuanceHelper* can be initialized with revocation parameters.

Besides offering helper methods for running the issuance protocol, the *IssuanceHelper* is also capable of producing templates of issuance policies with updated revocation information.

9.1.3.3 RevocationHelper

The *RevocationHelper* wraps the revocation ABC Engine. It is initialized with a list of *RevocationReferences* consisting of a revocation authority UID and URLs for the web services exposed by the revocation authority. These web services must either be taken from the the generic web services described in Section 9.1.2, or follow the REST method signatures defined here when implementing your own web service.

Inside the helper, the UID defining a revocation authority is checked for existence, and will be generated and exported if it is not present.

9.1.3.4 InspectorHelper

The *InspectorHelper* generates inspector key pairs based on a list of inspector UIDs and exports the public part for the user ABCE. When initializing, the list of credential specifications relevant for inspection must be supplied.

9.1.3.5 VerificationHelper

The *VerificationHelper* imports parameters supplied by issuers and revocation authorities and initializes the different stores inside the ABCE. Besides having the obvious *verify* method, it also has a few utility methods.

It can be used as a template engine for producing static presentation policies where only the nonce and maybe a simple text in the application data differs for each presentation, and if dealing with revocable credentials it can fill out revocation information in the policies.

9.1.3.6 UserHelper

The *UserHelper* is initialized with the parameters from issuers, revocation authorities and inspectors.

Unlike the other helpers, the *UserHelper* is does not wrap the internal methods of the user ABCE, but exposes the different stores and managers for direct access.

9.1.4 Generating Parameters

When designing a system using ABC4Trust from the scratch, the first set of parameters that must be generated are the system parameters. These parameters describe the basic cryptographic primitives that the other parameters must be built on. The system parameters are generated given a key length defining the security of the system. A discussion on the key length and security level can be found in Chapter 4. All entities' ABCEs in a setup must use the same system parameters in order to ensure compatibility. For instance, if two issuers use difference system parameters, presentation proofs based on credentials from both would not be possible.

When generating service specific parameters, i.e. issuer parameters, revocation authority parameters and inspector public keys, a unique *uid* must be specified. If the *uid* is reused in any subsequent calls to a *setup-X* method, a new set of parameters will be produced, however, the services will not update their private key material accordingly, resulting in the new parameters being invalid. Note that a single ABCE service can serve as an engine for a number of different logical entities, e.g. a bank could use the same issuer service to issue both Visa and MasterCard credentials. It is therefore recommended to encode a version into each *uid*.

9.1.5 Example Applications

To demonstrate various features of Privacy-ABCs, we have developed a couple of example applications that implement Issuer, Verifier and Inspector roles to run a sample scenario where a hotel guest can book a room. The scenario involves issuance and presentation of credentials as well as inspection of presentation tokens. The Issuer can also act as Revocation Authority so that revocation of credentials can be tested (see section 9.1.8).

Besides the hotel booking scenario, the example application includes an age verification example where the birthdate attribute from the credentials can be compared to a date entered in the web application.

For the end user side, we reuse the same user client as the pilots. As we want to reduce the complexity of the user client setup, the user client is configured to simulate the real smart card using a "software smart card".

9.1.6 The Hotel Booking Demo Scenario

9.1.6.1 Issuer application

Using the issuer application, one can create and maintain a list of Users called "Persons" and assign credentials of various types to them (see Figures 9.3 - 9.5).

The data model for Person is very simple and contains only First Name, Last Names, Gender and Birthdate. The credentials are also designed to be very simple and the attribute values can be either obtained from Person or automatically generated in the case of unique identifiers or expiration dates.

Person List

Person Id	Firstname	Lastname	Gender	Birthday	PIN
1.000.000.000	John	Doe	M	1976-07-21	14776
1.000.000.001	Alice	Von Nextdoor	F	1981-02-03	53281

Fig. 9.3 The issuer administration application

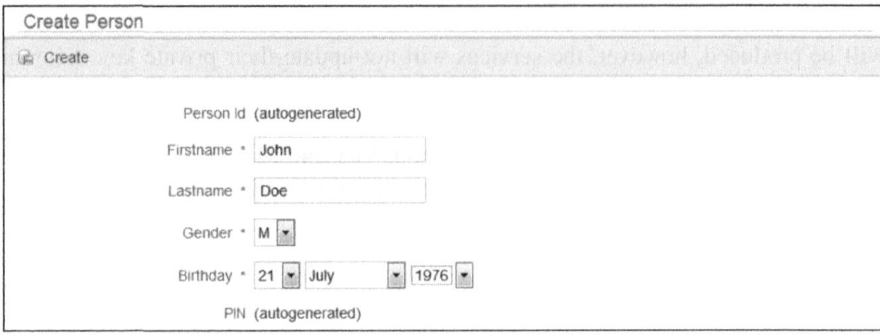

Fig. 9.4 Adding a new "Person" to the issuer's database

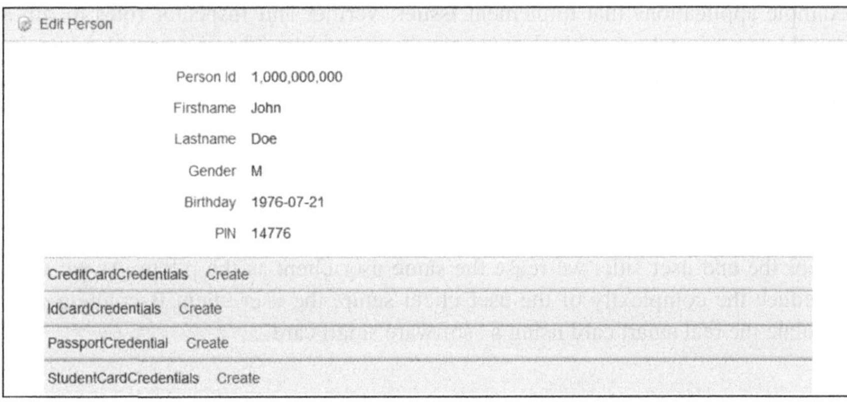

Fig. 9.5 A new "Person" has been created and the Id and the PIN have been assigned

For a credit card credential, the type (see Figure 9.6) and for passport credentials the country must be specified.

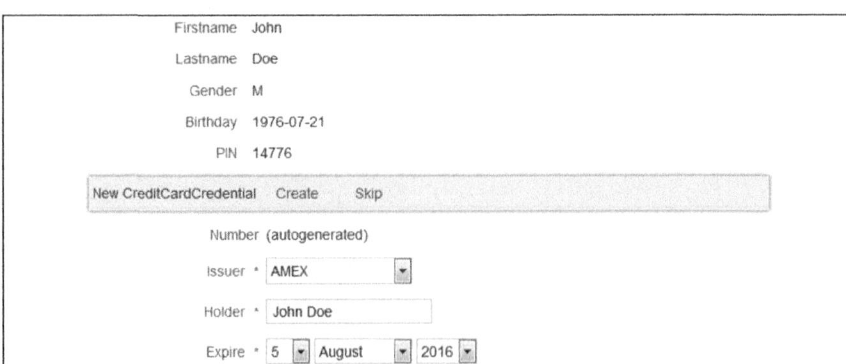

Fig. 9.6 Adding a credit card credential

In the issuer application, one can select a Person to get an overview of the assigned credentials and their states (Figure 9.7), and view the details by clicking on them (Figure 9.8).

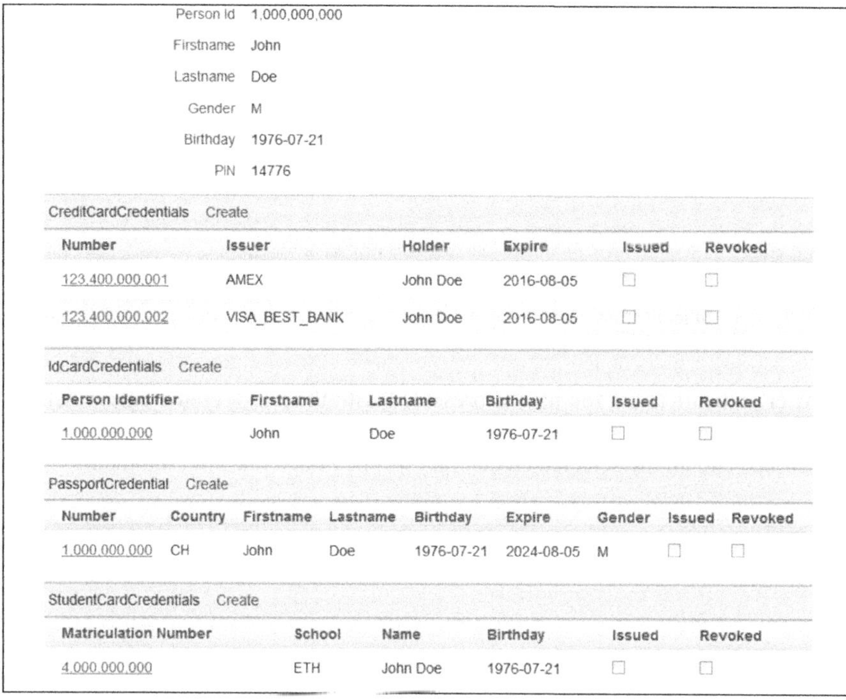

Fig. 9.7 The credentials assigned to the user

Fig. 9.8 Details of a credential

9.1.6.2 Obtaining credentials

When the credentials are assigned by the issuer, the end user can visit the issuer application to get the credentials issued (see Figure 9.9). The user enters her Person Identifier and her PIN. In the real world, the user would know this identifier from their country's exiting id scheme, and the PIN could be handed over in a secure way, e.g. sent to their official address as a "PIN Letter".

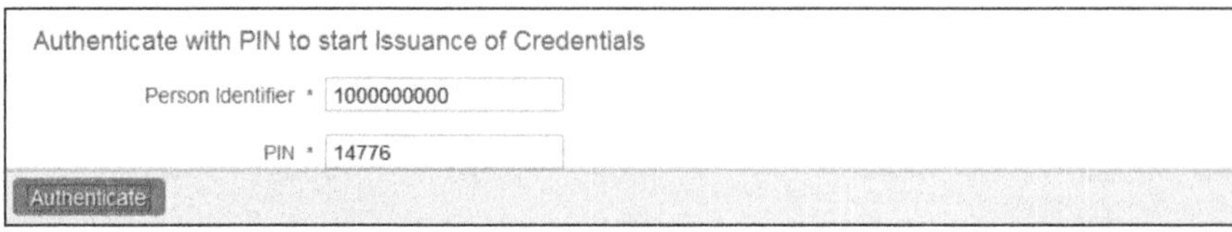

Fig. 9.9 User Authentication

After authentication, the user is presented with the list of credentials which are ready for issuance (see Figure 9.10). By pressing the start button, the user client will be invoked and all the selected credentials will be issued one after another.

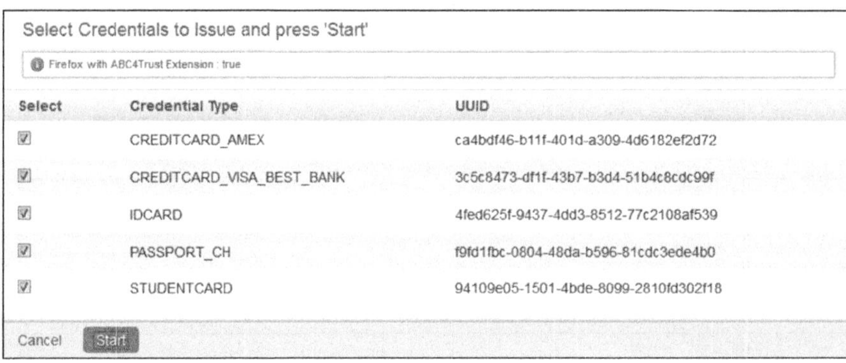

Fig. 9.10 User selects which credentials should be issued

As credentials are stored on a "software smart card", the user must enter the smart card PIN to access it (see Figure 9.11). For each credential the user has to confirm and accept the issuance policy (see Figure 9.12).

Having issued all the credentials, the user can now open the credential manager from the user client and view details of the credentials (see Figure 9.13).

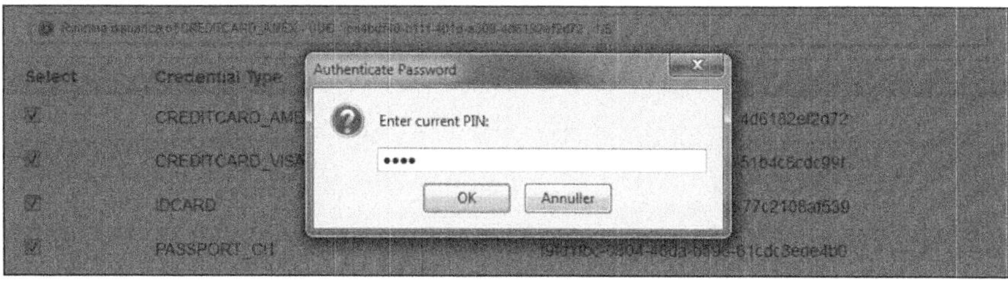

Fig. 9.11 User enters the smart card PIN

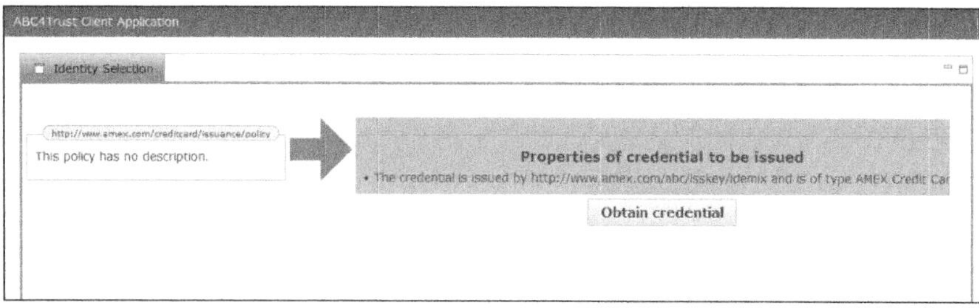

Fig. 9.12 User accepts the issuance policy

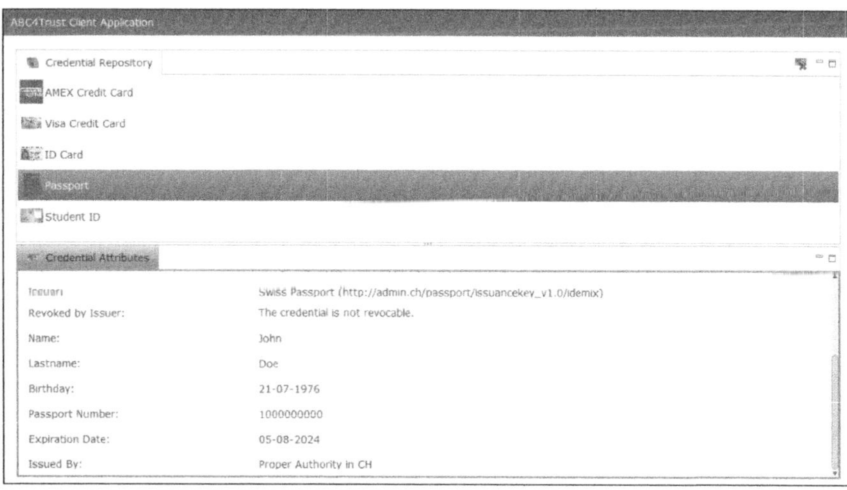

Fig. 9.13 Credentials have been issued

9.1.6.3 Booking a hotel room

The user is now ready to book a room at the Sweet Dreams Suites Hotel and selects the desired room type and the check-in date (see Figure 9.14). In the next step, a confirmation page is presented (see Figure 9.15), where the user is informed about the free-cancellation policy of the hotel.

Fig. 9.14 User books a hotel room

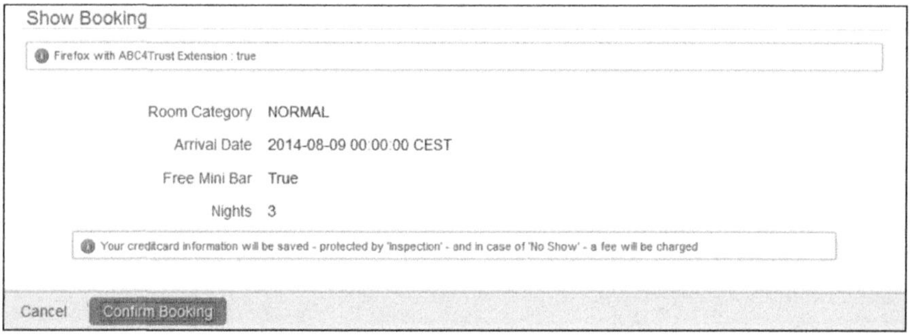

Fig. 9.15 Booking confirmation page

When confirming the booking, the user client browser plugin is invoked and the user is presented with the Identity Selector. The user must be able to present a valid passport and a credit card (see Figure 9.16). The user will also get informed that the credit card number is delivered not in clear form but as an inspectable token.

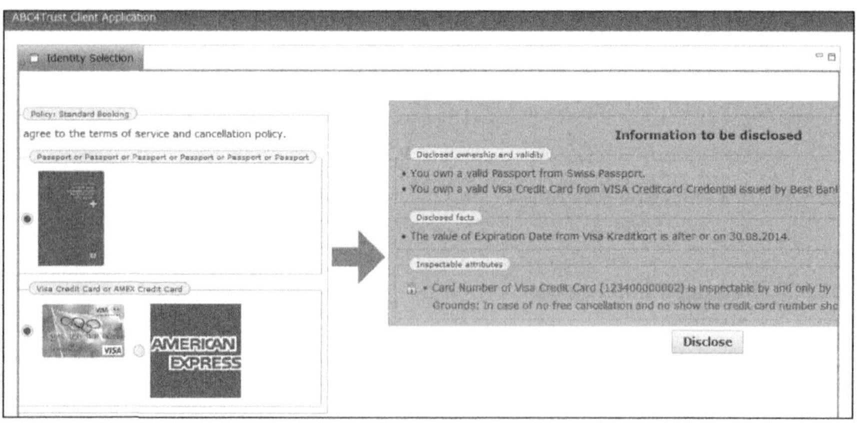

Fig. 9.16 User selects which credentials to be used

Fig. 9.17 Booking is accepted by the hotel

Clicking on *Disclose*, the user client sends the presentation token to the hotel application to validate the token. After validation the presentation token is stored at the hotel administration database, so that it can be used later for payment processing. After verification, the hotel guest is redirected to the status page (see Figure 9.17).

9.1.6.4 The guest not showing up

If the customer does not show up on the check-in date and does not cancel her room in time, the hotel is entitled to charge the fee. The hotel staff can look up the booking in the hotel administration application (see Figure 9.18) and confirm that the customer did not show up (see Figure 9.19). In this case, the presentation token of the booking can be forwarded to the inspector (see Figure 9.20) using a simple web service.

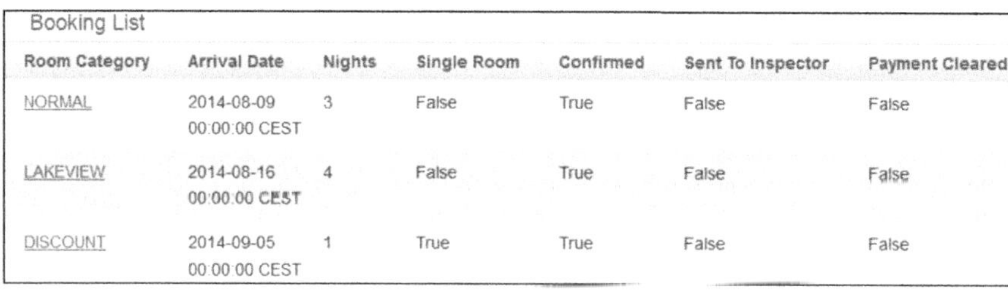

Booking List

Room Category	Arrival Date	Nights	Single Room	Confirmed	Sent To Inspector	Payment Cleared
NORMAL	2014-08-09 00:00:00 CEST	3	False	True	False	False
LAKEVIEW	2014-08-16 00:00:00 CEST	4	False	True	False	False
DISCOUNT	2014-09-05 00:00:00 CEST	1	True	True	False	False

Fig. 9.18 Looking up booking entries

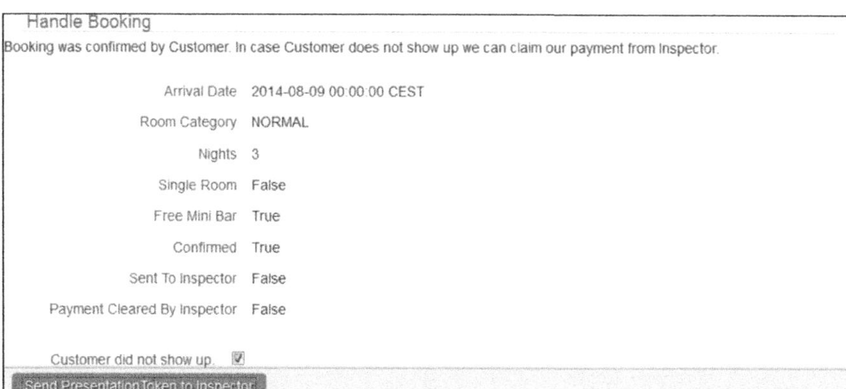

Fig. 9.19 Sending the presentation token to the inspector

Fig. 9.20 Presentation token sent to Inspector

9.1.6.5 Inspector clearing the payments

The Inspector, which in this scenario we could consider it to be a credit card clearing house, receives the presentation tokens from its clients (see Figure 9.21).

Fig. 9.21 Overview of the inspection requests (before inspecting the token)

The inspector can selected a specific request and invoke the inspection method to extract and decrypt the credit card number from the presentation token (see Figures 9.22 - 9.24). The inspector has to of course act according to the inspection policy agreed upon between the inspector, the user and the verifier.

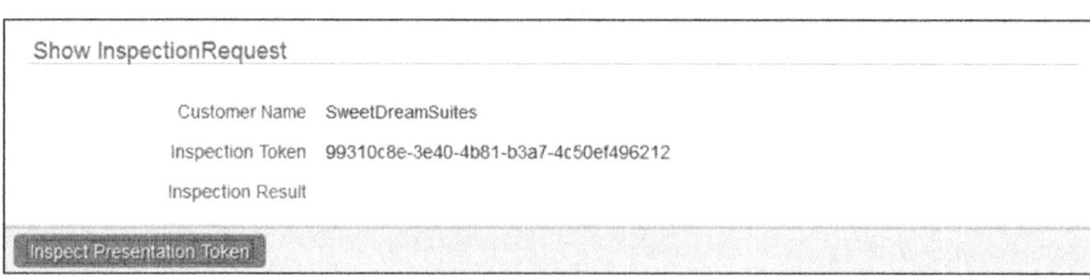

Fig. 9.22 Viewing an inspection request

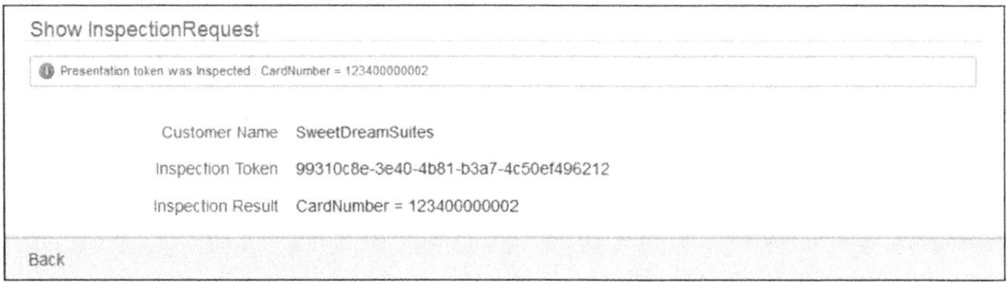

Fig. 9.23 Credit card number has been decrypted

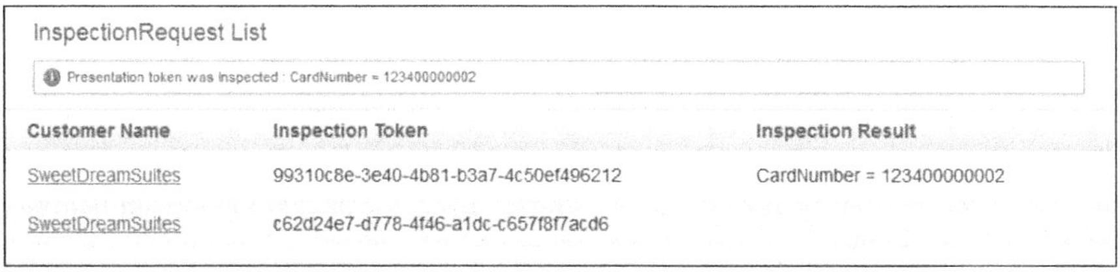

Fig. 9.24 Overview of the inspection requests (after inspecting the token)

9.1.6.6 Hotel retrieving the payment status

Back at the hotel, the staff can now send a request to the inspector and check if the payment has been *cleared* for a specific booking (see Figures 9.25 and 9.26). Again the hotel administration application contacts the inspector using a web service.

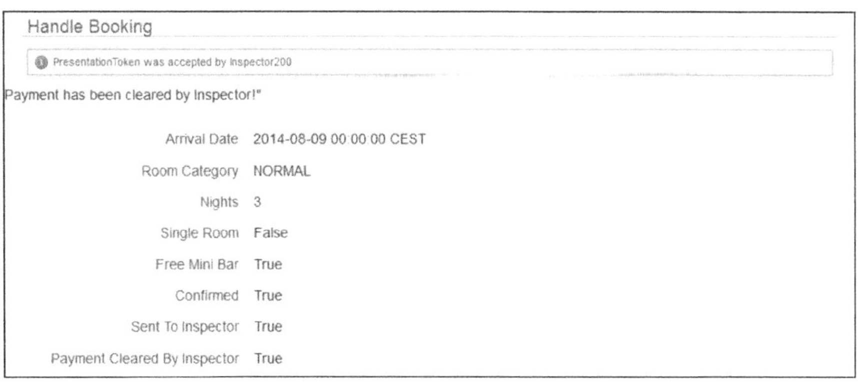

Fig. 9.25 Hotel checks if the payment has been cleared

Booking List

Room Category	Arrival Date	Nights	Single Room	Confirmed	Sent To Inspector	Payment Cleared
NORMAL	2014-08-09 00:00:00 CEST	3	False	True	True	True
LAKEVIEW	2014-08-16 00:00:00 CEST	4	False	True	True	False
DISCOUNT	2014-09-05 00:00:00 CEST	1	True	True	False	False

Fig. 9.26 Overview of the bookings (after clearing the payment)

9.1.6.7 Hotel booking scenario afterwords

The number of data fields used in the hotel booking scenario was deliberately kept as minimum as possible, as it was meant to show the steps. For a real world application, one may need a few more fields to be stored and presented in the application, such as *booking reference*.

Whether the name of the hotel guest and the passport number should be disclosed in a readable form or as inspectable token could be dictated by the local jurisdiction. Privayc-ABC users may appreciate minimal or at least protected (via inspection) data collection.

9.1.7 Access Control Based on Birthdate

For many Privacy-ABC use cases verifiers may want to perform an age verification based on the birthdate attribute in the credentials before granting users access to the resources. A flexible way would be to compare the birthdate with a reference date.

To demonstrate this, we have created a dynamic birthdate test application. Using the user client credential manager, the user can check the birthdate attested on their credential. In the web application the user can specify a reference date to which the credential must be compared (see Figure 9.27).

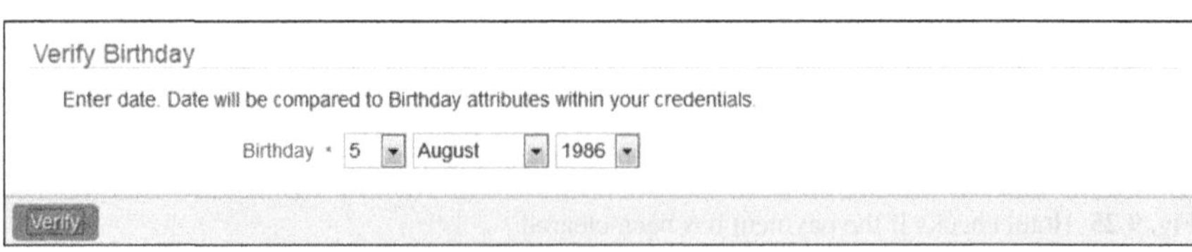

Fig. 9.27 Specifying the reference date

Having specified the reference date, the user continues to the confirmation page (see Figure 9.28) where the user client can be invoked by pressing *Start*.

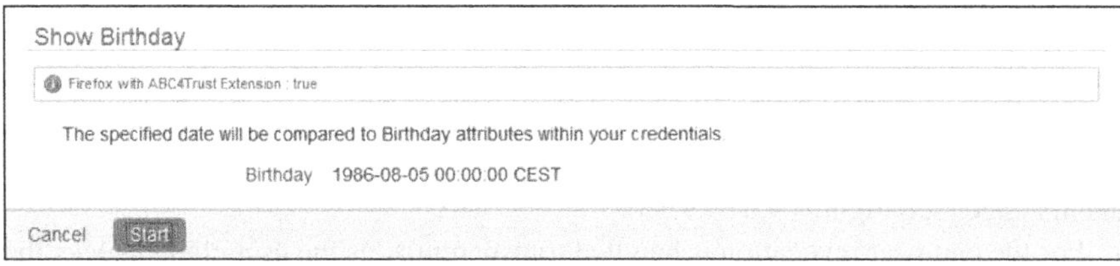

Fig. 9.28 Starting the birthdate comparison

The policy sent to the user contains policy alternatives for all 6 "comparison predicates", namely *equal-to*, *not equal*, *before*, *before-equal*, *later* and *later-equal*, so the user can choose the one she would like to test (see Figure 9.29). For example, comparing John Doe's birthdate 1976-07-21 to 1986-08-05 the policies for *not equal*, *before*, *before-equal* can all be satisfied. In our example, the user selects the policy proving that the birthdate is *before* 1986-08-05.

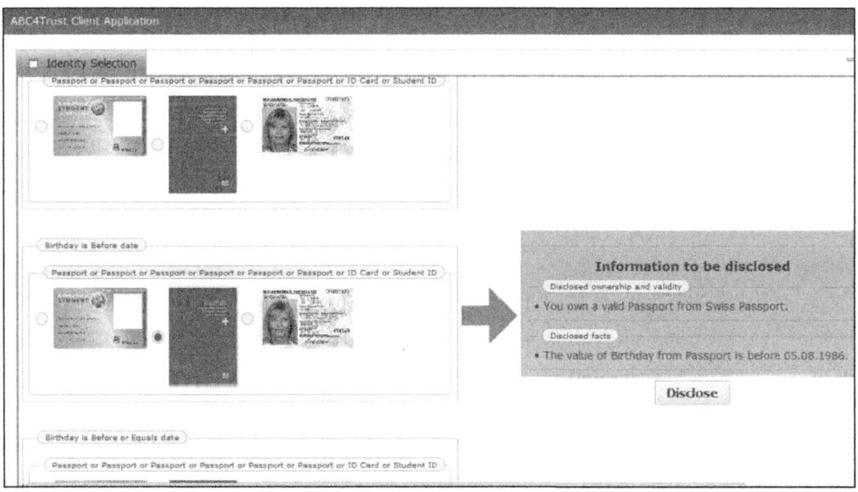

Fig. 9.29 User selects the policy alternative and the credential

After the presentation is completed, the user will be redirected to a page showing the result (see Figure 9.30).

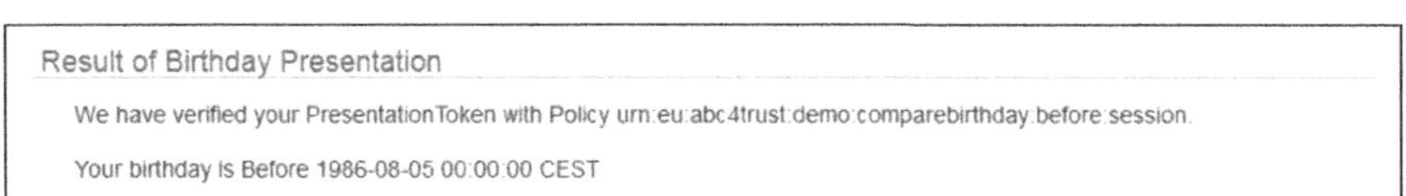

Fig. 9.30 Result of the Birthdate Test

9.1.8 Handling Revocation

The issuer demo application can be configured to use revocable credentials. In this case, the issuer will get the option to revoke the issued credentials on the credential details page (see Figures 9.31 - 9.33).

For the end user revocation is handled transparently, as the user client checks the revocation status before using the credential. So if a credential is revoked, it will not appear in the Identity Selector and cannot be used to satisfy a given policy.

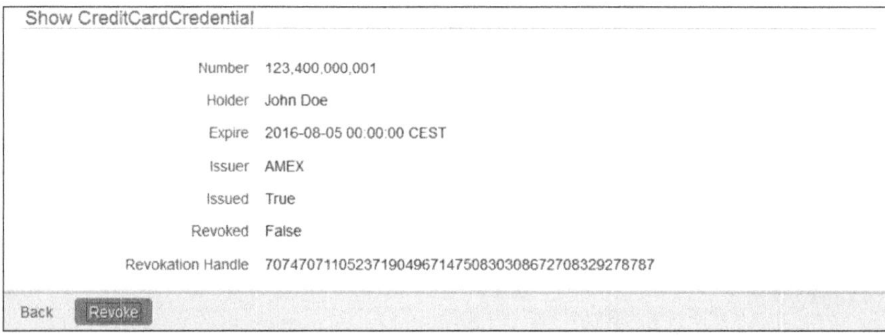

Fig. 9.31 Credential details when revocation is enabled

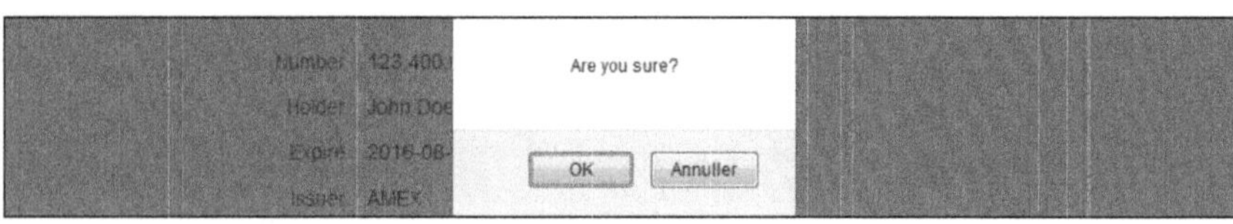

Fig. 9.32 Revocation confirmation window

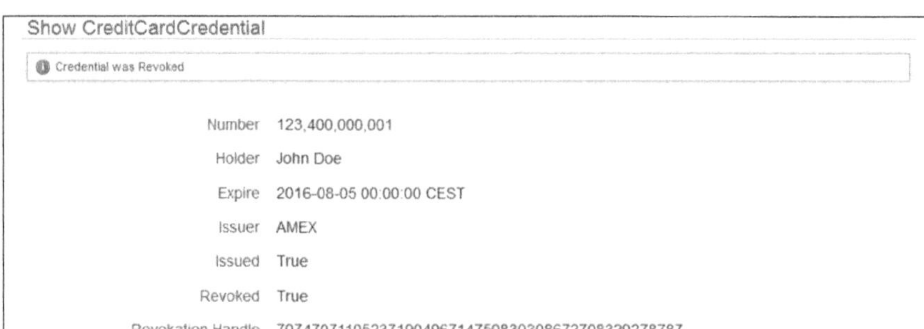

Fig. 9.33 Credential revocation report

9.1.9 Setting Up Your Own Test Privacy-ABC System

To setup your own Privacy-ABC system using the example applications, you must first setup an Issuer to generate parameters for Issuer, Inspector and Revocation Authority.

Then the public parameters must be copied to the Verifier application and prepared to be included in the user client.

Further information on how to build, configure and run the example applications and build an installer for the user client can be found in README files included in the demo applications.

9.1.10 Implementation Considerations

When implementing your own Issuer and Verifier service, you must make sure that the status of the issuance or verification processes are taken from the ABCEs and linked to the web session of the user. You cannot rely on the result status reported by the user client and javascript, as this could be compromised. Thus for websites using Privacy-ABC verification, the steps would be as follows:

1. The user visits the web site using ABC4Trust technology.
2. The web browser is coupled to a web session.
3. The session can either be stored in a cookie or explicitly added as part of the URL the web page sets up for the browser plugin.
4. A presentation policy is generated, made unique by adding *nonce*, and stored along with the web session before sending it to the browser.
5. When receiving the presentation token [4] it has to match the session. Then the verification is performed and the result of the verification is stored on the web session.
6. Browser plugin notifies the web application that the presentation has finished.
7. The web application retrieves the status of the presentation from the session before going forward.

A similar approach must be applied in an Issuer application to make sure that the correct attribute values are assigned to the credentials.

[4] In the case the user is not able to satisfy the policy or cancels the presentation the token will not be sent.

9.1.11 Obtaining the ABC4Trust Demo Applications

The demo applications are available together with the reference implementation on the ABC4Trust source code page[5].

9.2 ABC4Trust in Smart Cards

In the ABC4Trust project, smart cards have been introduced for increased security and mobility. The security is increased because smart cards can protect the user's secret key material much better than if the same key material was stored on the users' computers. The mobility is increased because with the personal data of the user stored on the smart card the user can use any computer with a smart card reader and the user ABCE installed.

Smart cards can be utilized in two different ways in a Privacy-ABC setup. Either the smart card contains the complete user side of the Privacy-ABC system, or the user side of the Privacy-ABC is implemented in software running on the users PC with the smart card securely storing the user's secret key. In the case where everything is implemented on the smart card, the smart card communicate directly with the verifier. Due to the low computing power and lack of display on smart cards, this results in a very basic functionality. In the other case with most of the user side of the Privacy-ABC system implemented in software on the user's PC, the smart card is used for securely storing the user's secret key, and the key never leaves the smart card as the card makes all computations involving the secret key. In this setup the secret key is as secure as in the previous case, however, at the same time the computational power and possibilities of interaction with the user supplied by the PC makes much more advanced functionalities possible. In the ABC4Trust project we have only focused on the latter case.

9.2.1 Privacy-ABCs on Smart Cards: Prior Art

There have been several approaches to implement Privacy-ABCs on smartcards. Bichsel [Bic07] and Balasch [Bal08] focused on providing the arithmetic functionality required, *i.e.* fast modular arithmetic. Balasch implemented the arithmetic using AVR microcontrollers, whereas Bichsel used the JCOP platfom. Later, Bichsel et al. presented the first practical implementation of a Camenish-Lysyanskaya-based Direct Anonymous Attestation scheme on a Java Card 2.2.1 [BCGS09] with a performance close to 7.5 seconds. Tews and Jacobs [TJ09] considered U-Prove and succeeded in performing a presentation proof in about 5 seconds for 2 attributes and 8s for 4 attributes. Batina et al. [BHJ$^+$10] suggest to use self-blindable certificates

[5] https://github.com/p2abcengine/

and put forward an implementation that requires about 1.5s to perform presentation for 1 attribute. In 2011, Mostowski and Vullers implement U-Prove on a MultOS card and reach about 0.5s (resp. 0.8s) for 2 (resp. 5) attributes.

In all these works, the verifier's security policy and the number of attributes is fixed in advance. We are not aware of any embedded implementation that provides a flexible and federated framework for Privacy-ABC systems.

9.2.2 *Introducing ABC4Trust Lite*

ABC4Trust has defined a smart card reference implementation referred to as ABC4Trust Lite to support the device-binding feature of Privacy-ABC systems. Throughout the project, the ABC4Trust Lite application has evolved in a number of ways; the first Patras pilot relied on version v1.0 based on a ZC7.5 BasicCard, whereas the Söderhamn pilot and the second Patras pilot respectively made use of versions v1.1 and v1.2 based on a MultOS card with a larger non-volatile memory. The latest version (v1.2) of ABC4Trust Lite is the one put forward as reference. Its sources are publicly available under GitHub [6] as well as its user manual [BDP14].

ABC4Trust Lite v1.2 is a dual-interface smart card application that implements the device-binding versions of both U-Prove and IdentityMixer in a federated way, thereby supporting also other discrete-log-based, device-bound Privacy-ABC systems. The card also features a number of customized functionalities that were required by the pilots, such as counters and encrypted backups. These features can be easily removed or modified to fit other specific needs.

The rest of this section is dedicated to providing a technical insight on how ABC4Trust Lite v1.2 works and how it extends the reference implementation by integrating a secure hardware device into it.

9.2.2.1 The smart card platform

The target platform selected to implement ABC4Trust Lite v1.2 is a MultOS ML3 card with the following characteristics:

- the MultOS exact reference is ML3-36K-R1. The chip belongs to the Infineon SLE78 family and is equipped with a cryptoprocessor supporting modular and non-modular arithmetics.
- Available non-volatile memory (EEPROM): 64 KB,
- Available RAM: 1088 bytes (dynamic RAM) + 960 bytes (public RAM),
- Dual interface communications (contact T=0, T=1 and contactless T=CL),
- MultOS 4.3.1 Operating System running a MEL virtual machine and providing a number of native cryptographic APIs.

[6] https://github.com/p2abcengine/p2abcengine

The sources of the application are written in ANSI C and compiled using the MultOS development tool chain .

9.2.2.2 The life cycle of a card

The card's life cycle is as follows:

Virgin mode. At delivery time, the card is in virgin mode. Its data memory is empty and the card is ready for personalization. Upon presentation of a 64-bit password via the dedicated APDU command SET ROOT MODE, the card switches to root mode.

Root mode. Only in this mode personalization can be performed by initializing the various objects the card requires to run properly (4-byte global PIN, 8-byte PUK code, device private key, algebraic contexts, on-card issuers, settings of the on-card prover, possibly on-card credentials, etc). After personalization, sending a SET WORKING MODE command irreversibly switches the card to working mode.

Working mode. In working mode, the card interacts with issuers, verifiers and the card holder through the ABCE. The card holder has access to a number of PIN-protected commands that create, operate and remove on-card credentials.

Locked mode. The card will switch to locked mode if an incorrect PIN is presented 3 times in a row. It can be unlocked by presenting the personalized 8-byte PUK code.

Dead mode. The card falls into dead mode if an incorrect PUK code is presented 3 times in a row; a dead card is unusable.

9.2.2.3 High-level view of handled objects

As depicted on Figure 9.34, the ABC4Trust Lite application manages a number of device-specific variables, several types of Privacy-ABC related objects and a free storage area called the BlobStore. These objects have the following purpose and meaning.

- **Algebraic contexts or groups:** a group is a collection of arithmetic parameters required to carry out algebraic computations. In addition to a modulus and optionally a group order and a cofactor, each group can also contain a number of group generators or bases. Privacy-ABC systems defined over the same group but making use of different generators may therefore share the same group structure and just register their own generators to that group.
- **On-card issuers:** an on-card issuer is meant to reflect the existence of an external issuer. It is a container (*i.e.* a structure) that merely defines a working context for all credentials attached to it, namely: a group for conducting issuance and presentation of credentials, whether credentials should use two generators (as in

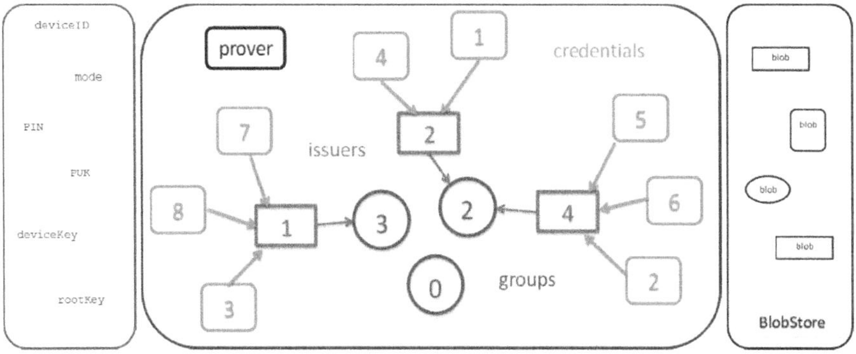

Fig. 9.34 Persistent objects residing in the ABC4Trust Lite v1.2 card

Idemix) or just one generator (as in U-Prove), and how many times credentials can be presented before they expire. Several issuers may relate to the same group.

- **On-card credentials:** an on-card credential contributes to the issuance and presentation of a full-fledge credential handled by the ABCE. It can be invoked at issuance or presentation time to provide parts of zero-knowledge proofs (commitment and response) that serve as inputs to the full-fledge protocols operated by the ABCE. An on-card credential is attached to a unique on-card issuer.
- **On-card prover:** the on-card prover orchestrates proof sessions wherein one or several credentials are sollicited to provide their commitment and response. The prover ensures that, once a proof session is open, the commitment of all involved credentials will share a common randomness. This allows the card to support proofs across multiple credentials. Pseudonyms and scope-exclusive pseudonyms can also be involved in proof sessions.

Credentials can be managed directly by the card holder as they are just PIN-protected. All the other Privacy-ABC related objects can only be created and stored when the card is in root mode.

- **Blobstore:** the Blobstore is a PIN-protected free storage space allocated by the card. The Blobstore manages data under the form of key-value associations – very much like in associative arrays – that are referred to as blobs. The application provides commands to store, update, read and remove blobs from memory. The Blobstore is used by the ABCE to store full-fledge credentials and other user-related parameters directly on the card. The card does not attempt to interpret the contents of the Blobstore.

9.2.2.4 Card personalization

Incoming and outgoing data (in the usual card-centric terminology) are transmitted back and forth between the card and the terminal application. The card allows write access to an internal input buffer referred to as `buffer`. The card supports extended APDUs, so that arbitrary byte streams of up to 512 bytes can be written into `buffer` to provide data material to the card. This is done using the APDU command PUT DATA.

Personalization is performed in three stages:

Stage 1 (root authority): the card is switched to working mode by sending a SET ROOT MODE command containing a 64-bit password. An RSA public key, referred to as the root key, must then be provided to the card using the SET ROOT KEY command. The root key serves as a means for the card to public-key encrypt data to the root authority in the case where the rest of the personalization is performed by a third party. The root authority makes use of the private part of the root key as a decryption key. The encryption scheme is detailed in [BDP14].

Stage 2 (third party): the command INITIALIZE DEVICE initializes the PIN and PUK codes to random values and returns them encrypted under the root key. This allows the delegation of personalization by the root authority to some untrusted third party without endangering the confidentiality of the card holder's PIN and PUK codes. INITIALIZE DEVICE also initializes the device private key x (that never leaves the card), various size parameters and a device identifier the access to which will be PIN-protected in working mode.

Stage 3 (third party): the personalizer plays a series of APDU commands that create groups and on-card issuers, configure the on-card prover and possibly store blobs and/or create on-card credentials in the card's non-volatile memory. When the personalizer is done programming all Privacy-ABC related objects, the command SET WORKING MODE is played to put the card in working mode.

9.2.3 Functional Model for Privacy-ABC Systems

9.2.3.1 Algebraic contexts (groups)

An algebraic context or group is a set of arithmetic parameters indicating how to perform algebraic computations. It is made of several components:

- a group identifier `groupID` $\in [0,255]$,
- a modulus m,
- a group order q optionally set to the empty symbol $\perp$,
- a cofactor f optionally set to the empty symbol $\perp$,
- one or several generators $g_1, g_2, \ldots, g_t$ with $t \in [1,255]$.

Groups of unknown order

These are given by an RSA modulus $m = n$, the group order q and cofactor f are not provided, meaning that these two components are left empty. When computing zero-knowledge proofs, the card will compute responses as $s = k - cu$ over the integers, where k is the random integer used in the commitment, c the challenge and u the secret discrete log.

Groups of known order

These are given by a prime modulus $m = p$, a group order q (a factor of $p-1$) and a cofactor $f = (p-1)/q$. The order and cofactor are to be provided as arithmetic components. When computing zero-knowledge proofs over groups of known order, responses $s = k - cu$ are computed modulo q (with the same notation as above).

Group 0

The group with identifier `groupID` $= 0$ is dedicated to contain the so-called system parameters required to operate pseudonyms and scope-exclusive pseudonyms. The group 0 must provide a modulus m and at least one generator. However, the group order q and cofactor f remain optional components, making it possible to use a group of unknown order. Pseudonym-related operations automatically rely on group 0 for algebraic computations, but nothing refrains an on-card issuer to also refer to that group to perform credential-related operations.

The two following APDU commands require a preliminary PUT DATA command:

SET GROUP COMPONENT (`groupID`, `type` $\in \{0,1,2\}$)

> populates the group `groupID` with the current value of `buffer` according to the component type `type` (0 indicates the modulus, 1 the group order, 2 the cofactor). If the group was previously undefined, this implicitly creates a new group with identifier `groupID`.

SET GENERATOR (`groupID`, `genID`)

> populates the group `groupID` with a generator with identifier `genID` $\in [1,255]$, the value of which is taken from the current contents of `buffer`.

The detailed format of APDUs (class and instruction bytes, semantics of incoming and outgoing data fields, etc.) can be found in [BDP14].

9.2.3.2 On-card issuers

On-card issuers in ABC4Trust Lite are just containers that provide a context for credentials attached to them. As depicted on Figure 9.35, an issuer provides references to an algebraic context needed by credential-related operations. More precisely, an on-card issuer is composed of the following components:

- an issuer identifier `issuerID` $\in [1,255]$,
- a group identifier `groupID` $\in [0,255]$,
- an identifier for a first generator `genID1` $\in [1,255]$ in group `groupID`,

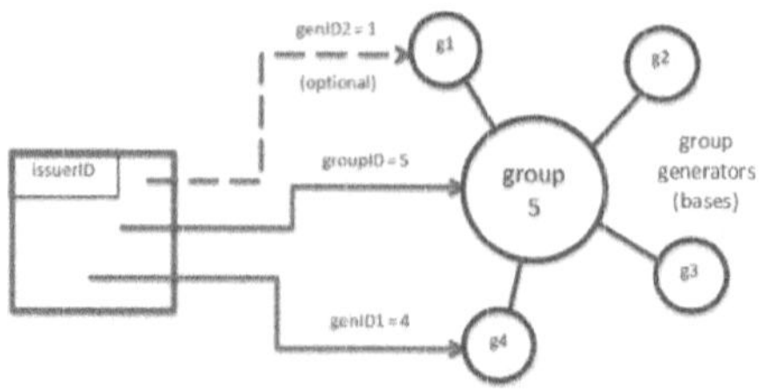

Fig. 9.35 Components of an on-card issuer. The group serves as an algebraic context to operate issuance and presentation of all credentials attached to the issuer.

- an identifier for a second generator `genID2` $\in [1,255]$ (double-base setting) or set to 0 to indicate absence of this component (single-base setting),
- a maximum number of presentations `numpres` $\in [1,255]$, optionally set to 0 to indicate an unlimited number of presentations for attached credentials.

SET ISSUER `(issuerID, groupID, genID1, genID2, numpres)`

creates a new issuer (or reconfigures an already created issuer) and initializes its components to the given values.

9.2.3.3 The on-card prover and the life cycle of proof sessions

The on-card prover is a container meant to supervise the generation of zero-knowledge commitments and responses. When the prover starts a new proof session, credentials and pseudonyms are orchestrated by the prover so that they will share a common randomness, thereby enabling proofs over multiple credentials and pseudonyms. The on-card prover is composed of:

- size parameters `ksize,csize` $\in \left[1,2^{16}\right]$,
- a large integer k_x of `ksize` bytes,
- a large integer c of `csize` bytes,
- a status flag `proofstatus` $\in$ {`'undefined'`, `'commitment stage'`, `'response stage'`}.

SET PROVER `(ksize, csize)`

initializes `ksize` and `csize`. The `proofstatus` flag is set to `'undefined'`.

Proof sessions are carried out in two stages, a commitment stage and a response stage.

Commitment Stage

When a proof session is started, the prover performs the following:

1. Randomly select $k_x \xleftarrow{\$}$ RandomBytes`(ksize)`.
2. Set `proofstatus` = `'commitment stage'`.
3. Update k_x and `proofstatus` in the prover.

From that moment on, any on-card credential, pseudonym or scope-exclusive pseudonym can potentially be involved in the session. If the terminal requests a commitment (for either issuance or presentation) from some on-card credential, that on-card credential will compute its commitment using k_x so that all the commitments produced within the same proof session share the same value for k_x.

START COMMITMENTS `(pin)`

if `pin` = `PIN`, updates the prover with $k_x \xleftarrow{\$}$ RandomBytes`(ksize)` and `proofstatus` = `'commitment stage'`.

Any sequence of

GET ISSUANCE COMMITMENT, GET PRESENTATION COMMITMENT,
GET DEVICE COMMITMENT, GET SCOPE-EXCLUSIVE COMMITMENT

commands (see below) may then be played to collect all the commitments from credentials and pseudonyms involved in the proof session.

Response Stage

When the response stage is started, the terminal sends a challenge `input_challenge` to the on-card prover which does the following:

1. Report an error if `proofstatus` ≠ `'commitment stage'`.
2. Report an error if size`(input_challenge)` ≠ `csize`.
3. Set c = `input_challenge`.
4. Set `proofstatus` = `'response stage'`.
5. Update c, `proofstatus` in the prover.
6. Compute and send $s_x = k_x - cx$ where x = `deviceKey`.

As in the commitment stage, any response (issuance and presentation alike) requested by the terminal to any credential within the session will be based on the components (k_x, c) stored in the prover.

START RESPONSES `(pin, input_challenge)`

if `pin` = `PIN`, `proofstatus` = `'commitment stage'` and size`(input_challenge)` = `csize`, updates the prover with c = `input_challenge` and `proofstatus` = `'response stage'`. The response $s_x = k_x - cx$ is computed over the integers and sent back to the terminal.

Any sequence of GET ISSUANCE RESPONSE command and GET PRESENTATION RESPONSE command may then be played to collect all the responses from credentials involved in the proof session. This only makes sense for credentials in the double-base setting since START RESPONSES already provides the session-wide response $s_x = k_x - cx$ to the ABCE.

9.2.3.4 On-card credentials

On-card credentials are objects that reflect the device-bound counterpart of full-fledge credentials handled by the ABCE. An on-card credential is operated according to the algebraic context imposed by its issuer. Credentials are created, operated and removed by the card holder upon presentation of the PIN. A credential is a container with the following components:

- a credential identifier $\texttt{credentialID} \in [1,255]$,
- an issuer identifier $\texttt{issuerID} \in [1,255]$,
- an integer v, called the credential's private key, set by default to the empty symbol $\perp$,
- an integer k_v set by default to the empty symbol $\perp$,
- a status flag

$$\texttt{status} \in \left\{ \begin{array}{l} \texttt{'just created'}, \\ \texttt{'issuance committed'}, \\ \texttt{'presentable'}, \\ \texttt{'presentation committed'}, \\ \texttt{'expired'} \end{array} \right\},$$

- a presentation counter $\texttt{prescount} \in [0,255]$.

At creation time, a credential is attached to an on-card issuer. If the issuer uses a 2-base setting (*i.e.* $\texttt{genID2} \neq 0$), the credential uses the group specified by that issuer to initialize its private key v.

SET CREDENTIAL (`pin, credentialID, issuerID`)

> if $\texttt{pin} = \texttt{PIN}$, creates a new credential (or resets an already created credential) and initializes its identifier and issuer identifier to `credentialID` and `issuerID` respectively. If $\texttt{issuerID.genID2} \neq 0$, the field v is initialized to a random byte array of size `xsize` (so v is left empty if the issuer `issuerID` imposes a single-base setting). The field k_v is set to the empty symbol $\perp$ while `status` is set to `'just created'` and `prescount` is initialized to 0.

LIST CREDENTIALS (`pin`)

> if $\texttt{pin} = \texttt{PIN}$, returns the concatenated identifiers of all the credentials available on the card.

READ CREDENTIAL (`pin, credentialID`)

> if $\texttt{pin} = \texttt{PIN}$, returns the 3-byte array $\texttt{issuerID} \| \texttt{status} \| \texttt{prescount}$.

Note that the data fields v and k_v are private to the credential and therefore not readable.

9.2.3.5 Life cycle of on-card credentials

Here are the operations performed on a credential, in chronological order.

Creation

The credential is created by playing the SET CREDENTIAL command. After creation, and at any time, the credential may return its public key

$$\texttt{pubKey} = \begin{cases} g_1^x \mod m & \text{if } \texttt{issuerID.genID2} = 0 \\ g_1^x g_2^v \mod m & \text{if } \texttt{issuerID.genID2} \neq 0 \end{cases}$$

where $x = \texttt{deviceKey}$, g_1 and g_2 are the generators with respective identifiers `issuerID.genID1` and `issuerID.genID2` in group `issuerID.groupID` and m is the modulus of group `issuerID.groupID`.

GET CREDENTIAL PUBLIC KEY `(pin, credentialID)`
 if `pin` = `PIN`, computes and returns `pubKey` as above. The `status` field of the credential is unchanged.

A credential's public key is recomputed on the fly each time this command is sent to the card. The ABCE may use the BlobStore to save it as a blob for quick access.

Issuance

At issuance time, the ABCE of the user agent interacts with the external issuer to generate a full fledge credential. During that process, the ABCE delegates some of these computations to the on-card credential in the following manner.
1. Compute an issuance commitment as

$$C = \begin{cases} g_1^{k_x} \mod m & \text{if } \texttt{issuerID.genID2} = 0 \\ g_1^{k_x} g_2^{k_v} \mod m & \text{if } \texttt{issuerID.genID2} \neq 0 \end{cases}$$

where $k_v \xleftarrow{\$}$ RandomBytes `(ksize)` and k_x is as stored within the on-card prover.

GET ISSUANCE COMMITMENT `(pin, credentialID)`
 if `pin` = `PIN`, `status` = `'just created'` and the current proof session is in commitment stage *i.e.* `proofstatus` = `'commitment stage'`, computes and sends C as above (possibly initializing k_v along the way in the double-base setting) and sets `status` = `'issuance committed'`.

2. Compute an issuance response as

$$s_v = \begin{cases} \perp & \text{if } \texttt{issuerID.genID2} = 0 \\ k_v - cv & \text{if } \texttt{issuerID.genID2} \neq 0 \text{ and } q = \perp \\ k_v - cv \mod q & \text{if } \texttt{issuerID.genID2} \neq 0 \text{ and } q \neq \perp \end{cases}$$

where q is the order of group issuerID.groupID and c is as stored within the on-card prover.

GET ISSUANCE RESPONSE (pin, credentialID)

if pin = PIN, status = 'issuance committed' and proofstatus = 'response stage', computes and sends the response s_v as above and sets status = 'presentable'.

Presentation

At presentation time, the ABCE of the user agent interacts with the relying party and performs presentation with the help of the card. Presentation also has a commitment and a response stage where the same outputs C and $\{s_v\}$ are produced for refreshed values of k_x and $\{k_v\}$. Also, the credential's presentation counter is incremented and checked against its maximal value programmed in the on-card issuer.

GET PRESENTATION COMMITMENT (pin, credentialID)

if pin = PIN, status = 'presentable' and proofstatus = 'commitment stage', computes and sends C as above (possibly initializing k_v along the way in the double-base setting) and sets status = 'presentation committed'.

GET PRESENTATION RESPONSE (pin, credentialID)

if pin = PIN, status = 'presentation committed' and proofstatus = 'response stage', computes and sends the response s_v as above to the terminal. prescount is incremented by 1 and if prescount $\geq$ numpres > 0 then status = 'expired', otherwise status = 'presentable'.

Destruction

Once it has been presented numpres times, a credential expires and becomes useless. If the issuer specifies that numpres $= 0$, an infinite number of presentations is allowed. The credential may also become useless for other reasons, in which case the ABCE can just remove it from the card's memory.

REMOVE CREDENTIAL (pin, credentialID)

if pin = PIN, removes the credential with identifier credentialID.

9.2.3.6 Pseudonyms

Once the card is initialized, the device public key and arbitrarily many pseudonyms and scope-exclusive pseudonyms can be derived from the device private key deviceKey. The group used for generating pseudonyms is the one with identifier $\texttt{groupID} = 0$ personalized in the card. The group 0 shall supply a modulus m and at least one generator but may be of known or unknown order. The generator g used by pseudonym-related operations is the one with identifier $\texttt{genID} = 1$.

Full-fledge pseudonyms are managed by the ABCE of the user agent who delegates the device-bound part of computations to the card. The card can prove its knowledge of the device private key in an interactive, zero-knowledge way and provides the ABCE with a couple of APDU commands in order to do that. Here are the operations provided by ABC4trust Lite to support pseudonyms:

Device public key

At any time, the card may compute and return its public key

$$\texttt{devicepubKey} = g^x \bmod m$$

where $x = \texttt{deviceKey}$, g is the generator with identifier $\texttt{genID} = 1$ in group $\texttt{groupID} = 0$ and m is the modulus of that group.

GET DEVICE PUBLIC KEY (pin)

if $\texttt{pin} = \texttt{PIN}$, computes and returns $\texttt{devicepubKey} = g^x \bmod m$ as above.

The device public key can be recovered by the terminal and saved in the card's BlobStore for later quick access. This could also be done at personalization time.

Commitment

To prove knowledge of the device private key, the card provides the commitment $C = g^{k_x} \bmod m$ where k_x is the randomness currently in use by the on-card prover.

GET DEVICE COMMITMENT (pin)

if $\texttt{pin} = \texttt{PIN}$ and $\texttt{proofstatus} = \texttt{'commitment stage'}$, computes and returns $C = g^{k_x} \bmod m$.

Response

The session-wide response $s_x = k_x - cx$ is already provided by the START RESPONSES command.

9.2.3.7 Scope-exclusive pseudonyms

Scope-exclusive pseudonyms are similar to the above, except that the generator g is replaced with a dynamically computed, scope-exclusive group generator

$$h(\texttt{scope}) = \begin{cases} \text{SHA-256}(\texttt{scope}) \bmod m & \text{if } f = \perp \\ \text{SHA-256}(\texttt{scope})^f \bmod m & \text{if } f \neq \perp \end{cases}$$

where m is the modulus and f the cofactor of the group $\texttt{groupID} = 0$. As for pseudonyms, all operations take place over the group 0. The card can prove possession of a scope-exclusive pseudonym in a zero-knowledge way through the following operations.

Compute scope-exclusive pseudonym

At any time, the card may take `scope` as input and return

$$\texttt{se-pseudo} = h(\texttt{scope})^x \mod m$$

where $x = \texttt{deviceKey}$.

GET SCOPE-EXCLUSIVE PSEUDONYM `(pin, scope)`

if $\texttt{pin} = \texttt{PIN}$, computes and returns $\texttt{se-pseudo} = h(\texttt{scope})^x \bmod m$.

The scope-exclusive pseudonym can be computed in advance and saved in the card's BlobStore for quick access.

Commitment

To prove possession of a scope-exclusive pseudonym, the card provides the commitment $C = h(\texttt{scope})^{k_x} \bmod m$ where k_x is the randomness currently in use by the on-card prover.

GET SCOPE-EXCLUSIVE COMMITMENT `(pin, scope)`

if $\texttt{pin} = \texttt{PIN}$ and $\texttt{proofstatus} =$ `'commitment stage'`, computes and returns $C = h(\texttt{scope})^{k_x} \bmod m$.

Response

The session-wide response $s_x = k_x - cx$ is already provided by the START RESPONSES command.

Finally note that

- commands related to scope-exclusive pseudonyms do not attempt to store the scope-exclusive generator $h(\texttt{scope})$. It is therefore re-generated on the fly whenever necessary,
- arbitrarily many scope-exclusive pseudonyms can be involved in the same proof session in a concurrent manner.

9.2.4 *Instantiating U-Prove, Idemix and other Privacy-ABC Systems*

Instantiating U-Prove

U-Prove makes use of groups of known order and requires only one generator, which amounts to define a prime modulus $m = p$, a group order q, a cofactor f and a single generator g. U-Prove issuers are therefore created with `genID2` $= 0$ at personalization time (single-base setting).

Instantiating Idemix

Comparatively, Idemix makes use of groups of unknown order and requires two generators g_1, g_2. Idemix issuers are personalized accordingly *i.e.* with `genID2` $\neq 0$ (double-base setting).

Instantiating other Privacy-ABC systems

Our applicative architecture allows to support other device-bound Privacy-ABC systems. Those can be categorized according to their algebraic context (known or unknown order) and whether issuers are in the single-base or double-base setting. ABC4Trust Lite supports the 4 categories of Privacy-ABCs shown on Table 9.1.

Table 9.1 Device-bound Privacy-ABCs Supported by ABC4Trust Lite.

Group of	known order	unknown order
single-base issuers	U-Prove	also supported
double-base issuers	also supported	IdentityMixer

9.2.5 *The "Counter" Mechanism*

To avoid multiplying the number of class attendance credentials to be issued, a counter-based mechanism has been implemented in the first Patras pilot. This mechanism may have practical interest in a wide range of other use cases, and we now give a brief description of how it works.

- The notion of a counter object is added to the application. The object is implemented as a container composed of
  - a counter identifier `counterID` $\in [1, 255]$,
  - an authentication key identifier `keyID` $\in [0, 255]$,

  - an incremental index `index` $\in [0,255]$,
  - a threshold value `threshold` $\in [0,255]$,
  - a 4-byte time-measuring variable `cursor`.

- The counter is meant to prevent the presentation of some on-card credentials by making sure first that `index` $\geq$ `threshold`. If so, the counter is said to be mature. On-card issuers now include an additional field `counterID` that indicates which counter is attached to that issuer, with the convention that `counterID` $= 0$ indicates that no counter is attached. Several issuers may refer to the same counter. Like groups and issuers, counters can be only be created in root mode.
- When an issuer is attached to a counter, all credentials assigned to that issuer are now submitted to an extra check at presentation time. Presentation occurs only if the counter is mature, otherwise an error is returned to the terminal.
- The `index` variable of a counter can be incremented by 1 upon presentation of a more recent value of `cursor` public-key signed by an external authority. To this end, authentication keys are added to the application. Very much like the root key, RSA public keys can be installed in the card at personalization time and an RSA-based signature scheme with message recovery is added [BDP14]. A counter then refers to one of these keys in its `keyID` field, with the convention that the key with `keyID` $= 0$ is the root key. Several counters may relate to the same authentication key.

The following APDU commands are then defined to support the mechanism.

SET AUTHENTICATION KEY (`keyID`)

> sets the authentication key with identifier `keyID` (or redefines it if already defined) to the current value of `buffer`. If the size of the provided RSA public key does not lie within a prescribed range, it is not memorized in the card and an error is returned. Only works in root mode.

SET COUNTER (`counterID, keyID, index, threshold, cursor`)

> creates a new counter (or resets an already created counter) and initializes its components to the given values. Only works in root mode.

A counter can be incremented by any designated entity who has registered an authentication key in the card. The private key corresponding to the authentication key is used by that designated entity to sign counter increments.

INCREMENT COUNTER (`keyID, sig`)

only works in working mode. The input data contains a public-key signature `sig` which is checked against the authentication key with identifier `keyID`. If valid, the signed message recovered from the signature is parsed as `counterID`||`newcursor`. The card accesses the counter with identifier `counterID` and makes sure that its `keyID` component is equal to the given `keyID`. It then checks the value of its `cursor` component against `newcursor`. If `newcursor` > `cursor`, the card sets `cursor` = `newcursor` and increments `index` by 1. When `index` is not incremented, the command does not report an error. However, authentication failure is reported as an error.

READ COUNTER `(pin, counterID)`

if `pin` = `PIN`, returns the 7-byte array `keyID`||`index`||`threshold`||`cursor`.

9.2.6 Summary of the APDU Command Set

APDU Command	virgin	root	working	locked	dead
GET MODE	✓	✓	✓	✓	✓
SET ROOT MODE	access code				
SET WORKING MODE		✓			
PIN TRIALS LEFT		✓	✓	✓	✓
PUK TRIALS LEFT		✓	✓	✓	✓
CHANGE PIN		PIN	PIN		
RESET PIN		PUK	PUK	PUK	
INITIALIZE DEVICE		✓+ROOT			
GET DEVICE ID		PIN	PIN		
GET VERSION	✓	✓	✓	✓	✓
GET MEMORY SPACE		PIN	PIN		
PUT DATA		✓	✓		
SET ROOT KEY		✓*			
SET AUTHENTICATION KEY		✓*			
SET GROUP COMPONENT		✓*			
SET GENERATOR		✓*			
SET ISSUER		✓			
SET COUNTER		✓			
READ COUNTER		✓	PIN		
INCREMENT COUNTER			KEY		
SET PROVER		✓			
START COMMITMENTS		PIN	PIN		
START RESPONSES		PIN*	PIN*		
SET CREDENTIAL		PIN	PIN		
LIST CREDENTIALS		PIN	PIN		
READ CREDENTIAL		PIN	PIN		
REMOVE CREDENTIAL		PIN	PIN		
GET CREDENTIAL PUBLIC KEY		PIN	PIN		
GET ISSUANCE COMMITMENT		PIN	PIN		
GET ISSUANCE RESPONSE		PIN	PIN		
GET PRESENTATION COMMITMENT		PIN	PIN		
GET PRESENTATION RESPONSE		PIN	PIN		
GET DEVICE PUBLIC KEY		PIN	PIN		
GET DEVICE COMMITMENT		PIN	PIN		
GET SCOPE-EXCLUSIVE PSEUDONYM		PIN	PIN		
GET SCOPE-EXCLUSIVE COMMITMENT		PIN	PIN		
STORE BLOB		PIN*	PIN*		
LIST BLOBS		PIN	PIN		
READ BLOB		PIN	PIN		
REMOVE BLOB		PIN	PIN		

$\checkmark$: the command is not protected, PIN: the command is PIN-protected, PUK: the command is PUK-protected, ROOT: the command output is encrypted under the root key, KEY: the incoming data must be public-key signed, $\star$: the command requires a preliminary PUT DATA.

We refer to [BDP14] for more detail.

9.2.7 *Potential Extensions*

A possible extension consists in supporting elliptic curve operations in addition to multiplicative integer groups. To this end, one may enrich the format of group containers to include components for the curve parameters a and b (classical groups would leave these two components empty), and use the modulus to store the field characteristic. The components for the group order q and co-factor f would be unchanged. Group generators would now store either integers or points on the curve, using some format for parsing the point coordinates (concatenation would do). The low-level arithmetic API would then automatically select the appropriate operations depending on the nature of the algebraic settings.

Another approach is to embed full-fledge Privacy-ABC systems in the card. This would be a major change as the application would then manage attributes locally and more generally would support more or less the same services as the ABCE. This means that the card must be able to parse XML security policies (maybe a more card-friendly format can be defined to express policies in that context), perform credential matching on its own and handle the issuance and presentation of full-fledge credentials. Such an application (say, ABC4Trust Pro) would be far more intricate to design and implement efficiently, it would however also be much more powerful.

9.3 ABC4Trust on Smartphones

Modern smartphones are general-purpose computing devices with computing power close to that of desktop computers. Users can install third party applications on them, and can use them to communicate through a number of channels, for example the Internet, Bluetooth and NFC.

Many users are carrying such a smartphone with them at all times, which enables many new, exciting use cases. One of these use cases, one which is interesting from the perspective of the ABC4Trust project, is the possibility of using a smartphone as an *identity hub*, to store credentials and keys, for authentication and authorization in both online and the physical world, and as a trusted device for cryptographic computations.

The basis for such an identity hub could easily be Privacy-ABC technology, and as part of the ABC4Trust project, we have investigated the feasibility of realizing the reference implementation on smartphone platforms and have implemented proof-of-concept implementations. To investigate the feasibility is here understood as determining whether both the hardware and software platforms of smartphones have the necessary features to run such an implementation. This has so far been approached as three different projects:

1. A feasibility study and implementation of the "user client" of the reference implementation on the Android platform.
2. A feasibility study and implementation of U-Prove in JavaScript for execution in web browsers.
3. A proof-of-concept implementation of an Android app using NFC to emulate the smart cards used in the pilots in Söderhamn and Patras.

In the following sections, we will discuss these projects in greater detail. The user is also referred to [Jen14] for even further details on these projects.

9.3.1 ABCE on Android

In order to analyse the possibility of realising parts of the reference implementation on smartphone platforms, we have implemented the part of the reference implementation that is supposed to run on the user's device as an app for the Android platform. We focus on the User ABCE since the only entity using a mobile device in a setup involving Privacy-ABC technologies in most use cases will be the user. However, the implementation could easily be adapted to make the mobile device act as other entities, e.g. Issuer or Verifier. Android was chosen over other platforms, such as iOS and Windows Phone, for two reasons: It is the most common smartphone platform, and it is possible to develop applications for Android using Java which was already used for the reference implementation.

The implementation is a slightly simplified version of the User Client from the reference implementation as it does not support the use of a smart card for storing the user's credentials and keys. Instead this is stored in the device's memory. Furthermore the only Crypto Engine supported so far is IBM's Identity Mixer, as this is developed in Java and therefore easily portable to the Android platform.

In order to make things easy for application developers, the reference implementation is implemented as an *ABC4Trust app* which is able to engage in issuance and verification on behalf of any third party application, which only has to implement a very simple API, and not deal with any of the cryptographic details. The communication flow when performing a presentation is as follows and is as depicted in Figure 9.36:

1. The user requests access to a service through a third party application.
2. The Service Provider determines what policy the user has to satisfy in order to access the service. A URL for where the policy can be found and the verifier's URL are returned from the service provider to the third party application.
3. The application sends the URLs to the ABC4Trust app.

4. The ABC4Trust app uses the given URL to retrieve the policy and makes (if possible) a token based on the credentials the user has stored with the ABC4Trust app. This token is then sent to the given verifier URL.
5. The verifier checks if the token is valid. If not, the protocol ends here, but if it was valid, the verifier generates a session key and notifies the Service provider on what policy the user was able to satisfy, what attributes the token revealed and the session key.
6. The session key is sent back to the ABC4Trust app.
7. The ABC4Trust app sends the session key to the third party application, who can now use this to authenticate when communicating with the service provider.

Between step 3 and 4 the ABC4Trust app provides a GUI which tells the user exactly what information and to whom is about to be revealed, and allows to either proceed or to stop the protocol.

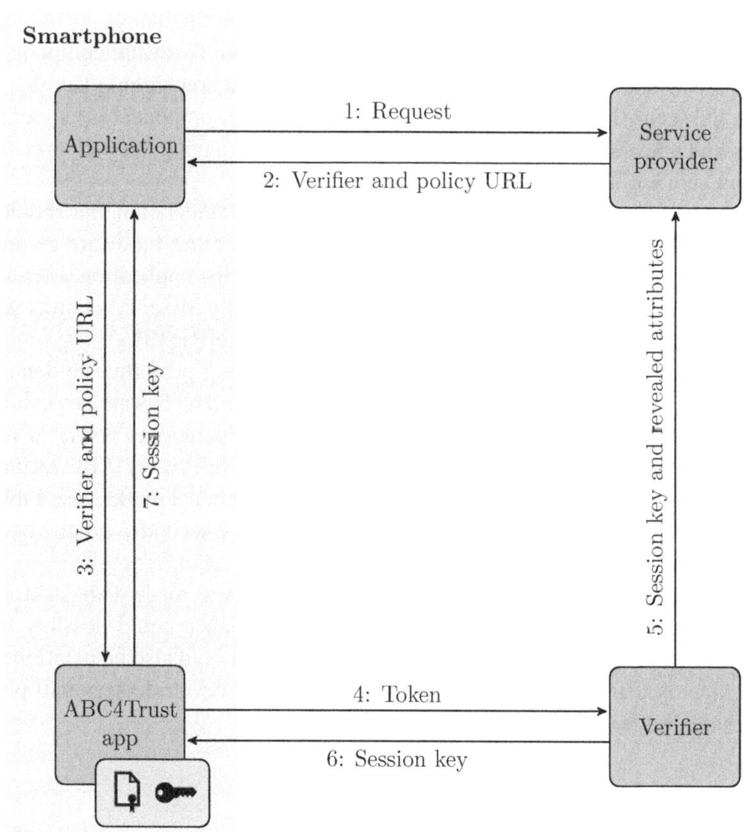

Fig. 9.36 The communication flow when performing a presentation through the ABC4Trust app.

9.3.1.1 Security Model of the ABCE on Android

The security model when looking at applications on smartphones is in many ways comparable to that of a traditional client-server application on a PC platform. The platforms are comparable in the way that the smartphone also runs a complex operating system where security flaws are continually discovered, and the User is able to install applications. The applications are validated by the major providers of mobile operating systems (Google, Apple, and Microsoft), but multiple examples exists of malicious applications being available for download through their individual application stores. These aspects make a smartphone vulnerable to many of the same attacks that is available on PC platforms. Furthermore, there is at least one threat that is more present on smartphones: The possibility of a malicious adversary gaining physical access to the device, and if this happens the whole device, including it's memory, is compromised. In our setting, where the user's private key and credentials are stored in the device's memory, this means that the adversary has access to all the user's information.

It is, however, possible use a solution where a secure hardware component (eg. ARM TrustZone) is used to sign information using a secret signing key that never leaves the secure component. Assuming that this secure component is tamper proof, this would give security comparable to that obtained by having the user store private keys and credentials on a smart card.

Our implementation is only a proof-of-concept implementation, but should it be developed further into an actual application, using a secure hardware component would be imperative, greatly increasing the security of the application. Fortunately, using such components is possible for both IBM's Identity Mixer (via Direct Anonymous Attestation [BCC04]) and for Microsoft's U-Prove[Paq13].

Another thing that has to be considered when porting performance demanding applications, is that even though modern smartphones and tablets are powerful computing devices, they do still not possess the same computational power as laptops and desktops. The cryptographic calculations involved in Privacy-ABC technology are typically rather computationally intensive, but our benchmarks, see Table 9.2, show that creating a presentation token takes about six seconds, which should be acceptable in many situations.

It is worth noting that the reference implementation was made with desktops and laptops and not smartphones in mind, so the performance could possibly be improved with a smartphone specific implementation. It should also be mentioned that the device used for the benchmarks is from 2011, and newer devices will perform remarkably better.

9.3.2 Privacy ABCs in JavaScript

The smartphone world is, compared to the PC world, very fragmented. There are several common platforms, e.g. Android, BlackBerry, iOS and Windows Phone,

Table 9.2 Performance of the ABC4Trust Reference Implementation on an Android Smartphone When Creating a Presentation Token Revealing One Attribute from an Identy Mixder Credential

Key size	Performance
1024 bits	5794 msecs
2048 bits	6587 msecs

Note: The smartphone used is a Samsung Galaxy Nexus with a 1.2 GHz ARM Cortex-A9 CPU and 1 GB RAM running CyanogenMod 10.2.0.

and developers will have to implement an application on all these platforms to reach all users. However, one thing all these platforms, as well as laptop and desktop platforms, have in common is that they are packed with a web browser that is able to execute JavaScript code. So a possible way of reaching all platforms is to develop the application in JavaScript, which also has the advantage that the user does not have to install any applications or browser plugins on their device.

As a proof-of-concept and for feasibility studies, we have implemented the user client for Microsoft's U-Prove[PZ13]. What we have implemented is a very basic stand alone crypto engine, without support for the policy language and other features available in the ABC4Trust ABC Engine.

Since the cryptographic calculations involved in Privacy-ABC's are rather computationally heavy, the main drawback of JavaScript in this context is that it does not perform as good as native applications. Furthermore, our tests show that the performance differs greatly from platform to platform, and that on a few platforms it is not feasible to obtain a decent performance. On most platforms, however, the performance is acceptable, so it is possible for a JavaScript application to run and perform acceptable on a wide range of platforms. The performance measures are shown in Table 9.3.

Table 9.3 Performance for Creating a U-Prove Presentation Token Using JavaScript on Different Devices and with Different Key Sizes

Device	Browser	256 bits	384 bits	521 bits
Laptop	Chrome 33	73	189	408
Laptop	Firefox 27	94	181	437
Laptop	Safari 7.0.2	1841	5675	13093
Android	Android Browser	903	2537	5528
iPhone	Mobile Safari 7	9068	27705	69396

Note: The key sizes can not be compared to the key sizes in Table 9.2 since we here use elliptic curves instead of subgroups of Z_p. The laptop used is a MacBook Pro with 2.8 GHz Intel Core i7 and 16 GB 1600 MHz DDR3 RAM running OSX 10.9.2. The Android device is the same as in the benchmarks in Table 9.2, and the iPhone is an iPhone 5 with 1.3 GHz dual core CPU and 1 GB LPDDR2-1066 RAM running iOS 7.0.4. All timings are in milliseconds.

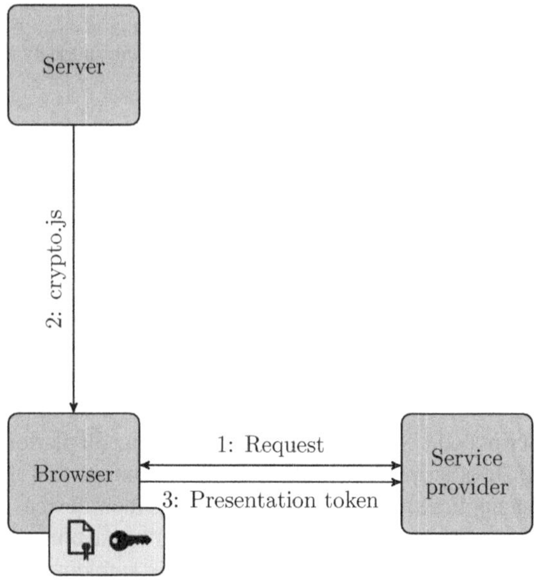

Fig. 9.37 This shows a possible communication flow when the user uses a JavaScript script to create presentation tokens in his browser.

For that reason we do find it feasible to extend the proof-of-concept implementation into a full ABC application that could be implemented in actual use cases, allowing the use of ABC-technology in services accessed from a webbrowser without the need to install any plugins or extensions. At a high level, the communication flow could be as depicted in Figure 9.37.

1. The user directs a webbrowser running on some device to an online service she wishes to access, and the service provider responds with a policy the user should satisfy to access the service and a web page containing an iframe pointing to some script, crypto.js, which is able to create presentation tokens and is stored on another server.
2. The user retrieves the script, crypto.js, from the server. Note that the request for the script comes from the user's browser, so the server does not know what service the user is trying to access.
3. Using crypto.js and the user's keys and credentials, which has previously been stored in the browser's local storage by a script running on the same domain as the browser, the user creates a presentation token based on the received policy, and sends it to the service provider.

If the user wants to make sure that the script received from the server is valid, we could introduce a fourth party, trusted by the user, which checks the source code of the script and signs it. The user can now check that this signature matches the received script. In this way the user is certain that he receives the same script as all other users and not some script specially designed for him

The memory of a mobile device is vulnerable to malware attacks, and this includes also the local storage of the user's web browser. Depending on the threat model, a possible protection against such an attack is to secret-share the private key and credentials with a cloud service, making it impossible to create presentation tokens without having both the share stored in the local storage and the share stored in the cloud.

9.3.3 Smart Card Emulation

Smart cards have played a key part in the implementation of the ABC4Trust reference implementation (see Section 9.2). Some smartphones contain an NFC-chip (Near-Field-Communication), making it able to communicate with other NFC-enabled devices and smart card readers, and in particular it enables it to emulate a smart card.

Using a smartphone to emulate a smart card has some advantages.

- A user is not required to carry around yet another card, but can use a smartphone which many users are already carrying with them at all times.
- Smart cards have to be handed out physically to users, making deployment cumbersome compared to the ubiquity of mobile devices and having a user installing an application on such.
- Smartphones, which unlike smart cards, have their own power supply, are computationally much faster than a smart cards.

As proof-of-concept, we have implemented an Android app which emulates the smart cards used in the pilots in Söderhamn and Patras. A smartphone running this implementation can be used interchangeably with a real smart card, and a presentation with a smartphone is almost six times faster than with a smart card [Jen14].

The main reason for using smart cards is that they are tamper proof, meaning that the user can store his key on a smart card, and it is not possible to read this key from the smart card. As discussed earlier, in Section 9.3.1, the memory of a smartphone is not tamper proof, and the user's key and credentials could be retrieved by malware installed on the phone or a malicious adversary with physical access to the device, but using a secure hardware module embedded in the smartphone will solve this issue and give a security comparable to that one would get using a smart card.

9.4 Perturbation Analysis

The objective of the "perturbation analysis (PA) activity" is to experimentally assess the robustness of the ABC4Trust's reference implementation. *For the purposes of*

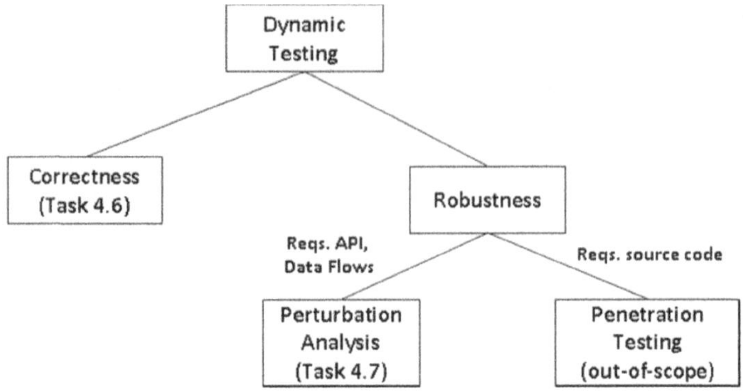

Fig. 9.38 Dynamic testing classes

this document, robustness will be understood as "the implementation's correctness (in particular availability and integrity) in the presence of failures".

Following the functional test cases (i.e., unit testing) that verify the correctness of the implementation, the perturbation analysis plans campaigns to inject outlier test cases, stress cases, and a range of perturbations to ensure that the architecture is resilient per se.

The main objective of a PA is to investigate how a system, or parts of a system, behave under anomalous (i.e., perturbed) operational conditions. A perturbation analysis is capable of demonstrating what sort of outputs a system produces under anomalous circumstances. Often a perturbation analysis will simulate scenarios that represent deviations from the system specification (also called "misuse cases"). The common assumption is that these misuse cases have not been considered at design-time, and as such a corresponding reaction might not have been specified. Contrary to traditional functional testing (correctness) and penetration testing (where usually a stable architecture, implementation and source code access is needed), the primary target of a perturbation analysis is assessing the system's robustness (Figure 9.38). It is important to highlight that a perturbation analysis does not target determining correctness, but empirically assesses if the system's robustness mechanisms actually work.

9.4.1 Overall Approach

The perturbation analysis is based on the framework shown in Figure 9.39 where an Evaluation Target (ET) is exposed to a perturbation in order to assess the system's robustness. In the proposed framework, an ET is selected according to the following criteria:

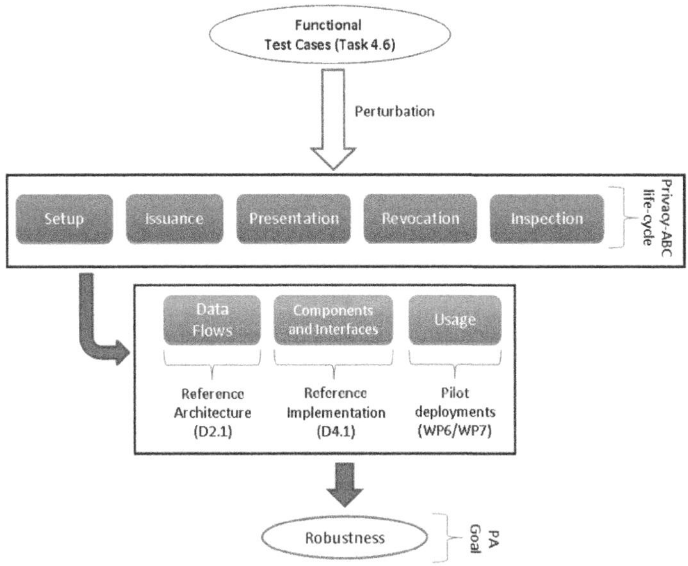

Fig. 9.39 Evaluation target

1. First, by focusing on a particular stage of the Privacy-ABC's life cycle (i.e. Setup, Issuance, Presentation, Revocation and Inspection as documented in [BCD+14]).
2. Second, by selecting the (i) flows taking place at the reference architecture level, (ii) components and interfaces and (iii) pilot experiences.

The perturbations in [LSP+14] are based on a set of functional tests with the goal to assess the correctness of the reference implementation.

Thanks to the framework proposed in [LSP+14], it is possible to achieve a comprehensive approach with perturbations being tested at all levels of the system: design, implementation and operational (including end-users). It conceptually incorporates perturbations derived from system specifications on the different levels of abstraction during the construction of the system, as well as feedback from operational conditions anticipated from the pilot deployment. ABC4Trust adopts existing perturbation frameworks that target the ET's assessment of availability and integrity in the presence of failures (e.g., software or network-related).

9.4.2 Overview of the PA Methodology

The method that implements the framework presented in the previous section consists of the steps shown in Figure 9.40. At a glance, the methodology starts by identifying the ET based on the framework (Step 1, in Figure 9.40. - Evaluation Target),

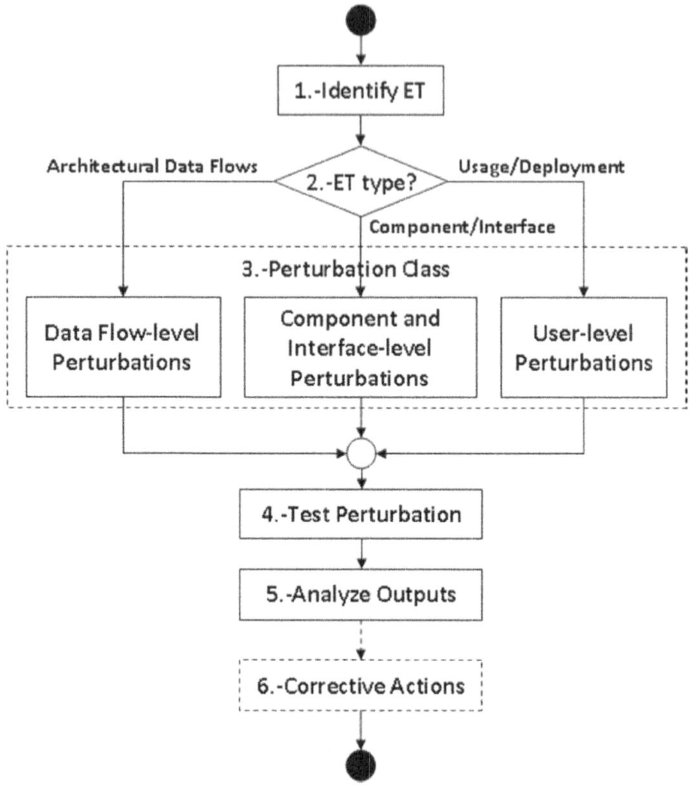

Fig. 9.40 Perturbation Analysis Methodology

that is, the Privacy-ABC life-cycle and associated flows/components & interfaces. In Steps 2 - 4 the ET is classified so the corresponding perturbation campaign is put together and applied. In Step 5 the results of the performed perturbation are analyzed. Finally, in Step 6 the foreseen corrective actions are feedback to WP2 and WP4 for the design and development of the final reference implementation ([BBE$^+$14]).

It is best-practice to document each perturbation as "misuse case scenarios", where design details are specified about the applied perturbations, observed results, and even with respect to the mitigation/corrective actions that have been taken. In the literature, there is no commonly agreed way to document a misuse case. Thus, in Table 9.4 we propose a template to be used in the rest of this document. Such a template gathers the most important information to e.g., trying recreating the failure once a corrective action has been deployed.

Table 9.4: Perturbation Analysis Template

Scenario [no.]: Name of the misuse case scenario	
Summary	Short description of the scenario

Continued on next page

Continued from previous page

Evaluation Target (ET)	Describe the ET (e.g., interface name, specific data flow, ...)
ET Class	Classify the ET as any of the following: 1. Architecture Data Flow (Arch); 2. Component/Interface (Comp); 3. Usage/Deployment (Usage).
Normal flow	Describe the normal (i.e., "correct") flow/usage of the ET.
Perturbation	Describe the perturbation to test in this misuse case (e.g., send to the Verifier a malformed presentation token).
Perturbation Class	Classify the perturbation to test in any of the following: 1. Data flow-level: any of Stress cases (DF-S) or Outlier cases (DF-O); 2. Component and Interface-level: Data-Type cases (C-DT) or Outlier cases (C-O); 3. User-level: any of Misuse (U-M) or Abuse (U-A). The difference being that, the former (U-M) are actually unintended, whilst the latter (U-A) are intentional.
Base functional test case (Task 4.6)	The designed perturbation will depart from a valid functional test case (cf., Task 4.6 "Test case development and testing"). The documented test case (or a reference to it) will be added in this section of the template.

Continued on next page

Continued from previous page

Output old arch.	Document the output/result of the tested perturbation in the old crypto architecture. The result of a test can be any of: • *Compliant*: if its execution follows the documented specification i.e., detects the failure by triggering an exception, or, alternatively, if the observed behavior does not show any evidence of uncontrolled resource consumption. • *Non-compliant*: if its execution does not follow the specification i.e., the test does not detect a fail-safe and no exception is triggered. Or, alternatively, if the observed behavior shows evidence of uncontrolled resource consumption. • *Inconclusive*: if it cannot be determined if the specification was followed or not, possibly because the test's execution time exceeded a prefixed amount of time.
Output new arch.	Document the output/result of the tested perturbation in the old crypto architecture. The result of a test can be any of: • *Compliant*: if its execution follows the documented specification i.e., detects the failure by triggering an exception, or, alternatively, if the observed behavior does not show any evidence of uncontrolled resource consumption. • *Non-compliant*: if its execution does not follow the specification i.e., the test does not detect a fail-safe and no exception is triggered. Or, alternatively, if the observed behavior shows evidence of uncontrolled resource consumption. • *Inconclusive*: if it cannot be determined if the specification was followed or not, possibly because the test's execution time exceeded a prefixed amount of time.

Continued on next page

Continued from previous page

Mitigation/Corrective action	Document the action(s) taken to either mitigate or correct the observed fault (e.g., applied some specific patch to the Application Server). If the perturbation was correctly handled by the ET, then just document in this field the correctness of the implemented mechanism.

9.4.3 Detailed Methodology

The detailed explanation corresponding to each step shown in Figure 9.40 is presented in this section. The methodology consists of seven steps. In Step 1, it identifies the ET based. In Steps 2 to 4, the ET is classified so the corresponding perturbation campaign is put together and applied. In Step 5, the results of the performed perturbation are analyzed. Finally, in Step 6 the foreseen corrective actions are feedback for the design and development of the final reference implementation.

9.4.3.1 Step 1: Identify the ET

The PA starts by analyzing the whole system in order to select those elements that are relevant/critical to the system's goals. For example, applying a perturbation to an API call's URL parameter would be less critical than applying it to a Private Key parameter.

9.4.3.2 Step 2: Classify the ET

With the ET identified by Step 1, now the analysis is focused on classifying it into any of the available categories (i.e., architecture flow, implementation component/interface or usage) in order to select the adequate perturbations to test in the following stage of the methodology. The categories defined by this document are:

- Architecture flow e.g., issuing a credential from scratch.
- Component/Interface e.g., ABCE API's initIssuanceProtocol() method.
- Usage e.g., student waiving her smartcard in front of the NFC reader (WP7).

It is worth noting that PA at the Component/Interface level will be focused on the ABCE API located underneath the context specific application, e.g., the User application or Issuer web application. This is a convenient point to inject faults before any cryptographic primitive is used (e.g., at the transport level). This approach (originally proposed by Nik [LMX04, LX03a]) allows us to gain the control needed to apply the perturbations.

9.4.3.3 Step 3: Select a perturbation class

The classes of perturbation are selected from the list in Table 9.5. Each class defines a group of tests. Each test is designed starting from valid functional test cases, and then derived according to perturbation class. DF-S tests were derived by introducing sustained concurrent requests. DF-S tests will consider two parameters: the number of concurrent requests k and the time interval in second t. The test keeps k concurrent requests during a period of t seconds. C-DT and C-O tests are performed by selecting inputs over a set of invalid inputs. Invalid inputs are identified by combining the syntax and semantics of the API function parameters. The selection is done manually and by using a uniform distribution function.

9.4.3.4 Step 4: Test perturbation

Once the perturbation has been fully defined, it is time to test it on the ET. This might require access to the system (physical/remote), code intrumentation, etc. In any case, the perturbation analysis should guarantee that the perturbation is repeteable under the conditions documented in the misuse case. In general, it is expected for an ET exposed to a perturbation to observe a "fail-stop" behavior. Such reaction to a perturbation will disallow the propagation of the failure (e.g., to other components in the ABCE) and, compromising the ABCE's availability/integrity.

9.4.3.5 Step 5: Analyze outputs

After testing the perturbation the output should be monitored and documented as part of the misuse case. This is a critical step, because corrective actions will be designed and deployed based on these observations.

9.4.3.6 Step 6: Take corrective actions

The final step in the proposed methodology refers to the actual set of actions that should be taken in order to correct/mitigate the observed effects of the perturbation. This might require patching the software, changing the system's specification, etc. This step usually falls outside the scope of traditional perturbation analysis (cf., Voas [VM95] and Nik [LMX04]), although for the sake of completeness is mentioned in the methodology proposed in this document. In ABC4Trust, the implementation of corrective actions will take place once the initial PA round has been executed.

Table 9.5 Perturbation Classes

ET Class	Perturbation Type	Comment/Example
Architecture data flow		
	Stress Case (DF-S)	Perturbations aimed towards taking a system to an extreme operation mode (close to its DoS border). For example, to keep a sustained overload on the Revocation Authority by constantly requesting the maximum tolerated number of revocation evidences.
	Outlier Case (DF-O)	These are perturbations testing values that appear to deviate markedly from other members of the sample in which it occurs. For example, if all credentials being issued have only 5 attributes, then an outlier case might consider credentials with a much larger number of attributes.
Component/Interface		
	Data Type (C-DT)	These perturbations test values that are valid for the type of parameter (e.g., -128 to 127 for Java's byte data type), but that are invalid for the specification. For example, typical DT perturbations [LMX04, LX03b] for an integer parameter include: param–, param++, 1, 0, -1, INT_MAX and INT_MIN. In Service Oriented Architectures, the use of DT perturbations is both useful and more efficient than other techniques (e.g., bit flipping) for testing fault tolerance mechanisms [LMX04].
	Outlier (C-O)	As defined in DF-O, these are perturbations testing values that appear to deviate markedly from other members of the sample in which it occurs.
Usage		
	Misuse (U-M)	Refers to a perturbation introduced accidentally by the user of the system due to some incorrect (violating the specification) use of it. For example, a user selecting the wrong set of credentials when requesting from the Issuer a new one with carried-over-attributes
	Abuse (U-A)	Contrary to the previously defined perturbation, this one refers to malicious users trying to abuse the system. For example, a user trying to crash the system by inserting her smartcard multiple times in the reader.

9.4.4 Detailed Overview of the Results

This section details the PA conducted on the ABCE component (and other core-components that are invoked through the ABCE API calls) of the reference implementation documented in [GN12] and [CKL+11] (i.e., "old crypto architecture") in order to assess its robustness. The goal is to identify those elements that need to be further analyzed and improved (from a robustness perspective), before integrating into the next version of the implementation (i.e., the "new crypto architecture" in [BBE+14], [BCD+14]). The PA started with the analysis of the whole system documented in [CKL+11] in order to identify the ET that can compromise the over-

Table 9.6 Scenarios and Test Cases (TCs) grouped by TE types.

Class	Setup		Issuance		Presentation		Revocation		Inspection	
	Scen.	Cases	Scen.	Cases	Scen.	Cases	Scen.	Cases	Scen.	Cases
Data flow	1	2	4	5	1	2	2	5	1	2
Component	9	13	3	9	3	15	0	-	1	5
User-level	0	-	0	-	0	-	0	-	0	-
Total	10	15	7	14	4	17	2	5	2	7

all robustness of the system. Then, the PA classified the ET into architecture flow, implementation component/interface, and usage. The classification allows selecting the type of perturbations to apply. Third, tests are executed against the implementation. The results of a test can be one of the following: *Compliant*, *Non-compliant*, and *Inconclusive*. A test is Compliant if its execution detected a fail-safe behavior, or, alternatively, if the observed behavior does not show any evidence of uncontrolled resource consumption. If a test does not detect a fail-safe, then the test is Non-compliant. A test is Inconclusive, e.g., it cannot be applied to a component, or its execution time exceeds a prefixed timeout. Finally, the PA identified and suggested the proper action to be taken in order to mitigate the findings in the next version of the reference implementation (i.e., [BBE$^+$14]).

In total, the PA consisted of 25 perturbation scenarios containing in total 58 test cases. Tests were designed starting from valid functional test cases, and then introducing perturbation inputs. The selection of inputs is done using both a uniform distribution function and manual selection over a set of outlier inputs. Invalid inputs are identified by combining the syntax and semantics of API function parameters. Table 9.6 reports the total number of perturbation scenarios (column Scen.) and test cases (column TC) grouped by ET Type. Test cases are distributed in: (i) 16 flow and stress test cases, (ii) 42 component and interface test cases.

As mentioned before, the scope of this PA is to assess the robustness of the reference implementation of ABC4Trust. The PA does not apply security testing techniques, such as penetration testing. Moreover, this PA does not perform any benchmark and does not define metrics for it. Software benchmarks and metrics are addressed in WP2 and WP3.

Table 9.7 shows the results of the test execution. The result of a test can be Compliant (column S), Non-compliant (column T), and Inconclusive (column I). The number of successful tests is 31 out of 58, while the number of failed tests is eight. The remaining 19 tests are inconclusive. Inconclusive tests can be classified in unresponsive tests (i.e., reached the timeout condition), the component under test is not implemented (i.e., it is specified, but the implementation is missing), and limitation of the testing platform (i.e., test and component resides on the same JVM instance).

31 tests out of 60 were compliant. It is important to consider that (a) the perturbation analysis does not claim completeness as an experimental methodology and (b) the test platform restrictions often do not allow tracing the stress cases and loads reaching the ABCE and its CE. This is a natural limitation of any PA approach where one needs to constrain elements such as length of inter-component propaga-

Table 9.7 Test case execution results grouped by result

Class	Setup				Issuance				Presentation				Revocation				Inspection			
	Cases	C	N	I	Cases	C	N	I	Cases	C	N	I	Cases	C	N	I	Cases	C	N	I
Data flow	2	1	1	0	5	4	0	1	2	1	0	1	5	4	0	1	2	1	1	0
Component	13	10	3	0	9	8	1	0	15	2	2	11	0	-	-	-	5	0	1	4
User-level	0	-	-	-	0	-	-	-	0	-	-	-	0	-	-	-	0	-	-	-
Total	15	11	4	0	14	12	1	1	17	3	2	12	5	4	0	1	7	1	1	5

C=Compliant, N=Non-compliant, I=inconclusive (e.g., timeout errors)

tion flows or the level of detail of a perturbation case. Thus the validity of the PA and designated success is based around the class of considered perturbations either as outliers, high-likelihood or nature of interface/data-flows for a target. Naturally, it must also be noted that these results do not imply that the implementation is secure. As shown in Figure 9.38, the PA aims at the robustness of the implementation. Although robustness issues may imply security issues as well, the PA did not explicitly targeted security properties of the implementation. Indeed, the PA did not apply security testing techniques, such as penetration testing, and they were considered out of scope.

The total number of non-compliant tests in the old architecture is 8, which indicate the presence of issues that may affect the robustness of the application. They were executed also against the new architecture: two of them were solved, one is considered unreachable by an external entity (e.g., an attacker), one is no longer applicable, and the remaining foud are still marked as fail however the corrective actions have been identified.

The total number of inconclusive results is 19. Four of them are due to a test execution timeout when testing the U-Prove cryptographic engine; and finally, 15 are due to the limitation of the testing platform.

References

[Bal08] Josep Balasch. *Smart ard Implementation of Anonymous redentials.* PhD thesis, KATHOLIEKE UNIVERSITEIT LEUVEN, 2008.

[BBE+14] Thomas Baignères, Patrik Bichsel, Robert R Enderlein, Hans Knudsen, Kasper Damgård, Jonas Jensen, Gregory Neven, Janus Nielsen, Pascal Paillier, and Michael Stausholm. Final Reference Implementation. Deliverable D4.2, The ABC4Trust EU Project, 2014. Available at `https://abc4trust.eu/download/D4.2%20Final%20Reference%20Implementation.pdf`, Last accessed on 2014-11-08.

[BCC04] Ernie Brickell, Jan Camenisch, and Liqun Chen. Direct anonymous attestation. In *Proceedings of the 11th ACM conference on Computer and communications security*, pages 132–145. ACM, 2004.

[BCD+14] Patrik Bichsel, Jan Camenisch, Maria Dubovitskaya, Robert R. Enderlein, Stephan Krenn, Ioannis Krontiris, Anja Lehmann, Gregory Neven, Janus Dam Nielsen, Christian Paquin, Franz-Stefan Preiss, Kai Rannenberg, Ahmad Sabouri, and Michael Stausholm. Architecture for Attribute-based Credential Technologies - Final Version. Deliverable D2.2, The ABC4Trust EU Project, 2014. Available at https://abc4trust.eu/download/Deliverable_D2.2.pdf, Last accessed on 2014-11-08.

[BCGS09] Patrik Bichsel, Jan Camenisch, Thomas Groß, and Victor Shoup. Anonymous credentials on a standard java card. In *Proceedings of the 2009 ACM Conference on Computer and Communications Security, CCS 2009, Chicago, Illinois, USA, November 9-13, 2009*, pages 600–610, 2009.

[BDP14] Thomas Baignères, Ccile Delerablèe, and Pascal Paillier. *Programming Privacy-ABCs on the ABC4Trust Lite v1.1 Smart Card*, 2014.

[BHJ+10] Lejla Batina, Jaap-Henk Hoepman, Bart Jacobs, Wojciech Mostowski, and Pim Vullers. Developing efficient blinded attribute certificates on smart cards via pairings. In *Smart Card Research and Advanced Application, 9th IFIP WG 8.8/11.2 International Conference, CARDIS 2010, Passau, Germany, April 14-16, 2010. Proceedings*, pages 209–222, 2010.

[Bic07] Patrik Bichsel. Theft and misuse protection for anonymous credentials. Master's thesis, ETH Zürich, Switzerland, 2007.

[CKL+11] Jan Camenisch, Ioannis Krontiris, Anja Lehmann, Gregory Neven, Christian Paquin, Kai Rannenberg, and Harald Zwingelberg. Architecture for Attribute-based Credential Technologies - Version 1. Deliverable D2.1, The ABC4Trust EU Project, 2011. Available at https://abc4trust.eu/download/ABC4Trust-D2.1-Architecture-V1.2.pdf, Last accessed on 2014-11-08.

[GN12] Hans Guldage and Janus Dam Nielsen. Initial Reference Implementation. Deliverable D4.1, The ABC4Trust EU Project, 2012.

[Jen14] Jonas Lindstrøm Jensen. Smartphone Feasibility Analysis. Deliverable D4.4, The ABC4Trust EU Project, 2014. Available at https://abc4trust.eu/download/Deliverable_D4.4.pdf, Last accessed on 2014-11-08.

[LMX04] N. Looker, M. Munro, and J. Xu. Simulating Errors in Web Services. *International Journal of Simulation Systems, Science & Technology*, 5(5):29–37, December 2004.

[LSP+14] Jesus Luna, Neeraj Suri, Giancarlo Pellegrino, Heng Zhang, and Michael Bladt Stausholm. Final Perturbation Analysis of the Implementation. Deliverable D4.3, The ABC4Trust EU Project, 2014. Available at https://abc4trust.eu/download/D4%203_PerturbationAnalysis_final.pdf, Last accessed on 2014-11-08.

[LX03a] Nik Looker and Jie Xu. Assessing the Dependability of SOAP RPC-Based Web Services by Fault Injection. In *Object-Oriented Real-Time Dependable Systems, 2003. WORDS 2003 Fall. The Ninth IEEE International Workshop on*, page 163. IEEE, October 2003.

[LX03b] Nik Looker and Jie Xu. Assessing the Dependability of SOAP RPC-Based Web Services by Fault Injection. In *Object-Oriented Real-Time Dependable Systems, 2003. WORDS 2003 Fall. The Ninth IEEE International Workshop on*, pages 163–163, Oct 2003.

[Paq13] Christian Paquin. Privacy and accountability in identity systems: the best of both worlds. TechReport MSR-TR-2013-85, Microsoft Corporation, September 2013.

[PZ13] Christian Paquin and Greg Zaverucha. U-prove Cryptographic Specification v1.1 (Revision 2). Technical report, Microsoft Corporation, 2013.

[TJ09] Hendrik Tews and Bart Jacobs. Performance issues of selective disclosure and blinded issuing protocols on java card. In *Information Security Theory and Practice. Smart Devices, Pervasive Systems, and Ubiquitous Networks, Third IFIP WG 11.2 International Workshop, WISTP 2009, Brussels, Belgium, September 1-4, 2009, Proceedings*, pages 95–111, 2009.

[VM95] Jeffrey M Voas and Keith W Miller. Software testability: The new verification. *IEEE Software*, 12(3):17–28, 1995.

Chapter 10
Privacy-ABC Usage Scenarios

Joerg Abendroth, Marit Hansen, Ioannis Krontiris, Ahmad Sabouri, Eva Schlehahn, Robert Seidl, and Harald Zwingelberg

Abstract The decision to employ Privacy-ABC systems and operate them is highly dependent on the business model, requirements and capabilities of the potential adopters. Nevertheless, more knowledge about various use cases of Privacy-ABCs and the problems that can be addressed by them may influence the benefits perceived by the decision makers.
In this chapter, we present additional scenarios, beyond the pilots described in Chapters 6 and 7, and discuss their issues that can be resolved by Privacy-ABCs. These scenarios include eIDs, anonymous participation in decisions and polls, use of cloud services within enterprises, bank as Identity Service Provider, and preventing tracking the relying parties.

This chapter takes a high level view on Privacy-ABC technologies and the scenarios in which they can be used. We begin with reviewing the ABC4Trust actors from a business perspective (for technical details please refer to Chapter 2). Then, a summary of the actors is presented along the examples and how they will likely be operated. Then in Section 10.2, we introduce different example scenarios, namely:

- eIDs (10.2.1)
- Anonymous Participation in Decisions and Polls (10.2.2)
- Use of Cloud Service within Enterprises (10.2.3)
- Bank as Identity Service Provider(10.2.4)

Joerg Abendroth and Robert Seidl
Nokia, Sankt-Martin-Straße 76, D-81541 Munich, e-mail: {Joerg.Abendroth, Robert.Seidl}@nsn.com

Marit Hansen, Eva Schlehahn, and Harald Zwingelberg
Unabhängiges Landeszentrum für Datenschutz Schleswig - Holstein, Germany, e-mail: {ULD6, ULD67, ULD2}@datenschutzzentrum.de

Ioannis Krontiris and Ahmad Sabouri
Chair of Mobile Business & Multilateral Security, Goethe University Frankfurt, Germany,e-mail: ahmad.sabouri@m-chair.de

K. Rannenberg et al. (eds.), *Attribute-based Credentials for Trust*,
DOI 10.1007/978-3-319-14439-9_10

- Do-Not-Track Relying Parties (10.2.5)

Each scenario is explained along with the issues that need to be solved and the advantages of deploying Privacy-ABC technologies.

10.1 Review of the Main Actors from a Business Perspective

Prior to discussing typical Privacy-ABC scenarios, a high level view of the activities and the interactions in the Internet will be provided in order to better understand the need for privacy protection.

As shown in Figure 10.1, typical users (Item 4) visit a website that provides a service (Item 1). This service can be immaterial, such as social networks, web search, or discussion groups. Moreover, the service can also result in a material delivery to the users, such as printed pictures, or other products purchased online. The business of service providers is typically built on the users interacting and ultimately paying for the services.

Besides providing goods or services, marketing and advertising (Item 3) are common elements in conducting a business. Two companies may provide a similar product but the company with better marketing and customization to people's needs will, ultimately, achieve higher financial benefits. Thus, knowing users' habits and characteristics becomes an important business element. Similar to the issue of adver-

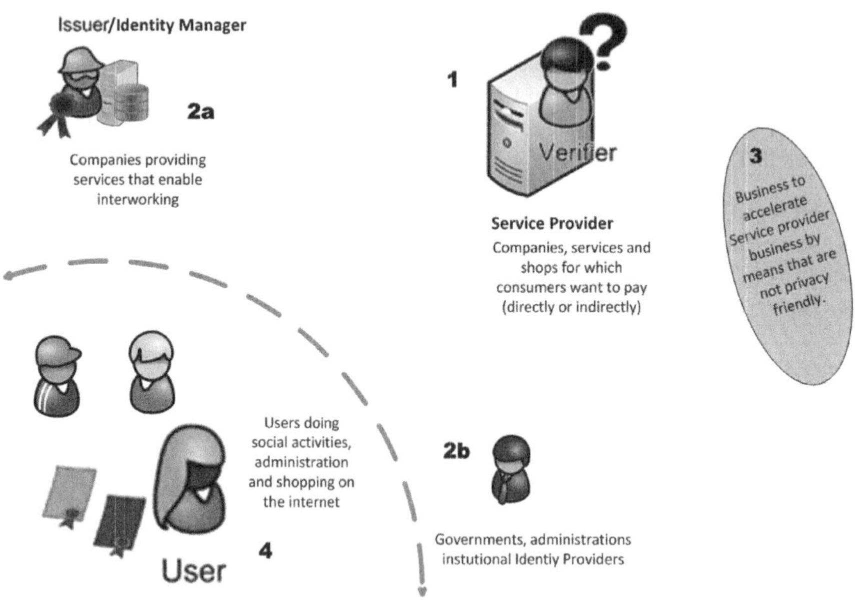

Fig. 10.1 High-level view of User activities on the Internet

tisement, all scenarios that benefit from Privacy-ABCs show that there is a common conflict of competing interests that motivates entities to ignore the privacy of users (or other entities). Increased knowledge about the users enables their identification. Examples of user information about which business operators may wish to know include ownership of a car, family status, recent visits to certain types of electronic services. Governments or administrations (Item 2b), identity service providers (Item 2a) as well as companies that provide services[1] (Item 1) are interested in collecting (and, ultimately, collect) information on users. It seems that in particular the heavy competition and the intensity of the business interests at stake influence the desire to profile users.

While infrastructure services (Item 2a/b) may be able to compete among themselves by offering stronger privacy protection to their users, in general companies and service providers (Item 1) have little intrinsic interest to not profile the user, since profiling is seen as a possibility to maximize profits. Thus, it becomes important that a user cannot be recognized as a specific returning customer or even as the same customer, by combining the information of various services she visited in the past. This anonymization and privacy protection can be achieved elegantly by Privacy-ABC technologies.

Compared to existing standards (see also Chapter 2), such as OAuth, SAML, OpenID, Privacy-ABCs have built-in mechanisms that allow users not only to select which information (or attributes) they wish to or need to disclose towards a service provider but also to keep the remaining information confidential. At the same time, standardization of privacy protecting protocols is slowed down due to the low number of well established underlying privacy-preserving technologies. Nonetheless, Privacy-ABC technologies can improve this situation as well.

10.1.1 User

The User (Item 4 in Figure 10.1) is typically the entity seeking to gain access to a resource. In this regard, she needs to authenticate towards the service provider and prove her eligibility for using the service or the resource. If the User wants to have her privacy preserved, she can benefit from of the Privacy-ABC technologies. During an authentication session, a Privacy-ABC User proves facts about herself using the credentials she obtained from the legitimate and trustworthy Issuers. Any application, such as a web browser, a cloud agent, or a standalone application performing the Privacy-ABC operations on behalf of the User is part of the User's domain.

The client side deployment is more complicated than a simple storage of credentials, as it has to support secure storage of the User's secret keys and perform cryptographic operations to produce the presentation tokens while providing adequate interfaces for credential management and selection.

[1] Identity Service Providers are seen as infrastructure providers

10.1.1.1 Examples of a User

In almost all scenarios, the Users are the consumers, even though there may be exceptions. Whenever Users are consumers of a good or customers of a service, they are the entities whose privacy is being protected. In Section 10.2, several examples of users are given.

10.1.1.2 Operations of a User

From the operational perspective, the actions of a Privacy-ABC User do not differ from any actions of other credential-based systems, such as InfoCard. The User needs to manage her credentials and pseudonyms with the help of a software agent, and upon authentication request, she has to select which from the possible options are to be used for the generation of the presentation token.

The User may need to go through some other out-of-band authentication processes in order to validate her attributes by the Issuer and bootstrap the issuance of her credentials.

10.1.2 Verifier

The Verifier (Item 1 in Figure 10.1) receives a presentation token from the User, allowing her to check whether the User possesses certain attributes. In other words, the Verifier is the entity verifying the information the user includes in the presentation token. This information may be a complete attribute (i.e. exact birth date), but may also be only a relevant fact about certain attributes (e.g. adult individual over 18 years old).

The Verifier usually provides some kind of access to restricted services for which the User is required to prove her eligibility to access by revealing relevant and certified attribute values. Providing a privacy-friendly access control will be beneficial in terms of legal compliance and customer trust especially when servicing consumers. However, the business model of the Verifier is not necessarily dependent on Privacy-ABC technologies.

10.1.2.1 Examples of a Verifier

Any service provider servicing consumers may become a Verifier. Service providers with a large number of different customers can perform statistical analysis as part of their business and benefit greatly from the results. This is due to the Privacy-ABC technology protecting their customers' privacy, and creating trust towards the service provider. Service providers in social networks often provide services that let users of similar interest join and find each other. Still, those services do not need to know all interests of the users unless the users deliberately reveal them.

An advanced form of a Verifier is similar to the RP-STS (Relying Party Secure Token Service) known from the Web Service technology. In that case, the service provider does not need to implement the Verifier functionality on its own, but may rely on an intermediate party to do so. The intermediate party implements a Verifier functionality, evaluates the presentation token according to the policy defined by the service provider, and hands back the result in a proprietary or standardized protocol (e.g. XACML Request/Response [Org05]). However in this case the intermediate party gets to know the attribute value of the user, so the user needs to know about this and the intermediate party must enjoy a level of trust from the users that is similar to that of the verifier.

10.1.2.2 Operations of a Verifier

The Verifier needs to have one or several presentation policies, which need to be defined before enabling access control for a service. A presentation policy determines which attributes need to be shown to gain access to that service. Moreover, the presentation policy includes whether certain attributes need to be proven in an inspectable way. If sub-areas of the application require a more specific access policy, then additional presentation policies need to be defined.

In addition to the basic access, a Verifier may need to handle pseudonyms created by the User, including their respective scope. With a pseudonym, a user can be recognized as "being the same as before", without the verifier being able to recognize the real user identity. For example in the School Pilot (Söderhamn), there were long time chats (wall), in which the same user could post several times using the same alias. In this case impersonation of the users had to be prevented (i.e. a pupil takes over an alias of another pupil). Privacy-ABCs provide the feature of pseudonyms, and enforcing them in this way is part of the presentation policy. However, the verifier is not responsible for managing the pseudonyms of the users. If the Verifier would keep track which pseudonym a user can use, there would be a privacy issue.

Another example of pseudonyms concerns the Patras pilot. In this pilot, it was necessary to ensure that each user could deliver only one course evaluation to prevent manipulation of the evaluation results. For this purpose, "scope-exclusive pseudonyms" were used. The Verifier provided the scope and ensured that each user could possess only one pseudonym within this scope.

10.1.3 Issuer (with or without IdM)

The role of the Issuer (Item 2a/b in Figure 10.1) is often combined with the role of the Identity Manager (IdM). As the role of the IdM has no specific Privacy-ABC function, we discuss IdM together with the Issuer.

Issuer: The Issuer provides the User with credentials containing the user attributes. Hence, it is the domain where the bootstrapping from the offline world occurs. In the Privacy-ABC ecosystem, the Issuer is an authoritative entity[2], similar to the IdM[3] in a state-of-the-art IdM ecosystem. Thus naturally an IDM is predestinated to take on the role of an Issuer. The Issuer takes its position either by implementing an interface where relevant parties can input information (e.g. which students belong to a specific class), or by having an interface to an IdM. Nevertheless, using advance issuance techniques, the Issuer can blindly transfer attributes (without learning the attribute values) from the other credentials that a user holds into a new credential and augment them with new attributes.

IdM: The IdM role changes compared to the state-of-the art systems, where it was the only authoritative entity. Now the IdM shares this role with the Privacy-ABCs Issuer by feeding authentic data to it. An Issuer may be installed beside the traditional IdM to enable authentication based on Privacy-ABCs. In this case, the Issuer fetches the information of the user profiles from the IdM and delivers them to the users in form of Privacy-ABCs. The IdM may be also patched with a Verifier in order to feature access control using Privacy-ABCs.

In a nutshell, an Issuer attests the attributes of a credential and vouches for their correctness. However, the Issuer has to establish trust relationships with Verifiers so that they rely on the credentials by that Issuer. In this regard, the Issuer shall be in a legitimate position for the credentials that it issues. For instance, a university usually may not setup an Issuer for driving licence certificates beyond the university campus.

Ecosystem participants being holders of user attribute databases, which are supposed to serve other services in a privacy-preserving way, can take in the full advantages of the Privacy-ABCs Issuer role. However, in some business scenarios, it is not always necessary to issue credentials based on the stored attributes. Depending on the use case, the source of the attributes may vary. They may be provided by the User herself, verified by the Issuer offline, fetched from the trusted sources (e.g. IdM), or transferred from the other credentials that the user holds. Moreover, attribute values may also be generated "jointly random"[4], which may be useful for specific scenarios.

10.1.3.1 Examples of an Issuer

The Issuer provides knowledge about the user (e.g. whether he or she is in a certain class, her birth date or gender) in form of credentials. Using these credentials, Users

[2] Authoritative with respect to the attributes the Issuer can provide to the user. There may be several authorities for one or different attributes.

[3] In the OpenID standard based system, the entity knowing the user might have less authority than in traditional IdM systems; still, this authority replies on behalf of the user.

[4] "jointly random": This element indicates that a specific attribute of the newly issued credential must be generated jointly at random, i.e., so that the Issuer does not learn the value of the attribute, but so that the User cannot bias the uniform distribution of the value.

can demonstrate certain facts about themselves and prove their fulfilment of certain requirements. It is conceivable that different Issuers exist for different domains, for example the vehicle examination office issues credentials about "road worthiness" of a car, while the insurance company issues credentials for cost coverage in case of accident.

An Issuer can provide a kind of notary service to the users, so that they can have credentials with self-claimed attribute values. In state-of-the-art IdM systems like Microsoft's InfoCard [Inf], these attributes are known as self-certified attributes. This is also possible in Privacy-ABC systems. In addition to this, Privacy-ABC Users can run an Issuer themselves for issuing credentials out of their self-claimed attributes.

10.1.3.2 Operations of an Issuer

The Issuer must prepare one or several issuance policies, which indicate what attributes a user has to reveal or what facts she has to prove in order to get the credential issued. The issuance policy may be empty if the user is authenticated out-of-band.

The Issuer may require the following actions in the setup phase:

- Connecting to the database holding the attributes (e.g. the IdM),
- Setting up the Privacy-ABCs' libraries and initialize them to issue credentials,
- Configuring the interface to the other entities such as Revocation Authorities,
- Publishing the public parameters and make them available to the other parties.

Typically, administrative intervention during the issuing process is not necessary. The User can use self administration to obtain credentials when attributes are available in the source databases. However, change of attribute values may need the administrators' attention. Moreover, depending on the scenario, some administrative effort may be needed to initiate the revocation process when it is desired.

10.1.3.3 Operation of an IdM

During a set-up phase, trust relations of the IdM component need to be initiated, e.g. by means of exchanging certificates and agreeing on the SAML protocol, or by enabling one of the authentication modules.

In the next step, the database has to be filled with the users' data, including the information used later for issuing credentials. This process is called provisioning. It can be done manually, one-by-one, or as mass provisioning, utilising a CSV [5] -File. Other possible methods of provisioning include pulling the data from another IdM system, or having the data pushed into the system.

[5] Comma Separated Values

Users may want to change their profiles, thus a self-administration portal would help to provide flexibility. The profile consists of permanent data (e.g. name or date of birth) and data which may change in time (e.g. address or telephone number).

10.2 Some Typical Privacy-ABC Scenarios

In this section we present different use cases of Privacy-ABCs beyond the two pilots of ABC4Trust described in Chapters 6 and 7. Since the different scenarios highlight different privacy protection goals, it will be possible for the readers to compare our scenarios with theirs and, thus, deduce which of the optional high level building blocks are necessary to their applications. It should be noted that each of our scenarios should also include or achieve the protection goals of the others. However, for the sake of simplicity, we restricted each scenario to one protection goal.

10.2.1 Scenario: eIDs

Electronic Identity (eID) smart cards are rapidly emerging in Europe and are gradually gaining a broader user acceptance. As an authentication token and personal data container, an eID card is a gateway to personal information. This, however, entails certain risks to the privacy of the citizen, through the unwanted disclosure of personal information and its subsequent misuse. As the information in official eID documents is verified by an entity trusted by most market participants this, in addition, adds a new quality to the data in comparison to ID information provided by the Users themselves. It improves the accuracy of the data but also deprives Users from acting under self-chosen pseudonyms [Zwi11]. These privacy risks could become even more prominent in the future, if citizens would be using their eIDs not only for e-government services, but also in e-commerce for shopping online, booking rooms at hotels, renting cars online, managing bank accounts, etc.

Several European countries have taken extra care to protect their citizens against these risks [NH08]. A notable example is the German eID card. The German eID card provides a set of features to protect the user's privacy. Before gaining access to a German eID, the Service Providers must perform a checking procedure done by the German federal authority and prove that the personal data requested is necessary for the requested service[6] (for details on the process please refer to [Zwi11]). This serves as basis for obtaining a digital certificate, which is also used to identify the Service Provider and display the purpose of the processing to the user. Furthermore, it establishes a secure identification process at the Service Provider's side first[7]. Additionally, the possibility of obliging the User to reveal only parts of the attributes, so

[6] See 21 German Personalausweisgesetz (German law on eIDs), online: http://www.gesetze-im-internet.de/pauswg/BJNR134610009.html

[7] See 18 Sec. 4 German Personalausweisgesetz.

that the User has full control of his personal data, is another important requirement. Moreover, citizens must consent to every attempt, by service providers, to access their personal data. On-card verification supports use cases, such as anonymous age verification and proof of place of living as well as selective disclosure of attributes. Finally, service-specific pseudonyms allow a secure re-identification of users while being unlinkable across different services they have used in the past.

The European Commission published a proposal for a "Regulation of the European Parliament and of the Council on electronic identification and trust services for electronic transactions in the internal market" (herein: eIDAS)[8]. This proposal aims at removing existing barriers to the digital development in Europe by providing the legal basis for a wider acceptance of electronic identification and authentication means, as mandated by the Digital Agenda[9]. The Regulation (EU) $N°910/2014$ on electronic identification and trust services for electronic transactions in the internal market (eIDAS Regulation) was adopted by the co-legislators on 23 July 2014[10].

Achieving cross border interoperability is also an important goal. However, the Regulation should not be implemented in a way that it, essentially, prevents privacy preserving solutions from being applicable by Member States due to cross-border legal and technological differences among the EU countries. The privacy legislation experts within the ABC4Trust project have performed an analysis addressing these obstacles in detail also proposing solutions for the lawmakers. In [ZS13] the authors discuss the legal prerequisites that must be met in order to deploy Privacy-ABCs directly as a part of the officially issued eIDs, which would be our first option. However, at the moment, neither the EU Member States nor the market are sufficiently advanced to adopt such a solution while even the strongly privacy-preserving German eID framework would require a major update of its technology to directly support Privacy-ABCs. For this use case we, therefore, would rather address a solution that allows a combination of Privacy-ABCs with existing national eID schemes, where Privacy-ABCs can act as intermediate solution. If this approach is adopted by EU countries, then it will be easier for all Member States to introduce eID schemes with direct support of Privacy-ABCs.

10.2.1.1 Issues to solve

The non-privacy ABC proposal to instantiate eIDAS has steps to protect user's privacy in eID, however several security and privacy concerns still remain. These prob-

---

[8] For the proposal text and other related legislative documents see: `http://ec.europa.eu/prelex/detail_dossier_real.cfm?CL=en&DosId=201689`.

[9] Key Action 16 reads: "Propose a Council and Parliament Decision requesting Member States to ensure mutual recognition of e-identification and e-authentication across the EU based on online 'authentication services", in A Digital Agenda for Europe, COM (2010) 245final, online: `http://eur-lex.europa.eu/LexUriServ/LexUriServ.do?uri=CELEX:52010DC0245:EN:NOT`.

[10] See `http://eur-lex.europa.eu/legal-content/EN/TXT/?uri=uriserv:OJ.L_.2014.257.01.0073.01.ENG`

lems originate from the fact that authentication schemes follow passive authentication protocols with bearer tokens. Bearer tokens (security tokens) containing user's claims are delivered by the eID server to the service provider without user intervention. Unless each relying party operates its own eID server, which is a resource intensive task, this model is subject to several threats, as further discussed [BKPR14]:

- The eID server knows all user transactions. Even though the eID server does not necessarily need to know where the user is authenticated and which service she is requesting, this knowledge is passed, by design, to the eID server in the current eID solutions. More specifically, the eID server is involved each time a user authenticates herself to a service provider using her eID and, thus, it is able to keep track of the user actions. This enables the eID server to trace and link all communications and transactions of each user (user profiling).
- The eID server knows all the customers of a service provider. Reversing the above threat, the involvement of the eID server in every user authentication constitutes a threat for the service providers' business secrets as well, since the eID server learns who are the customers using a specific service. Especially if the eID server is operated by a private company, it might be a threat to its competition, if it can learn all the customers of another company (i.e. the service provider).
- User impersonation. Since the user does not perform an active role in the information exchange between the eID server and the service provider, there is a high security risk of user impersonation by insider attackers at the eID server or outsider intruders who can gain access to the eID server's resources. An eID server under the control of an external or internal attacker has the ability to impersonate every user at applications using eIDs for authentication. For example, insiders can copy or alter users' credentials and, thus, steal their identities. In general, in a federated eID environment, the insiders or outsiders who acquire a user's credentials can impersonate the user and get access to the assets at different services belonging to the federated domain.
- Availability. The eID server becomes a business critical component (single point of failure) as it is needed for every transaction the user performs with the service applications. Denial of Service attacks towards the eID server will impact all applications using the service. Attacking this component may have a huge economic impact because the attack can then spread over many different services.

All of the above problems become even more critical when there are only a few eID servers operating instead of a fully scalable, distributed model.

Meanwhile, the requirement that the eID providers must not be able to track the behaviour of eID holders is becoming more prominent. In the evaluation assessment of the recent proposal of a Regulation "on electronic identification and trusted services for electronic transactions in the internal market" it is stated that a solution to this tracking problem should be aligned with the current on-going revision of the Data Protection Directive and include specifically privacy-by-design rules. Next section discusses specifically how the above threats can be addressed within the privacy-by-design model.

On the legal side, now, there is a major issue to solve as well. The initial version of the German law on eIDs ("Personalausweisgesetz"[11] = PAuswG) strictly prohibited that a relying party professionally (German "geschäftsmäig") transfers the obtained information. The objective of this rule was the prevention of, e.g. address brokers from obtaining and selling personal data without their owners' consent and control[12]. The law was amended in 2013 and now allows the transfer of the obtained information to previously defined third parties[13]. However, it is still not allowed, by the provisions in this law, to have an identity broker obtaining personal data, since ID brokers ("geschäftsmäig") transfer the data by profession.

Progress can be made if we allow yet another amendment to the German law stating that specific ID brokers are allowed. Then, these must either transfer the data only on behalf and under control of the user to third parties or issue credentials to the user based on the obtained personal data.

10.2.1.2 Advantages of a Privacy-ABCs solution

Privacy-ABCs have a significant potential to enhance existing eID smart-card based privacy solutions. Their integration with existing infrastructures is realizable today, although modifications of some of their elements may be required. For example, enhancing German eID servers with the capability of issuing Privacy-ABCs would make the eID server act as a Privacy-ABC Issuer. Deploying the Privacy-ABC Issuer applications can promote Privacy-ABC Tokens as they provide unlinkability and anonymity to the users.

In more detail, Figure 10.2 shows the entities involved in such a case. In particular, the combined eID/Privacy-ABC Issuer has the capability of issuing Privacy-ABCs. With this combination we achieve an interesting solution of high assurance on the identity of individuals through their eIDs and full anonymity when using a service. User anonymity is possible since the presentation token cannot be linked to the true identity of the user. This identity was verified during her authentication at the eID server but, afterwards, Privacy-ABC tokens were used to transfer the information. Privacy-ABCs ensure the unlinkability between the issuance of the credential and its usage through the presentation proof. For the sake of completeness, we would like to point out that in [Bjo10, BKPR14] a different architecture is proposed. The architecture is close to the scenario in 10.2.3, as the eID server is treated as a separate entity from the Privacy-ABC Issuer. However, the fast time to market of this architecture is achieved at the risk of the Privacy-ABC Issuer altering the eID attributes during transformations.

---

[11] http://www.gesetze-im-internet.de/pauswg/BJNR134610009.html

[12] See 21 Para. 2 Nr. 2 German PAuswG.

[13] The amendment adding 21 Para. 2 Nr. 2a German PAuswG as ratified in the Gesetz zur Förderung der elektronischen Verwaltung sowie zur Änderung weiterer Vorschriften (EVerwFG) as in force since August 1st. 2013.

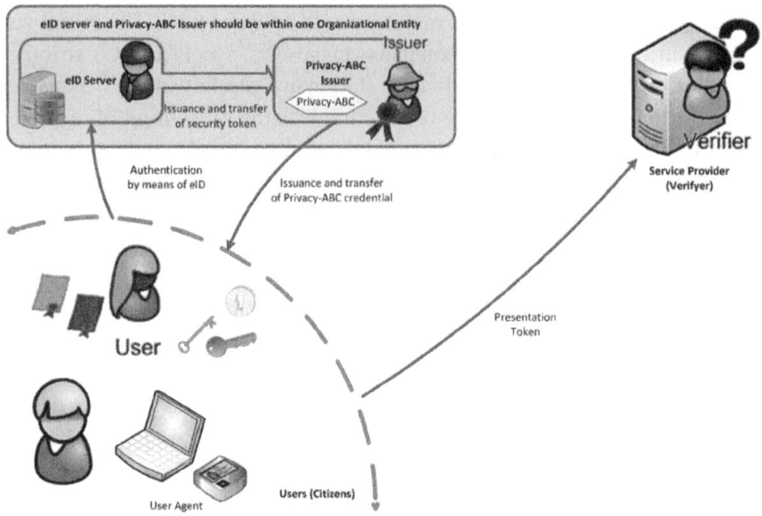

Fig. 10.2 Overview of an eID scenario using Privacy-ABCs

10.2.2 Scenario: Anonymous Participation in Decisions and Polls

In times of low participation in election procedures and widespread political disinterest, an increase participation in governmental decision processes can be considered of an utmost value in itself. This includes opinion polling and decision making processes on any aspect of people's daily lives.

At the same time, the wide availability of inexpensive networked devices, such as smart phones, TV-sets or video games, brings a large part of the earth population online. A consequence of this is the idea to deploy electronic communication means and devices to trigger an increase of people's participation in decision making processes. The use of such means and devices may also result, as an added benefit, in the inclusion of people who are otherwise hindered to participate in these processes such as handicapped people as well as people who cannot afford to travel to the places where decision making processes are held. Other reasons that hinder participation include professional or family obligations as well as avoidance of the burden to travel long distances within a limited time period. Many of these deterrents could be removed if it was possible to hold decision making processes online.

However, the deployment of Privacy-ABCs for eVoting processes is not recommended. While some European Union Member States already have online elections, others are highly reluctant to deploy electronic processes for general elections. For example, the German Constitutional Court has set very high requirements regarding the transparency of the voting and counting processes as well as the verifiability of the results by independent observers[14]. These demands can barely be met by

[14] Bundesverfassungsgericht judgement of March 3rd 2009, 2 BvC 3/07, 2 BvC 4/07, See in particular reasons para. 105 et seq., German text of the judge-

most e-voting machines and processes existing today. As political elections are the fundamental cornerstone of any democracy, this decision in German law should be respected and taken as an opportunity to trigger further research into eVoting with regards to its transparency. While Privacy-ABCs may remedy some shortcomings of existing eVoting processes, it is not the aim of the ABC4Trust project to propose or develop a legally compliant eVoting mechanism.

Privacy-ABCs are an effective approach to motivate European citizens to a higher participation in democratic processes. The best approach would be to start with non-critical decisions or polls, e.g. in societies or on municipality level. Furthermore, it is possible to influence legislation with petitions or initiatives[15].

Existing processes tend to require authentication of participants with their complete identifying information. As the Users/Citizens do not know the details of operation of the polling system, it is not possible for them to know whether their particular opinion or vote is linked to their identity or whether some mechanism for anonymity is in operation. Even worse than the mere collection identifying information from citizens appears that some systems can even publish the names of supporters of specific opinions, unless the voters actively opt for a pseudonym[16].

10.2.2.1 Issues to solve

Making decisions online and participating in polls requires trust in the underlying mechanisms that they preserve the participants' anonymity and the confidentiality of their votes. Moreover, it is also necessary to ensure the equality of voters by preventing people from voting more than once. Some existing systems solve the latter problem by keeping clear text lists containing voter identifying information. This, however, poses the risk that individuals are linked to their opinions. This is especially crucial where the mere act of participation can, potentially, reveal information on the opinion of the user. This can occur, for instance, in petitions where the only action allowed to participants is to support a single fact (the petition subject). In this case, every one listed as a participant is, automatically, known as a supporter of the issue at stake.

---

ment: http://www.bundesverfassungsgericht.de/entscheidungen/cs20090303_2bvc000307.html. English press release, available online: http://www.bundesverfassungsgericht.de/pressemitteilungen/bvg09-019en.html. The court ruled the use of Nedap voting machines unconstitutional due to the lack of publicity of the voting process (the publicity principle refers to the necessary transparency that allows observers to verify the correctness of the procedure).

[15] For instance, in the context of the European Citizens' Initiative, which is based on Article 11, Paragraph 4, citizens may propose opinions on issues of concern to the European Commission if they see a legal act of the Union as necessary. For such an initiative, at least one million signatories are required. Privacy-ABCs would allow collecting signatures anonymously.

[16] See, for instance, the privacy policy of the petition system of the German Bundestag, online: https://epetitionen.bundestag.de/epet/service.$$$.rubrik.datenschutz.html

Furthermore existing solutions that allow anonymous participation in voting procedures can often not verify that a voter has a particular attribute such as, for example, membership of a club or the management board of a company. This implies that the verification of the attribute can only be achieved through the disclosure of the full identity of the voter.

Another problem of anonymity systems as well as for eParticipation systems is in general the unknown size of the, so called, anonymity set. It is known that whether or not a person is identifiable, depends, to a large extend, on whether the person is indistinguishable within a group of people. This group is called the anonymity set ([PH10], p. 9). According to the concept of k-anonymity, with k being the number of entities that share the same attributes of the examined entity (see e.g. [Swe02], p. 9) , the larger the set is, the less likely it becomes that a particular user can be identified even if additional information is obtained and linked to the existing data sets. E-participation solutions, thus, must avoid storing information that could allow re-identification and links to other databases. For example time-stamps, birth dates, or ZIP-codes could be used in connection with information stored in service or in log files of other data controllers to identify a participant.

10.2.2.2 Advantages of Privacy-ABCs solutions in eParticipation

The special privacy needs of participation processes lead to a series of requirements which, we believe, can be fulfilled better with Privacy-ABCs than other mechanisms.

In this context, the participation in petitions, polls or surveys whether they are organized by private entities or governmental agencies should be possible even for emotionally debated topics such as abortion, same-sex marriage, or governmental measures infringing upon civil rights. This is an important issue since such controversial discussions in society have the potential of hindering citizens' will for participation in decision making. There is a variety of reasons for this, such as fear of potential identification by political opponents or negative consequences in life stemming from discrimination.

Thus, an anonymity preserving eParticipation method is necessary to address such concerns and eliminate reluctance towards participation. In conclusion the unlinkability feature of Privacy-ABCs can exactly provide the technical solution, needed for combining anonymity and authentication. While anonymity is necessary, it must still be ensured that Users may not participate more often than they are entitled to this can be solved by use of pseudonymity. Here, the scope exclusive pseudonym feature of Privacy-ABCs may be used. Within this scope, e.g. each separate poll or process, it is possible to see if a user accesses the service several times. Thereby the casting of multiple votes can be prevented effectively.

Being able to participate in the election from any place and not, necessarily, from a protected voting booth, where anonymity and secrecy of the votes can be imposed, implies the risk of interfering with the participant's decision either through coercion or vote buying. As a countermeasure, the participant can change her vote as many times as she likes, until the end of the voting period with only the last vote taken into account. Here, the scope exclusive pseudonym feature of Privacy-ABCs may be used, allowing overwriting previous votes.

Finally, regarding the issue of having a large anonymity set, Privacy-ABCs offer a solution as well. The possible strict limitation to the necessary data, irrespective of other potentially linkable information that may be contained in typical credentials, allows reducing the revealed information and, consequently, enlarging the anonymity set. The possibility to provide proof of attributes such as, for instance, a proof that the user belongs to a certain age range instead of revealing the exact birth date further supports the formation of large anonymity sets. For eParticipation instances where re-identification may be necessary, e.g. to modify votes, Privacy-ABCs require information that is only known to the user and can link the new action to the previous one. Nonetheless, even in these cases it does not become easier for an attacker to link the actions of the user. In an ideal case, the anonymity set includes all persons eligible to participate irrespective of their place of living, sex, birth date, or other attributes typically contained in authentication tokens. Furthermore, the previous participation can neither be verified nor denied without the specific secret known only to the user. In general the size of the anonymity set depends on the number of eligible persons a size usually known before participation. With this feature, Privacy-ABCs also enhance the transparency due to the ability to estimate the anonymity set's size.

In summary these requirements may be seen as a protective wall preventing an organisation from identifying users or establishing a connection between users and their particular opinions stated in the poll. The eParticipation use case could take advantage of the Privacy-ABCs feature of anonymous authentication of attributes and unlinkability of the provided tokens to verify that a participant is eligible for participation[17].

For a schematic view of an eParticipation system, comprising the necessary features for secure and anonymous participation, see Figure 10.3. The dotted line forms a protective wall making it impossible for the participation system to learn the identity of the Users or even link a particular vote to a specific User. Whenever such linking is necessary, only the User has the required secret information that allows a valid re-authentication towards the system. Depending on the use case, the Verifier may also act as an Issuer, e.g. municipalities issuing state eIDs used for eParticipation on a local level, companies issuing eIDs for their employees, which may, also, be used for participation in other decision bodies within the company.

[17] Alternatively one could use the feature of anonymous one-show credentials which allow identifying the same credential which has been used more often than the allowed number of times. This has been proposed for eCoins under Identity Mixer but is currently not supported by the ABC4Trust architecture.

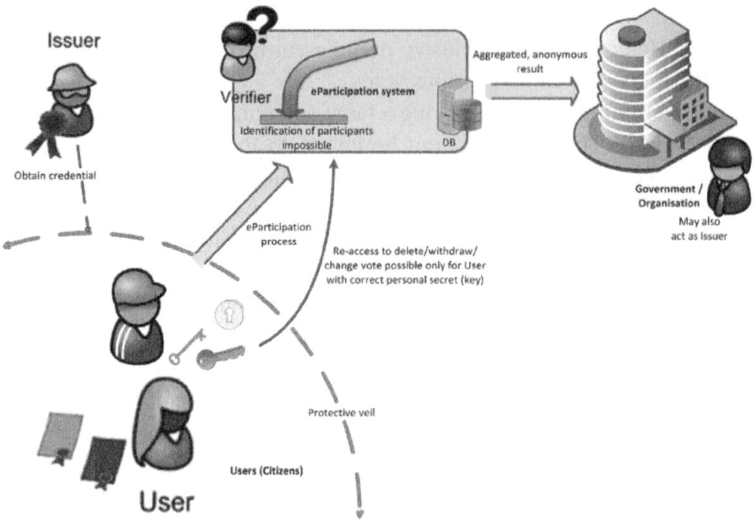

Fig. 10.3 Overview of eParticipation use case

10.2.3 Use of Cloud Service within Enterprises

Along with the rapid growth in adoption of cloud services, there have been developments towards a new emerging concept, called Identity Management as a Service (IdMaaS). As the internal IT systems were not designed for externals, the IT solutions from the cloud can solve the challenges of connecting enterprises to the outer world and consequently, bring all the benefits of the cloud-based services to them.

A comprehensive list of the drivers and the blockers to uptake cloud services has been surveyed in [CA14, HY10]. Their results show that the drivers extend well beyond cost savings; In addition to the lower cost of ownership, over 50% of their respondents have recognized better working practices for the employees, improved efficiency, easier external interactions, and access to specialized and affordable applications to be significant or very important drivers.

In this regard, IdMaaS enables easy federation of applications from different cloud service providers for all types of users, IdMaaS is easily scalable and can be expanded or contracted based on the need, and IdMaaS improves productivity of employees as it provides easy access to wide range of resources for all employees, including those working remotely. More interestingly, the findings of [CA14] show that the potential of IdMaaS is widely recognised even by those with pure on-premise IdM deployments, which gives hope to see further transitions towards IdMaaS in future.

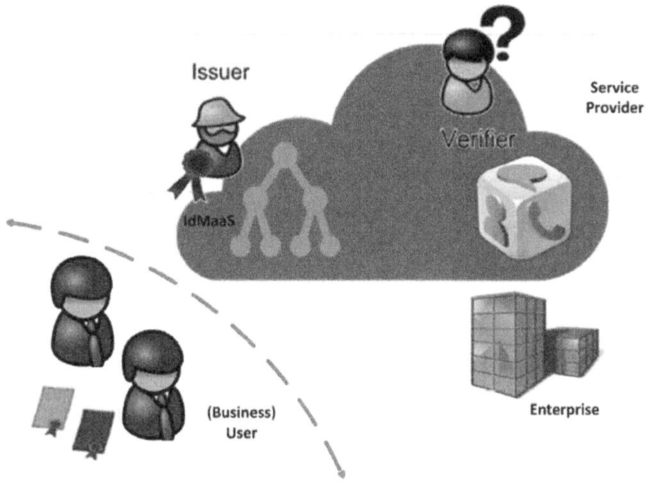

Fig. 10.4 IdM as a Service used by Enterprise

10.2.3.1 Issues to solve

Besides all the benefits and motivations mentioned about IdMaaS, Identity Management in the cloud comes with a set of challenges with regard to its security and privacy. As it is shown in Figure 10.4, having Identity Management of an enterprise outsourced to the cloud, the setting resembles a four-corner model where User, Enterprise, IdMaaS Provider and Cloud Service Provider (CSP) are the involved entities. This reflects the basic difference to the traditional three-corner model where IdMaaS and Enterprise were represented by a single entity called Identity Service Provider (IdSP). There are several privacy concerns in the new model that must be addressed. But before moving to this discussion, it is important to understand that the trust relationships have changed, compared to the case of on-premise deployment of services (e.g. applications) and IdM Systems. In a full on-demand deployment of IdMaaS, IdM capabilities and cloud services are being operated by external entities and not the enterprise itself. Therefore, additional measures are needed to deal with the emerging privacy issues. More specifically, these privacy issues are the followings:

1. IdMaaS must not learn about the services that the users are authenticating to: Due to the fact that the IdMaaS Provider is not the same entity as the enterprise, tracking the services accessed by the enterprise's users might introduce threats to the enterprise's business.
2. CSPs must not be able to link a user to her identity: The CSPs are not operating in the domain of the enterprise and therefore the minimal disclosure obligation implies that they should be provided with the necessary information only. In this regard, the CSP only needs to ensure that the user is authorized by the enterprise to access the licensed service.

3. CSPs must not be able to profile a user based on her different accesses: Similar to the case of IdMaaS Provider, building a profile of the users by an external entity is not desired by the enterprise and can be considered as the threat.
4. Enterprise should be able to audit the use of resources and services while the CSPs are blinded to this information: To avoid misuse and fraud cases, the enterprises demand for mechanisms to monitor the access to the resources. However, the minimal disclosure principle requires these mechanisms to limit monitoring capabilities only to the enterprise and avoid leaking extra information to the external parties operating the resources and services on the cloud.

10.2.3.2 Advantages of Privacy-ABCs in the Use of Cloud Service within Enterprises

In [CHHY12], the authors list the following desirable security/privacy properties for authentication in the cloud. We consider this list as the basis for our analysis of the interactions between Users, IdMaaS Provider, Cloud Service Providers (CSPs) and the Enterprise.

- Unlinkability: In cloud computing, a user may access multiple services associated with the same or different CSPs. Unlinkability ensures that no CSPs, even if they collude, can link different transactions, whether they are of the same service or different services, of the same user. In addition to this definition by [CHHY12] , another functionality is needed, which concerns the IdMaaS learning about the verification services that a user accesses. This functionality is also known as untraceability in the literature and it is required in our model because the IdMaaS Provider is considered as an external entity for the Enterprise. The Enterprise might not be content if IdMaaS Provider profiles its employees or users.
  One of the key properties of Privacy-ABCs is that the presentation sessions are not linkable to the issuance sessions. Therefore none of the Verifiers can profile a user or map different transactions of the same user even if they collude. In addition to that, The IdMaaS is not involved in the presentation process at all; therefore it will not learn about the presentation sessions and the services a user gets access to.
- Delegatable Authentication: In case that the service offered by a CSP, is a combination of services by some other CSPs, the authentication should be delegatable such that the CSP behind the scene can authenticate a user without a direct communication with either the user or the IdMaaS Provider, and without fully trusting the CSP in front.
  In our model, the CSP in front can easily act as an intermediate proxy between the user and the CSP behind the scene and help them to exchange the Presentation protocol messages. The secondary CSP can perform the authentication using only the public information available about the IdMaaS.
- Anonymity: The users should be able to anonymously authenticate themselves, as authorized users to the CSP, without letting the CSP know about their real identity or exact attributes.

Another key feature of the Privacy-ABCs is minimal disclosure. If the presentation token does not include identifiable information, the anonymity of the user is preserved.

- Accountability: The users may abuse their anonymity. If needed, a trusted party can inspect or revoke the anonymity so the users can be held accountable for their malicious actions.
  The Inspection feature of Privacy-ABCs enables the Enterprises to securely log and audit the access to the resources. Using this feature, the CSPs can force the users to include encrypted identifiable information in the authentication token. Since nobody else other than the actual user can create such a token, the user will be responsible in cases of misuse.
- User Centric Access Control: Users should be able to control what information they want to reveal about themselves over the cloud or to a CSP, and to control who can access that information, and how this information will be used in order to minimize the risk of identity theft and fraud. For example if an attacker running his own service provider is unable to obtain enough information, due to selective revealing in Privacy-ABCs, the identity theft cannot take place.
  Users of Privacy-ABCs are in control of their credentials. Before any presentation takes place, users get notified about the information that the access policy requires them to disclose. They can fully control what kind of information they give out. Furthermore, since the user is actively involved in the presentation phase, nobody else (not even the IdMaaS Provider or the Enterprise) can impersonate the user.
- Single Registration: The users need to register themselves only once for obtaining the credentials without the further need of contacting the IdMaaS every time authentication is needed.
  Once the users obtained their credentials, they can perform authentications until their credentials are revoked. However, for some concrete realization of Privacy-ABCs like U-Prove, the credential consists of a number of unlinkable U-Prove tokens. When the user runs out of tokens, she has to how reload the credential with more tokens.

10.2.4 Scenario: Bank as Identity Service Provider

Financial institutions are normally trusted and reliable sources of information about their customers, since it is crucial that their information is accurate and up-to-date. Therefore, the idea of having financial institutions (e.g. banks) as Identity Service Providers is being actively discussed over the last decade[18]. The implementation of such a scenario gives the opportunity to service providers to rely on the information provided by the financial institutions and delegate the authentication process to them.

[18] e.g. in Austria and Sweden

10.2.4.1 Issues to Solve

A very important factor for financial institutions in evaluating their customers' credibility and ability to meet their financial obligations is their job status. Now, imagine Bob loses his job and goes to the job search portal to look for appropriate job positions. The portal requires Bob, the User, to login via his bank using a typical federated identity infrastructure allowing the portal to acquire proof about Bob's identity. Consequently, the bank learns about the contact with the job portal. Due to this transaction, the bank may suspect that something has happened with Bob's career and that he is now looking for a new job. This extra information can negatively impact Bob's credibility assessment for his next loan application at the bank.

10.2.4.2 Advantages of a Privacy-ABC solution

Deploying Privacy-ABCs, as shown in Figure 10.5, can easily resolve this issue since the two phases of Issuance and Presentation of the credentials are unlinkable. As a result, the Identity Service Provider would not learn where the user shows his authentication tokens and which services he visits. At the same time, the Relying Party makes sure that it receives authentic claims issued by the corresponding Issuer. In our scenario, Bob, a user, can obtain Privacy-ABCs from his bank and later use them to authenticate towards the job search portal. In this case, Bob's bank will not be involved in the later phase and, therefore, will not learn about the fact that Bob is looking for a new job.

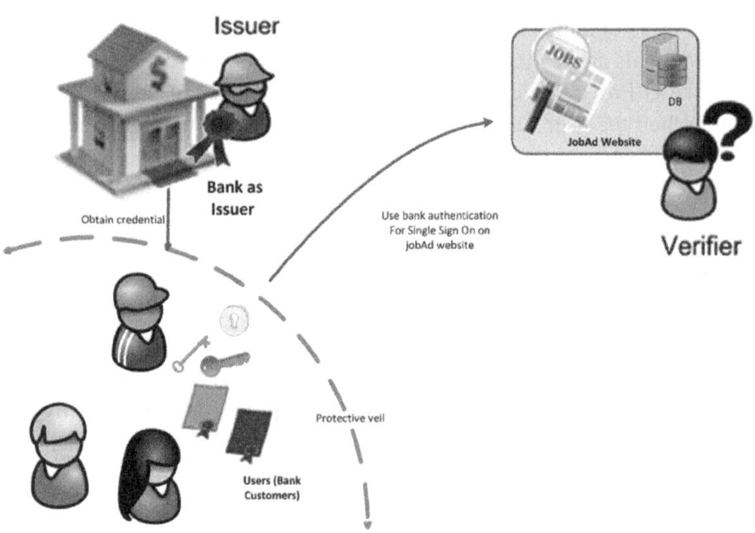

Fig. 10.5 Bank as Identity Service Provider using Privacy-ABCs

The Bank as Identity Service Provider is a straightforward authentication example without any special sub cases. Users obtain identity credentials from their banks and use them to authenticate towards the Verifiers. The credentials can become invalid (revoked), but inspection is not needed.

10.2.5 Scenario: Do not Track Relying Parties

Today, the wish to customize web sites according to the needs of the visiting users often requires an optimization of the site's accessibility and usability. This includes the modus operandi of login to the services offered to the customer. To enable a smooth and simplified user experience, it is therefore desirable for any service provider to offer the possibility of using a single login interface to obtain access to various services. Therefore, in the current ecosystem of digital services and goods, an easily implemented single-sign-on function through market-leading and popular service providers (like Facebook, Google) is often made available. However, such a monopoly log-in-functionality may pose issues concerning competition or privacy-compliance, which require attention.

Figure 10.6 shows an example of such a login shared across sides (service providers). In these cases, the small companies (service providers) rely on the authentication of the big company's main web service (e.g. a social network) while being integrated into the look and feel of the big companies page, see Figure 10.6. For users, this convenient single-sign-on has advantages, but a small company's business may be threatened.

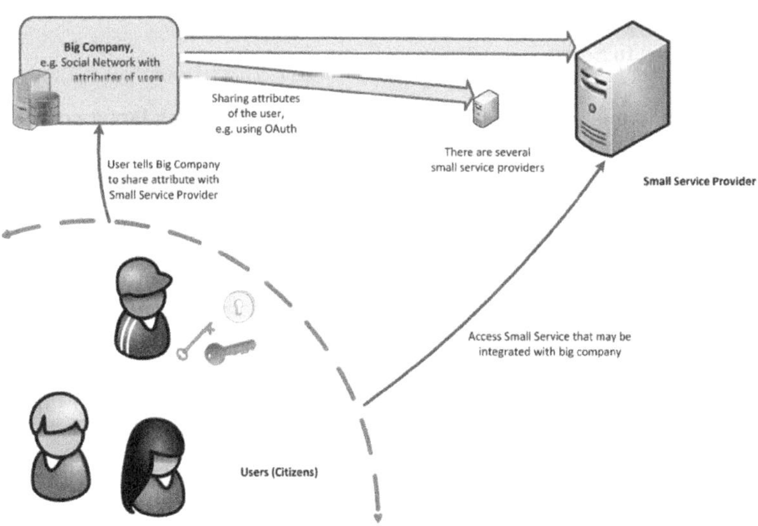

Fig. 10.6 Scenario without privacy protection

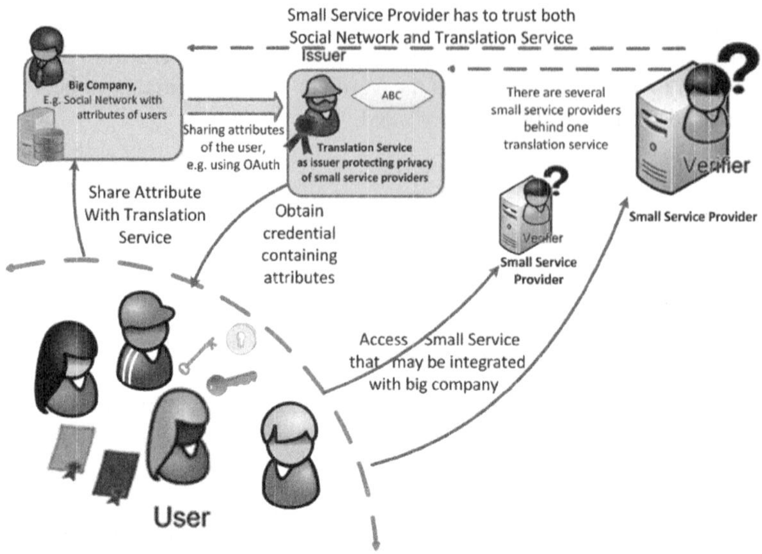

Fig. 10.7 Scenario with protection of small companies' privacy

By utilizing Privacy-ABC the architecture changes for the small service provider and an additional translation service is introduced, see Figure 10.7. For the big company no change of the interface is necessary. This architecture supports the goal of a user-friendly login-function while still preserving the privacy (and proprietary information) of the small service providers in a satisfactory way.

10.2.5.1 Issues to Solve

Let's assume, in this scenario, that a small company relies on a larger company for providing a single-sign-on functionality. The small company may or may not pay a fee for this authentication service. If the service by the small company is innovative, most probably it will have many users. The service may be easy to provide, but the large company may not have noticed its potential before. Thus, the small company may have a good business, at almost no additional cost. With current technologies, the large company will be able to notice how well the small company's business is doing, by seeing the number of authentications it performs for the small company. It may even be possible to infer the interest level of the users by the number of repeated authentications or attributes shown. Moreover, the involvement of the larger company poses a threat to the users of the smaller company's services, because their attributes are revealed, resulting in a disclosure of personal information. Such a revelation may encompass not only the user's identifying information, but may also uncover details about the services requested by the user. All of these aforementioned issues result in a fear of the small company, which is relying on the larger company, that the large company may use the obtained information in some way to eventually become a competitor. Finally, the wider problem of a reduced number of innovations, due to an uncertain business environment, exists. Since many innovations are built on top of each other, this scenario is important.

10.2.5.2 Advantages of a Privacy-ABC solution

The Privacy-ABC technology with its unlinkability feature can solve the issues described above. However, this has a certain precondition: in a basic setup phase, the large company would need to adopt Privacy-ABC technologies. But such a basic setup may not be established, for at least two reasons: First, additional implementation costs will incur on the large company, without any added value for itself, and second, the large company will no longer be able to process and analyze the obtained information routed through its own systems for its own purposes. Therefore, it has to be assumed that these disadvantages for the large company pose a major obstacle to the deployment of Privacy-ABC technologies, despite its obvious benefits for the privacy of the users as well as for the smaller company.

Hence, this scenario needs to be instantiated with a slightly more complicated setup, in a more realistic business background. Instead of the large company implementing the service, a third party will implement a kind of "translation service". This party will be an entity sitting as an intermediary between the smaller and the larger company. As such, this entity can implement a Privacy-ABC system and translate the user information into privacy-preserving credentials which are, then, presented to the larger company.

This new business model of the translation service aims at providing privacy for the users as well as business-related confidentiality for the smaller service provider. The translation service will most likely need a compensation in return for the service and, therefore, needs a functioning economic model. The trust model, with respect to the correctness of identity proofs, dictates that the translation service is trusted by the small company as well as the large company (e.g. both are trusted not to generate fake credentials). Still, additional safeguards could eventually be needed to enable the corroboration of this trust, because this third party will become an additional entity learning the user's personal information. For the large company, the translation service will appear like a successful small company. But further evaluation of information, especially aimed at the access to user's personal data as well as an assessment which of the small companies behind the translation service is the most successful, will be effectively hindered.

However, this model depends on the large company accepting the translation service as a Relying Party. Since this is not, initially, a desirable action for the large company, the question remains how such an interaction model can be established. Eventually, further legislative advances, especially in the fields of data protection and competition law may be required to hinder the exploitation of market power and monopoly position by large companies. Despite these difficulties, the establishment of such an intermediate attribute translation service may be an opportunity to introduce Privacy-ABCs into the market and, in the process, enhance the privacy of users. At the same time, the interests of small and medium enterprises (SMEs) offering digital services and goods will be protected.

Figure 10.7 shows the full communication structure for both the large company's traditional IDM and the small company, being protected by the translation service. The social networking service, normally providing the information directly to the small service provider, now interacts with the translation service. The small service provider interacts, and trusts, the translation service which protects its privacy towards the social networking service.

Finally it is worthwhile to observe that, although being in the centre, the translation service cannot disrupt the privacy of the users, as it acts as the Issuer for Privacy-ABCs and such Identity Service Providers cannot profile their users.

From the perspective of implementation the do-not-track-the-relying-party scenario may appear more complicated, as there are two parties that have knowledge about the users. Nonetheless, in its core it is a basic attribute issuing use case. The third party provider is a special form of Issuer that does not have its own attribute database, but only translates the information that it receives from others. Figure 10.7 shows this relation by incorporating the social networking site as an extra domain on the left side of the Issuer. It is worth noting that a current enhancement for the German eID [BKPR14, Bjo10] utilizes this approach to avoid organizational integration with the eID servers.

Acknowledgement

Acknowledgements We would like to thank Norbert Götze, Eva Schlehahn, Daniel Deibler and Ronny Bjones for comments, input and helpful discussions in relation to this chapter.

References

[Bjo10] Ronny Bjones. eParticipation Scenario Reference Guide. Technical Report Tech. Rep., Oct 2010, Microsoft, 2010.

[BKPR14] Ronny Bjones, Ioannis Krontiris, Pascal Paillier, and Kai Rannenberg. Integrating anonymous credentials with eids for privacy-respecting online authentication. In *Privacy Technologies and Policy*, pages 111–124. Springer, 2014.

[CA14] CA. The adoption of cloud-based services: Increasing confidence through effective security. `http://www.datacenterresearch.com/whitepaper/the-adoption-of-cloud-based-services-increasing-confidence-4822.html`, 2014. Last accessed on 2014-10-20.

[CHHY12] Sherman SM Chow, Yi-Jun He, Lucas CK Hui, and Siu Ming Yiu. Spice–simple privacy-preserving identity-management for cloud environment. In *Applied Cryptography and Network Security*, pages 526–543. Springer, 2012.

[HY10] Rolf Harms and Michael Yamartino. The economics of the cloud. *Microsoft whitepaper, Microsoft Corporation*, 2010. Last accessed on 12.01.13.

[Inf] Information Cards Foundation. Information cards.: Information cards foundation. http://informationcard.net/.

[NH08] Ingo Naumann and Giles Hogben. Privacy features of european eid card specifications. *Network Security*, 2008(8):9–13, 2008.

[Org05] Organization for the Advancement of Structured Information Standards (OASIS). extensible access control markup language (xacml) version 2.0, 2005.

[PH10] Andreas Pfitzmann and Marit Hansen. A terminology for talking about privacy by data minimization: Anonymity, unlinkability, undetectability, unobservability, pseudonymity, and identity management. http://http://dud.inf.tu-dresden.de/literatur/Anon_Terminology_v0.34.pdf, 2010. Last accessed on 2014-11-08.

[Swe02] Latanya Sweeney. k-anonymity: A model for protecting privacy. *International Journal of Uncertainty, Fuzziness and Knowledge-Based Systems*, 10(05):557–570, 2002.

[ZS13] Harald Zwingelberg and Jan Schallaböck. The Proposal for a Regulation on Electronic Identification and Trust Services under a Privacy and ABC4Trust Perspective. Deliverable H2.4, The ABC4Trust EU Project, 2013. Available at https://abc4trust.eu/download/ABC4Trust-H2.4_Privacy_Perspective_on_the_eIDAS_regulation.pdf, Last accessed on 2014-11-08.

[Zwi11] Harald Zwingelberg. Necessary Processing of Personal Data: The Need-to-Know Principle and Processing Data from the New German Identity Card. In *Privacy and Identity Management for Life*, pages 151–163. Springer, 2011.

Chapter 11
Establishment and Prospects of Privacy-ABCs

Marit Hansen, Hannah Obersteller, Kai Rannenberg, and Fatbardh Veseli

Abstract In this chapter, a glance into the future is taken. In 2014, the European Regulation on Electronic Identification and Trust Services came into force. This will have influence on future usage of Privacy-ABCs (Section 11.1). Support for the adoption and distribution of Privacy-ABCs that help users' privacy could be provided by various stakeholders as sketched in Section 11.2. One main driver can be standardization. Section 11.3 presents an overview of the most relevant standardisation projects for ABC4Trust, discusses concrete contributions to these standards, and gives some insights on how to achieve a higher degree of trustworthiness in the Privacy-ABC technologies through certification.

The ABC4Trust project has worked on the federation and interchangeability of technologies that support trustworthy yet privacy-preserving Attribute-based Credentials (Privacy-ABCs). In the previous chapters, advantages and achievements through the employment of Privacy-ABCs were discussed. Those speak for them-selves, but further steps must be taken.

11.1 eIDAS Regulation and ABC4Trust

In 2014 the Regulation on electronic identification and trusted services for electronic transactions in the internal market the so-called eIDAS Regulation came into force in the European Union [eIDb]. This regulation aims at ensuring mutual recognition

Marit Hansen and Hannah Obersteller
Unabhängiges Landeszentrum für Datenschutz Schleswig-Holstein, Germany, e-mail: {ULD6, ULD66}@datenschutzzentrum.de

Kai Rannenberg and Fatbardh Veseli
Chair for Mobile Business & Multilateral Security, Goethe University Frankfurt, Germany e-mail: {kai.rannenberg,fatbardh.veseli}@m-chair.de

K. Rannenberg et al. (eds.), *Attribute-based Credentials for Trust*,
DOI 10.1007/978-3-319-14439-9_11

and acceptance of electronic identification across borders as well as giving legal effect and mutual recognition to trust services. It is designed as a follow-up law to the e-Signature Directive 1999/93/EC which will be replaced by the regulation, but it widely extends the scope. The eIDAS Regulation "(a) lays down the condition under which Member States recognise electronic identification means of natural and legal persons [...]; (b) lays down rules for trust services, in particular for electronic transactions; and (c) establishes a legal framework for electronic signatures, electronic seals, electronic time stamps, electronic docu-ments, electronic registered delivery services and certificate services for website authentication." (Art. 1, [eIDb]). In a first step the regulation addresses cross-border use of identification means for the public services, but it also aims at encouraging the private sector.

The eIDAS Regulation sets the frame for mutual recognition of electronic identification: Member States can choose to notify to the Commission one or more of the electronic identification schemes used at national level to access at least public services. All Member States are required to recognise means of electronic identification falling under those notified schemes provided that the identity assurance level that is the degree of confidence in electronic identification means in establishing the identity of a person is sufficient for the online service in question (e. g. "substantial" or "high"). This will facilitate natural and legal persons to use the same identification schemes for cross-border access of (at least public) services as at national level.

Obviously attribute-based credentials could play an important role in the European framework on electronic identification and trust services, e. g. as a paragon for national eIDs or for considering their data-minimising functionality. Therefore the ABC4Trust project team diligently analysed the European Commission's proposal for an eIDAS Regulation from June 2012 [eIDa], considered options for Privacy-ABCs on that basis and communicated the main suggestions for improving the eIDAS Regulation to the European Parliament [ZS13]. In the following we will summarise the proposals from the ABC4Trust project and elaborate how far the final legal text takes these into account. Further, we will show how Privacy-ABCs could fit into a landscape shaped by the eIDAS Regulation.

11.1.1 Suggestion "Emphasise the Concept of Authentication instead of Identification"

The underlying model of the eIDAS Regulation both of the proposal and the final version is the use of "person identification data" in the electronic identification schemes that are to be notified by the individual Member States. In the pro-posed version from 2012 authentication was seen as "the possibility to check the validity of the electronic identification data" [eIDa]. The obvious interpretation would be reading out the entire set or a uniquely identifying subset of the attributes provided by an eID system, e.g. electronic ID cards issued by the Member States. However, authentication could and as the ABC4Trust context proves this right should be understood in a wider sense to clarify that properties such as unlinkability of transactions or context-specificity of authentication may be favourable in many situations.

The ABC4Trust project suggested to clearly distinguish between identification and authentication and proposed the following amendments for the definition part:

" **'transaction'** means the particular session or contact between the person and a relying party;

'unlinkable electronic authentication' means the process of using data in electronic form describing attributes of a natural or legal person where the provided attributes and any additionally available information do not allow to link the transaction to a person or any other transaction;

'context specific electronic authentication' means the process of using data in electronic form describing attributes of a natural or legal person where the provided attributes allow verification that the same person has electronically authenticated in the same context in a previous transaction;

'electronic identification' means the process of an electronic authentication using identification data in electronic form unambiguously representing a natural or legal person

(a) where the identification data can only be used by the relying party for identifying the person if specified conditions are met (conditional electronic identification) or

(b) where the identification data can be used by the relying party for identifying the person (**unconditional electronic identification**);

'identification data' means any set of attributes the knowledge of which al-lows to get hold of a single person, e.g. the set of name and an address allowing for service of documents or any information leading to these information, e.g. a unique person number. " [ZS13].

Although these farsighted and future-oriented amendments were not directly taken up, the final eIDAS Regulation adds in Recital 11: "authentication for an online service should concern processing of only those identification data that are adequate, relevant and not excessive to grant access to that service online" [eIDb]. Also, it introduces a definition for "identification data" which was not existent before:

" 'person identification data' means a set of data enabling the identity of a natural or legal person, or a natural person representing a legal person to be established " (Art. 3(3) [eIDb]).

Surely this definition raises further questions since "enabling the identity" is not clarified throughout the legal text. This may be related to the reference to identity management system in Recital 12: "This Regulation does not aim to intervene with regard to electronic identity management systems and related infrastructures established in Member States." [eIDb]. Possibly these changes address eID systems such as the German eID card that provides attribute selection, attribute aggregation for birthdate and residence as well as use under pseudonym. Hence, this offers an opportunity for Privacy-ABCs, too.

11.1.2 Suggestion "Remove Barriers for Privacy-preserving eID Solutions"

Online authentication between a user and a relying party can work without integrating entities in the middle of the communication which is preferable from the privacy perspective since no "man-in-the-middle" can collect information on us-age patterns. However, this solution would likely require some software to be in-stalled on the devices at the user and the relying party, e. g. cryptographic libraries for the validation process [ZS13]. But the draft of the eIDAS Regulation explicitly forbid Member States to "impose any specific technical requirements on relying parties established outside of their territory intending to carry out such authentication" (Art. 6(d)). It was argued that this prohibition was created in the spirit of technology neutrality, but, as the ABC4Trust project pointed out, it is not technology-neutral at all if privacy-preserving approaches are being excluded.

This message not only from the ABC4Trust project, but also from Member States whose eID systems are working without integrating "man-in-the-middle" parties was well received. The wording of the final version of the eIDAS Regulation is in Art. 7(f) [eIDb]:

"Member States shall not impose any specific disproportionate technical requirements on relying parties intending to carry out such authentication, where such requirements prevent or significantly impede the interoperability of the noti-fied electronic identification schemes".

Now, it may be debated what "disproportionate technical requirements" should mean here, at least regarding privacy functionality, the data protection authorities should have a say. However, the naïve and not at all privacy-friendly solution of introducing a limited number of centralised gateways that are technically able to snoop on all authenticated cross-border transactions is not excluded in the eIDAS Regulation; some may interpret the liability obligations imposed in Art. 11 of the regulation even as a valid legal ground for storing metadata of the authentication for a long time. This would create the risks of national inventories of relevant communication metadata that are neither necessary nor proportionate at the sight of available privacy-preserving solutions provided that these are implemented on the Member State level.

11.1.3 Suggestion "Clarify Applicability of Data Protection Requirements also for eID Services"

The proposal for an eIDAS Regulation stated in its Article 11 "Data processing and protection" that trust service providers shall "process personal data according to Directive 95/46/EC" (the European Data Protection Directive), that the processing shall be "strictly limited to the minimum data needed to issue and maintain a certificate or to provide a trust service", and that they shall "guarantee the confidentiality and integrity of data related to a person [...]" [eIDa]. An obligation for data protection is appreciated, but the focus on trust service providers would have been understood as excluding other areas covered by the eIDAS Regulation. Therefore the ABC4Trust report asks for clarification that data protection requirements apply for those other areas where personal data are being processed, specifically eID services [ZS13].

The final eIDAS Regulation does not limit data protection requirements to trust service providers. Instead, in its Article 5 it lays down as a general rule that processing of personal data "shall be carried out in accordance with Directive 95/46/EC" [eIDb]. Further, according to Article 12(3) the establishment of the interoperability framework shall not only ensure compliance with Directive 95/46/EC, but facilitate "the implementation of the principle of privacy by design" [eIDb]. This principle will most likely be incorporated in the upcoming General Data Protection Regulation, but has not been part of the European Data Protection Directive from 1995. Taking the principle of privacy by design seriously would prevent centralised "man-in-the-middle" entities as discussed in the previous section.

Another aspect is the use of pseudonyms: Whereas the draft only discussed pseudonyms in electronic signature certificates, the final eIDAS Regulation explicitly states: "Without prejudice to the legal effect given to pseudonyms under national law, the use of pseudonyms in electronic transactions shall not be prohibited." (Art. 5(2) [eIDb]). However, since pseudonyms in the eIDAS con-text are mainly regarded as substitutes for the name of a signatory which has to be clearly indicated, it is not clear whether the kind of pseudonyms that Privacy-ABCs realise fall into the scope or not.

11.1.4 Privacy-ABCs in the eIDAS Landscape

The eIDAS Regulation has come into force in 2014. Still, it will take some more time until the European Commission has adopted the necessary delegated or implementing acts that will define further operational aspects. Recital 72 states "the Commission should take due account of the standards and technical specifications drawn up by European and international standardization organisations and bodies" [eIDb]. The visibility of Privacy-ABCs in standards as well as in policy discussions will be crucial for their uptake in the delegated or implementing acts and in the general interpretation of the legal text.

However, the construction of the interoperability eIDAS framework builds on top of the identification schemes to be notified by the Member States. This means that Privacy-ABCs need to be considered at the Member State level before they can influence the interoperability framework outlined by the eIDAS Regulation. Since Member States can notify more than one identification scheme, Privacy-ABCs could constitute one of those. Even Germany that has deployed an eID card with similar, though less flexible, properties could support the full flavour of Privacy-ABCs in another identification scheme; and even the more those Member States that have not implemented privacy features in their schemes, yet. An analysis of the practicability of Privacy-ABCs on an eID card is shown in [BKPR14].

The eIDAS Regulation aims at openness for innovation (see Recital 26 [eIDb]) , and it explicitly demands the cooperation of Member States concerning "examination of relevant developments in the electronic identification sector" (Art. 12(6)(d) [eIDb]). Here Privacy-ABCs should definitely play a role to advance the availability and deployment of privacy-preserving electronic identification and authentication systems. The envisioned timeline for the factual implementation of the eIDAS Regulation is to finalise the necessary implementing acts by end of 2015 and kicking of mandatory mutual recognition of notified identification schemes by end of 2018.

11.2 How Stakeholders Can Support Privacy-ABCs

In the Swedish pilot project (cf. Chapter 6) ABC4Trust showed that it is possible to set up a communication network that offers the possibility to discuss with others while staying completely anonymous. The Greek pilot project (cf. Chapter 7) of ABC4Trust implemented a university course evaluation system which proved that it is possible to run an anonymous poll online. But many more applications for Privacy-ABCs are thinkable.

11.2.1 "State of the Art" and "Best Practice"

Although the application of Privacy-ABCs is certainly not explored to its full potential, it is appropriate to ask, in how far Privacy-ABCs are already, or at least can become, "state of the art" and therefore should be considered when implementing privacy-protecting techniques.

"State of the art" is a term used in the European legislation concerning data protection. Art. 17 (1) of the Directive 95/46/EC (Security of Processing) reads as follows:

"Member States shall provide that the controller must implement appropriate technical and organisational measures to protect personal data against accidental or unlawful destruction or accidental loss, alteration, unauthorized disclosure or access, in particular where the processing involves the transmission of data over a network, and against all other unlawful forms of processing. Having regard to the state of the art and the cost of their implementation, such measures shall ensure a level of security appropriate to the risks represented by the processing and the nature of the data to be protected." [Eur95]

As already mentioned in Section 5.1.2 , the Data Protection Directive is going to be replaced by a General Data Protection Regulation [GDP]. Since the final text was not available when writing this book, we refer to the version the European Parliament voted on the 12th March 2014. This version does not only keep the term "state of the art", but also defines more precisely what a data controller shall assure. The Paragraphs 1 and 2 of its Art. 23 (Data protection by design and by default) read as follows:

1. *"Having regard to the state of the art and the cost of implementation, the controller shall, both at the time of the determination of the means for processing and at the time of the processing itself, implement appropriate technical and organisational measures and procedures in such a way that the processing will meet the requirements of this Regulation and ensure the protection of the rights of the data subject.*
2. *The controller shall implement mechanisms for ensuring that, by default, only those personal data are processed which are necessary for each specific purpose of the processing and are especially not collected or retained beyond the minimum necessary for those purposes, both in terms of the amount of the data and the time of their storage. In particular, those mechanisms shall ensure that by default personal data are not made accessible to an indefinite number of individuals."* [GDP]

There is no universal definition of the term "state of the art" in connection with data protection legislation. Commonly, "state of the art" can be understood as a certain degree of development of a technique that is reached at a certain date.

A legal definition can be found in the patent law. Art. 54 (1) of the European Patent Convention (EPC [EPC]) defines the term "novelty" as something that "does not form part of state of the art". Art. 54 (2) EPC defines "state of the art" as follows:

"The state of the art shall be held to comprise everything made available to the public by means of a written or oral description, by use, or in any other way, be-fore the date of filing of the European patent application."

Given that, according to the wording of the law it is not necessary to yield the scientific proof that an invention does actually work to apply a patent, it is unlikely that the definition is transferable to the data protection law. While the EPC's ratio legis is to protect an idea (even though it is not "usable" yet), for the purposes of the data protection law it does not make sense to consider techniques that are not (yet) implementable.

Based on the common understanding, Privacy-ABCs can be identified as the current "state of the art", since they are implementable and they work. Further-more, they meet the requirements of Art. 23 (2) Draft-GDPR: data-minimisation by design (*"implement mechanisms (...) only those personal data are processed which are necessary for each specific purpose of the processing"*). Privacy-ABCs enable the user to make a decision on how much information she is willing to reveal. If her identity, e. g. understood as name, address and exact date of birth, is not required for the online service she desires to use, she can choose to act anonymously. They thereby help to protect the user's "net identity" in other words: the data subject's rights and therefore comply with the requirements set up by the European law. But, as mentioned before, the technique is not mature yet. So even if one would define Privacy-ABCs as "state of the art", they do not meet all requirements yet: The legislative demand of having regard to the "state of the art"-technologies is explicitly restricted by the costs of implementation, respectively described more precisely as *"appropriate technical and organisational measures and procedures"*. Taking this into account, it seems likely that the goal the legislator aims for is what is called "best practice". Best practice means that a certain procedure is generally recognised as the most appropriate. It is not a "standard" (concerning standardization cf. Section 11.3 below) since not officially set, but a proven and cost-efficient method that has already been used successfully. At this point Privacy-ABCs are only tested in comparatively small experimental setups. Given that, it is obvious that they cannot be claimed as "best practice" yet. But as the results are promising, it seems a question of time and appropriate support by different stakeholders that Privacy-ABCs make it to marketability and finally to the state of "best practice".

Concerning the issue of which techniques would fulfil the legal requirements there is an approach by ENISA, which suggested establishing an official guidance to "Best Available Techniques" (BATs). BATs are defined as a "particular combination of technologies, protocols, standards, practices, etc., that can provide a reasonable level of privacy protection in a particular area" ([ENI], pp. 8, 35).

The idea is taken from the European legislation on integrated pollution prevention. Directive 96/61/EC [CD-] deals with this term BATs and defines it precisely. An adequate definition is missing in the General Data Protection Regulation (like before in the Directive) and furthermore, the definition is not directly transferable since it is likely that the different term ("state of the art") was chosen knowingly. Additionally, the areas regulated by the abovementioned legislation are very different. But since the problem is similar, the idea is still worth to be discussed. So far, it has not been picked up yet.

11.2.2 Support of Stakeholders

To establish Privacy-ABC technology as "best practice" the support of all thinkable stakeholders is needed. The user cannot use what is not provided. The provider cannot offer what is not developed. The developer (or the industry) will not develop when there is no market. A market arises from demand, which can be promoted best if supported by the legislator and/or public authorities.

Since currently a wide range of online service providers live on collecting, processing and selling of their users personal data (for the purpose of personalised advertisement), it is obvious that there are strong commercial interests to hinder the process of enforcing data subject's rights, respectively the consequent compliance and enforcement of the Privacy Protection Goals, e. g. data minimisation. Still, it is considerable whether user-friendly concepts based on truly informed, educated and responsible consumers can be a (perspectively even better) business model. With respect to the purpose of the law, to create a data protection legislation that focuses on the protection of the user as the data subject and her fundamental rights, the only correct answer must be "yes". The following section focuses on the support by specific stakeholders. Concerning possible achievements through standardization activities, see Section 11.3 below.

- *Users:* Be aware of the threats. That you do not see it does not mean that it is not there. The topic "data protection" has reached a new level of public awareness since the espionage activities of several international secret services were revealed. This general impression could be verified by evaluating the ABC4Trust pilot projects (cf. Chapter 8). Although the pilot's reference groups, consisting of pupils and students, represent a comparatively young audience, the evaluations show that this group is aware of risks relating to the revelation of personal data in the internet. This contradicts the often heard thesis that users do not accept privacy-preserving technologies because they do not see the need of self-protection or do not care at all. It indicates that users will choose privacy-preserving technologies if they know the facts and have an actual choice.
- *Service Providers:* Help the users to protect themselves as they desire to do. It is required by the law to indicate the purpose of every single data processing anyway. This means that clearly and precisely formulated privacy policies, containing exact information about which personal data is going to be disclosed, are indispensable (cf. Section 5.2.1). But Privacy-ABCs are not necessarily a one-way-road. They also allow you to ask the user for more information (than needed for a specific service) in a law-abiding way, since the user can choose for every single attribute if she wants to reveal it or not. Tap into new markets. The user might be interested in e. g. personalised advertisement if she can choose the range.
- *Developers/Industry:* The Source Code for the ABC4Trust engine is available on the ABC4Trust website (`https://abc4trust.eu/`). Chapter 10 refers to ideas on further application scenarios.
- *Legislator/Politics/Public Authorities:* Of course, the existing and upcoming legal framework needs to be enforced as effectively as possible. Legal texts concerning technical requirements are not self-explaining. To encourage developers (and the industry as a whole) to support research activities in the field of privacy and data protection and to develop feasible applications it would be helpful to collect and publish regularly examples for and references to best practices and best available techniques (cf. Section 11.2.1, [ENI]). The European Commission would be empowered to do so according to Art. 23 (3) Draft-GDPR. It is also desirable to foster a long-term project dealing with e. g. the setup and maintenance of a website that provides open source codes of privacy-protecting techniques and at the same time help and guidance to developers who are interested in implementing those techniques. Best ideas and approaches concerning new applications do not necessarily come from the industry, but maybe from some private developer who just needs some support. This might also lead to a broader dissemination of Privacy-ABCs.

  The new Regulation makes specific provisions in case of law violation, e. g. it provides the possibility of imposing a fine. According to experience the threat of sanction has no effect if there is no pressure to prosecute. In this regard it is also appropriate to develop European standard forms for complaints to simplify the reporting of violations. But true to the motto "Better safe than sorry" at the same time incentives should be provided. Audits and trustworthy certification schemes for obtaining privacy seals can encourage data controllers to comply with the data protection law. The objective should be to establish commonly accepted certifications as a commercial advantage meanwhile the first certification criteria catalogue for assessing data protection principles and requirements acknowledges the potential of Privacy-ABCs [ULD]. For both purposes the Member States have to provide their data protection authorities with the necessary resources, both financial and human.

11.3 Standardization and Certification

Standardization is an important outreach and dissemination activity and it is therefore important for innovative solutions such as the ones ABC4Trust deals with are properly addressed. Also, standardization can influence the interoperability of technologies, which can be important for the diffusion of Privacy-ABC technologies. In this regard, the aim is to target international standardization organizations so that the main concepts and features of Privacy-ABCs are taken into account, especially those dealing with privacy frameworks and architectures.

11.3.1 Framework Standardizations

In the search for the most relevant international standardization projects on privacy architectures and frameworks, two projects within ISO/IEC JTC 1/SC 27/WG 5 on Identity Management and Privacy Technologies were identified. Therefore ABC4Trust has established a liaison with this group and has actively participated in those projects. The two projects are the ISO/IEC 24760 multipart standard on an identity management framework, and ISO/IEC 29101 on a privacy architecture framework. The following section presents an overview of the focus of these projects and the main challenges, which ABC4Trust has identified and addressed.

11.3.1.1 Identity management frameworks standardization — ISO/IEC 24760

ISO/IEC 24760 Information technology Security techniques A framework for identity management is a multi-part standard that addresses the issue of efficient and effective implementation of systems that make identity-based decisions. This standard consists of three parts, namely Part 1: Terminology and concepts, Part 2: Reference architecture and requirements, and Part 3: Practice. Most of ABC4Trust's contribution went to Part 2 and Part 3, as Part 1 is already published as an International Standard.

Part 2 of ISO/IEC 24760 [ISO14a] describes the lifecycle model of identity information, providing guidelines for the implementation of systems for the management of identity information, and specifying requirements for the implementation and operation of a framework for identity management. The topic is very close to ABC4Trust, so we contributed to the definitions of the terms and processes, making sure privacy features of Privacy-ABCs where considered. A particular contribution for ISO/IEC 24760-2 from ABC4Trust was the inclusion of the concept of *"presentation tokens"* of Privacy-ABCs, which was usually understood to be the same as the credential of the User. Indeed, in many identity systems this is the case, but for Privacy-ABCs, one of the key privacy features is the possibility to hide subset of attribute values from the credential and instead present a different token, which includes a conversion step, thus enabling the User to only reveal the (minimal) set of required attributes.

Another important factor is the changing of the existing concept of an identity management scheme where the Issuer is constantly involved during the authentication of the User to the Verifier. While this approach is understandable for some prominent federated identity management schemes in use nowadays, this approach considers only "short-lived" credentials, whereas it excludes other options of "longer-lived" credentials, such as Privacy-ABCs, which provide the additional privacy benefit for the User, enabling a better control on their privacy by avoiding such traceability by the Issuer.

Finally, Part 3 of ISO/IEC 24760 [ISO14b] provides a more practical approach on guiding the design, implementation, and operation of systems for identity management. For this purpose, it was deemed also relevant for inclusion of the ABC4Trust architecture. This part is designed to contain a list of best examples of technologies and architectures that comply with the privacy architecture framework defined in Parts 1 and 2. So the current draft of this standard now contains a description of the architecture and the main components of an identity management system that uses Privacy-ABC technologies phrased in the language of ISO/IEC 24760-1 and ISO/IEC 24760-2. This way, the draft of this standard currently shows Privacy-ABC technologies, namely the architecture of ABC4Trust as one of the best practice examples to achieve privacy in identity management systems.

11.3.1.2 Privacy architecture standardization – ISO/IEC 29101

"ISO/IEC 29101: Information Technology Security Techniques Privacy Architecture Framework" [ISO] "describes a high-level architecture framework and associated controls for the safeguarding of privacy in information and communication technology (ICT) systems that store and process personally identifiable information (PII)." Because of the topical overlap with the focus of ABC4Trust, this project is also considered to be of a strategic importance. ISO/IEC 29101 identifies several views on the architecture of identity management schemes with a particular focus on the exchange of personally identifiable information (PII) within the architecture.

The main effort has been showing how the architecture of ABC4Trust and the features of Privacy-ABC technologies not only comply with the privacy frame-work, but also show a practical approach to achieving the goals of the standard. Furthermore, it shows that using Privacy-ABC technologies, only a small subset of the identified strategies, such as multi-party computation, or encryption technologies, can fulfil the privacy goals of this standard.

In particular, Annex C of ISO/IEC 29101 now shows an adapted version of the architecture of the course evaluation application from the Patras pilot, lists its components, and describes the ISO/IEC 29101 privacy components in this example architecture. Annex C depicts the main entities of the application, including the Student entity (i.e. the User), the Course Evaluation Application (the Verifier), and the University (the Issuer) described in the terminology of ISO/IEC 29101. It then describes in detail the ISO/IEC 29101 privacy components implemented in the architecture of this application and lists the provided privacy features, as re-quired in the standard. In short, the annex shows that the ABC4Trust inspired ap-plication architecture requires a minimal set of such privacy-components implemented, whilst providing compliance with the privacy architecture framework of this standard.

11.3.2 Certification of Presentation Policies

In this section, we discuss an important aspect of privacy, namely we identify potential risks that could be exploited by malicious Verifiers, and propose mitigation mechanisms against those. The proposed mitigation mechanism against such privacy risks describes an approach using certification of presentation policies.

11.3.2.1 Identification of potential privacy risks

In the architecture of ABC4Trust [BCD$^+$14], but also in any other system that requires authentication of the Users, the Verifier (Relying Party) defines the conditions that must be fulfilled in order for the User to get verified or authenticated. In the ABC4Trust architecture, this is done through the *presentation policy*, which defines, among other things, also the attributes of the credential(s) that the User must disclose.

Privacy-ABCs enable *selective disclosure* of attributes, which is one of the privacy features of the technology behind Privacy-ABCs. In line with the respect for users' privacy and avoiding collection of excessive amounts of personal data beyond the legitimate purpose, a Relying Party should only require disclosure of those attributes proportionate to the purpose of such disclosure.

Nevertheless, there is some potential to violating the privacy of the users even when using Privacy-ABC technologies. One of such potential risks to users' privacy may come from malicious Verifiers, who may ask for excessive amount of attributes to be disclosed during presentations. Technically, a Verifier could define such presentation policies, which would request the User to reveal all or more than necessary attributes.

Furthermore, even in the case when not all attributes are asked for, not all credential attributes have the same identification power. While some attributes may be similar for more people, it may be that some of the attributes may uniquely identify a User, as can be the case of a unique identifier of a credential, e.g. *a revocation handle* used to revoke a credential [BCD+14]. Therefore, a presentation policy should never ask for the revocation handle, as this would then kill some of the main privacy-features of Privacy-ABCs, namely this would enable linkability of user's transactions on a different level. While the architecture of Privacy-ABCs explicitly states that such unique attributes should never be disclosed (or asked for), it does not specify technical means to limit such misuse scenarios per-se.

Needless to say, the above-mentioned privacy risks are not specific to Privacy-ABC technologies, but they could deserve attention in order to avoid potential risk of malicious Verifiers promoting the use of Privacy-ABC technologies, whilst at the same time exploiting them in ways they were not designed for.

11.3.2.2 Certification and standardization as a solution

To protect from such a privacy risk in practice, we propose a mechanism, which would be built on top of the existing architecture framework of Privacy-ABCs. This would involve establishing separate, independent and trusted entity, which would *certify presentation policies* of Verifiers. This relates to the increase of technical trustworthiness of the systems using Privacy-ABCs and a better transparency in general.

For a similar purpose, the new German eID scheme [Fed10] was designed and equipped with a special security mechanism (TA - Terminal Authentication), which protects the data (credential attributes) in the card from being read from an unauthorized terminal (i.e. at the Verifier). In particular, some of the attributes which are considered to be more sensitive are restricted to a number of authorised parties only, e.g. biometric data, such as photo or fingerprints, are denied to all entities, except for "sovereign authorities", such as law enforcement agencies during border control. In consequence, the terminal needs to explicitly show that it is authorized to read the specific data (attributes) by showing a particular certificate [Fed10]. At a more abstract level, the purpose of using this mechanism is similar, namely to prevent the Verifiers from reading unnecessary attributes from the user's credential by having certified read authorizations for specific authorized Verifiers. Although Privacy-ABC technologies can also be applied in additional scenarios besides eIDs, the principles of the architecture design can be similarly applied in any other scenario where such a protection mechanism is desired.

What entity would be most suitable for certifying such presentation policies in practice certainly depends on the application scenario. As an example, in the case of the German eID card, a government institution, the Issuing Office for Certificates (*Vergabestelle für Berechtigungszertifikate* (VfB), which is part of the Federal Office of Administration, (in German: *Bundesverwaltungsamt* (BVA)), is set up and made responsible for the authorization certificates to the service providers. In order to be able to read the eIDs, the service provider would have to submit evidence on the reason why access to specific personal data is necessary for the execution of the service [Mar]. A certificate issued by the Issuing Office enables the service provider to access the card for basic operations, such as age verification (without reading the birthdate), but may also specify fields of personal data (attributes) that the Service Provider is authorized to access.

To summarize, it is important to avoid scenarios, which could enable Verifiers or other entities to get access to data, which would violate privacy features of attribute-based credential technologies, namely selective disclosure or unlinkability of (otherwise unlinkable) Privacy-ABC tokens. This is also in line with the EU Directive on privacy and electronic communications [Eur02], which demands service providers to *"limit the amount of personal data necessary to a strict minimum"*, and the EU Data protection directive, which requires that *"the data must be adequate, relevant and not excessive in relation to the purposes for which they are processed"* [Eur95].

This is not a typical standardization action per-se, but it can prove to be a de-facto standard in certain areas of everyday life, particularly in cases that require a stronger protection of citizens' privacy. In addition to this, one could also create practical standards for most-commonly used presentation policies. These could potentially ease the adoption of Privacy-ABC technologies if some of the most commonly used types of proofs are standardized, such as, e.g. having standard presentation policies for showing that a person is of a certain age.

There are certainly other ways to achieve similar goals, such as reputation-based mechanisms, where Users or some other entity could review different Verifiers in terms of appropriateness of their presentation policies. Nevertheless, the main point is to make clear the possibility of having additional mechanisms in place to assure the protection of the promised privacy for the Users. Finally, having the infrastructure support these privacy assurance mechanisms would hopefully increase the trust on the technology, and ensure that the promised privacy features are well preserved.

References

[BCD$^+$14] Patrik Bichsel, Jan Camenisch, Maria Dubovitskaya, Robert R. Enderlein, Stephan Krenn, Ioannis Krontiris, Anja Lehmann, Gregory Neven, Janus Dam Nielsen, Christian Paquin, Franz-Stefan Preiss, Kai Rannenberg, Ahmad Sabouri, and Michael Stausholm. Architecture for Attribute-based Credential Technologies - Final Version. Deliverable D2.2, The ABC4Trust EU Project, 2014. Available at `https://abc4trust.eu/download/Deliverable_D2.2.pdf`, Last accessed on 2014-11-08.

[BKPR14] Ronny Bjones, Ioannis Krontiris, Pascal Paillier, and Kai Rannenberg. Integrating anonymous credentials with eids for privacy-respecting online authentication. In *Privacy Technologies and Policy*, pages 111–124. Springer, 2014.

[CD-] Council Directive 96/61/EC of 24 September 1996 concerning integrated pollution prevention and control. Official Journal L 257, 10.10.1996, pp. 26 - 40 (1996).

[eIDa] Proposal for a Regulation of the European Parliament and of the Council on electronic identification and trust services for electronic transactions in the internal market. COM(2012)0238 2012/0146(COD). http://eur-lex.europa.eu/legal-content/EN/TXT/?uri=CELEX:52012PC0238.

[eIDb] Regulation (EU) No 910/2014 of the European Parliament and of the Coun-cil of 23 July 2014 on electronic identification and trust services for electronic transactions in the internal market and repealing Directive 1999/93/EC (eIDAS Regulation). Official Journal of the European Union, 28.08.2014, L 257/73-114.

[ENI] ENISA Ad Hoc Working Group on Privacy and Technology: Technology-induced challenges in Privacy & Data Protection in Europe. October 2008 (2008).

[EPC] Convention on the Grant of European Patents (European Patent Convention) of 5 October 1973 as revised by the Act revising Article 63 EPC of 17 December 1991 and the Act revising the EPC of 29 November 2000 (2000).

[Eur95] European Commision. Directive 95/46/EC of the European Parliament and of the Council of 24 October 1995 on the protection of individuals with regard to the processing of personal data and on the free movement of such data. *Official Journal of the EC*, 23(6), 1995.

[Eur02] European Commision. Directive 2002/58/EC of the European Parliament and of the Council of 12 July 2002 concerning the processing of personal data and the protection of privacy in the electronic communications sector (Directive on privacy and electronic communications). *Official Journal of the European Communities*, 2002.

[Fed10] Federal Office for Information Security (BSI). Innovations for an eID Architecture in Germany, September 2010. Available at `http://www.personalausweisportal.de/SharedDocs/Downloads/EN/Flyers-and-Brochures/Broschuere_BSI_innovations_eID_architecture.html?nn=3610692`, Last accessed on 01-11-2014.

[GDP] European Parliament legislative resolution of 12 March 2014 on the proposal for a regulation of the European Parliament and of the Council on the protection of individuals with regard to the processing of personal data and on the free movement of such data (General Data Protection Regulation) (COM(2012)0011 – C7-0025/2012 – 2012/0011(COD)).

[ISO] ISO/IEC. ISO/IEC 29101:2013 Privacy Architecture Framework.

[ISO14a] ISO/IEC JTC 1. Text for ISO/IEC DIS 24760-2: Information technology Security techniques A framework for identity management Part 2: Reference architecture and requirements, 2014.

[ISO14b] ISO/IEC JTC 1/SC 27. ISO/IEC 24760-3 (2nd CD): Information technology Security techniques A framework for identity management Part 3: Practice, 2014.

[Mar] Marian Margraf. The New German ID Card. Federal Ministry of Interior.

[ULD] Unabhängiges Landeszentrum für Datenschutz Schleswig-Holstein: Anforderungskatalog v 1.3 fr die Begutachtung von IT-Produkten im Rahmen des Gü-tesiegelverfahrens beim ULD SH. https://www.datenschutzzentrum.de/download/anford.pdf(2014).

[ZS13] Harald Zwingelberg and Jan Schallaböck. The Proposal for a Regulation on Electronic Identification and Trust Services under a Privacy and ABC4Trust Perspective. Deliverable H2.4, The ABC4Trust EU Project, 2013. Available at https://abc4trust.eu/download/ABC4Trust-H2.4_Privacy_Perspective_on_the_eIDAS_regulation.pdf, Last accessed on 2014-11-08.

Chapter 12
Further Challenges

Kai Rannenberg, Jan Camenisch, Ahmad Sabouri, and Welderufael Tesfay

Abstract ABC4Trust was able to progress the vision of privacy-friendly identity management being widely used and protecting privacy in a digital world several steps further. However there are still challenges open. In this chapter we outline some of them.

As a backdrop two general issues seem to be important for privacy-friendly identity management:

- The views of the respective stakeholders need to be considered (Multilateral Security). Typical examples are the quest for anonymity by people who are requested to deliver content, e.g. an assessment of a service or an explanation of a critique, and the interest of the people, who need to process the content, to learn as much as possible about its background and especially the background of the editor of the content.
- Partial Identities are an important instrument for people to maintain the different spheres of their lives. So it is important to respect the separations of domains, that "before" had been separated either naturally or by intention. This is to some degree counter-intuitive, if one takes the perspective of information processing, as it has always been the aim of information processing to integrate information from different sources. A related buzzword that has often been used in the identity management sphere is "overcoming silos". However, as silos actually have a function to protect their respective content, the different domains of different identity attributes in Partial Identities have been protecting the multiple facets of the respective individuals. With ever-growing bandwidths, communication speed, and interoperability possibilities the transfer of information be-

Kai Rannenberg, Ahmad Sabouri, and Welderufael Tesfay
Chair of Mobile Business & Multilateral Security, Goethe University Frankfurt, Germany, e-mail: {kai.rannenberg, ahmad.sabouri, welderufael.tesfay}@m-chair.de

Jan Camenisch
IBM Research – Zurich, Switzerland, e-mail: jca@zurich.ibm.com

K. Rannenberg et al. (eds.), *Attribute-based Credentials for Trust*,
DOI 10.1007/978-3-319-14439-9_12

yond domains has become much easier than in the past, however this means, that reasonable boundaries between domains (e.g., health care information and job-related information) need to be protected.

Considering the importance of Partial Identities and following the approach of different stakeholder perspectives, we group the further research challenges into the following two categories:

1. Challenges to enable users to manage their identities and the identity management process;
2. Challenges to encourage the (commercial) usage of Privacy-ABCs by relying parties and service providers.

Addressing these challenges should help the adoption of Privacy-ABCs.

12.1 Enabling Users to Manage Their Identities and the Identity Management Process

While Privacy-ABCs by themselves are a very useful and mature technology, it is still not easy for users to manage their identities and the identity management process. Therefore users can not yet take full advantage of Privacy-ABCs. Partially this is due to the lack of some pieces needed for the integration of Privacy-ABCs into existing environments; partially it is a consequence of the need for progress in related areas.

12.1.1 Devices Suitable for Managing Identities

Devices such as Smartphones, personal security assistants, or smart cards are ideal to provide users with functionality to influence the character and degree of identification. To do so, however, such devices need to offer a combination of properties that is not easy to find in the current market.

Secure Storage and Processing. The device will store and process credentials (including cryptographic keys) and other sensitive information of the users. It will thus need to protect this information against attackers that have physical access to the device (if it is lost), control malware on the device, or just are able to communicate with the device. There are a number of initiatives that try to achieve this, including the "Global Platform" (www.globalplatform.org). The following are the main properties that need to be achieved from the point of view of using Privacy-ABCs.

- Being able to verify counterparts, especially other entities that request data from the device: This verification should not depend on the communication channel with the counterpart, as one often has it with smart cards that have no other contact to the environment than the respective smart card reader that tries to read them.

- A portfolio of communication channels for redundancy: in case one communication channel to the environment (e.g. WLAN) would be disturbed there should be other channels (e.g. GSM) available, e.g. to check the validity of the certificate of counterpart, that tries to get information.
- Sufficient access control mechanisms to protect relevant data such as certificates.
- Sufficient processing power for complex operations, in particular, cryptographic calculations.

Secure Interaction with the User. To allow users to control the use of their credentials and the information that is revealed to other parties when authenticating, the communication channel to and from the secured parts of the devices and the user need to be secure as well.

So, in summary, a device should provide a secure platform to its user. While the same is true for other devices such as laptops, the challenges for smaller devices are different. Smart Cards are easier to protect than PCs as their complexity w.r.t to functionality and interfaces is less overwhelming, but sometimes they lack the power for adequate protection, when strong computation and storage facilities are needed. Then PCs are in a better position. Mobile phones are somewhere in between these poles: A cynic may say they combine the Smart Cards' lack of power with PCs' high complexity in the design of the system; and often they have even more interfaces.

12.1.2 Interfaces for Identity Management

Often users feel overwhelmed by the need to manage their identities and attributes and especially by the complexity of cryptography-based security mechanisms. For the users in our pilots this issue could be overcome by carefully analysing the use cases and integrating the management of identities and attributes into the normal work flows. However to overcome this issue in general, more practical, usable, understandable, and maybe even nicer looking interfaces for identity management are needed. This entails addressing the following challenges:

- Appropriate integration into processes that require authentication such as log-in to a portal or requesting a resource;
- More consideration of non-experts and user-groups that prefer not to play around with a device to understand it, such as older-age people;
- Making it easier for users to understand the consequences of their actions when they are selecting their credentials and other options for authentication;
- Motivating users to manage their credentials and identities, e.g. by exploring the potential of gamification, as gamification seems to make people enjoy also

other relatively tedious processes in daily life such as managing one's weight and nutrition household by game-like apps on smartphones.

12.1.3 Minimizing the Installation Effort

Users seem to perceive the relative simplicity of typing a user name and a (single) password as the reference for any effort for identity management. Thus, any alternative solution for authentication should not be substantially harder to use and to install. In particular, the following hurdles need to be overcome:

- The use of a security element such as a smart card is currently preventive because it requires in most situations the installation of special drivers and the user of smart card readers. Solutions are required that do not have an additional hardware token or at least do not require additional items.
- For most users it is a pain to install and maintain any additional software components. Offering such additional components as apps that can be installed by a single click and that update themselves addresses this issue to some extent. Nevertheless, ideally the installation of additional components should not be needed.
- Ease switching between different devices, e.g. one's own smartphone, tablet, and laptop, but also the PC at a location one visits: this would especially mean to remove the need to install specific client software on a device.

12.1.4 Additional Services that Help the Users to Manage Their Data and Protect Their Privacy

Some processes cannot simply be dealt with between a user and her device, as they involve other entities. One example are the life-cycle management processes for credentials, either to preserve credentials that only exist in a user device against loss or to reduce the effort for getting a credential back that after loss can be reissued by the issuer. A special challenge are backup and restore features to deal with cases of stolen, broken or lost devices, that preserve the secrecy of the backup images but at the same time prevent manipulation, e.g. cloning or doubling of cards or vouchers. For the pilot trials adequate solutions could be found, but transferring them to other cases is not trivial, as it requires a detailed threat analysis for the respective environment.

Another example are educational sites that inform the users in an entertaining way about on-line privacy, how to protect it, and how Privacy-ABCs can be used.

12.2 Usage of Privacy-ABCs by Relying Parties and Service Providers

Switching from the currently used authentication and authorization mechanisms to ones that are based on Privacy-ABCs will require investments by relying parties and service providers. Thus, to foster the adoption of Privacy-ABCs, the benefits of using Privacy-ABCs must be made as large and clear as possible and the related costs may need to be reduced. One could chose the easy option to wait for more incidents with existing technologies and to profit from the fear thereafter. However this may be not the best approach from a point of view of common welfare. Moreover in any case for adoption an adoption roadmap is needed. It should cover the whole value chain and reward progress with appropriate incentives. In the following we discuss a number of elements to be considered for such a roadmap, grouped by typical factors for the adoption of technology.

12.2.1 Boundaries between Different Domains

Originally, a user had a different identity or even many identities with each service provider. Then, to make their business processes easier and to improve customer service, service providers started to deploy server-side identity management to be able to recognize the same user in different transactions within the enterprise and later across different domains. This trend is a major obstacle to privacy-friendly user-controlled identity management. Thus, one needs to find incentives for companies to respect and possibly enforce boundaries between separate domains and make privacy-friendly user-controlled identity management commercially attractive. Examples include:

- Improving regulation to avoid, that users get forced to transmit information about themselves (attributes), that is not really needed (cf. also Chapter 11);
- Inventing business models that take advantage of the fact that the information, that is provided via Privacy-ABCs, is better assured and that at the same time enterprises do not need to store and protect unnecessary personal data. This could include developing sector specific examples to showcase business processes taking full advantage of Privacy-ABCs (cf. also Chapter 10).
- Establishing ecosystems such as a "personal data economy," that encourage users to consider what they get and do not get for providing personal data.

One approach to the latter two points could be new mechanisms for ad-paid services. So for instance, rather than having a server to profile users by trying to learn as much information about a user as possible, such profiling could happen on the users' platforms. Then only the resulting profile is sent to auction advertisements to this user. Of course, the process must ensure that cheating is not (easily) possible.

12.2.2 Interoperability and Compatibility with Existing Technologies

Identity management systems are not trivial to deploy. They require business process and application designers to understand the principles of identity management. Also the reference implementation provided by ABC4Trust requires understanding, especially for privacy-friendly authentication. Moreover application developers and implementers need to learn the specific data formats that are used. These requirements on people working with the technology don't promote its adoption. To overcome this, the protocols and data formats should be further simplified, at least for the most common specials cases, so that Privacy-ABCs become more interoperable and compatible with their environment. More precisely, the following items should be addressed:

- Integration with currently popular technologies such as OpenID, X.509, or SAML so that Privacy-ABC technologies can be used with no changes of the existing infrastructure. This will of course not allow to take full advantage of all features that Privacy-ABCs offer but will still provide the basic privacy-enhancing features such as selective disclosure of attributes or pseudonyms.
- Enabling easy use of Privacy-ABC by providing to Relying Parties cloud-based services that remove the need for installations and can be easily configured. This would allow to take full advantage of Privacy-ABC while lightening the burden of installation, configuration, and integration.
- Tailored solutions for specific but popular cases to, e.g. reduce the effort for authoring ABC4Trust presentation policies (access control policies) through template policies and default policies. Template polices such as "over a certain (to be defined) age" or "identified by (to be defined)" allow the implementer to define a policy, e.g. which age is required for granting access to which resources. Default policies, such as "of legal age", or "over 16", or "possessing a valid identity card" allow to make use of best-practice examples or predefined proposals, that may have been successful elsewhere.
- Integration with established environmental infrastructures such as national eID initiatives.
- Encouraging the integration of Privacy-ABCs into business processes by equipping example applications with Privacy-ABCs, e.g. a customer loyalty process.
- Offering the exchange of experiences and best practices within adopter groups to ease the overcoming of potential difficulties and create a stimulating community.

12.2.3 Enabling Prototypes and Trials

Currently, testing and evaluating the use of Privacy-ABCs and integrating them into applications requires downloading, compiling, and installing the reference implementation of ABC4Trust. This proved to be a hurdle for some early adopters.

Therefore more supporting materials for the reference implementation such as more best-practice-examples may be useful. Moreover, a running public demonstrator infrastructure of issuers and relying parties could prove very helpful. On the one hand, this would allow to play with the technology without installing any software and, one the other hand, if one decides to install and use the technology, these services could be used for testing one's own installation.

12.2.4 Standardization

Some of the properties of Identity Management relevant to Privacy-ABCs such as the separation of presentation tokens and credentials are covered by standards, e.g. ISO/IEC IS 24760 (developed in ISO/IEC JTC 1/SC 27/WG 5 "Identity Management and Privacy Technologies"). However, the majority of the data and protocol formats are not standardized yet and a lot of work in this area remains. This is not a trivial task at all, and the same holds for deciding, which aspects of the reference implementation should be standardized. This may require broader experience with the reference implementation.

Appendix A
ABC4Trust Workpackages and Deliverables

A.1 Workpackages

WP No.	WP Name
WP 1	Management
WP 2	Architecture
WP 3	Comparison
WP 4	Reference Implementation
WP 5	Application Requirements
WP 6	Community Interaction Among Pupils
WP 7	Course Rating by Certified Students
WP 8	Dissemination

K. Rannenberg et al. (eds.), *Attribute-based Credentials for Trust*,
DOI 10.1007/978-3-319-14439-9

A.2 Deliverables

Del. No.	Deliverable Name	Lead	Date
D2.1	Architecture for Attribute-based Credential Technologies Version 1	GUF	M13
D2.2	Architecture for Attribute-based Credential Technologies Final Version	GUF	M45
D2.3	Benchmarking criteria WP2	GUF	M43
D3.1	Scientific comparison of ABC protocols	MCL	M42
D3.2	Guidance on selection and complementarity of ABC	MCL	M45
D4.1	Initial Reference Implementation	ALX	M19
D4.2	Final Reference Implementation	IBM	M45
D4.3	Final Perturbation analysis of the Implementation	TUD	M45
D4.4	Smartphone feasibility analysis	ALX	M45
D5.1	Scenario Definition for both Pilots (incl. Credential Definition)	CTI	M15
D5.2	Description of the "common denominator" elements	NSN	M19
D5.3	Experiences and Feedback from the Pilots	NSN	M42
D6.1	Application Description for the school deployment	EDOC	M16
D6.2	Necessary hardware and software package for the school deployment	EDOC	M27
D6.3	Evaluation of the school pilot	EDOC	M42
D7.1	Application Description for students	CTI	M16
D7.2	Necessary hardware and software package for the student deployment	CTI	M24
D7.3	Evaluation of the student pilot	CTI	M42
D8.1	Public website (https://abc4trust.eu)	GUF	M4
D8.2	Project presentation	ULD	M5
D8.3	Plan for Use and Dissemination of Foreground V1	ULD	M13
D8.4	Architecture for Standardization V1	GUF	M16
D8.5	Reference Implementation for Standardization V1	GUF	M22
D8.6	First Reference Group Meeting and Summary of Reference Group Feedback	ULD	M18
D8.7	Second Reference Group Meeting and Summary of Reference Group Feedback	ULD	M28
D8.8	Plan for Use and Dissemination of Foreground V2	ULD	M25
D8.9	Standardization Workshop	ULD	M28
D8.10	Plan for Use and Dissemination of Foreground V3	ULD	M37
D8.11	Third Reference Group Meeting and Second Summary of Reference Group Feedback	ULD	M40
D8.12	Architecture for Standardization V2 (Final)	GUF	M48
D8.13	Reference Implementation for Standardization V2	GUF	M48

Continued on next page

Continued from previous page

Del. No.	**Deliverable Name**	**Lead**	**Date**
D8.14	Final Event	ULD	M52
D8.15	ABC4Trust Book	GUF	M52
D8.16	Plan for Use and Dissemination of Foreground V4	ULD	M52

Appendix B
ABC4Trust Consortium

The ABC4Trust Consortium comprises the following 12 organisations, being situated in 7 European countries:

1. GUF - Johann Wolfgang Goethe-Universität Frankfurt am Main: Chair of Mobile Business and Multilateral Security, Germany
2. TUD - Technische Universität Darmstadt, Germany
3. ALX - Alexandra Institute AS, Denmark
4. ULD - Unabhängiges Landeszentrum für Datenschutz, Germany
5. CTI - Computer Technology Institute & Press - DIOPHANTUS, Greece
6. EDOC - Eurodocs AB, Sweden
7. IBM - IBM Research - Zurich, Switzerland
8. CRX - CryptoExperts SAS, France
9. MCL - Miracle A/S, Denmark
10. MSNV - Microsoft Belgium NV, Belgium
11. NSN - Nokia Solutions and Networks, Germany
12. SK - Söderhamn Kommun, Sweden

GUF - Johann Wolfgang Goethe-Universität Frankfurt am Main: Chair of Mobile Business and Multilateral Security

GOETHE UNIVERSITÄT FRANKFURT AM MAIN

The Chair of Mobile Business and Multilateral Security (www.m-chair.de) is part of the Institute of Business Informatics. Enjoying endowment sponsorship by Deutsche Telekom (the leading German telecommunications provider), the chair focuses its research on innovative mobile networks and their applications, as well as on related issues of privacy and security. Its mission is to find business models and technologies enabling the secure and privacy enabled use of mobile devices and mobile communication for applications and businesses. The Chair of Mobile Business and Multilateral Security coordinated the Network of Excellence (NoE) Future of Identity in the Information Society (FIDIS),

K. Rannenberg et al. (eds.), *Attribute-based Credentials for Trust*,
DOI 10.1007/978-3-319-14439-9

lead the Work Package "Evaluation" in the Project PRIME and the Activity "Infrastructure" in the Project PrimeLife. Moreover, the Chair coordinated the project "Privacy in Community Services" (PICOS) and the project "Attribute-based Credentials for Trust" (ABC4Trust) and lead the Work Package "Architecture".

TUD - Technische Universität Darmstadt

TU Darmstadt is Germany's premier Technical University and especially for Computer Science. TU Darmstadt has developed to become one of the leading research centers for IT security and dependability in Europe through its CASED (Center for Advanced Security) and EC-SPRIDE (European Center for Security & Privacy by Design) Centers that integrate multiple security/dependability groups at TU Darmstadt.

Prof. Suri's TU Darmstadt's DEEDS - Dependable Systems & Software Group is an integral member of both CASED and EC-SPRIDE and specifically researches design, assessment and validation as an infrastructural basis for trustworthy systems and services. The group is internationally renowned for its dependability/security research in (a) Fault Injection based experimental validation of trust which was also DEEDS core activity in ABC4Trust, (b) formal approaches to trust specification and verification, (c) covert channel attacks, (d) quantification of trust covering security metrics, and (e) SLA based specification, comparison and negotiation of Cloud/Storage level trust provisioning.

The dependability/security research of the DEEDS group has garnered extensive support from the European Commission with some relevant FP7/H2020 projects being: COMIFIN, ISNPIRE, BIC, ABC4Trust, SPECS, SLA-READY, ESCUDO among others. In addition, its research support has come from NSF, DARPA, ONR, and multiple international industry such as Airbus, Audi, Boeing, Daimler, GM, Hitachi, IBM, Intel, Microsoft, NASA, Saab, Volvo etc. Further details of DEEDS activities are available at: http://www.deeds.informatik.tu-darmstadt.de/

ALX - Alexandra Institute AS

The Alexandra Institute Ltd. has 15 years of experience in establishing working relationships between researchers, companies and end users.

We focus on matchmaking between public and private organisations, based on deep respect for the interests of the parties involved. Businesses participate to accelerate their innovation and achieve growth, researchers to gain new knowledge, insights and inspiration.

Our research and innovation projects constitute the engine that creates new knowledge of benefit to the participants in the projects. We also bring this knowledge into play in our consultancy services and our innovation networks. In this way, the Alexandra Institute contributes to improving the innovation processes in organisations and to enhancing their competitive position.

Our work is organised across a number of different labs, one being the Security Lab, which work with advanced security solutions with a particular view towards applied cryptography. This includes e.g. attribute-based credentials and multi-party computation.

The Security Lab also advises private and governmental organisation about security and privacy.

ULD - Unabhängiges Landeszentrum für Datenschutz

Unabhängiges Landeszentrum für Datenschutz (ULD, Engl. Independent Centre for Privacy Protection) is the Data Protection Authority of Schleswig-Holstein, the northernmost Federal State of Germany. Its office with 40 employees is located in Kiel, Germany. The Privacy Commissioner of Schleswig-Holstein, Dr. Thilo Weichert, is head of ULD. ULD is responsible for both data protection and freedom of information in Schleswig-Holstein. The basis for the work of ULD is laid down in the State Data Protection Act Schleswig-Holstein. This act is one of the most progressive ones worldwide and includes among others provisions on a seal of privacy for IT products and on privacy protection audits for public authorities. In addition to the privacy seal based on German national and regional law, ULD has founded the European Privacy Seal initiative EuroPriSe for evaluating compliance with European data protection regulation which is being performed by EuroPriSe GmbH since 2014.

CTI - Computer Technology Institute & Press - DIOPHANTUS

The Computer Technology Institute and Press Diophantus, or CTI for short, is a leading research organization in Greece supervised by the Greek Ministry of Education. CTI is fulfilling its goals based on an efficient administrative structure and an experienced highly qualified research and administrative staff.

Among CTI's main goals is to conduct basic and applied research in theoretical as well as applied Computer Science in a variety of domains covering foundational research, cryptography and ICT security, ad-hoc and sensor networks, distributed computation, signal processing, applications of ICT in medicine, among others.

CTI is, also, the technological pillar of the Greek Ministry of Education for the support of ICT in the educational domain as it is responsible for the publishing of printed and electronic materials, and for the administration of the Greek School Network

EDOC - Eurodocs AB

Eurodocs AB is a next generation IT Company developing smart, innovative and cost effective digital convergence solutions in the areas of privacy preservation and identity protection. For over a decade, Eurodocs has striven to remain at the forefront of Internet safety and online privacy issues. Through its participation within ABC4Trust, Eurodocs has participated in cutting edge research and development activities toward the creation of IT products that can be best described as WebS^4 where the "S" stands for Smart, Secure Social Services.

In today's interconnected world of online participation and representation, it is more critical than ever that netizens have a means by which their identity can be not only protected, but also verifiable. Eurodocs provides these solutions with a new dimension of Internet security tools for improved electronic identification, privacy preservation and digital authentication. Our products empower users to make more informed decisions over what personal data may be shared while being confident that their identity is safeguarded and privacy is upheld.

IBM - IBM Research - Zurich

IBM Research - Zurich is a European branch of IBM's Research Division. The lab employs researchers from more than twenty countries working on projects in computer science, communications, optoelectronics, and physics. The privacy and security group of IBM Research - Zurich played a leading role in the development of IBMs Enterprise Privacy Architecture (EPA), and has several research projects related to privacy- friendly technologies, e.g., Identity Mixer (a privacy-enhanced pseudonym-based public-key infrastructure), EPAL (a language and architecture for defining and enforcing enterprise privacy policies), and CDIM (a set of protocols for browser-based attribute exchange and federated identity management). The lab has actively participated in several research projects funded by the European Union including ABC4Trust, FutureID, PrimeLife, PRIME, ECRYPT, FIDIS, and OpenTC.

CRX - CryptoExperts SAS

CryptoExperts is a young start-up company founded by widely recognized industrial and academic researchers in IT security and cryptography. The company offers externalized R&D and consulting services in a wide variety of security areas, including advanced security evaluation of cryptographic software, products and services. The cryptographic expertise of the company includes: proof-based analysis of cryptographic systems and protocols, on-demand design of new cryptographic systems (access control, e-passports, secure storage, electronic commerce and e-cash systems, electronic voting, e-government applications, broadcast encryption and traitor tracing, digital signatures and encryption with specific properties), practical applications of cryptography, security architectures, design and implementation of cryptographic libraries for embedded systems on specific hardware (crypto-processors, smart cards, USB tokens, HSM, etc), and security evaluation of cryptographic implementations (side-channel and fault-based analysis).

CryptoExperts has a research group of well-recognized experts in cryptography. Research areas include provable security for security infrastructures and application; the design and security evaluation of cryptographic functions, schemes and protocols; secure implementations and the physical security of embedded systems. Therefore the group's technical expertise simultaneously covers theoretical and very practical aspects of cryptographic systems.

User privacy and anonymity, and applications thereof (e.g. e-cash, e-vote) are long-lived research topics for the group members.

MCL - Miracle A/S

Miracle A/S (MCL) was founded in the year 2000 in a garage near Copenhagen and has been proliferating significantly since. Today Miracle approaches 120 employees and delivers IT services to more than 250 diverse companies in Denmark. Miracle is a total supplier of IT operation, implementation, and development, and our core output consists of project development, database administration, consultancy services, mobile development, ERP solutions and hosting services.

Miracle was formerly known as the no. 1 Oracle database expert in Denmark, however, while still upholding this unofficial status, Miracle now possesses significant expertise within Microsoft SQL Server as well, and employs some of the countrys most acute experts within both fields. Apart from 24/7 support, emergency consulting and problem solving, Miracle's operations department offers regular online checks, and our experts have many years of experience in conducting databases, application servers and operating systems.

In recent years Miracle's development units have taken on increasingly large projects in the public sector and in the corporate world and business critical enterprise solutions has become one of Miracle's specialities. Miracle develops tailored software solutions on a series of platforms including Microsoft .Net and a variety of open source platforms counting Java, Sun, Scala, and JBoss within which Miracle employs some of the country's most specialised developers and architects. Lately Miracle has been successful in developing mobile applications for several costumers both on iPhone, Windows, Phone, Android and Blackberry platforms.

Miracle Buddyshop, a subsidiary company to Miracle, is an IT consultancy employing more than 100 consultants, which provides extra resources for Miracle to draw on if necessary or if requested by customers.

Miracle Hosting, another subsidiary company to Miracle, is an integrated part of Miracle and their modern facilities, located in Miracle's headquarters, include a new data centre.

MSNV - Microsoft Belgium NV

Microsoft was founded in 1975 and has been committed ever since to helping people and businesses throughout the world realize their full potential. Our software innovations and cloud services generate opportunities for the technology sector, businesses, public sector and consumers worldwide. We are dedicated to improving and extending access to education, supporting job training and fostering innovation, as well as protecting the online safety and privacy of individuals, families and businesses.
www.microsoft.com

NSN - Nokia Solutions and Networks

Nokia invests in technologies important in a world where billions of devices are connected. We are focused on three businesses: network infrastructure software, hardware and services, which we offer through Nokia Networks; location intelligence, provided through HERE; and advanced technology development and licensing, pursued through Nokia Technologies. Each of these businesses is a leader in its respective field.

Nokia Networks is the world's specialist in mobile broadband. From the first ever call on GSM, to the first call on LTE, we operate at the forefront of each generation of mobile technology. Our global experts invent the new capabilities our customers need in their networks. We provide the world's most efficient mobile networks, the intelligence to maximize the value of those networks, and the services to make it all work seamlessly.

The research group involved in this project participates regularly in EU research projects and transfers its results into the relevant business units. Recent involvements in European projects include SIMPLICITY, SPICE, SERVERY, FI-WARE, 5G-PPP, NESSI and SASER.
http://networks.nokia.com

SK - Söderhamn Kommun

Söderhamn is an active municipality in terms of ICT and school issues. Söderhamn has large commitment and are working hard to increase the number of ICT technology in teaching. As an education provider with responsibility for children up to the age of 20 (according to national legislation the municipalities have a responsibility for children/young people up to the age of 20) it is important for us that our students can feel safe in their ICT usage and therefore the ICT security and issues relating to student privacy is paramount.

Contributors

Abendroth, Joerg
Joerg Abendroth received a diploma in communication engineering from the University of Applied Science in Dieburg (formerly owned by Deutsche Telekom) and the Ph.D. from the Distributed Systems Group of Trinity College Dublin, Ireland. In 2003, he received a Marie Curie Fellowship, which enabled him to work at the BRICS (Basic Research in Computer Science) research institute in Denmark. He joined Siemens AG Corporate Technology, later NSN and now Nokia in 2004. His research interests include privacy, access control mechanism and models, as well as mobile malware detection.

Bcheri, Souheil
Souheil Bcheri is the founder and CEO of the Swedish company Eurodocs, AB. He has a Master's Degree in mathematics and statistics from Umea University, Sweden. Additional areas of educational experience have included extensive coursework relating to cyber-crime and computer forensic investigations. Mr. Bcheri boasts more than 20 years of experience within the sectors of large data analysis and IT security, with specific expertise within the fields of digital identification, encryption and digital signatures. Souheil has a long track record of accomplishments in projects dealing with topics relating to online anonymity and personal data protection issues.

Benenson, Zinaida
Zinaida Benenson is a Lecturer in Computer Science at the Friedrich-Alexander University of Erlangen-Nuremberg (FAU), Germany, where she leads the Human Factors in Security and Privacy Group. Her research interests include usability of security- and privacy-enhancing technologies, decision making and risk perception in security and privacy, and also technical security issues in distributed systems, especially in wireless sensor networks and in pervasive computing. Zinaida Benenson received her PhD in Computer Science from the University of Mannheim, Germany, on the topic of cryptographic access control protocols for wireless sensor networks.

K. Rannenberg et al. (eds.), *Attribute-based Credentials for Trust*,
DOI 10.1007/978-3-319-14439-9

Bichsel, Patrik

Dr. Patrik Bichsel studied electrical engineering and information technology at ETH Zürich got an M.Sc. degree in November 2007. In 2008, Patrik joined IBM Research - Zurich as a PhD Student and started to work on the design of cryptographic protocols for privacy. Patrik also engaged on the design and implementation of Identity Mixer which was later transformed into the ABC4Trust crypto layer. Patrik was awarded a PhD from KU Leuven in 2012 for his thesis entitled "Cryptographic Protocols and System Aspects for Practical Data-minimizing Authentication. Patrik has left IBM Research - Zurich in 2014 and now works as a consultant at Innovation Process Technology.

Bieker, Felix

Felix Bieker, LLM.Eur is legal researcher and consultant at the Unabhängiges Landeszentrum für Datenschutz (ULD). Upon completion of his Master at the University of Edinburgh in 2013, he has been working on the EU-funded ABC4Trust research project within ULD. Since 2014, Felix also works as a research and teaching assistant for European law at the Walther Schücking Institute of International Law at the University of Kiel. There, he is currently writing his doctoral thesis on European fundamental rights and data protection.

Camenisch, Jan (i.a. editor)

Jan Camenisch is a Principal Research Staff Member at IBM Research - Zurich. He holds a Diploma in Electrical Engineering Science and PhD in Computer Science both from the ETH Zurich (1993). From 1998-1999, he has been a Research Assistant Professor in Computer Science at the University of Aarhus, Denmark. He published extensively in cryptography and security and was a chair of a few and a member of numerous scientific program committees. He also teaches a course on technologies for privacy protection at ETH Zurich. Dr. Camenisch was the technical leader of the interdisciplinary research projects PRIME and PrimeLife funded under the 7th framework programme of the European Commission. He is an IEEE Fellow and has received a number of awards for this work on privacy-enhancing technologies including the 2013 IEEE Computer Society Technical Award and the 2010 ACM SIGSAC Outstanding Innovation Award. His research interests include cryptography and privacy enhancing technologies.

Damgård, Kasper

Kasper studied computer science at Aarhus University and got his masters degree in 2011 with a thesis in cryptography. Kasper has been employed at the Alexandra Institutes security lab since 2011 where he has worked mainly with developing new security solutions. He has been working with the ABC4Trust project since his employment at Alexandra and has contributed to both code and deliverables.

Deibler, Daniel

Ass. iur. Daniel Deibler, LLM is legal researcher at Unabhängiges Landeszentrum für Datenschutz (ULD). Already during his Law studies in Germany Daniel concentrated on privacy and data protection law and subsequently graduated with core subjects concerning the law of the informational society. After passing his First State Examination in Law he specialised further on international and European human rights law during his LLM studies at the University of Exeter, UK. After graduating Daniel completed his postgraduate legal trainingship back in Germany and joined the ULD. Daniel has been working on several national and international projects and in particular on the EC-funded project ABC4Trust.

Dubovitskaya, Maria

Dr. Maria Dubovitskaya received her Master's degrees in *Information Security* in 2007 and in *Economics and Business Management* in 2008 from Moscow Engineering Physics Institute, Russia. In 2007, Maria started at IBM Science and Technology Center in Moscow, as a Staff Software Engineer on storage systems for Mainframes. Maria joined IBM Research - Zurich in 2010 and since then she has been working on provable cryptographic protocols for privacy protection and their real-world applications. In 2014, Maria received a PhD from ETH Zurich for her thesis entitled "Cryptographic Protocols for Privacy-Preserving Access Control in Databases."

Enderlein, Robert R.

Robert R. Enderlein received his master's degree in Communication Systems from the Swiss Federal Institute of Technology in Lausanne (EPFL). He is currently employed as a pre-doctoral researcher at IBM Research—Zurich and pursues a PhD in cryptography as an external student of the Swiss Federal Institute of Technology in Zurich (ETH). His research interests include privacy-preserving cryptography and universally composable security.

Girard, Anna

Anna Girard is a doctoral candidate at the Institute for Marketing, Ludwig-Maximilians-University (LMU) Munich. In her research she focuses on the influence of ambient scents in service and retail environments. Besides her doctoral studies, Mrs. Girard is a part-time research associate at the Human Factors in Security and Privacy Group at the Computer Science Department of the Friedrich-Alexander University Erlangen-Nuremberg (FAU). Prior to her doctoral studies, she worked as a research and teaching assistant at several research institutes, as well as for an international retailer. Anna Girard holds a B.Sc. with honors in Business Administration and a Master of Business Research with honors from the LMU Munich.

Götze, Norbert
Norbert Götze obtained a degree in electrical engineering from the University of Applied Sciences in Constance in 1987. Within Siemens, he began his career as hardware developer and designed boards for public telephone switching systems. Norbert entered software development in 2001 and took part in the implementation of voice and maintenance services for Siemens' SURPASS system. In 2005, he switched tasks and focused on software hardening and security of the "Integrated Multimedia System" (IMS). As member of the Program Control Team in 2006, he was responsible for the security of the FMC (Fixed Mobile Convergence) system of Nokia Siemens Networks. From 2009 until today, Norbert is active in Nokia research, covering security, privacy and cloud topics.

Guldager Knudsen, Hans
During the last decade Hans Guldager Knudsen has been designing and building cryptographic based solutions in areas as PKI for authentication and digital signatures for public sector websites and internet banking, mobile payment on GSM/SIM backed by central HW crypto solution, electronic ticketing for delegating trust between websites and a server based solution for central handling of secure email. Hans worked on the reference implementation in the ABC4Trust project, and had a major role integrating the reference implementation with other systems in the pilots.

Hansen, Marit
Dipl.-Inform. Marit Hansen is Deputy Privacy & Information Commissioner of Land Schleswig- Holstein, Germany, and Deputy Chief of Unabhängiges Landeszentrum für Datenschutz (ULD). Within ULD she is in charge of the "Privacy Technology Projects" Division and the "Innovation Centre Privacy & Security". Since her diploma in computer science in 1995 she has been working on privacy and security aspects especially concerning anonymity, pseudonymity, identities management, biometrics, multilateral security, privacy by design and privacy by default from both the technical and the legal perspectives. In several projects she and her team actively participate in system design in order to support privacy technologies and give feedback on legislation.

Jensen, Jonas Lindstrøm
Dr. Jonas Lindstrøm Jensen received a PhD degree in mathematics from Aarhus University in 2012, based on research in number theory, diophantine approximation and dynamical systems. From 2012 to 2013 he worked as a software engineer at CCI Europe, and has since 2013 been employed as innovation and research specialist at Alexandra Institute Centre for IT Security

Krenn, Stephan
Stephan Krenn holds a Master's degree in mathematics from Vienna University of Technology, and a PhD in Computer Science from University of Fribourg. After a first postdoc at IST Austria he joined IBM Research – Zurich as a postdoc in 2013, where he is mainly working on quantum-resistant protocols and privacy enhancing cryptographic primitives.

Krontiris, Ioannis
Ioannis Krontiris (ikrontiris@gmx.de) received his diploma in Electronic and Computer Engineering from Technical University of Crete, Greece, in 2001. He holds a Master degree on Information Networking from Carnegie Mellon University, USA and a PhD degree in Computer Science from Mannheim University, Germany. He has worked several years as senior researcher at University of Frankfurt focusing his research on privacy in pervasive systems as well as identity management. He has served as technical coordinator of the EU project ABC4Trust, while he was involved in several other EU projects. He has also served as the chair of IFIP WG 11.2 - Pervasive Systems Security till June 2014.

Læssøe Mikkelsen, Gert
Gert Læssøe Mikkelsen holds a PhD. in computer science and cryptography from Aarhus University ("On the Protection of Digital Identities through Threshold Cryptography"., 2011). Since 2011 hi has been working at the Alexandra Institute's Centre for IT Security with research and innovation in the field of cryptography based identity management technologies.

Lehmann, Anja
Dr. Anja Lehmann is a researcher in the security group at IBM Research Zurich, where she is involved in the ABC4Trust, FutureID and FI-Ware projects. Her work mainly deals with the development of new cryptographic protocols with provable security guarantees, and the deployment of privacy-enhancing technologies in real-world applications and infrastructures. Before joining IBM in 2010, she obtained her PhD in Marc Fischlin's research group at Darmstadt University of Technology, Germany.

Lerch, Jimm
Jimm Lerch is a Project Manager at Eurodocs, AB. He obtained his Master's Degree in International Policy Studies from Monterey Institute of International Studies, USA, and has completed additional graduate studies at Uppsala University, Sweden. Over the years, Mr. Lerch has worked with policy issues within the realms of online privacy, Internet security and web governance principles with specific regard given to their respective interrelationships with each other as well as with ICTs.

Liagkou, Vasia
Vasia Liagkou holds a B.Sc. from he Computer Engineering and Informatics Department, University of Patras, Greece, and a M.Sc. in Foundations of Computer Science and a PhD in Cryptography and Cryptanalysis of Secure and Trust communication protocols from the same department. Her Ph.D. was focused on theoretical issues of random communication networks and secure ICT technologies. She is also, an Adjunct Professor at the Department of Management of Cultural Environment and New Technologies of University of Ioannina. She has extensive experience in cryptography, ICT security as well as Privacy Enhancing Technologies (PETs).

Luna, Jesus
Jesus is the Research Director of the Cloud Security Alliance EMEA, and security group leader with TU Darmstadt. His main responsibilities include the internal scientific/technical management of EU funded projects. Jesus has worked in the ICT security field for more than 17 years with both industry and academia in U.K., Germany, Spain, Greece, Cyprus and Mexico. Jesus obtained his PhD degree (Cum-Laude) in Computer Architecture from the "Technical University of Catalonia" (2008), and has published more than 30 scientific papers in prestigious venues.

Neven, Gregory
Dr. Gregory Neven is a scientific researcher at IBM Research - Zurich. His research focuses on provably secure cryptography, privacy, and policy languages. Gregory holds a PhD in applied sciences (2004) and a Master of Engineering in computer science (2000) from Katholieke Universiteit Leuven, and has worked as a visiting researcher at University of California, San Diego and at Ecole Normale Supérieure. He published over 40 research papers and patents in the field of cryptography and information security, several of which appeared in top-ranking conferences and journals.

Nielsen, Janus Dam
Janus Dam Nielsen received the M.Sc. degree in computer science and the Ph.D. degree in programming languages from Aarhus University, Aarhus, Denmark, in 2006 and 2009, respectively. Since then, he has been with the Alexandra Institute A/S, Aarhus, Denmark, where he is currently Senior Security Architect. His main areas of research interest are it-security, identity management, and secure computation.

Obersteller, Hannah
Ass. iur. Hannah Obersteller studied law with focus on commercial criminal law at the University of Potsdam. After the First State Exam in law, she conducted her legal internship inter alia at the civil chamber for banking and insurance law of the Landgericht Potsdam and the Ministry of the Interior of the German State of Brandenburg. After the Second State Exam in law she worked for an insolvency office in Hanover before joining the Unabhängiges Landeszentrum für Datenschutz (ULD) and the ABC4Trust project as legal researcher and consultant.

Østergaard, Michael
Michael Østergaard works with software development, cryptography, penetration testing and other IT security related activities at Miracle A/S. He was a member of the IT security and cryptography group at the University of Aarhus, where he completed in PhD in May 2008. He is the co-author of research papers related to authentication, privacy and digital signatures. In the ABC4Trust project he worked primarily on formal analysis and definitions of Privacy-ABC schemes.

Paillier, Pascal
Pascal Paillier is a public-key cryptography expert and has more than 16 years of industrial experience in IT security, with a specific interest for designing and developing side channel/fault-resistant cryptographic software for embedded architectures such as smart cards. His favourite research works include the design of public-key primitives, security proofs and more recently the design of hash functions (co-conceptor of the SHABAL hash function submitted to the NIST SHA-3 competition). Until 2009, Pascal was heading the Cryptography & Innovation expert group at Gemalto, the worldwide leader in smart card technologies. Co-founder of CryptoExperts, Pascal has published over 60 research papers and filed about 25 patents, most of which are commonly implemented in the smart card industry. Pascal is also an active member of ISO SC27 WG2, the expert group that defines ISO/IEC cryptography standards.

Paquin, Christian
Christian is a Principal Program Manager in Microsoft Research's Security and Crypto group, responsible for incubating emergent cryptographic technologies. Christian has more than 15 years of experience in the field; his main area of focus is to improve security and privacy in identity and federated systems. He currently is leading the development of the award-winning U-Prove technology, and manages its integration in various products and services. Prior to joining Microsoft in 2008, Christian was Credentica's Chief Security Engineer, where he help design and develop the U-Prove technology. Christian started his career as a crypto engineer implementing anonymous remailers and digital signature products. He holds a M. Sc. from University of Montreal in cryptography.

Pellegrino, Giancarlo
Giancarlo Pellegrino is Postdoctoral Researcher at Technical University of Darmstadt. He holds a Ph.D. in computer network and security from Telecom ParisTech/EURECOM, France. He was a member of the S3 research group at EURECOM in Sophia-Antipolis (France) and of the "Security and Trust" group at the SAP Research. He contributed and is contributing to EU FP7 funded projects, e.g., AVANTSSAR, SPaCIoS, and SPECS. His research interests are concerned with the development of testing techniques in order to detect vulnerabilities in application and system software by combining security testing, formal methods, and model-based testing techniques.

Preiss, Franz-Stefan

Franz-Stefan Preiss was born in Zwettl, Austria. He received master's degrees in *Software Engineering & Internet Computing* and in *Computer Science Management* from the Vienna University of Technology in 2007. In 2008, he joined the Security and Cryptography group at IBM Research – Zurich to perform research related to security, privacy, and identity management. While working at IBM, Franz-Stefan wrote a doctoral thesis on minimizing the information disclosure in authentication transactions. In 2012, he received a doctoral degree in engineering (PhD) from KU Leuven, Belgium.

Pyrgelis, Apostolos

Apostolos Pyrgelis holds a BSc from the Computer Engineering and Informatics Department at the University of Patras, Greece, and an M.Sc. from the same department on privacy and security issues of ad-hoc sensor networks. He has in depth knowledge of Privacy Enhancing Technologies (PETs) and their practical implementation for supporting privacy preserving Web services. His interests lie in cryptography, ICT security, privacy technologies, sensor networks and key management schemes in ad-hoc networks.

Rannenberg, Kai (i.a. editor)

Kai Rannenberg holds the Deutsche Telekom Chair of Mobile Business & Multilateral Security (www.m-chair.de) at Goethe University Frankfurt since 2002. Before he was working with the System Security Group at Microsoft Research Cambridge on "Personal Security Devices & Privacy Technologies". 1993-1999 Kai coordinated the interdisciplinary "Kolleg Security in Communication Technology", sponsored by Gottlieb Daimler & Karl Benz Foundation researching Multilateral Security. After an Informatics-Diploma at TU Berlin he had focused his PhD at Freiburg University on IT Security Evaluation Criteria and the protection of users and subscribers. Since 1991 Kai is active in ISO/IEC standardization in JTC 1/SC 27/WG 3 "Security evaluation criteria". 2007 he became Convenor of SC 27/WG 5 "Identity management and privacy technologies". 2009 Kai became an IFIP Councillor and 2014 the Chair of the IFIP Publications Committee. From 2007 till 2013 he chaired IFIP TC-11 "Security and Privacy Protection in Information Processing Systems", after having been its Vice-Chair since 2001. Kai is also active in the Council of European Professional Informatics Societies (CEPIS) chairing its Legal & Security Issues Special Interest Network (LSI) since 2003. 2004 till 2013 Kai served as the academic expert in the Management Board of the European Network and Information Security Agency, and is now a member of ENISA's Permanent Stakeholder Group.

Sabouri, Ahmad (i.a. editor)

Ahmad Sabouri holds an M.Sc. degree in Information Networking from the Carnegie Mellon University (USA) and a B.Sc. diploma in Software Engineering from the University of Tehran (Iran), and is currently perusing a doctoral degree at the Chair of Mobile Business & Multilateral Security, Goethe University Frankfurt, with a focus on Privacy-respecting Identity Management. Since 2011, he has a key role in various activities within the ABC4Trust EU project, including project coordination, architecture design, management of the pilots and dissemination. Ahmad participated in various research and industrial projects such as Petrofuzzy (IR. PEDEC), Core-Banking (IR. Trade Bank), Mid-capacity Router Design (Uni. of Tehran), Hermes (FP7), My-eDirector 2012 (FP7), and GINI-SA (FP7).

Schlehahn, Eva

Ass. iur. Eva Schlehahn is legal researcher and consultant at Unabhängiges Landeszentrum für Datenschutz (ULD) in Kiel, Germany. Since 2010, she has been working in various EC-funded FP7 R&D projects focused on privacy and cloud computing, identity management, accessibility, usability, and security. Her research interest is involving interdisciplinary requirements analysis, balancing and evaluation, specifically taking into account data privacy, legal privacy requirements, and Privacy by Design solutions. Her work includes the factual compliance of IT systems related to the European data protection framework.

Seidl, Robert

Robert Seidl studied Electrical Engineering at the Munich University of Applied Sciences. He received his diploma in 1993. Joining Rohde & Schwarz for a first period of practice he was involved in the introduction of digital cordless phones in Germany. Since 1995 he has been with Siemens AG in Munich. After 7 years of hard- and software development he entered the mobile network division in 2001. In 2007 he joined Nokia Siemens Networks (NSN) and has mainly been involved in the area of identity management, reliability, service access control and simplified access to services and heading the group on Identity Management within NSN research. Today Mr. Seidl works in the research group of Nokia and is heading a team responsible for Data Analytics and Privacy.

Stamatiou, Yannis

Yannis Stamatiou holds a B.Sc. degree from the Computer Engineering and Informatics Department, University of Patras, Greece, and a PhD on Theoretical Computer Science from the same department. He is currently Associate Professor at the Department of Business Administration of the University of Patras, Greece and Consultant at the ICT Security Sector of the Computer Technology Institute & Press ("Diophantus") in Patras, Greece. His research interests are focused on cryptography, cryptanalysis, modeling of the spread of computer viruses and ICT security with a focus on Privacy Enhancing Technologies (PETs).

Stausholm, Michael
Michael Stausholm received the M.Sc. degree in computer science from Aarhus University, Aarhus, Denmark in 2011. Since then, he has been working with IT security and secure multiparty computation at the Centre for IT Security at the Alexandra Institute A/S, Aarhus, Denmark, as an innovation and research specialist.

Suri, Neeraj
Suri is a Chair Professor of "Dependable Systems and Software" at TU Darmstadt, Germany and also with the University of Texas at Austin. Further professional details can be found at: http://www.deeds.informatik.tu-darmstadt.de/suri

Tesfay, Welderufael B.
Welderufael B. Tesfay received his Master of Science degree in Computer Science and Engineering with specialization in Mobile Systems from Lulea University of Technology and Bachelor of Science in Computer Science and Engineering from Mekelle Institute of Technology (MIT-Ethiopia). He has been involved in projects such as ABC4Trust (EU project) at Goethe University Frankfurt, Sense Smart City (Skelleftea, Sweden), and Electronic eID (Ethiopia). He also worked for ABB Corporate Research (Vsters, Sweden) and NEC Labs Europe in Heidelberg in the areas of mobile computing and telecommunications. Currently, he is pursing his PhD at Goethe University Frankfurt with research interests in mobile/pervasive computing, privacy enhancing technologies (PETs) and human factors of PETs.

Vateva-Gurova, Tsvetoslava
Vateva-Gurova is a PhD candidate at the "Dependable Systems and Software" group at TU Darmstadt, Germany. She obtained her BS and MS in Computer Science and IT Management (in 2012) from the TU Darmstadt. Her research focuses on trust quantification security in virtualized environments, side and covert-channel attacks and benchmarking security. Further information can be found at: www.deeds.informatik.tu-darmstadt. de/deeds/homepages/tsvetoslava/

Veseli, Fatbardh
Fatbardh Veseli has a rich international background, both in the education and work experience. He received his Master's degree in Information Security at Gjøvik University College (Norway), a Bachelor degree in Computer Science, and another one in Management and Informatics from the University of Prishtina (Kosovo). He has been involved in security- and privacy-related research projects, such as the European project "ABC4Trust" at Goethe University Frankfurt, and commercial industry projects. His experience also includes working in the banking and software development sector, as well as work in public services. Currently, he is doing research at the Goethe University Frankfurt, where he is working on security and evaluation frameworks, standardization, usability, and acceptance of privacy technologies.

Zhang, Heng
Heng Zhang is currently a PhD candidate at the "Dependable Systems and Software" group at Technische Universität Darmstadt, Germany. He obtained his Bachelor's degree in Telecommunications Engineering (in 2007) from Hubei University in China and his Master's degree in Computer Science (in 2013) from the Høgskolen i Gjøvik in Norway. At the end of 2013 he joined the "Dependable Systems and Software" group. His work focuses on security and trust quantification in cloud. His primary research interests are related to cloud security monitoring, security quantification and benchmarking.

Zwingelberg, Harald
Ass. iur. Harald Zwingelberg is head of the division for data protection in public entities, eGovernment and freedom of information. Until March 2014 he was a researcher in the EC-funded projects ABC4Trust, PrimeLife and FIDIS. He focused on legal questions related to privacy-enhancing technologies, identity management and eGovernment. Before joining Unabhängiges Landeszentrum für Datenschutz (ULD) Harald Zwingelberg gained legal experience as an advocate. He teaches data protection law at the University of Applied Sciences Kiel.

The manufacturer's authorised representative in the EU is Springer Nature Customer Service Centre GmbH, Europaplatz 3, 69115 Heidelberg, Germany. If you have any concerns regarding our products, please contact ProductSafety@springernature.com

Printed and bound by CPI Group (UK) Ltd, Croydon, CR0 4YY
30/09/2026
02225570-0014